THE END OF
DIVERSITY?

A volume in the series

Cornell Studies in Political Economy

EDITED BY PETER J. KATZENSTEIN

A full list of titles in the series appears at the end of the book.

THE END OF DIVERSITY?

Prospects for German and
Japanese Capitalism

EDITED BY

Kozo Yamamura
and
Wolfgang Streeck

Cornell University Press

ITHACA AND LONDON

First published 2003 by Cornell University Press

First printing, Cornell Paperbacks, 2003

Printed in the United States of America

Library of Congress Cataloging-in-Publication Data

The end of diversity? : prospects for German and Japanese capitalism /
edited by Kozo Yamamura and Wolfgang Streeck.
    p. cm.—(Cornell studies in political economy)
Includes bibliographical references and index.
    ISBN 0-8014-4088-2 (cloth : alk. paper)—ISBN 0-8014-8820-6
(pbk. : alk. paper)
    1. Capitalism—Germany.   2. Germany—Economic policy.
3. Capitalism—Japan.   4. Japan—Economic policy.   I. Yamamura,
Kåozåo.   II. Streeck, Wolfgang, 1946–   III. Series.
    HC286 .8   .E49 2003
    330.943—dc21

                                        2002151026

Cloth printing   10 9 8 7 6 5 4 3 2 1
Paperback printing   10 9 8 7 6 5 4 3 2 1

Contents

Tables and Figures

Tables

Figures

Contributors

Robert Boyer is an economist at the Centre d'Études Prospectives d'Économie Mathématique Appliquées à la Planification and a senior researcher at the National Center for Scientific Research in Paris.

Erica R. Gould is an assistant professor of politics at the University of Virginia.

Gregory Jackson is a fellow in the Research Institute of Economy, Trade and Industry in Tokyo. He recently completed his Ph.D. in sociology at Columbia University and was formerly a research scientist at the Max-Planck-Institut für Gesellschaftsforschung in Köln.

Ulrich Jürgens is director of the unit on the Regulation of Work at the Wissenschaftszentrum Berlin für Sozialforschung and adjunct professor in the Political Science Department of the Freie Universität Berlin.

Peter J. Katzenstein is the Walter S. Carpenter, Jr., Professor of International Studies at Cornell University.

Herbert Kitschelt is a professor of political science at Duke University.

Stephen D. Krasner is a senior fellow at the Institute for International Studies and Graham H. Stuart Professor of International Relations at Stanford University.

Ikuo Kume is a professor on the Faculty of Law at Kobe University.

Wolfgang Streeck is director at the Max-Planck-Institut für Gesellschaftsforschung in Köln.

Kathleen Thelen is associate professor of political science at Northwestern University.

Sigurt Vitols is a research fellow at the Wissenschaftszentrum Berlin für Sozialforschung.

Steven K. Vogel is an associate professor of political science at the University of California, Berkeley.

Kozo Yamamura is Job and Gertrud Tamaki Professor of Japanese Studies, professor of East Asian Studies, and adjunct professor of economics and international business at the University of Washington.

Preface

We had to have more than our share of good luck to be able to organize and complete a multiyear international and interdisciplinary research project and at the end publish this book and its companion, *The Origins of Nonliberal Capitalism: Germany and Japan in Comparison* (Streeck and Yamamura 2001).

First, we—the coorganizers of the project, who also coedited both volumes—were lucky to have met in Hawaii in summer 1995 at a conference on land-use regimes in different types of market economies, where we presented papers on the essential institutional characteristics and the changing economic performance of postwar Germany and of postwar Japan. The many similarities and no less intriguing differences between the two countries, as well as their differences from Anglo-American "standard" capitalism, became the subject of our long conversations during coffee breaks and over meals. Soon we found ourselves contemplating the possibility of jointly undertaking a comparative interdisciplinary study of Germany and Japan, two countries that had succeeded in transforming their war-torn economies and becoming leaders in global competition on the strength of their distinctive institutions, but that in the 1990s were both facing serious crises of performance and confidence.

Of course, as evident as the desirability of a broad comparative study of economic institutions in the two countries was, undertaking it was a daunting prospect given the analytical challenges it would face and the very substantial logistical difficulties and financial needs we had to expect. Still, by the final evening of the conference, we were sufficiently inspired by the dramatic sunset and a good bottle of wine that we resolved to explore the feasibility of a joint project, which we did by countless emails and in meetings in San Francisco and Seattle. In April 1996, we scheduled a planning workshop, which was to convene in June of the same year in Köln.

There were several reasons why the early phase of the project progressed so unexpectedly smoothly. First, we quickly learned to work together, demonstrating that neither of us deserves the reputation, propagated apparently by our colleagues and even our spouses, of never being likely to receive even an honorable mention in a contest for congeniality.

Second, we had little difficulty identifying a number of eminent scholars in Europe, the United States, and Japan who had published on or were in the midst of studying the issues and institutions in Germany and Japan in which we were most interested. Better still, almost all of them indicated their willingness to participate in the project in various capacities. In particular, among the participants in the planning workshop were Ronald Dore, Peter Katzenstein, Herbert Kitschelt, Stephen Krasner, Gerhard Lehmbruch, and T. J. Pempel—all leading scholars who continued to contribute to the project either by writing papers or by providing critical counsel and support.

Third, we were most fortunate in being able to obtain the necessary financial support. The Tamaki Foundation of Seattle provided a generous three-year grant, and the Max-Planck-Institut für Gesellschaftsforschung, Köln, offered both financial and administrative assistance. Although we like to think this was strictly because of the merits of the project, we cannot deny that two propitious facts played a role: the president of the foundation, Meriko Tamaki, is the daughter of a German-Japanese marriage and takes a strong personal interest in promoting studies of her parents' nations, and Wolfgang Streeck had moved in 1995 from the University of Wisconsin to become codirector of the Max-Planck-Institut.

Fourth, our good luck continued as the project progressed. In April 1997, we held the first conference in Seattle at the University of Washington, which agreed to defray the local costs. Participants included those who had attended the planning workshop. They were joined by a number of others who presented papers-in-progress or proposals for comparative studies (Robert Boyer, Gregory Jackson, Ikuo Kume, Philip Manow, Kathleen Thelen, Sigurt Vitols, and Steven Vogel) or acted as discussants (Theo Eicher, John Haley, Fumio Kodama, Mikio Matsui, Yukio Noguchi, and Tsutomu Tanaka).

Two other successful conferences followed, one in January 1998 at the Japanisch-Deutsches Zentrum Berlin (JDZB), which provided a generous subsidy, and the other in June 1999 at the Max-Planck-Institut in Köln. Either as paper givers or as resource persons and discussants, the following scholars attended, some of them at both conferences: Masahiko Aoki, Harald Baum, Angelika Ernst, Heidi Gottfried, Erica Gould, Susan Hanley, Anke Hassel, Kenji Hirashima, Ulrich Jürgens, the late Frieder Naschold,

Jacqueline O'Reilley, Thierry Ribault, Mike Shalev, Karen Shire, Akira Takenaka, and Hajo Weber. In Berlin, we also held a public session with business representatives, union leaders, and journalists on the future of the German and the Japanese models. In particular, we had the good fortune of being joined by Dr. Klaus Murmann (former president of the German Employers' Confederation, BDA), Kazo Nukazawa (Keidanren), Noriko Hama (Mitsubishi Research Institute, London), Dr. Rainer Hank (Frankfurter Allgemeine Zeitung), Prof. Hans-Jürgen Krupp (Landeszentralbank Hamburg), Tsutomo Tanaka (Chuo University, Tokyo) and Prof. Norbert Walter (Deutsche Bank Research) as speakers, as well as by others from business, academia, and government who attended the session and took part in the discussion.

Finally, we were blessed with the capable and dedicated assistance of Martha Walsh in Seattle and Greg Jackson in Köln. Working with two project directors as demanding as we are is not easy to begin with. But the burdens Martha and Greg had to carry became even heavier when the project turned out to encompass not only the present, main volume of papers as initially envisioned, but also the *Origins* volume, as it came to be called in our internal jargon. As a result Martha Walsh's duties—turning Germanic or Japanese and jargon-laden English into readable English, reminding authors to respect logical consistency and accuracy of facts, and use accepted translations and terms, not to mention all manner of administrative tasks—also doubled. The same applied to the workload we imposed on Greg, who acted as the majordomo of the project as a whole. We still wonder how he managed to get all this done while at the same time contributing a major chapter to each of the two volumes and completing his Columbia University doctoral dissertation.

As codirectors, the only way for us to conclude this preface is to thank the goddess of probability for our luck and, of course, to express our deepest appreciation to all those who helped us, including the many others whom we do not have the space to mention by name. We can only hope this volume and its companion justify all the support we have received in so many forms from so many individuals and organizations. Personally, we are amazed at having survived in good health the task of editing the two volumes, the miserable cold and wet snow of Berlin, and the Japanese restaurant there for which there is no appropriate adjective. And we may be permitted to add that we are pleased to report that after nearly five years of meeting so often and exchanging innumerable emails, we have developed what can be best called an acquired fondness for one another.

WOLFGANG STREECK
KOZO YAMAMURA

Köln and Seattle, July 2001

THE END OF
DIVERSITY?

Introduction: Convergence or Diversity? Stability and Change in German and Japanese Capitalism

Wolfgang Streeck and Kozo Yamamura

Postwar Germany and Japan represented distinctive versions of nonliberal capitalism embedded in, and managed through, national institutions supported to different degrees by a strong nation-state. Although differing from one another in numerous ways, German and Japanese capitalism also differed substantially from the Anglo-American model of a capitalist economy and seemingly violated core prescriptions of neoclassical economic theory.[1]

The superior postwar performance of the German and Japanese economies attracted wide admiration, particularly in the 1970s and 1980s when the two countries became world leaders in the race for international economic competitiveness. Although from an Anglo-American as well as a neoclassical theoretical perspective the success of the two countries was a vexing mystery and even a threatening enigma, dissenters from neoclassical orthodoxy felt confirmed by it. In a period when Britain and the United States went through serious economic crises, the German and Japanese economies thrived, supported by their socially embedded economic institutions and the long-term commitments and mutual trust among economic agents these fostered. The lesson for the Anglo-American economies, dominated by market-driven transactions focused on short-term gains and apparently burdened with the dead-weight costs of rampant opportunism, seemed to be that they had in one way or other

We are grateful to Gregory Jackson for his competent help, comments, and criticism.
1. On the historical origins of the specific institutional configurations that define the German and Japanese models of capitalism, see Streeck and Yamamura (2001).

to emulate or adopt the institutions of the more socially integrated economies of Germany and Japan.

Emphasizing the two countries' rejection of core assumptions of the Anglo-American model of a market economy, much of the popular literature of the 1970s and 1980s placed the German and Japanese economies in the same category, for example in Lester Thurow's (1992) communitarian capitalism or in Michel Albert's (1993) Rhine model. However, although the German and Japanese economies share many significant similarities, such as institutions maintaining long-term cooperative relations among economic agents and a lower concern with short-term allocative efficiency and the elimination of monopoly rents, they differ in numerous ways. Whereas the institutions of the Japanese postwar political economy were designed to help the country catch up with and surpass the West, the predominant concern in West Germany was the construction and protection of national social cohesion and solidarity. This is why we distinguish between Japanese developmentalism, on the one hand, and the German consensus economy,[2] on the other, as two different versions of a nationally embedded, nonliberal capitalist political economy.

The discussions in this book are informed by and contribute to the academic literature on varieties of capitalism (Aoki 2001; Crouch and Streeck 1997; Hall and Soskice 2001; Hollingsworth and Boyer 1997; Jackson 2002b; Whitley 1999). This literature takes national differences in economic institutions seriously in that it relates them to different economic performances. It also implies that the different national varieties of a capitalist economy seek to maximize the internal coherence of their distinctive institutional configurations because complementarity between institutions increases their productivity. Economic change is regarded as closely intertwined with institutional change, which in turn is seen as mostly conditioned by functional interdependence between the institutions that make up a given capitalist system. Most political-economic change is therefore seen as path dependent—with past institutional structures being the principal determinants of future ones. Important issues in the debate are how tightly coupled national institutional configurations are and how much space they leave for fundamental change, for example for convergence between previously different varieties of a capitalist market economy.

In the present book, just as in the one that preceded it (Streeck and Yamamura 2001), our main distinction is between *liberal capitalism* of the

---

2. The concept is not ideal because developmental capitalism, too, involves a major concern with the preservation of social consensus. Alternative terms might be "social cohesion economy," "social market economy," and "social-democratic capitalism." But the first is not very distinctive either, the meaning of the second is unclear, and the third suffers from the fact that German capitalism in its present form was influenced at least as much by Christian as by social democracy.

Anglo-American sort and different versions of *nonliberal capitalism,* including its German and Japanese versions. By *economic liberalism* we mean a social order that "sets economic transactions free from obligations other than to serve the interests of those immediately involved; it also tends to be suspicious of collective support of economic action as it may breed collusion and monopoly" (5). Nonliberal economic regimes, by comparison, place little trust in self-regulating markets in which relative prices are allowed freely to fluctuate. "Instead they rely on various forms of hierarchical and organizational coordination that sometimes require heavy injections of public authority, . . . often overriding contractual exchanges as entered into by private agents on their own volition, discretion, and calculation" (6). In nonliberal political economies, transactions are supposed also "to serve other than economic purposes" and are "constrained by noneconomic objectives, such as social cohesion or national defense." Moreover, they are regarded as legitimately supported by particularistic social relations and by "enforceable social obligations that engender trust among economic actors" (2).

"Nonliberal" is not an ideal concept, but neither are for various reasons its closest alternatives (Streeck and Yamamura 2001, 6). As a synonym for nonliberal capitalism, we sometimes speak of nationally embedded, organized, managed, or institutionalized capitalism, again referring to both Germany and Japan. This is to emphasize that typically in the twentieth century nonliberal capitalism was organized or managed by, as well as embedded or institutionalized in, national states and institutions directing the economy to serve nationally defined social or political objectives. Because liberal capitalism was much less governed by market-modifying institutions and national purposes, and much more governed by the free play of market forces, it might among other things be better prepared for economic internationalization than nonliberal, nationally embedded capitalism. At least this is one of the hypotheses explored in this volume.

Since the early 1990s, German and Japanese capitalism has been facing a deep and lasting performance crisis. After having been highly successful in international competition for decades, the two economies are finding it unexpectedly difficult to cope with accelerating technological change and globalization in the post–cold war world order. To many, this crisis originated in a mismatch between the two countries' economic institutions and the demands of a changed economic and political environment. Both within and outside of Germany and Japan, there is growing belief that the socially embedded institutions of the two countries' economies have changed from assets into liabilities. Strong pressures have built for nationally managed capitalism to restructure, so as to fit better with a much less regulated international political economy. In particular, there are vociferous demands in the two countries for institutional change in the direction of a less regulated, Anglo-American sort of capitalist economy—the same economic model that a short time before appeared hopelessly in decline. As a result, what once seemed to be robust and static national models of political economy have become fluid and uncertain.

The crisis of the German and Japanese political economies offers an intellectually exciting and highly practically relevant subject of speculation that is much in need of theoretical and empirical analysis. The core question is whether Germany and Japan, confronted with the political and economic exigencies of technological revolution and economic internationalization, must thrust aside their distinctive institutions and the competitive advantages they have yielded in the past or whether they will be able to adapt and retain such institutions and preserve the social cohesion and economic competitiveness of their societies.

The paramount theoretical issue underlying this question is that of convergence and divergence in the institutional makeup of industrial societies and of the possibility of the coexistence of distinct capitalist systems in a global economy that is becoming steadily more integrated. The first postwar convergence theories were technologically deterministic: they expected industrial societies to become more similar as industrial technologies spread (Crouch and Streeck 1997). Later, social scientists emphasized the social and political malleability of technology and made a strong case for continued national and even subnational diversity based in different institutional resources, strategic choices, and collective politics (Bendix 1956; Dore 1973; Granovetter 1985; Maurice, Sellier, and Silverstre 1986; Sorge and Warner 1986). In the 1990s the theoretical pendulum has swung sharply back to convergence, although this time the principal engine for change is assumed to be market forces rather than a universal technological logic (Guillén 2001). Market-driven convergence is believed to occur at an accelerating pace because of increasing economic interdependence and the growth of international arrangements such as the European Union and the World Trade Organization, supposedly forcing divergent national systems of social and economic organization into a common mold because resisting convergence may mean a loss of international competitiveness and, as a consequence, a declining standard of living. Germany and Japan are the ideal sites for exploring the interplay between the new forces of convergence and the social conditions and economic effects of resistance against them.

In the following sections we briefly summarize the main symptoms of the crises of performance and confidence that have beset German and Japanese capitalism and revived the issue of competitive convergence to an Anglo-American pattern of economic organization. Next, we explain the organization of the book and present an initial review of its chapters, each of which offers a comparative investigation of the current problems and future prospects of the two countries with respect to selected aspects of national economic performance. The general message the chapters convey is one of considerable institutional resilience and of path-dependent incremental change at best, to the good or the bad, and in particular one of lasting differences between nonliberal and liberal capitalism, in spite of instances of liberalization in the former and hybridization with elements of the latter. We close with a discussion of how to distinguish observed stability from stagnation and incremental from radical change and of whether incremental change within a framework of lasting diversity might not after all, in the longer run, add up to radical change and convergence.

The Crisis of Japanese Developmentalism

Although significant changes have occurred since the 1970s, Japan's political economy has remained developmentalist (Murakami 1996, 183–228; Yamamura 1982) in its fundamental characteristics. Studies of the Japanese economy have emphasized, among other factors, the historical legacies of post-Restoration catch-up industrialization (Murakami 1982), the institutions created around 1940 to control and mobilize resources for the war economy (Okazaki and Okuno-Fujiwara 1999), the pervasive power of economic ministries deployed to achieve plan-rational economic growth, and the use of state power to promote the rapid adoption of ever more advanced technology (Johnson 1982).

Japanese developmentalism was based in a national belief in the importance of catching up with and surpassing the advanced economies of the West. It also rests on a firm conviction of the superiority of political-economic and social institutions that promote long-term economic performance and on a widely shared assumption that market forces cannot bring about such performance. A crucial tenet of Japanese developmentalism is that high long-term performance of the economy can be most effectively maintained by increasing exports of successively more advanced manufactured products. To achieve this, the state with its proactive bureaucracy and many private organizations engage in activities that foster mutual trust and cooperation among economic actors to reduce both political and economic transaction costs. The welfare of citizens is judged on the basis of long-term growth of real incomes; short-term rents accruing to individuals and organizations that happen to have political or market power are viewed as some of the necessary costs of achieving long-term income growth. Developmentalism also made Japan support the Pax Americana because it maximized Japanese access to foreign markets while minimizing international entanglements and the costs of national defense.

There are three main interdependent and mutually reinforcing relations of cooperation in the developmentalist Japanese economy, each
based in institutional arrangements that have for a long time successfully
reduced political and economic transaction costs: close relations between
the government—the Liberal Democratic Party (LDP) and the bureaucracy—and industry; long-term, intensive, and multifaceted relations
between firms (vertical and horizontal *keiretsu*); and labor-management
relations in large firms, characterized by permanent employment, the
seniority wage system, and enterprise unions. They all worked because the
parties involved gained from them. For example, large firms benefited
(the larger, the more) from a wide range of progrowth policies intended
to enhance the ability of the manufacturing sector to adopt new technology as rapidly as possible. Examples are the numerous prosaving
policies aiding rapid capital formation; industry-specific subsidies handed
out under many different guises; preferential allocation of loanable funds
to the largest manufacturing firms on the condition that they adopt new
technology (i.e., firms in targeted industries expected to increase productivity, and thus exports, rapidly); dispensations from the Antimonopoly
Law allowing firms to form price cartels; and protection for domestic
industries through trade policies, especially the reluctant liberalization of
imports of manufactured products and capital.

Similarly, the LDP, which had no grassroots organizations, obtained all
its funds for maintaining its apparatus and for funding its campaigns from
industry. It was able to remain in power because of the rapid growth of
targeted and other industries, which enabled the Japanese economy as a
whole to achieve sustained export-led growth, assured nearly full employment, and raised the real income of a large majority of the electorate. And
finally, the bureaucracy, as a result of the close cooperation between
government and industry, gained power and turf, arguably unmatched by
its counterparts in other large capitalist democracies. The economic
ministries drafted almost all legislation enacted by the Diet, exercised
the extensive powers given to them by that legislation, and in addition
engaged in extensive administrative guidance, applying extralegal power
and authority. Industries and firms accepted such guidance either because
they were ordered to do what they themselves wanted (e.g., forming cartels
and restricting imports) or because they feared being penalized later on
other issues, as shown by examples from the iron and steel, shipbuilding,
machinery, chemical, and other industries.

Similarly, cooperation among firms through the three types of *keiretsu*
became established because all participating firms benefited from it.
Membership in an enterprise group (a horizontal *keiretsu*, such as Mitsui
and Sumitomo), which consists of large firms in different industries, provided companies with a "main bank" from which they received the largest

share of their loans; with stable shareholders in the form of fellow *keiretsu* firms engaging in cross-shareholding; and with opportunities to engage in joint activities in research and development (R&D), foreign investment, and marketing that minimized costs and risks.

Likewise, a vertical *keiretsu*, which consists of subcontracting relations between a large parent manufacturer and a number of small and medium-size suppliers, became a main feature of the Japanese economy, as shown by the high outsourcing ratio of Japanese automakers. Intensive and almost daily personal contacts within a vertical *keiretsu*, together with various forms of share ownership by the parent company, technological guidance and collaboration, managerial assistance, and so on, reduced transaction costs and otherwise increased productive efficiency, for example, by promoting complementary investment in physical and human capital. Relations of this kind made possible the famous *kanban* system in the automobile industry. The third type of *keiretsu*, in distribution, provides dependable sales outlets and customer information to parent companies and also contributes to increasing the productive efficiency of manufacturing firms.

The institutions that sustain cooperation in the Japanese economy together constitute a unified social framework for Japanese developmentalism. Participants in any one of the three main cooperative relationships depend on the other two being successfully maintained. Cooperation between government and industry, premised on the sustained success of large manufacturing firms making for continued export-led growth, cannot be maintained without extensive, mutually beneficial, and efficiency-promoting subcontracting relationships. The latter, a key reason for the international competitiveness of Japanese manufacturing firms, relies in turn on the labor-management relationship in large firms and the main bank system, with banks rather than shareholders providing the largest part of corporate finance through loans and, in turn, monitoring company management.

Cooperation, and as a consequence developmentalism, worked also because it did not entirely stifle competition; the Japanese shared the national goal of rapid growth; and Japan was able to borrow technology from abroad, which enabled it to maintain export-led growth by steadily increasing its productive efficiency. A growing and more efficient economy, by producing gains that could be shared, minimized political and economic conflicts and thereby reinforced the cooperation that underpinned Japanese postwar developmentalism.

Two examples illustrate how cooperation did not stifle the competition necessary for long-term economic performance. Both legal and extralegal (i.e., administratively guided and illegal) cartels were almost always short-lived because of strong incentives to defect, deriving primarily from firms being able to reduce costs by adopting new technology or by taking advantage of economies of scale and learning by doing. Even when price cartels were in effect, cartel members competed for market share by improving product quality and service and offering more attractive delivery schedules and terms of finance. This was why, even when imports were still restricted in various ways, fierce nonprice competition characterized the markets for most manufactured products in postwar Japan. Also significant was competition among employees to "climb the ladder of hierarchy," that is, to be promoted to positions that offered them more responsibilities and higher wages within the seniority wage system.

During the 1970s, various reactive adjustments were made in Japanese institutions to cope with increasingly pressing problems that originated mainly in the very success of Japanese developmentalism. State-industry cooperation for rapid growth had to respond to more and more vociferous public demands for effective environmental policies. Expenditures for the social safety net had to be increased for those who failed to share in the gains of rapid growth. The appreciation of the yen and American restrictions on Japanese exports had to be accepted as prices of Japan's export drives, embarked on to overcome the oil-shock recessions of the decade. Penalties against cartels were raised, if only by a little; the Ministry of International Trade and Industry (MITI) was reprimanded by the Tokyo High Court for its guidance in the fixing of prices for petroleum products; and the Ministry of Finance (MOF) had to yield some of its power to guide interest rates and restrict the activities of banks and other financial institutions.

No fundamental change occurred in the working of the *keiretsu*. The slower pace of technological change and the recession yielded fewer gains to be shared between parent firms and subcontractors. Still, subcontractors chose to accept parent-firm demands for price reductions because doing so seemed preferable to losing all the benefits of *keiretsu* relations. Labor-management relations and patterns of corporate governance did not change much either. Even in the recessions of the decade, firms reduced the salaries of their managers before resorting to employee dismissals and stockholders did not gain much influence. The interdependent cooperative arrangements of Japanese developmentalism held up basically because the economy was performing well in comparison to the West, especially the visibly declining U.S. economy. During this decade Japan began to be called an economic superpower and exported increasing quantities of technologically advanced products to the United States and indeed to all corners of the global economy.

This continued in the 1980s, in spite of increasingly frequent challenges from outsiders, domestic and foreign, to the principles of national cooperation. The economic policy of the Ronald Reagan administration led to sharply increased Japanese exports of goods and capital to the United States, and the Plaza Accord of 1985 resulted in the boom associated with the bubble economy. As the economy continued to prosper, most of the tensions within Japan's developmentalist institutions were muted and could be dealt with by administering painkillers as required by imminent necessity.

Despite Japan's huge trade surplus, especially vis-à-vis the United States—which brought on the Structural Impediments negotiations in 1989—the export dependence of the Japanese economy remained unchanged. The capital market was further liberalized, but the scope of liberalization was determined less by international constraints than by the demands of domestic financial institutions, coordinated by MOF, for more freedom to export capital and to offer new types of financial instruments within Japan. The other economic ministries also relaxed their regulatory grip over their respective domains. In no case, however, was there an indication that fundamental change was about to occur in the character of Japan's central bureaucracy. Because of easy access to capital—equity capital at home and loans floated abroad—in the bubble years, the main bank system grew weaker but was far from defunct.

Keiretsu relationships too remained alive and well. Exports to Asia and elsewhere were booming and increased the demand of parent firms for the products of their subcontractors. And, because the economy remained robust, there was little reason for labor-management relations to change. In the bubble years, it seemed that developmentalist cooperation in Japan could continue forever. At the close of the 1980s, the Nikkei index had risen to almost 40,000 points, and more than a few scholars and pundits were discussing the possibility of a Pax Japonica emerging in the next century.

As the 1990s began, however, it became quickly and brutally evident that the bubble boom had in fact been the twilight of Japanese developmentalism. Despite increasingly larger injections of deficit-financed fiscal stimuli, the economy remained mired in a prolonged recession causing many to call the 1990s "a lost decade": the real growth of GDP hovered at 1 percent because of stagnant investment and consumption, unemployment reached 4.9 percent (which some believe was actually as high as 7 percent when adjusted for various inimitably Japanese employment practices and the method of data gathering), and both the numbers of firms and the total assets involved in bankruptcies soared. Japan's developmentalism is widely held responsible for the lost decade, both as direct cause of the prolonged recession—of the bubble itself and thus of the aftereffects of its collapse—and as underlying cause, because the entrenched institutions of developmentalism are proving too slow to respond to market signals and became vestiges of pervasive rent-seeking detracting from the performance of the economy in the 1990s.

Simply put, the rapid escalation of stock and land prices in the 1980s occurred essentially because Japan, especially after the Plaza Accord of 1985 and until 1990, relentlessly pursued both easy money and tight fiscal policies—which was the exact mirror image of the Reagan policies in the United States in pursuit of supply-side economic goals. The motivation for the Japanese policies was to minimize the appreciation of the yen and sustain a high level of investment so that Japan, continuing to increase productive efficiency and capacity, could boost exports to the United States, which absorbed nearly 40 percent of Japanese exports. An increasingly large trade surplus was invested in U.S. treasury bills and stocks, aiding a U.S. economy that was starved by high interest rates and suffering from ballooning fiscal and trade deficits. The export-led boom brought increased tax revenues, enabling the government to pay off outstanding national debt and support rapidly increasing foreign direct investment, mostly in the United States and in Asia. The boom prolonged the LDP's hold on power and effectively muted the criticism of developmentalist institutions that had been steadily on the rise since the 1970s.

The bubble, however, was destined to burst. The Bank of Japan finally became alarmed by the runaway prices of stocks and land and raised its discount rate in 1990; stock prices began to fall in 1991 and the price of land, which served as the most important collateral for bank loans, followed suit. As the 1990s proceeded and stock and land prices plummeted, it became evident that the Japanese economy had begun to pay the price for the opportunistic monetary and fiscal policies of the 1980s that had given rise to excesses in many forms and to vast entrepreneurial misjudgments and malfeasance. In addition to the bleak economic conditions of the decade, the by-now-familiar list of notable economic disasters includes nonperforming loans exceeding $1 trillion that bankrupted nearly fifty large and small financial institutions, huge excess capacities in several key industries, and a massive national debt—the largest as a proportion of GDP among all Organization for Economic Cooperation and Development (OECD) economies—that rose sharply in a series of vain efforts to stimulate the economy.

Two conflicting realities of the 1990s—the sputtering and deflationary Japanese economy caught in a liquidity trap (rendering monetary policy ineffectual despite the Bank of Japan's zero-interest policy and other measures to revive the economy by increasing money supply) and the high performance sustained by the U.S. economy—reinvigorated the criticism of Japanese cooperative institutions. As the decade proceeded, the assessment of cooperative institutions as relics of the catch-up era detrimental in the new age of the digital revolution and economic globalization grew more and more vociferous. This was the development that validated and promoted deregulation, including the Big Bang of the capital market;

erosion of long-cherished employment practices such as permanent employment and seniority-based wages; and a weakening of entrenched bank-firm and interfirm ties, in particular the main bank system, cross-share-holdings, and various other *keiretsu* ties. The Americanization of corporate governance, especially the greater consideration of shareholder value and transparency of corporate decision making and accounting, was demanded and legal changes were enacted to meet the demand. Because of these and other developments, by the end of the 1990s market signals were more important in both capital and labor markets than at any time in the preceding decades. In 1993, the LDP lost the dominance in Japanese politics it had enjoyed since 1955, and since then it has clung to power only with the aid of coalition partners.

Still, no judicious observer would conclude that the changes reported daily in the mass media will inevitably amount to a remodeling of Japanese cooperative institutions on the U.S. system. In fact, although significant erosion and adaptation have taken place, the core characteristics of the Japanese institutional configuration are still intact. Despite deregulation, the state, and especially the bureaucracy, wields far more power than in the Anglo-American economies. Although the recession and the dictates of global economic competition have significantly increased the risks of employment and income, a vast majority of employees, especially of large firms, still continue to enjoy secure employment and an income enviable to many U.S. workers. Even with all the changes in the ties between banks and firms, as well as between firms, it is possible to argue that although such ties are being made more market-responsive and strategic (as exemplified in inter-*keiretsu* mergers creating financial megainstitutions and in the creation of *keiretsu*-based holding companies), they retain the long-term character that makes them qualitatively different from similar ties in Anglo-American economies and even in Germany. And whether substantive institutional change will follow the legal changes remains to be seen.

The Crisis of the German Consensus Economy

Postwar German capitalism was the product of a complex historical compromise between liberalism and two competing countervailing forces, social democracy and social Catholicism; between traditionalism and two opposed versions of modernism, liberalism and socialism; and of course between capital and labor. This compromise was struck, and became firmly institutionalized, in the immediate postwar years when both the communist wing of the labor movement and the authoritarian faction of German business were, for different reasons, excluded from political participation (Streeck 1997c).

The "social market economy" that began to form in the 1950s was instrumental in integrating West Germany as a society, overcoming the deep internal divisions inherited from the past, and pulling the country together in its confrontation with the German Democratic Republic, a client state of the Soviet Union on German territory. The West German postwar political economy was above all geared to social balance—not just between the classes but also between regions, industrial sectors, small and large firms, industrial centers and the countryside, and the native population and millions of refugees from the east. Such balance was accomplished through a set of distinctive socioeconomic institutions, some of them new and others with a long tradition, in particular socially regulated markets with a high floor under them; labor-inclusive firms with codetermination and patient capital; a vertically and horizontally divided state, weak in direct intervention but strong in arranging for negotiated compromise; and a densely organized civil society, articulated through well-established interest associations with recognized rights and capacities for self-government giving rise to a bargained economy across the board (Katzenstein 1987).

The German consensus economy was hugely successful in rebuilding the country socially and economically. In the 1970s and 1980s in particular, its institutional structure conditioned and sustained a distinctive pattern of economic performance that happened to be highly competitive in world markets (Streeck 1992). High costs originating in socially regulated labor markets and in extensive provisions for status protection of various social groups ruled out price-competitive production and forced firms to seek survival in quality-competitive international markets. Here, the same institutions that made the German economy unable to compete on price gave it competitive advantage, in that they enabled firms to achieve quality-competitiveness through the continuous upgrading and customization of their products.

In particular, while placing German firms under constraints that made low-cost production prohibitively costly, German economic institutions also offered them rich opportunities for adjustment to the requirements of what has been called diversified quality production (Streeck 1992). Unions and business associations, given an extended social welfare state, negotiated management under codetermination, and almost complete coverage by collective bargaining, found it in their common interest to deploy their safely established quasi-public powers to help firms move into quality-competitive markets through the jointly promoted upgrading of skills, work organization, technology, and products. Although the bargained economy accounted for the fact that only very few German industries remained price-competitive, collectively negotiated cooperation made for high-quality competitiveness in German manufacturing. The success of this system is indicated by the fact that, especially before unification, this sector was proportionately larger than in any comparable country, in spite of its much higher wages. It also was and remained internationally competitive across a uniquely broad range of products, making Germany the world's most diversified export economy.

German industrial upgrading is typically continuous but also slow and gradual, reflecting an institutional infrastructure that, while fostering long-term orientations, makes for long decision times. The resulting pattern of innovation is more likely to generate improvements of existing products in existing firms and sectors than to give rise to new sectors (Nelson 1993; Porter 1990). Generally, sticky decisions, steady commitments, and delayed responses in German institutions make for slow fluctuations, up or down, in economic activity and performance; for flat cyclical movements, especially compared to the United States; and for low dispersion of outcomes. Averages are typically high, coefficients of variation are low, and extreme cases are rare at both ends.

The broad migration of the German economy in the 1970s and 1980s into quality-competitive markets was helped by the traditional preference of German consumers for high quality. Social traditionalism contributed also to a high saving rate, which helped generate the patient capital needed for the continuous upgrading of products and production factors. Within firms, patient capital and committed labor, both having access to voice as an alternative to exit, enabled management to take the long view, based on stable bargains with and between all those concerned. In politics, a divided and immobile economic government enshrined a currency regime that foreclosed devaluation to restore price-competitiveness and offered investors insurance against electoral volatility.

Above all, the success of the German model, as long as it lasted, was due to the way it used social demands for an egalitarian distribution of economic outcomes to generate an egalitarian distribution of productive capabilities, the latter enabling the economy to underwrite the former. Turning social and political constraints on market relations into productive opportunities, and thereby creating a pattern of production capable of sustaining a socially desirable but economically improbable pattern of distribution, the political economy of the German model, as it had emerged by the 1970s, managed to combine competitive efficiency with high equality and social cohesion.

By the early 1990s at the latest, however, the previously successful German model had moved into a severe performance crisis. High and persistent unemployment was beginning to undermine the very social cohesion the institutions of the German political economy had been designed to ensure. Not only was unemployment beginning to generate deep inequalities that threatened to exclude a significant part of the population from the economic mainstream, but the rising costs of unemployment, in addition, undermined the social welfare state and the systems of solidaristic redistribution that were part of it.

Three factors seem to have converged to draw the continued viability of the German consensus economy in question. First, the industrial strategy of broad incremental innovation ceased to generate sufficient advantage in nonprice-competitive markets for the full employment of the German labor force at the high wages and the low wage dispersion that had become the hallmark of the German consensus economy. When other countries, in particular Japan, learned to produce at the same quality level as German firms but at lower costs, the traditional German market niches became smaller or disappeared. Moreover, as leadership in innovation began to require ever faster development and speedier marketing of new products, the German innovation mode of continuously upgrading existing products began to appear outdated.

In the 1980s the employment gap in the German economy was for a while covered up by successful but costly measures of rationing the labor supply, especially through the reduction of working hours and early retirement. But this could not be done indefinitely. Although Germany has one of the lowest participation rates of all major industrial countries and an average working time that is shorter than in all competitor countries, unemployment, and in particular long-term unemployment, continues to be very high. Among the unemployed are a rising number of unskilled or low-skilled workers who fail to meet the qualification requirements of quality-competitive production, and their number has risen together with rising standards and rising investment in training.

Second, unification imposed additional burdens on the German consensus economy. Rising taxes and the growing national debt caused by the need to rebuild East Germany detracted from German economic performance, as they would have in any other country faced with a similar task. But the problems were vastly exacerbated by the West German decision to conduct unification as a wholesale transplantation of the entire array of West German institutions to the former East Germany. This approach was supported by all forces in West German society, including business, labor, the conservative government, and the Social Democratic opposition. Immediately after unification, unions and employer associations formally committed themselves to raising East German wages to West German levels within a few years, ruling out the establishment of a low-wage area in the east. In part this reflected a shared belief that however low East German wages might be, German industry could never be price-competitive. But there may also have been a fear that a low-wage regime in the east might erode the high-wage and high-skill regime of the west.

In any case, it was the institutional logic of the (West) German political economy, with its low tolerance for diversity and inequality, that forced the country to define the problems of unification in a way that made them even more difficult to resolve than they would otherwise have been. At a time when its wages were being raised far beyond its productivity, East German industry was included in the rigorous competition and hard-currency regime that West German firms had had four decades to learn to live with. This was bound to place the East German economy under potentially destructive adjustment pressures, with resulting prolonged mass unemployment. The latter, in turn, could only trigger massive financial transfers from west to east, given that among the institutions transplanted with unification was the West German welfare state.

By the mid-1990s, united Germany was engaged in the largest wealth transfer in economic history, having committed itself for at least a decade to subsidize the *neue Länder* at a level of about $100 billion a year to cover infrastructural investment, pension supplements, and, not least, unemployment benefits. Still, there is no guarantee that this extraordinary redistributive effort will not in the end be self-defeating. Public debt exploded after 1989 and was reined in only by cuts in public investment, especially in R&D effort—cuts that are in more than one way obstructive of a quality-competitive social market economy. And world markets for German products, hardly large enough to provide for full employment in West Germany, and shrinking perhaps for reasons of their own, have so far proven too small for Germany as a whole.

Third, the postwar German bargain between labor and capital, or between the German society and its capitalist economy, was conditioned on the limited mobility of production factors across national borders. At its core was an institutionally mediated accommodation of capital and labor markets—both themselves highly organized by government intervention and associative self-regulation—that turned less-than-perfectly mobile capital into an infrastructure for a production pattern compatible with social objectives such as low inequality. In exchange, capital was provided with a labor supply willing and able to satisfy the economic requirements of high competitiveness in international quality markets.

Economic internationalization undermined the German consensus economy in more than one way. By increasing the mobility of capital and labor across national borders, it not only extricated the labor supply from national control but also enabled the financial sector to refuse to do service as a national utility. Also, a rising number of unskilled migrant workers weakened the socially imposed labor constraint that had in the past so forcefully promoted industrial upgrading toward a high-wage economy with low wage dispersion. Moreover, as German capital became more cosmopolitan and could more easily emigrate in pursuit of higher and faster profit, large German firms began to extricate themselves from the tutelage of their *Hausbanken*, the German equivalent of the Japanese main banks.

Banks, in turn, restructured to become more like Anglo-American investment banks. As a result, their willingness and capacity to monitor company performance and promote prudent long-termism declined. This, in turn, was bound to affect relations between capital and labor. In particular, the core institution of the German consensus economy, codetermination, might be less than perfectly compatible with the emerging spirit of placing shareholder value first (see the essay by Gregory Jackson in this volume; see also Höpner 2002).

International markets are not subject to the complex class politics that gave rise to the social market economy. They are especially devoid of a social dimension, and indeed, although the German monetary and competition regimes were by and large transferred to the European Union, its domestic complement, the German social welfare state, was not. Nor have German corporate governance arrangements been transferable to Europe; to the contrary, the German system, whose strongest supporters have become the unions, has come under continuing pressure to change in an Anglo-American direction. Moreover, although the political independence of the Bundesbank provided the blueprint for the status of the new European Central Bank, the signature capacity of the German state to organize social cooperation and group compromise is absent at the European level. Indeed just as German *Marktwirtschaft* is being internationalized without its social correctives, German institutionalized monetarism has been transferred to the European Community without the associative self-governance that makes it socially compatible inside Germany.

In short, the characteristic competitiveness of the postwar German economy was of a kind that could be consensually negotiated between organized social groups under the roof of a facilitating national state at a level of social balance that was for a long time unique among large industrial societies. Many believe that the pattern of innovation that corresponded to the German bargained economy can no longer compete internationally and that the consensually managed arrangements for training and for the control of access to the labor market that were associated with it have become outdated or ineffective. The same may hold for the German model of collectively bargained industrial relations and corporate governance, which face the potential defection of formerly patient capital to the larger and less regulated circuits of the global economy. Rising and persistent unemployment, in itself the most threatening malfunction of a consensus economy, also undermines the public systems of social insurance designed to correct the outcomes of markets at a time when private industry is more than ever coming under the dictate of shareholder value. The shock of unification added significantly to problems that may already by the late 1980s have been endemic; this was magnified by the low tolerance of the German political economy for inequality and by the resulting need for political redistribution. Finally, although economic globalization promotes the internationalization of liberal German institutions, such as the competition regime or the Bundesbank, complementary institutions of consensual bargaining remain nationally confined. Due to their changed environment, they may turn into competitive liabilities.

The Chapters of This Volume

The ten chapters that follow this introduction deal with five subject areas that are of crucial importance for the future of nationally embedded capitalism: a country's integration into the international system, its use of technology and its capacity to generate and absorb technological innovation, its labor relations and production regimes, its financial regime and system of corporate governance, and its politics and electoral system.[3] Each subject is addressed by two chapters comparing the situations of Germany and Japan at the end of the twentieth century.

International Relations

Nationally organized capitalism can be understood only in its international context which to a large extent defines the capacities of the national state, including its role in relation to the national economy. This applies in particular to countries such as Germany and Japan, which were conquered by the United States in 1945 and were returned to sovereignty only after a deep transformation of their national institutions (Smith 1998). The two chapters that deal with the German and Japanese positions in the international system complement one another—Erica Gould and Stephen Krasner emphasize the relationship of the two countries to the United States, whereas Peter Katzenstein looks at the way Germany and Japan are embedded in their respective regional contexts.

Both chapters start out emphasizing the similarities in Germany's and Japan's international positions, which are related in complex ways to the similarities in the institutional structures of their economies. Germany and Japan entered the twentieth century as candidates not just for re-

---

3. Other issues that could have been addressed include welfare-state reform and macroeconomic policy. Although progress has been made in exploring the relationship among different production regimes and variants of the welfare state (Ebbinghaus and Manow 2001; on Germany and Japan see also Manow 2001a, 2001b), a macroeconomic policy analysis would have to explore the implications of European monetary union and the events leading up to it for German economic policy. We briefly comment on this in the present chapter. An in-depth discussion of the matter could, however, easily fill another volume.

gional dominance but for great power status. Whatever ambitions they may have entertained, however, were decisively defeated in World War II, and the two countries were included on the U.S. side in a new bipolar world order. To turn them into well-integrated members of the "free world," they had to be internally reorganized into parliamentary democracies and market economies, opening their societies and economies to U.S. influence. Gould and Krasner show, however, that quite early the United States began to tolerate the rebuilding of more traditional national structures to mobilize the resources of the two countries for anticommunist containment. It is at this point that the specific synthesis was allowed to take place between the new and the old, between the imported and the indigenous, that is at the root of the contemporary German and Japanese models of political economy.[4] That the resulting *mixta composita* became so successful was also in part due to U.S. policy—especially its willingness to accept asymmetry not just in trade, which laid the foundations of the two countries' postwar economic miracles, but also in the provision of national security, which freed up resources in the two countries and made them available for civil reconstruction and economic progress. Indeed Gould and Krasner locate the two countries' present difficulties—the pressures on their international and domestic postwar settlements—mainly in a declining tolerance of the United States for asymmetrical relations with former clients now turned into competitors.

How the new international conditions of the post–cold war era affect the two countries and how they respond to them is conditioned, according to both chapters, by the ways they were originally embedded in the postwar international order. A crucial difference here is that Germany chose, had to choose, or was able to choose to cede a portion of its sovereignty to a set of supranational institutions embracing Germany as well as its regional neighbors. In part this was because, unlike Japan, Germany emerged from the war divided, which made it smaller and more acceptable to surrounding countries. Moreover, with its eastern part cut off, postwar Germany was more amenable structurally than the Weimar Republic to internal democratization, liberalization, and indeed Westernization. And, even more important, Germany, and especially West Germany, was located in a regional environment in which it was big but not overwhelmingly big. Thus a process of regional institution building became possible, which, with the support of the United States, provided Germany with secure export markets without the need for military conquest and generally avoided a repetition of the historical mistakes of the Treaty of Versailles.

---

4. Clearly this was a fundamental transformation by way of large-scale "hybridization," as the term is used throughout this book.

The North Atlantic Treaty Organization (NATO) and European integration provided a framework within which Germany could prosper and live in peace, although and because it was allowed to recover its sovereignty only in shared, pooled form. In fact this framework proved capable of effectively "binding" even a united Germany after the end of the cold war. In particular, supranational institutions ensured compatibility between the new Germany's internal order and what Katzenstein calls its regional milieu. This it did by laying Germany open to Europeanization while opening up Europe to some degree of Germanization in the form of a progressive extension of German institutions beyond its borders, conditioned on Germany having firmly internalized the principles and structures of liberal democracy and a free market.

Japan's integration into its regional environment took a very different course. After World War II, the country remained undivided, being occupied by just one power, the United States, which saw no reason to share control of Japan with its Asian neighbors. With hindsight, this may have been a rather mixed blessing. The lasting result of the formative postwar situation of Japan was dependence on the United States, if only because U.S. supremacy was required to assure other countries in the region of Japan's commitment to peaceful, nonhegemonic relations. Moreover, whereas Germany over time began to blend into its European environment and especially the German state came to accept a condition of external as well as internal semisovereignty (Katzenstein 1987) as both legitimate and beneficial, Japan remained a distinct entity bent on restoring and defending its sovereign independence. National sovereignty, however, came at the price of lasting suspicions on the part of other countries in the region with respect to Japanese intentions.

Like Germany, Japan developed a distinct pattern of linkages with the countries in its region that included the United States as an important additional external participant. Asian regionalism, however, according to Katzenstein, was not and is not based on legal integration and joint supranational institutions but remains much more informal in character. As a consequence, it is much more dominated by the regional lead country, Japan, making it more vulnerable to resentment on the part of smaller countries. Indeed, as in Europe, Katzenstein observes, the Asian regional order strongly reflects the domestic order of its core nation in that informality and hierarchy take the place and perform the function in Asia of constitutionalism and the rule of supranational law in Europe.

These differences, the two chapters point out, have important consequences for international relations as well as national and international economic policy. With respect to the former, Germany and Japan face insistent U.S. demands to accept more "responsibility" for regional and global security. Acceding to such demands will require the two countries significantly to build up their military capabilities in line with their economic capacity while reneging on their respective postwar commitments to a nonmilitary, "pacifist" conduct of international relations. Such a change, however, might appear threatening to the two countries' regional neighbors unless, according to Gould and Krasner, the military forces of Germany and Japan are deployed strictly under U.S. control and in the service of U.S. (by definition peacekeeping) objectives. Indeed, given the firm integration of German troops in NATO and the presence of U.S. troops on German soil, German postwar pacifism seems to have become dispensable, making possible German participation in the "out-of-area" operations that provide the *raison d'être* for the U.S. military establishment in the post–cold war period. In the case of Japan, by comparison, U.S. pressures for a military buildup and for accompanying changes in the U.S.-sponsored Japanese constitution, to enable the country to support the projection of U.S. power in cases such as the Gulf War, Kosovo, or the expedition into Afghanistan, are bound to encounter Asian resistance because the binding of Japan to U.S. and Western objectives must appear much less complete and irreversible than in the case of Germany.

Concerning the economy, European integration has effectively opened up Germany and foreclosed any return to a policy of autarchy, with open regionalism (as Katzenstein puts it) allowing for strong links between Europe and the world economy at large, especially the United States. Moreover, as European integration proceeded in the 1980s and 1990s, it gradually extricated the national states of Germany and the other European countries from the governance of their internationalized economies, basically reducing them to a market-making and market-enforcing role. With the redefinition of the economic role of the nation-state, the economic constitution of integrated Europe increasingly became fundamentally liberal.

In the early postwar decades of German semisovereignty, it was mainly a variety of traditional para-state institutions, including in particular the associations of business and labor, that took the place of the strong state of the past in organizing German capitalism. But with Europeanization progressing, the societal foundations of the German model of political economy turned out to be only partly capable of extension to Europe as a whole and less so the more their function was to suspend or modify markets rather than to expand or defend them. In the absence of a European superstate replicating the interventionist national state of the postwar era of "embedded liberalism," Europeanization will remain identical with depoliticization, privatization, and disorganization—or, in other words, liberalization—of a less and less national European economy. The strong and often dominant German presence in the economy and society of Europe, although much more established, institutionalized, and secure than the

Japanese presence in Asia, comes at the price of a loss of national autonomy and of nationally distinctive modes of economic governance.

Japan, unlike Germany, retained its economic independence, as witnessed, among other things, by its national currency and continuing trade
disputes with the United States. In a period of economic internationalization, however, economic sovereignty may be more of a liability than an
asset. The fact that in the 1990s Japan was still formally in command of
the interventionist instruments of traditional nation-states allowed successive Japanese governments to try to overcome the economic crisis by lowering interest rates and inflating public expenditure, not least to protect the
country's postwar labor regime of lifelong employment. The result was
more than one and one-half decades of economic stagnation and a
national debt that will immobilize policy for a long time to come.

Germany, by comparison, was protected from similar temptations by the
European monetary system and later by the European Monetary Union
and the Stability Pact. By Europeanizing national economic policy,
European integration prevented the German state from adopting a
national course of action that might have been viable in a more closed
economy but was doomed to fail in the internationalizing world of the
1990s. The crisis of the labor market that resulted from German compliance with the new rules of the game in internationalized capital markets
could be explained to the electorate by the government as an inevitable
consequence of international commitments to privatization, budget
consolidation, and a free play of market forces. German adjustment to
globalization largely ended its national economic identity and, with it, its
postwar commitment to politically managed full employment. In Japan,
by comparison, the distinctiveness of the national economy and the up-
to-now largely successful defense of employment by national means was
bought at the expense of a deep crisis of capital markets and of lagging
adjustment to the realities of a new international economy.

Technology and Innovation

A second context that affects the performance of different variants of a
capitalist political economy is technological development and its changing
dynamics. The chapters by Kozo Yamamura and Robert Boyer share the
assumption that differences in national economic institutions make for
different capabilities with respect to technological innovation and the
application of technology. Simplifying somewhat, the German and
Japanese political economies seems to be predisposed toward incremental,
experientially based innovation that improves existing products; U.S. institutions seem to favor radical innovation that gives rise to new industrial
sectors. Indeed, as in international relations, the two countries in the post-

war period seem to have carved out niches for themselves in the capitalist world system in which their particular technological predispositions, grounded in their distinctive institutions, can be deployed and developed for national advantage (Hall and Soskice 2001). These niches have become less secure as increased international competition has lowered the defenses of national capitalist systems against international penetration, and a new technological dynamism has begun to redistribute the comparative advantages of competing national systems of innovation.

Boyer and Yamamura pose, and answer in the negative, the question of whether the present economic difficulties of Germany and Japan should make the two countries emulate the U.S. way of generating and adapting technological innovations. To the contrary, placing current events in a longer-term historical perspective, they warn against such attempts, urging instead that policymakers in the two countries rely on indigenous solutions that capitalize on proven strengths. But whereas Yamamura emphasizes the similarities of Germany and Japan in comparison to the United States, Boyer shows that the two countries at the same time differ considerably.

Yamamura offers two observations on which he bases his discussion of the issue of convergence. The first is that, since the beginning of the Industrial Revolution, there have been two long waves, or paradigms, of technological change. One was based on steam energy and steel and extended roughly from the 1780s to 1870s; the other was based on electricity and human-made new materials, beginning in the 1880s and continuing into the early 1970s. Each paradigm consisted of two phases that lasted approximately half a century: a breakthrough phase in which the new paradigm appeared and new institutions emerged helping its adoption and a maturation phase when innovation centered on making the new technology more productive and the resulting economic growth more sustainable.

Second, according to Yamamura, since the early 1970s the world has entered into the breakthrough phase of a third paradigm, the digital revolution based on information technology. In this period, the more market-driven capitalism of the Anglo-American mode is favored over the more socially embedded German and Japanese capitalisms that are less responsive to market signals. More generally, Yamamura argues that different institutional arrangements are differently well adapted to the different stages of the technological cycle. In times such as the end of the twentieth century when basic innovation predominates, the U.S. model has a comparative advantage and Germany and Japan lag behind. However, like its predecessors, the third paradigm will also eventually enter into a maturation phase and then the German and Japanese systems will be able to prosper from their specific capacities. To recover high economic performance in the future, therefore, both Germany and Japan would be well advised to preserve the cooperative capacities that have enabled their economies to excel in the postwar decades, which were the maturation phase of the last technological cycle.

In advancing his view, Yamamura discusses various examples of cooperative German and Japanese institutions, evaluating in comparison with U.S.-type institutions the long- and short-term gains and losses in productivity, distributional equity, employment, and income that are associated with them. Yamamura stresses the importance for both Germany and Japan of evolving a political consensus capable of distinguishing between the short-term reasons for the current crisis (such as structural fatigue and mismatch) and the essential strengths of the two countries' growth-promoting cooperative institutions. These, he argues, should not be sacrificed even though they may temporarily be somewhat out of step with current dynamics of change.

Boyer's chapter closely relates the dynamics of innovation to the issue of the variety of capitalism. Many authors have proposed various taxonomies based alternatively on the style of economic policy, the roles of state and market, and the opposition between uncoordinated and coordinated economies or between embedded and disembedded capitalism. Boyer argues that these criteria have to be pooled in order to characterize the basic institutional elements of economic systems, in particular the monetary regime, the wage-labor nexus, the form of competition, the nature of the relations between state and citizens, and the insertion of the national economy into its international environment. For *régulation* theory, Japan and Germany are variants of embedded capitalism with, however, quite distinctive growth regimes. German growth, according to Boyer, is based on a social-democratic institutional architecture that produces highly skilled workers, enabling the economy to compete on quality and product differentiation in world markets. In contrast, Japan has established what Boyer calls a companyist compromise, enabling it to play the more conventional game of mass production and consumption, with a growth regime founded on increasing returns to scale and on the polyvalence of workers providing flexibility and quality.

Why, then, did the German and Japanese success of the 1980s turn into a more uncertain macroeconomic condition in the subsequent decade? Whereas the German innovation system suffered from the costs associated with reunification and from the preparation for the launching of the euro, its Japanese counterpart was destabilized by the bursting of the financial bubble of the 1980s and the aftereffects of the 1997 Asian crisis. In other words, for Boyer the change in the economic fortunes of the two countries is not a consequence of the end of the catching-up period, of a lack of market competition, or of a failure to develop typically U.S. economic institutions. Each economy, he argues, has to realign its domestic institutions in its own way to accommodate the shift in the international system toward financial globalization, as well as a possible shift in the dominant technological paradigm linked to the diffusion of information and communication technologies.

It follows that, according to Boyer, we should not expect an institutional convergence of Japan and Germany on a market-led version of capitalism. First, national systems of innovation are more complementary to one another than competing with one another. Incremental reforms that preserve a system's historical style are therefore more promising than the destruction of existing institutions and their replacement by a replica of a foreign institutional architecture. Second, hybridization—that is, the transplantation of foreign institutions and their adaptation to the domestic context—is in any case much more likely than pure imitation. Third, the viability of a social system of innovation and its regulation mode depends on its complementarity with the economy's core institutional forms and not on its proximity to a market-led "best way" that has its own specific complementarities. Last but not least, concurring with Yamamura, Boyer argues that it is a mistake to extrapolate from the developments of the 1990s since a future stabilization of the world economy and the maturation of information and communication technology will hand competitive advantage back to German and Japanese institutional settings. Boyer concludes that, also for this reason, these will remain very different from the U.S. system, even though they are likely to be significantly transformed and reformed.

Labor Relations and Production

The next two chapters, one by Kathleen Thelen and Ikuo Kume and the other by Ulrich Jürgens, look at the German and Japanese systems of labor relations and production. Both systems are rooted in and reflect the two countries' specific postwar settlements and versions of class compromise, as well as the different niches they have found in world markets.

As already indicated by Yamamura and Boyer, the socially embedded capitalisms of Germany and Japan derived their outstanding economic performance in large part from social institutions that supported cooperation between capital and labor. Among other things, such cooperation made possible a kind of industrial innovation that comes from shop-floor workers safe enough in their positions not to be concerned about making themselves redundant. The essays by Thelen and Kume and by Jürgens explore how the institutions that underpinned labor-management cooperation in postwar Germany and Japan are changing, how the two countries' distinctive politics of production and productivity are being transformed by internationalization and changing markets and technologies, what the prospects are for Germany and Japan to continue using high social integration as an asset for their pursuit of economic prosperity and international competitiveness, and to what extent we can expect the two countries to resist pressures for convergence and defend their distinctive politics and social organization. Although the two chapters discuss different elements of the relationship between capital and labor and ask somewhat different questions, their findings overlap with one another and also with some of the conclusions of the two preceding chapters.

More specifically, although the authors do see changes, essentially they report a great deal of continuity, far more than envisaged in common speculations about nonliberal capitalism having to emulate wholesale what is currently widely regarded as "best practice." Indeed neither of the two chapters observes or anticipates radical breaks with the two countries' postwar regimes of industrial relations and production. In particular, Thelen and Kume find that those who expected the labor-inclusive institutions of Germany and Japan to be challenged by an employer offensive as soon as the power of labor was weakened by unemployment or international competition were proven wrong by the course of events. Although neoliberal rhetoric abounds in both countries, when it comes to the realities of production, employers in Germany and Japan appear to be as dependent as ever on their workers' goodwill. Even if they want to, it seems that employers in the two countries cannot afford to frustrate the settled expectations of workers for social protection, stable or even lifetime employment, codetermination and consultation, and so on because this would disrupt long-grown production arrangements and thereby undermine companies' market position precisely during a period of exacerbating competition. Employer dependence on social integration at the workplace, Thelen and Kume argue, makes for a resilience of labor-inclusive institutions not anticipated by traditional theories of political economy. In both Germany and Japan, the adoption in the past of a mode of production for which social peace is a productive asset militates for its continuation, simply because of the costs—including those of writing off past investment in consensual workplace relations—and the uncertainties of switching to a different mode.

This does not preclude change altogether, and in fact Thelen and Kume observe a lot of it. Especially in Germany, it appears that new lines of cleavage have begun to subvert the traditional politics of industrial relations, lines that are emerging within rather than between the two classes. Among employers, divisions arise between those willing and able to pay almost any price for social peace and those who feel exploited, not just by strong unions, but also by large firms negotiating high wage increases not only for themselves but, through the associations of employers, also for small and medium-size firms—which at the same time come under pressure from the large firms to cut the prices of the intermediate products they supply to them. Similarly, among labor there appears to be a broadening gap between a shrinking core of well-protected and safely employed workers in the primary sector and those who remain unemployed or are in other ways sidelined, for example in casual or low-wage service sector employment.

In terms of organized relations between management and labor at the industrial level, declining solidarity among employers paradoxically becomes a serious concern for German unions. Because these depend on functioning employer associations for the viability of industry-level collective bargaining, they must regard defections among employers from their associations or from the collective agreement as a threat to themselves. On the opposite side, employer associations feel increasingly powerless and less able than ever to resist union demands, in part because their large members, operating in ever more competitive world markets, have become unwilling to allow their association to order them to lock out their workforces. In this way, they deprive their associations of their principal weapon against union demands in a system of centralized bargaining.

What does this bode for the future? Are the dilemmas, tensions, paradoxes, and contradictions that Thelen and Kume observe in Germany just by-products of a normal institutional evolution or are they a first sign of a fundamental decline of the viability of social arrangements once designed to overrule market forces and to make the capitalist labor market amenable to collective regulation and political modification? And as far as Japan is concerned, is the shrinkage of the domain of the lifetime employment and seniority wage regime that the authors describe just a quantitative retrenchment that will be reversible in better times or will it, as it continues, at some point turn into a change in quality? Both systems show strains, both are undergoing a reconfiguration of their elements, both are becoming smaller although they remain dominant, and both are more present in the old sectors of the economy than in the new ones. If in Japan the share of firms that no longer pay all their workers on the basis of seniority rises in one year from 10 to 19 percent, this may, as the authors say, not be "a free fall into neoliberalism." But creeping change may in the end produce the same result. The authors rightly guard against overestimating latest events, paying too much attention to changes at the margins and overlooking that the center is still large and holding firm. But it is also true that it is precisely on the margins that the new shows first.

Those who read Thelen and Kume carefully will note that one change seems to be common to both countries, one that cannot be observed with complacency by believers in socially embedded and politically governed capitalism. Clearly in Germany and Japan, the realm of cooperative and labor-inclusive production has not just been shrinking, but the regimes that govern it seem to be losing their claim to universal applicability throughout the economy. More and more, the postwar labor regimes of nonliberal capitalism seem to be turning into peculiar institutions for selected sectors or firms in which they are becoming encapsulated—special cases in a growing diversity of employment relations whose institutional forms are driven less by the politics of class at the level of the society as a whole than by the particular pressures of product, capital, and labor markets operating on individual economic organizations. In the core, just as on the broadening and diversifying margins, employment relations seem to be less and less shaped by universal rights of industrial or social citizenship and more and more by a competitive search for the lowest possible transaction costs. In this way, what was—or was at least intended to be—a universal norm is being transformed into a variety of site-specific contractual arrangements that survive only as long as their benefits exceed their costs or as long as the expected losses associated with change exceed those associated with stability.

What Thelen and Kume report, then, may in the end amount to a quite radical change in the foundation of the German and, perhaps to a lesser extent, of the Japanese nonliberal systems of labor relations, regardless of the fact that on the surface we see mostly continuity. Markets, not politics, may already have become the driving force in the institutional evolution of German and Japanese labor relations. It is not a new class struggle that would then undermine the institutions to which we have become accustomed but, almost to the contrary, an intensification of cooperation in the economic core in response to competitive pressures, resulting in a gradual redefinition of rights into rewards for productivity and causing a growing gap between the core and the fringe, turning the core gradually into a special pattern among many others and in the end into just another fringe.

Drawing on the case of the automobile industry, Ulrich Jürgens investigates the fate of the German and Japanese models of industrial production in the 1980s and 1990s, the period in which automobiles became an internationally integrated and highly competitive global industry. Production models, the way the concept is used by Jürgens, comprise the norms and institutions that regulate work and labor relations in a country, the sociotechnical organization of work at the point of production, and the product strategies of firms. They result from the interaction among shop-floor workers and supervisors, engineers of various sorts, personnel managers, trade unionists, and specialists for production planning, product development, marketing, and so on. Comparing Germany and Japan to the United States, Jürgens covers the three leading automobile-producing countries of the period, looking at the evolution of their production models in terms of their endogenous development as well as of the effects of their mutual interaction.

Production models differ not just between countries, but also between companies. The rise of a national production model is in itself partly the result of a process of diffusion of company practices under the roof of supportive national institutions. Because companies are increasingly multinational, national models become ever more complex as companies try to set up their operations in different countries in ways that are amenable to central coordination. Moreover, more intense international competition and integration of firms across national borders increase the awareness on the part of management of differences in national production models, inspiring attempts to learn from others in order to improve competitiveness. It is in this perspective that Jürgens analyzes the development and the future prospects of the production models of Germany and Japan.

On the surface, the last two decades of the twentieth century were the period in which the Fordist-Taylorist production model that had evolved in the United States lost its status as "best practice" to be emulated worldwide. Jürgens mentions that for a short while the German model had some attraction in the United States. Overall, however, it was clearly Japan that moved into the position of the leader from which others, including the Germans, tried to learn.

Generally Jürgens's account projects an image of national models of production as being in permanent transformation, under the impact of changing market conditions and technologies as of well as their mutual encounter in markets and within multinational companies. That transformation, according to Jürgens, is governed by a logic distinctive for each model. In the right circumstances, the elements of a national model may form a virtuous circle, in which they reinforce one another in the service of high economic performance adapted to a given environment. But due to external or internal changes, virtuous circles may turn vicious and move a system into a downward spiral of deteriorating performance. Jürgens seems to imply that no production model can entirely escape this fate and that all will at some point require renewal and revitalization. Moreover, the examples Jürgens cites suggest that renewal often includes the importation of institutions and practices from other, competing models that achieve superior performance at a given time.

But does this mean convergence on a unified model of production, as some believe? Jürgens notes that in the decades of observation, Germany and especially the United States learned far more from Japan than Japan did from the two other countries—although a few elements of the German and U.S. models did become integrated into Japanese practice.[5] Convergence

5. Perhaps Japanese companyism may be easier to transplant, especially to the United States, because the German model requires the support of social institutions, such as industrywide collective bargaining and the vocational training system, that cannot be transplanted or constructed by individual firms. Elements of the Japanese model may therefore be particularly suitable to multinational companies striving to integrate their operations cross-nationally.

across the board, however, did not occur, and certainly not on the disembed-ded U.S. model, even though what the literature calls neo-American production arrangements did leave traces outside the United States. Instead of the wholesale replacement of one national model by another, Jürgens finds cases of the transplantation of elements between models. That such hybridization (a concept used also by Boyer to denote the adaptation of imported elements to requirements of system complementarity) often seems to work suggests that the configuration of institutions and practices that makes up a national model is less firmly locked together by functional interdependence than is often believed. Indeed there appears to be much space within national models of production for experimentation with new elements, including ones imported from other countries.

In any case, institutional change seems to entail a deconstruction of apparently coherent national models and their replacement with hybrid configurations better adjusted to rapidly changing circumstances in a competitive global economy. But what could perhaps be described as a softening up of interlocking complementarities in national production systems is obviously far from giving rise to identical arrangements. In part, as pointed out also by Thelen and Kume, this may be due to the sunk costs of investment in existing structures. Equally important, however, seems to be the fact that some elements of production systems are more nationally fixed than others and thus less at the disposition of, often multinational or international, system designers. As a result, these are forced to find ways of reconciling new imported elements with old indigenous ones. Particularly resilient to pressures for cross-national convergence seem to be the skill base on which production systems must draw and the institutions of industrial relations.

Put differently, although each of the three countries, including Japan, can to different degrees learn from the two others, such learning occurs under the constraints of local cultures and institutions (Streeck 1996). This may explain why the resulting hybrid systems, however much each may be changing over time, seem to remain recognizably different. Thus, when German auto manufacturers adopted some of the principles of Japanese lean production, this was negotiated with their workforces under codetermination. As a result, German lean production does not, for exam-ple, include the *kaizen* practice of a systematic and regular reduction of labor input both following and compelling improvements in productivity. Also, as Jürgens points out, each of the three countries is constrained by the resilience of its social relations and political contexts to invent its own distinctive solution to the problem, crucial especially for the German and Japanese modes of production, of how to induce shop-floor workers to contribute to productivity improvements that might make their current job redundant.

For the future, Jürgens expects change to be continuous and national models to become still more complex and heterogeneous, given the high potential for cross-national diffusion of selected system elements and the unmitigated tendency for producers to integrate cross-nationally. At the same time, the further evolution of production models will very likely not take the form of a race to catch up with one national leader. Companies and their experiments with different configurations of "best practices" will be even more important than they are already, and the same applies to the managerial skill of inventing new responses to evolving problems. No dramatic ruptures are foreseen and certainly not a wholesale Americanization of German and Japanese firms in a sector in which U.S. firms even in the 1990s remained behind their international competitors. But uncertainty will be considerable, not least concerning the viability and transferability of neo-American production arrangements that once more try to sidestep the problems of cooperation and social integration by relying on technological fixes.

Like Boyer and Yamamura, Jürgens does not predict that German and Japanese strengths will turn into weaknesses. But he does identify a series of problems. In part, these spring from the stickiness of established social institutions and traditional human resource endowments in the two countries. Jürgens mentions specifically the need for automobile producers to adjust the composition and distribution of skills, engage and excel in time-based competition, adopt new forms of supplier integration and modular production, "make progress in standardization of production while preserving motivations to innovate locally," and adjust labor relations to the possibility of a return of worker bargaining power. Even if these and other problems are successfully dealt with, however, this will, as in the past, not guarantee economic success. Success depends not just on the structure of production systems, but also on conditions external and unrelated to it, such as the international exchange rate—conditions which, in the terms used by Boyer, have nothing to do with a system's *virtú* and everything with its *fortuna*.

Financial Systems and Corporate Governance

Labor regimes in the sphere of production are matched in a capitalist economy to financial regimes in capital markets. The next two chapters, by Sigurt Vitols and Gregory Jackson, differ from standard analyses of financial systems and corporate governance in that they are acutely aware of this relationship.

Like other chapters in this volume, Vitols's account of the liberalization of the German and Japanese financial systems sets out from the difference between liberal and nonliberal versions of capitalism, without overlooking significant differences within the two categories. As others have done before him, Vitols observes that the nonliberal financial systems of Germany and Japan differ from the liberal financial system of the United States in that they are bank-based rather than market-based. Instead of selling securities and rights of control in an anonymous financial market, in the traditional German and Japanese systems firms typically mobilize financial resources through long-term relations with banks. These, in turn, are given the right to monitor from inside the firm the way in which management makes use of the credit provided to it.

Vitols points out that bank-based finance not only rests on specific social-structural foundations but also comes with governance arrangements that differ profoundly from those associated with liberal, market-based financial systems. Among the societal conditions that militate toward bank-based finance are a large share of small and medium-size firms in the national economy; a relatively low level of income inequality, requiring suitable instruments for saving and capital formation; a low level of public debt, making the funding of government activities independent from the existence of developed capital markets; and a pay-as-you-go pension system that works without large-scale capital accumulation.

As to governance arrangements, market-based financial systems tend to rely on independent regulatory agencies to enforce the compliance of market participants with general rules designed to prevent market failure. Germany and Japan, by contrast, have traditionally controlled the performance of their financial systems through corporatist institutions and state intervention, respectively. Whereas in Germany the setting of standards and the enforcement of good practice was largely left to corporatist arrangements in which the associations of the banking industry played a prominent semipublic role, in Japan MOF controlled the activities of the banks through administrative guidance, that is, informal advice by government bureaucrats made irresistible by the wide discretion of the ministry on a wide range of issues important to a bank's economic well-being.

Corporatist self-regulation and statist administrative guidance, Vitols indicates, laid open the two financial systems to politicization and made their operation subservient to the pursuit of public policy objectives, for example in the context of industrial policies aimed at growth and full employment. Politicization thus turned nonliberal financial systems into national economic infrastructures. Liberalization can then be seen as politically instituted depoliticization, or commercialization, of finance, relieving the financial sector of public responsibility and setting financial institutions free to act as normal private enterprises.

How far has the liberalization of financial regimes in Germany and Japan—the transformation of the financial systems of nationally embedded capitalism into an internationally integrated private industry like any other—progressed since the mid-1990s? Vitols describes the manifold pressures on the social foundations of bank-based finance, in particular rising inequality, an increase in public debt, a shift toward funded pension systems, and, in Germany, a reorientation in the business strategy of large banks in the direction of U.S.-style investment banking. But he also notes strong retarding forces, among them the persistence of a large sector of small and medium-size firms in the two countries that continues to be better served by relational banking than by arm's-length market finance. In addition, by looking at the historical origins of bank- and market-based financial systems, Vitols makes clear that a move from the former to the latter involves much more than simple deregulation, given that free financial markets require elaborate rules to attract customer confidence and to work efficiently. Deregulation and depoliticization of finance, in other words, in reality take the form of a complex process of reregulation, which is itself highly political and therefore susceptible to being derailed or compromised by opposing interests.

The liberalization of financial regimes, Vitols shows, is driven by banks in Germany and by the state in Japan. Whereas German banks find the old regime too constraining for their commercial ambitions, the Japanese state is seeking an adequate response to international pressures and to the need for more allocative efficiency in a depressed national economy. Vitols notes that although the erosion of the social foundations of bank-based finance has progressed faster in Germany than in Japan and although German politics was far more receptive to financial liberalization, not even in Germany is the process adequately described as one of convergence on an Anglo-American liberal pattern. In fact, reminiscent of Boyer and Jürgens, Vitols uses hybridization to signify the however tentative and perhaps fragile incorporation of liberal structures and practices into the nationally embedded financial systems of Germany and Japan.

"Hybridization," the way Vitols uses the term, involves an emergent dualism in financial systems between a liberal segment serving the financial needs of large, increasingly multinational companies and a relationship-based one catering to the many small and medium-size firms in the two countries. But the concept also seems to refer to a mixing of liberal and nonliberal elements in financial regimes due to the persistence, or at least the retarded disappearance, of a number of societal conditions supportive of and indeed demanding nonmarket financial arrangements, reinforced by strong political forces that oppose liberalization and successfully intervene in the complex politics of deregulation and reregulation. German corporatism, it appears, is more conducive to gradual liberalization than is Japanese state interventionism, although this may be explained less by the traditional absence of general rules in the Japanese system than by the contingent condition of the present banking crisis forcing the Japanese state de facto to nationalize most of the large banks. Moreover, whether or not the emerging melange of liberal and nonliberal, disembedded and embedded elements in the German financial system can become self-reproductive must remain an open question. Clearly the European Union, in the name of an integrated European financial market with free competition on a level playing field, is continuing to attack the special status of public and semipublic financial institutions in Germany, which in Vitols's scenario seems to be the mainstay of relational banking, obstructing total convergence to a market-driven system.[6]

Hybridization is a key concept also in Gregory Jackson's detailed analysis of the transformation of corporate governance in Germany and Japan. Jackson deals with corporate governance in a broad sense, referring to the totality of institutional arrangements at societal and company levels that link firms to their two main production factors, capital and labor, and allocate rights of control between them and management, the role of the latter being to organize the cooperation between capital and labor and mediate between the two.

Jackson begins by reconstructing the ideal-typical similarities and differences between the traditional nonliberal German and Japanese models of corporate governance. Central to both was a symmetrical correspondence between dedicated, patient, captive, committed capital, on the one hand, and a stable, equally dedicated labor force enjoying what Jackson calls rights of industrial citizenship, on the other. The two elements reinforced one another and were maintained in equilibrium by "contingent management." Common to nonliberal modes of corporate governance, Jackson points out, is that neither a firm's relations to capital nor those to labor are organized as anonymous market relations easily severed if relative prices change. To the contrary, because both capital and labor relations are long-term and particularistic, it is an important task of management to protect their stability against the fluctuations of the markets.

As for the differences between the two countries, Jackson's analysis of capital markets intersects with that of Vitols in that he emphasizes the

---

6. It should be noted that Vitols never mentions the contribution of the European Union to the liberalization of the German financial system, probably because it is so pervasive. As pointed out in Katzenstein's chapter, Germany as a national state has practically ceded control over its financial system to a supranational organization charged with and bent on opening up national economies. This development culminated in the completion of the monetary union and the introduction of the euro in 1999. The European Monetary Union prevented the German state in the 1990s from using fiscal or monetary expansion to fight rising unemployment in the wake of German unification. Although this may in the end have done more good than harm, the important point is that the Japanese state commanded and still commands a much greater degree of sovereignty, including the freedom to make mistakes, with respect to the governance of the national financial system and its use for national economic objectives.

importance of relational banking for the creation of patient capital in non-liberal capitalism while recognizing the different structural foundations, institutional supports, and political purposes of bank-based finance in the two countries. Also, Jackson shows that the institutions of industrial citizenship, on which corporate governance in Germany and Japan rests on the labor side, are quite differently constructed and have originated along different historical trajectories. Here, the mostly informally based enterprise communities of Japan are compared to a constitutionalized model of the firm in Germany, in which the firm's internal structure is to a major extent defined by legal rights and obligations instituted to provide for a socially acceptable balance between the classes and to secure a public interest in good, "socially responsible" company governance.

Jackson's chapter traces in detail how in the 1990s the institutional coherence between the capital and labor relations of German and Japanese firms, and in particular the correspondence between the nonmarket nonliberal arrangements linking the two to the firm as an organization and to its decision-making process, was upset by the liberalization of capital markets, especially the erosion of bank-based finance. Due to a number of complex interlocked developments, some related to internationalization and others not, firms in Germany and Japan have come under pressure to accord greater prominence to the interests of shareholders in the value of their investment, in many ways like firms in liberal Anglo-American environments. Jackson's central question is whether or to what extent the liberalization of capital relations in Germany and Japan is about to be followed by a liberalization of labor relations, in particular a disintegration of rights of industrial citizenship. Clearly this would, in an important respect, amount to the convergence of the German and Japanese models of corporate governance to a liberal Anglo-American model.

The answer Jackson offers is a highly qualified one. Corporate law and financial regimes were reorganized in liberal directions, new investors appeared on the scene with different expectations, banks lost or gave up their monitoring capacity, and market feedback began to take the place of relational banking, in Germany more than in Japan—with considerable impact on the governance of large firms in both countries, significant enough to be more than a continuation of the old logic in new forms. But there was no liberal convergence, at least as yet. Instead hybrid models began to emerge, firm by firm, that tried to accommodate increasingly market-driven capital relations with traditional industrial citizenship regimes. These too changed in the process, although they have proved far stickier than arrangements in capital markets. Due to this kind of asymmetrical change, institutional coherence declines, both within firms (whose capital and labor relations now follow partly different logics) and within national systems where different firms experiment with different ways of managing the new tensions and contradictions. Here Jackson's analysis again overlaps with that of Jürgens, who also finds growing diversity between firms within countries.

In summary, what Jackson sees forming in Germany and Japan is what he refers to as an "enlightened" or "weak shareholder-value model" succeeding the nonliberal corporate governance regimes of the past, differing enough from the latter to constitute something new, but also remaining distinct from the entirely market-driven liberal model of the Anglo-American tradition. In particular, while its influence is weakening on the margin, labor is still influential in German and Japanese firms, although in a new institutional configuration that is far from stable and seems particularly vulnerable to the further expansion of the market for control, in particular of opportunities for hostile takeover.

Rather than being coherently designed in one piece from above, the emerging new model is being negotiated mostly at the level of individual companies, in a process of widespread experimentation that is driven more by the market than by politics. Jackson argues that, historically, the economic efficiency of institutional arrangements—of corporate governance and others—often was an emergent phenomenon that was not and could not have been planned a priori. This leaves open the possibility that this time, too, some sort of unintended fit may develop between stable labor relations, however modified by market pressures, and a new form of capital relations that enables firms to satisfy demands for shareholder value and thereby attract sufficient investment to support stable employment for at least a core workforce.

Generally in his conclusions, Jackson expresses cautious optimism when he declares it "premature to assume that a stronger role of the capital market necessitates market-based labor relations with high external mobility and low participation rights." Reasonable as this must seem, however, it does suggest that the range of possible divergence from the liberal model has narrowed. Moreover, Jackson, like Jürgens, seems to predict that within the world of nonliberal, or less-than-fully-liberal, capitalism the national distinctiveness of institutional arrangements will decline. In particular, negotiated industrial citizenship responsive to market conditions and ultimately based in the competitive advantage to be derived from a stable and committed core workforce—which is clearly closer to the Japanese than to the traditional German pattern—is becoming the more likely version of nonliberal labor relations than politically based rights of participation granted regardless of considerations of efficiency in the pursuit of egalitarian social cohesion.

The Politics of Change

The final two chapters of the volume deal with the process of institutional change, in the two countries and elsewhere, in an effort to inform speculation about the likely future of nationally embedded capitalism in Germany and Japan by general theoretical reflection. Steven Vogel's essay directly follows on Jackson in its attempt to understand how, in the words of the subtitle, "the German and Japanese models are shaping their own transformations." Essentially, Vogel explicates the mechanisms underlying some of the changes described in detail in preceding chapters, especially those by Thelen and Kume, Jürgens, Vitols, and Jackson. He also concisely sums up the similarities and differences between the German and Japanese models; identifies a series of exogenous pressures to which the two systems must respond, such as the globalization of the economy, U.S. demands for market opening, and the rise of a new technological paradigm; and explains some of the differences in the pattern of change in Germany and Japan with reference to differences in national institutions.

Institutional change, according to Vogel, advances slowly and conservatively in the two countries, making it unreasonable to expect a dramatic departure from present patterns, not to mention convergence to an Anglo-American liberal version of capitalism. Drawing on evidence from the labor relations and financial systems of the two countries, Vogel suggests that whatever change may happen now or in the future inside the German or Japanese model will be "conditioned by the incentives and constraints of the model itself." Indeed Vogel implies that all institutional change, in liberal and in nonliberal systems, unless caused by a traumatic external shock, is bound to be gradual and (to use the favorite concept of the new historical institutionalism) path dependent, amounting in effect to the self-reproduction of the system and the preservation of its identity in changing external circumstances.

For this, Vogel offers a variety of reasons—economic, political, and social. Institutions, he argues, tend to be self-perpetuating because they make it rational for actors to invest in complementary arrangements and practices, thereby increasing both the usefulness of the institution itself and the costs of exiting from it. Moreover, institutions once they exist do not remain exogenous to the preferences of those acting within them but in fact shape those preferences to fit the constraints and opportunities they offer. As a result, the internal coherence and consistency of institutional configurations and of the practices informed by them, everything else being equal, are likely to grow over time as institutional structures are reinforced by increasingly compatible actor interests and preferences. Thus in an institutional context that traditionally places a premium on cooperation within long-term relations of mutual trust, adjustment to external pressures for change is likely to be negotiated with existing partners in a cooperative manner, rather than carried out unilaterally and in an effort to gain advantage over others, in order not to jeopardize the long-term benefits of trustful relations built at high costs in the past and because of preferences acquired in the meantime.

Institutional resilience is further increased by the dynamics of the political process and the effects of normative social integration. At the microlevel of individual actors, including corporate actors such as firms, adjustment to changing external conditions is constrained by politically enacted regimes at the macrolevel that must be changed if the adjustment in actor behavior is to be more than marginal. But regime change, according to Vogel, is even slower and more difficult to accomplish than behavioral change, due to the fact that politics normally offers numerous opportunities for special interest groups to veto reform, delaying and compromising it if not preventing it entirely. Indeed, as Vogel argues with reference to the subsequent chapter by Herbert Kitschelt, the political systems of Germany and Japan seem particularly prone to immobilism and deadlock. Although Vogel refrains from strong predictions given the uncertainty of the outcomes of the complex interaction between micro and macro adjustments in institutional regimes, he does not expect "a complete break with past patterns," not least because established practices tend to become valued for their own sake by social actors, making change even more unlikely.

Political competition, at least the way it exists in Germany and Japan, does not help. Herbert Kitschelt, whose chapter concludes the book, investigates the chances of liberal political reformism in the two countries—more precisely, of a politics that strengthens rather than blunts market incentives and increases the rewards for radical innovation. But rather than upsetting—as it were, from the outside—the conservative path dependence of their countries' economic institutions, German and Japanese democratic political and electoral competition, Kitschelt finds, are themselves deeply enmeshed in the two countries' postwar regimes of embedded capitalism. The result is that their possible outcomes are strongly predisposed toward the reproduction of existing institutional arrangements.

Why can party competition in Germany and Japan not become a source of policy innovation in the future? Kitschelt starts out with the proposition that the socially cohesive economic institutions of German and Japanese capitalism stifle innovation, especially of the radical sort that depends on high-risk trial-and-error experimentation. According to Kitschelt, and to some extent Boyer and Yamamura as well, however, it is exactly this kind of innovation that is needed to meet the new challenges of freer world markets and a new technological paradigm. Although governments may in principle be capable of changing the structure of economic incentives and disincentives in a country in a liberal direction, the incentives operating inside the German and Japanese political systems on party leaders and policymakers happen to be as conservative as those governing economic behavior in the two countries. To prove his point, Kitschelt recounts how governments in Germany and Japan have failed again and again in efforts to increase the flexibility of labor markets and end the misallocation of capital by a closed and politicized financial system.

Specifying a number of conditions for party competition bringing about fundamental change in economic policy, Kitschelt shows that they apply neither in Germany nor in Japan, although on the surface the political systems of the two countries seem quite different. Kitschelt suggests that the endemic conservatism of the two political systems is no accident because their formation was closely intertwined with the evolution of nationally embedded capitalism in the postwar period, shaping the pattern of political decision making so as to make it complementary to and supportive of the operation of the countries' economic institutions. The result is that, "Mass party organization in Germany and clientelist voter-party linkages in Japan both undercut the incentives for a large proportion of office-seeking politicians inside the relevant parties to support painful political-economic reform."

Obstacles to policy innovation seem greater in Japan than in Germany, although they are formidable there as well, as shown by the first period of office of the Gerhard Schröder government. Kitschelt does not categorically rule out radical change as a result of a severe economic crisis, a change in the mood of national electorates, or, in the German case, pressures for liberalization from the European Union. Generally, however, he concludes, in line with the other chapters, that a "radical break with cooperative market capitalism in favor of a liberal economic order is highly unlikely" in both countries.

Stability or Stagnation?

The common tenor in the institutionalist analyses collected in this volume is that Germany and Japan are not about to converge to the Anglo-American model. To the contrary, whatever changes may be observed on the surface of the German and Japanese models, the conclusion in all the chapters is that they will ultimately not undo the distinctiveness of the core institutions of nationally embedded and nationally managed capitalism. These include in particular cooperative labor relations, regimes of corporate governance that enable labor to participate in the decision making of large companies, and financial systems more attentive than those in liberal capitalist societies to the growth needs of local firms. What this apparent stability implies, however, is very much an issue of debate and contention.

Claims of an absence of convergence between Germany and Japan, on the one hand, and the Anglo-American world, on the other, are of interest only if the persistent differences called on to justify such claims are more than just ornaments on the outside of social systems that function essentially according to the same logic. The authors of the chapters of this book do not share in the esthetic anti-Americanism of some of the protesters against globalization, whose main concern seems to be with preserving the variety of diverse ways of life, as manifested in music, fashion, or regional cuisines. In the chapters we have reviewed, national distinctiveness refers to differences between national systems that matter for the way in which societies cohere and economies perform and especially for the way in which societies and economies are related to one another.

That Germany and Japan should retain their distinctiveness as nationally embedded versions of modern capitalism, therefore, can only be read to say that they were able, and will continue to be able, to defend the values that their institutions were designed to support. These include, in the one case, politically negotiated social cohesion and high social equality and, in the other, the protection of internal solidarity and external independence through politically guided economic development assuring equal status with the West, while avoiding the social disruptions associated with rapid modernization. More generally, nonconvergence of nonliberal and liberal capitalism implies that Germany and Japan will remain capable in the future of placing political compromise and national solidarity above market forces and of controlling the course of their economies by political intervention instead of submitting it, voluntarily or under pressure, to the free play of self-regulating markets. Or put the other way around, however different the institutions of Germany and Japan may continue to be from those of the Anglo-American world, such differences will be compatible with convergence theory unless they serve to defend normatively valued or politically willed social relations from erosion under market pressures and generally manage to contain the destructive effects of the "satanic mill" of the market (Polanyi 1944) on social cohesion and on the collective capacity to determine the national fate with political means.

Of course, if this is how we define nonconvergence, we can still hold different views of its consequences. For example, Vogel and Kitschelt would probably agree about the diagnosis that markets in Germany and Japan will continue for some time to be under a sort of political control that blunts their impact on social relations. But the same condition that Vogel describes as proof of a remarkable stability of national institutions in the face of adverse external pressures, Kitschelt regards as a potentially disastrous lack of capacity to face up to new challenges. What to one writer is a viable socioeconomic system capable of defending its identity, to the other is a sclerotic remnant of the past unable to adapt. Which of the two meanings of nonconvergence is the right one is difficult to decide, if only because up to a point they are not mutually exclusive. In a changing world, triumphant resilience in the short run may in the longer run be self-defeating rigidity. Stability and stagnation may be the same—at least until the costs of stagnation become so high that stability collapses.

Institutional stability, to Kitschelt, may be tantamount to failure to address new problems and exploit new opportunities. Whether this is the case—and whether resistance to liberalization in nationally embedded capitalism is a sign of healthy stability or of morbid stagnation—can ultimately be judged only on the basis of a system's economic performance. National economies may decide to use politics to blunt the impact of market incentives and to bind economic action to national political objectives such as social cohesion or collective self-determination. The question is to what extent this is associated with overall losses in welfare and performance, especially comparative performance in an open world market. Slower growth in production, employment, or productivity can for a while be accepted in the name of the collective values that the social embedding of the economy is supposed to serve. However, given the inevitable insertion of national economies in the world economy, economic underperformance is likely to result in external pressures and internal frictions—from exchange rate crises to the relative deprivation of consumers to the exit of disappointed investors—likely to make unsustainable institutions that trade prosperity for social or political objectives. In fact, low economic performance caused by nonliberal institutions that no longer fit a changed economic and technological environment may frustrate the attainment of precisely those values for whose sake nationally managed capitalism tries to keep market forces under control.[7] Long-term unemployment may give rise to a deep cleavage between insiders and outsiders in the labor markets of a society devoted to equality and social cohesion. Or a crisis of profitability or overinvestment may increase the difference between the leaders in technological modernization and a developmentalist country bent on catching up with them.

The nonconvergence of economic institutions, that is to say, may be regarded as a successful defense of identity if and only if the economy in question performs to expectations—just as it must be attributed to a rigid inability to adjust if, as a consequence, the economy suffers. Predictions as to how Germany and Japan will do economically if they continue to resist becoming more market-driven economies and societies such as the United

---

7. It is also possible that such values may, for reasons of their own, lose their *raison d'être*. German-style social cohesion and solidarity may make less sense in an open society with high immigration than in the ethnically homogenous society that Germany was in the 1950s. Or the sacrifices citizens are asked to make by a national policy of developmentalism may no longer seem legitimate once a country has found a safe place among the leading industrial societies.

States and Britain are, however, difficult to make.[8] A number of chapters in this book emphasize that national economic performance depends not just on an economy's internal institutional structure, but also on changing external circumstances beyond the control of national policymakers. Thus Yamamura points out that technological change may proceed in cycles, favoring more liberal capitalist systems at one point and more politically managed ones at another. From this Yamamura concludes that Germany and Japan should not now discard institutional capacities that they may want to be able to use for comparative advantage when the technological cycle turns again. The question, of course, is what to do in the meantime. The answer depends on when the dominant paradigm of technological development can be expected to again be favorable to nonliberal versions of capitalism. If temporary adverse conditions last too long, protracted economic underperformance may so emaciate the capacities of a national economy that they cannot be reactivated when more sympathetic conditions finally return.

Similarly, Boyer argues that, provided that a stable world economic order can be created in which countries may have confidence in their mutual economic relations, different national styles of innovation can coexist, each country specializing in what it does best and flourishing by working out a division of labor with other countries and entering into stable exchanges with them. But this, of course, is premised on the provision of a collective good (a reliable international economic order), which cannot be taken for granted. If international order can be restored, the stubborn defense of national values and identities may become a source of prosperity for all. If not, the potential comparative advantages of nationally embedded capitalist systems may not materialize and successful resistance to convergence will in effect amount to an inability to adjust to new conditions.

One general implication is the importance for national economic performance of international politics and economics, as reflected, for example, in the movement of the exchange rate. As Gould and Krasner indicate, the international political economy is a hierarchical system in which powerful actors such as the United States can deploy their political and military resources to shape the rules of the game so as to deny competing economies with nonliberal institutions their potential comparative advantages. Here, again, Boyer's reminder of the difference between *virtù* and *fortuna* is of help—that is, that it is not just on the virtue of a country's

---

8. There is also of course the possibility that change in an Anglo-American direction might be desirable but impossible, due to the dense coupling of existing institutions and the high associated transition costs that can for a long time be expected to exceed the costs of continued stagnation.

institutions that its economic success depends, but also, in a major way, on the good luck (or for that matter the bad luck) the country encounters in its external relations.

Another question that arises is whether social systems, in particular the socioeconomic systems of Germany and Japan, are indeed as robustly self-reproductive, or path dependent, as historical-institutionalist analyses (Thelen 1999a) tend to suggest. For example, although the evidence such analyses present often appears highly convincing, we might wonder whether the time frame within which change, or nonchange, is observed is too short. Analyses of contemporary developments inevitably suffer from the fact that the observations on which they are based are embedded in a continuous stream of events that is cut off at an entirely arbitrary moment, the time of writing. There also is the tendency of human observers to mistake the short term for the long term and to overestimate the length of the time and the finality of the events they have seen.

What if the trends in German and Japanese financial and labor relations that are described in this book were to continue at the same pace for another, say, ten years? And continue they do, with shareholder value further increasing in significance in Germany and lifetime employment further declining in Japan. What if, entirely within the logic of contemporary developments, impending tax reforms in Germany set off a wave of divestment of corporate cross-shareholding, as they likely will? If the European Union succeeded in further undercutting, step by step, the special status of public financial institutions in Germany? If more and more Japanese firms were forced to renege on promises of employment security? Clearly there must be a point when cumulative incremental change affects the identity of a socioeconomic system to such a degree that change must be recognized for all practical purposes as fundamental.

Moreover, we might ask whether what analyses of path dependence call a complete break with past patterns, only to show that it has not occurred in Germany and Japan, is not defined in such a way that it practically cannot occur at all, except perhaps in the most extreme circumstances. If this is so, the reassuring finding of self-reproduction of social arrangements may actually be a conceptual artifact. If the only change recognized as fundamental is of a sort that is practically impossible, social systems are stable almost by definition. Similar concerns apply to the concept of convergence. In the real world, however far convergence may go, some differences will always remain, making it possible to argue that the systems being compared have not become identical and convergence has therefore not taken place. Because convergence cannot result in identity and change comes always and only with continuity, everything depends on theory being able to distinguish major change from minor change, just as significant convergence must be recognizable short of complete identity.

Otherwise all change and all convergence, the real as well as the possible, is continuity and proof of stable difference, regardless of how much an existing institution or system of institutions is in fact transformed.

German codetermination, to take an example, is highly unlikely to disappear as an institution in any foreseeable future. But, as described by Jackson and others, it may be undergoing a transformation from a general legal right of industrial citizenship into an economically expedient device to improve a firm's competitiveness, differently organized in different workplaces to fit specific technological and market requirements and based more on contractual arrangements than on the traditional, public constitution of the workplace. An institutional analysis that fails to recognize such transformation as a major change, a change that affects the operation of the institution of codetermination in a fundamental way, misses the essence of what it observes. An institution need not disappear altogether for there to be fundamental change, and self-reproduction in a meaningful sense may stop well short of a complete breakdown, for which there are very few empirical examples anyway.

Furthermore, to the extent that institutionalist theories derive the tendency of social arrangements to reproduce themselves from the rational calculations of agents careful not to waste their past investment in institutional coherence, they must beware of attributing too much foresight to human actors. More often than not, actors may have no way of knowing exactly what action best fits a key institution that they want to preserve. Indeed, actors may be unaware of what the key institutions of their system are—for example, as in the case of the German unions and Social Democrats who for decades ritually denounced the "power of the banks." They may also be confused as to what the system is that a given institution is supposed to fit into—as in the case of the German social market economy, which is defined quite differently by employers and unions. Often all actors can do is gamble, at the risk of unintentionally introducing new elements into an institutional setting with which they may later turn out to be incompatible. Politicians, knowing their own lack of foresight and realistically discounting the certainties offered to them by their advisers, may reasonably behave like adventurers, taking measures whose compatibility with measures previously taken they have no way of assessing. The reason this may work for them is that, given how social systems operate, it usually takes some time for the effects of a lack of compatibility to show, making it possible to postpone complementary adjustments until emerging problems have finally become critical—if they emerge at all before the present officeholders retire.

Moreover, the problems actors confront are often neither self-explanatory nor paired with obvious or unique solutions. Systems have different problems when looked at from different perspectives, and in fact some people's problems may be other people's solutions and vice versa. Also, in social and political life causal textures are not so tight that every problem has one and only one solution. Even with the best available knowledge, actors may have to choose among alternative responses whose long-term effects, including those for the reproduction of the system in its present condition, may be both significantly different and impossible to know beforehand.

Uncertainty is a fundamental condition of social life in yet another respect. Although institutions embody constraints and opportunities, or rights and obligations, their exact meaning can never be completely clear because no social norm is ever unequivocal and capable of speaking for itself (Bendix 1956). Interpretations of what an institution demands or allows are not only typically contested, but may change over time as new facets of the institution are discovered. In fact what exactly an institution demands, makes possible, or penalizes is continuously redefined by the activities of what may be called interpretive entrepreneurs (Fligstein 2001)—for example, tax lawyers specializing in finding loopholes in a tax code that nobody else has found before and successfully defending in the courts their interpretation of what the law "really means." Thus, in the German system of industrial relations, works councils and employers continuously test the limits of their license to conclude workplace agreements supplementing or modifying the industrial agreement. Workplace agreements of a sort that seemed out of the question in the mid-1980s are entirely acceptable one and one-half decades later under the same, formally unchanged but collectively reinterpreted regime of centralized collective bargaining. In fact, such testing of the limits of the law, with the effect of a gradual but quite possibly fundamental change of its meaning, is to a large part what occurs in the complex interaction, mentioned by Vogel, between the company level and the regime level in national financial and labor relations systems.

Another factor that contributes to uncertainty is that social action, including that of the purposeful problem-solving sort, always has multiple effects that often cannot be anticipated equally well. Whereas some of these effects may be functional in terms of a given objective, others may be dysfunctional. Indeed in social life, as we learn from Robert Merton (1963), every function tends to come with a dysfunction, which makes for endemic tensions and contradictions in social systems that frustrate all attempts to ever make them fully coherent. The expectation that national systems of capitalism will grow increasingly identical over time as rational actors invest in the complementarity of institutional domains is then an illusion—not only because actors often do not know what is in fact complementary, but also because growing complementarity in one respect is inevitably accompanied by new frictions in others. In this way, what is initially a solution to a problem may with time become a problem itself. For example, using social security for the early retirement of redundant workers may suggest itself as a system-compatible response to employment problems in the German high-wage economy, with its urgent need for worker cooperation in productivity improvement. The more widely a response is adopted and the more generally it is accepted, however, the more incompatible it becomes with other objectives—in this case with budget consolidation and lowering the costs of labor to increase employment.

Socioeconomic systems, this implies, are even in the best of cases much less in functional harmony and structural equilibrium than we might think. To the contrary, they often seem beset with "dialectical" contradictions and riddled with self-made dysfunctions that can be fixed only provisionally, if at all, and in ways that themselves are likely to give rise to new tensions. Considering in addition the limited cognitive capacities of human agents and their inevitable errors of judgment about what will stabilize and destabilize a given social arrangement, a model of institutional change in which all major change results from exogenous shocks and endogenous change is limited by definition to incremental adjustments that increase the functional coherence and thereby strengthen the identity of the system seems unrealistic at best. To do justice to the complexities of the real world, institutionalist theories of change have to allow for fundamental endogenous change redefining core elements and values of social systems, including nationally embedded systems of capitalism (Deeg 2001). Such change may be brought about by internal dysfunctions that undermine institutional coherence and can be eliminated only by major reorganization; by actions restoring stability for the moment but inadvertently jeopardizing it for the future; by "wrong" decisions destroying important conditions of institutional continuity; by functional complementarities causing rising costs; by new opportunities for experimentation opened up by denser interaction with competing systems; or by a logic of action that unintentionally turns what was for a particular period a virtuous into a vicious circle, creating a need for a revitalization of the system through reorganization, often by grafting onto it elements of other, competing systems.

Internationalization, Liberalization, Hybridization

Gradual but, potentially, fundamental change in nationally embedded systems of capitalism is associated in the chapters of this volume with three concepts: internationalization, liberalization, and hybridization. As national economies and political systems move closer together, actors that experience their own system as partially dysfunctional are tempted to broaden their strategic repertoire by including in it elements of apparently better performing, competing systems. In Germany and Japan, pressures for institutional reform resulting from invidious comparison are likely to grow as the German employment crisis and the Japanese debt and profitability crisis continue and solutions that fit the past experience and present structures of nonliberal political economies appear either economically unsustainable or internationally unacceptable. Among the driving forces in this respect are likely to be new corporate actors with weak national loyalties or identities, such as multinational firms and international organizations.

As Jürgens makes clear, importing apparently superior practices or institutions from other countries in order to revitalize an underperforming national system normally requires adjustments to improve the fit of imported elements with their new environment. But it is not always and necessarily only the foreign transplant that is modified in the process of hybridization. A transplant from a foreign system may be so valuable to powerful actors inside or outside its new context that possible frictions with older elements are resolved by adjustment not just of the former, but also or even exclusively of the latter. This seems to be the case, for example, in the rebuilding of German codetermination in response to the ongoing importation of a more or less Anglo-American capital market regime into the German economy. As noted previously, social systems, being much less tightly coupled than conservative theories of institutional change assume, do seem to allow for considerable experimentation with new elements imported from the outside, also because their rejection time is long enough to accommodate the modifications to be made.

Internationalization refers to a widening of strategic horizons and an extension of the chains of social causation beyond national borders. It includes the immigration of foreign actors and practices in previously closed national systems, as well as emigration of actors and activities to foreign or supranational circuits. Generally, internationalization adds the world outside national states to the playing field of some, although not all, of the actors inside them. It increases the presence within national systems of their international environment; it reconfigures social actors, for example, by turning national into multinational firms; and it creates new opportunities and constraints for actors within and between national societies.

The trajectories of postwar German and Japanese capitalism differ fundamentally with respect to the insertion of the two systems in their international contexts. Whereas Japan continues to be a sovereign national state, German sovereignty is now irrevocably pooled in the European Union and dispersed over a multitude of supranational and intergovernmental agencies unrelated to any meaningful definition of a German national interest. National self-determination and survival, concepts that continue to play a central role in Japanese political life, have lost almost all meaning in Germany and have in fact practically disappeared from German public discourse. The same may soon be true for postwar ideas of economic equality underwriting social cohesion and national unity—ideas that in the face of high and potentially rising levels of immigration and under the conditions of an integrated European economy are rapidly losing their capacity to inform political decisions and support a national consensus. Unlike Japan, Germany as a country is for many practical purposes no longer a relevant unit of analysis or political decision making because important sectors of its economy and its polity have since the 1980s ceased to be German and become Europeanized.

Given the lasting critical weaknesses in the two countries' economic performance, Germany and Japan currently experience the hybridization of their institutions—as brought about by the increasing penetration of the international environment into their societies and economies—mainly as a broad process of liberalization. For both countries, liberalization in the form of the incorporation of Anglo-American institutions under external pressure is by no means a new experience. Indeed, what we have come to know as the German and Japanese models is, as Gould and Krasner in particular remind us, a synthesis of new liberal institutions implanted by the victors of World War II, especially free markets and parliamentary democracy, with older indigenous ones that were more or less willingly tolerated by the Allies (Streeck and Yamamura 2001). But liberalization did not stop when the postwar settlement stabilized in the two decades after 1945. By and large, the pressure was always for more rather than less liberal modes of economic and political organization, and internal pressures to this effect continued throughout the second half of the twentieth century to be reinforced by external pressures in the same direction.

International demands for domestic liberalization emanate from U.S. trade policy and global capital markets in the case of Japan and are in addition anchored in the unique institutional construct of the European Union in the case of Germany. The Japanese economy in its present unreconstructed, postdevelopmentalist condition suffers from manifold frictions in its intersection with an increasingly market-driven world economy. In Germany such frictions are largely eliminated by the European Union, which has successfully reorganized the political economies of western Europe to make them compatible with self-regulating international markets. One way in which liberalization works inside the European Union is that it changes the functioning of structurally unchanged nonliberal institutions by enveloping them within a dominant context of free markets that redefines what they can do—see, for example, the encapsulation of traditional German institutions of collective bargaining described by Thelen and Kume. The dysfunctions of liberalization show mostly at the lower end of the hierarchy of markets, such as in high levels of unemployment, which call for further liberalization.

Will liberalization, conceived as a continuing hybridization of traditional with liberal institutions under international pressure, ultimately result in convergence? A review of the history of the German and Japanese models in the twentieth century shows that, although liberalization was a long-term trend in both countries in periods of both continuity and discontinuity, with hindsight its results always appeared as a new stage in the evolution of recognizably national institutions of a nonliberal sort. Regardless of liberalization, the distinctiveness of the German and Japanese versions of capitalism did not disappear—even though at most times the changes that were to come would have been regarded by most actors and observers, had they known about them, as incompatible with national traditions or as a complete break (to use Vogel's term) with the past. Conceivably, what happens at the beginning of the twenty-first century is simply a continuation of this long-term process of liberalization—and again the natural conservatism of those deeply enmeshed in the present may be unable to imagine the creative mutations that actors will invent to defend the identity of their national institutions while at the same time adjusting them to changing circumstances. Once more, then, the sanguine prediction of nonconvergence, made by so many of the contributors to this volume, will come true.

Concluding on such a happy note may, however, overlook an important fact: throughout the second half of the twentieth century, the overall trend in the two countries clearly and always was toward more open markets and a greater role for parliamentary democracy and away from traditionalism, paternalism, corporatism, etatism, and the like. Having been effective for so long, that trend toward less institutional and more market governance inside nonliberal national models of capitalism might reasonably be expected at some point to culminate in a qualitative switch. Perhaps we have reached this point. After the demise in the 1970s of the international regime of embedded liberalism, with its delicate balance between national political autonomy on the one hand and the needs and constraints of free international trade on the other, and with the subsequent unraveling of the postwar settlement, not just between the classes but also between markets and politics, the time may now have come for a fundamental redefinition of the terms of the coexistence between markets and institutions in modern capitalism. Perhaps the unsettling of the postwar settlement that we have observed since the 1980s will be followed by a new, post–cold war settlement. But there are very good reasons to expect that this will be a great deal more liberal than its predecessor—perhaps liberal enough finally to render the categoric distinctions between the liberal and non-liberal models of capitalism obsolete.

Or, in the middle of triumphant liberalism, is a new synthesis possible—one that exposes the political economies of Germany and Japan to the mobilizing effect of market incentives, thereby overcoming economic stagnation without sacrificing the values of social solidarity and national survival that have informed nonliberal capitalism in the two countries? Clearly if this is to be possible, these values themselves will have to be redefined in the light of new historical circumstances. Japan, according to Yamamura, urgently needs an idea as to the purposes to which it wants to put its cooperative developmentalist institutions in the future—a redis-covery of the *raison d'être* of an institutional system that refuses to turn society over to the reign of self-regulating free markets. Something similar can clearly be said about Germany, where new meaning must be given to the value of solidarity after the end of postwar and post–cold war state building, the demise of the labor movement as an anticapitalist force, and above all the dissolution of the national state in the process of European integration.

A new policy of social cohesion into a Europeanized Germany can only be conceived in an interplay between national and European politics and collective identities, probably involving regional and local politics and identities as well. Institutional stability at the price of economic stagnation is not an option for a country as integrated into the world economy as Germany, something that surely applies in the long run to Japan as well. Not becoming "American" requires a new definition of the German and European welfare state that is compatible with the modus operandi of a changed international economy, which offers very few protections for re-gional or national institutions interfering in the free play of market forces. Very likely, a modernized European welfare state must accommodate the new supply-side constraints associated with more competitive world markets by helping societies make use of their opportunities, among other things by converting the remnants of national social cohesion into sources of "competitive solidarity" (Streeck 1999). Social policy will then be a vari-ant of economic policy, in that it seeks to help citizens find market niches that support a modicum of social stability within markets of unprece-dented flexibility and uncertainty.

Although this may not be impossible, it clearly is difficult—and is not made any easier by a European institutional context designed to weaken national political capacities through progressive liberalization. Perhaps upward denationalization—the transfer of national competences in areas such as competition and monetary policy to the European Union—may have to be countered, not by renationalization but by the downward dena-tionalization of social and educational policy to subnational regions, which may be better able than big countries to respond collectively to market signals through specialization instead of price competition. In any case, as the history of the twentieth century amply demonstrates, what may look ex post like a logical and even the only possible development in the liberalization, internationalization, and hybridization of nationally embedded capitalism, may appear impossible and may even be outright unimaginable ex ante.

Germany and Japan:
Binding versus Autonomy

Erica R. Gould and Stephen D. Krasner

Germany and Japan both flourished in the international environment of the cold war. With the crucial support of the United States, both countries rebuilt their economies and became models of economic success. Germany and Japan regained their regional stature and established their particular brand of economic organization—embedded capitalism. The post–cold war international environment poses different challenges for Germany and Japan. This essay focuses on the viability and robustness of German and Japanese policies in the face of decreasing U.S. tolerance for asymmetrical economic and security relations in the post–cold war world rather than on the challenges posed by technological change and the integration of international markets. Because Germany has bound itself in multilateral institutions, such as the European Union (EU) and the North Atlantic Treaty Organization (NATO), it is both less dependent on the United States and less threatening to its neighbors. By contrast, Japan has engaged in bilateral security and unilateral economic policies. Unbound and relatively autonomous, Japan is threatening to its neighbors regardless of the intentions of its leaders. Germany is in a more secure position than Japan because it has tied its hands.

Germany and Japan are both large industrialized democratic states. Japan has the second largest economy in the world, Germany the third. In the 1930s and 1940s, both attempted to dominate their regional environments; both failed and were occupied. In both cases the occupying powers, specifically the United States, facilitated the reconstitution of embedded capitalism. The Americans were willing, even eager, to support the reconstruction of Germany and Japan, a reconstruction that, as other authors in this project have argued (see Streeck and Yamamura 2001), was conditioned by previously established institutional arrangements. U.S. support was forthcoming because it bolstered the power of the Western alliance vis-à-vis the Soviet bloc, not because it maximized narrow U.S. economic interests or enhanced the relative position of the United States within the Western alliance. Without U.S. assistance both during and after the occupation, the success now characteristic of Germany's and Japan's embedded capitalism would not have been assured.

Later developments in many areas have brought new pressures on Germany and Japan. Challenges associated with technological change and globalization have put their embedded capitalisms at risk. In addition, the collapse of the Soviet Union has undermined the primary rationale for the postwar system of alliance and security arrangements within which Germany and Japan flourished. At least with regard to international political, economic, and security issues, however, Germany is much better situated than Japan. Germany has bound itself in a set of institutional arrangements that make even united Germany much less threatening to its neighbors. Japan has pursued a policy of independence that makes its position more brittle.

For much of the twentieth century, both Germany and Japan have been too big but not big enough—too big in that they have both posed threats to their neighbors and not big enough in that they have never been powerful enough to unilaterally establish their own regional, much less global, orders. Being too big but not big enough is an awkward position in the international system. States that are dominant, or at least dominant in their own regions, can create stable environments because their weaker neighbors have limited options—the United States vis-à-vis the Caribbean, Mexico, and Central America, for instance.

States that are too big but not big enough cannot dominate their neighbors outright, but they can threaten them, even if they are themselves committed to defensive and status quo rather than offensive goals. It may be impossible for states to distinguish between offensive and defensive weapons leading to arms races. Smaller states may be uncertain about the intentions of their larger neighbor because it is difficult to know whether leaders that profess their peaceful intentions are engaged in duplicitous cheap talk. Binding commitments are hard to make. It is not just a Germany led by Adolf Hitler but also a Germany led by Willy Brandt that must confront this awkward situation.

To mitigate this problem, states that are too big but not big enough must find a way to convince others that they are not a threat. If they attempt to maximize their power, as Germany and Japan did in the first half of the twentieth century, they will provoke countervailing balances by their neighbors. To be secure, states that are too big but not big enough must limit their own options; they must bind themselves to a nonthreatening course of action. This is no easy task. Protestations of innocent intentions are not enough.

Germany has been much more successful than Japan in resolving the inherent insecurity its size and power generate. Both states bandwagoned with the United States during and after the cold war in response to similar structural predicaments. But in addition the leaders of Germany have chosen to bind themselves, to tie their own hands by enmeshing their country in multilateral institutions from which extrication would be prohibitively costly. As a member of NATO and the EU, Germany has restricted its own autonomy and thereby made itself less threatening.

Japan, in contrast, has not enmeshed itself in multilateral institutions. Japan has unilaterally limited the size of its military (although its military power is, in fact, quite substantial). It has pursued a policy of comprehensive security that, while still involving ties with the United States, is designed to limit external vulnerability across a range of issue areas related to both economic well-being and national security. Japan has fostered mutual but often asymmetrical interests, first with the United States and later with Asia. Despite setbacks, its economic resources have been its single most important asset. Germany's policy of binding offers more security in the post–cold war world than Japan's policy of autonomy.

The post–cold war world will be more problematic for Japan than for Germany, even though Europe has experienced something close to war in the former Yugoslavia. Japan is unconstrained, giving its neighbors cause for worry. China is a rising power. Both economic stability and peace in Asia rely heavily on continued U.S. commitments, through open U.S. markets and the U.S.-Japan Security Treaty, whereas economic stability and peace in Europe no longer rely as heavily on U.S. participation. A more ambitious foreign policy and security role for the Western European Union (WEU) or the EU itself could maintain stability in Europe, including Germany. The maintenance of extant security relations is more difficult for Japan than for Germany. German use of military force is more acceptable both within Germany and to other states because Germany has embedded itself in a multilateral security structure. In contrast, greater militarization in Japan would be perceived as a threat by its neighbors.

Germany's pattern of economic engagement with the world is relatively symmetrical. Flows of capital, technology, and trade are more or less balanced. By contrast, Japan's unique pattern of economic involvement, its lack of symmetry in trade, investment, and technology flows, will continue to generate economic and security tensions with the United States. Japan, unlike Germany, is more subject to charges of violating international, and particularly World Trade Organization, rules. A key pillar of Japan's embedded capitalist model is its protectionist trade practices, which have helped shield corporations from international competition and amplified the government's role in managing economic development. By contrast, the Federal Republic of Germany (FRG) has demonstrated a consistent commitment to external liberalization, and its embedded capitalism is centered on labor management structures that are consistent with international rules.

If a country is large but not large enough, its best possible strategic option might be to tie its own hands. By credibly committing itself to forgo those policies that would yield the greatest short-term benefits given its current relative capabilities, a state may soften the suspicions of its potential rivals and increase the prospects of concluding mutually beneficial agreements that enhance its well-being in the longer run. By engaging in a policy of binding, Germany has left itself in a more secure international position than Japan, whose strategy of comprehensive security is designed to enhance rather than constrain its policy options.

Bandwagoning, Balancing, and Binding

States have several strategic options they can pursue in the international arena, including balancing, bandwagoning, and binding. States bandwagon by aligning with more powerful states. States balance against more powerful states by developing their own resources or by entering into alliances (Waltz 1979). States bind by making alternate courses of action prohibitively costly. Balancing or binding can be pursued through either unilateral or multilateral (including bilateral) policies. Bandwagoning can only be achieved through multilateral ties.

Balancing and bandwagoning have been extensively discussed in the international relations literature; binding has been less extensively analyzed. Binding is a policy by which a state ties its own hands, makes commitments its allies and enemies will take seriously. It is hard to make commitments in the international environment. If the rulers of one state say to those of another, "trust me, TRUST ME!" why should they be believed? There is no court system or police to enforce contracts. Rulers may say one thing today and do another tomorrow. Political leaders can bind themselves, either internationally or domestically, by taking actions that lock them into a certain policy stance, such that they have no incentive to change that policy.[1]

---

1. James Fearon (1997) distinguishes between two strategies to make a credible commitment in the international realm: tying hands and sinking costs. When leaders *tie their hands*, for instance through audience effects, they will incur prohibitively high costs ex post if they renege on their commitment. When leaders *sink costs*, they incur high costs ex ante, so high that they remove uncertainty about the leaders' intentions. In this discussion we focus mainly on tying hands binding mechanisms, but differentiate between international and domestic ex post costs.

In that case, a shift in policy would cause leaders to incur such high costs ex post, either in the international or domestic realm, that a shift will not be in their interest. For example, James Fearon (1994) has analyzed one binding mechanism that operates in the domestic arena, audience effects, and argues that it allows democratic states to make more credible commitments in the international arena. If a democratic leader makes a public promise or threat and then fails to carry it out, he or she may be subject to electoral sanctions. If the leader's electoral costs are high enough, for instance, losing office, then a foreign power can feel assured that the commitment or threat will be honored because the leader will lose more by reneging on the commitment.

A second way governments can be domestically bound to adhere to policy commitments is through the (perhaps inadvertent) creation of domestic constituencies that benefit from those policies. If a government adopts a certain policy, particularly an economic policy, that clearly benefits a key constituency whose support is both necessary and contingent on the continuance of this policy, then the government generally will not renege on that policy commitment. Reneging would result in the government being ousted, either by being voted out of office in the case of a democratic regime or through other, perhaps less apparent, means in the case of an autocratic regime.

States can also bind themselves internationally, such that they would be internationally worse off if they reneged on a policy commitment. In order to credibly commit not to engage in war, states can tie their hands such that they would be disadvantaged if they launched a military offensive or acted autonomously. For instance, by adopting only defensive weaponry, when and if offensive and defensive weapons are distinct, the security dilemma can be mitigated (Jervis 1978). A state could also structure its armed forces in ways that make it difficult for them to act independently. For instance, during the cold war the Soviet Union integrated the militaries of the satellite states into a multilateral force structure that precluded unilateral action (Jones 1984; Mackintosh 1984).

International institutions can also help states bind themselves, or commit themselves to a cooperative agreement, by altering the configuration of domestic interests, creating focal points, and making states' policy choices more transparent. For instance, by identifying a clear focal point, international institutions can publicize defections from that focal point, or a state's change of policy, and thereby make states' policy choices more transparent. In certain circumstances (for instance, prisoner's dilemma–type strategic problems), such information would lead other states to defect as well. If all states defected, they would all be worse off. Because the consequences of defection are visible to all actors, the existence of the institution can create a stable equilibrium that would not otherwise be available. Without the institution, rulers that want to convince their counterparts that they will not alter their policies (from those stipulated in the cooperative agreement) might not be able to do so because they will not be able to define and defend a focal point from which defection will be mutually disadvantageous.

States of different sizes tend to rely on different strategies in a given international environment. The policy options for small states are limited. Binding is not likely to be particularly consequential for small states dealing with larger powers. The modal strategy for small states is to bandwagon with more powerful proximate partners. Only rarely can a small state, such as Cuba during the cold war, escape from the dominance of its most puissant neighbor by allying with a more distant power. Occasionally small states will choose unilateral isolation, for example, Myanmar and Cuba in the late 1990s, usually a costly policy. Neutrality is also an option for small states. It can either be achieved by the mutual agreement of the major powers, for example, Belgium from 1830 until World War I, or by unilateral choice, for example, Switzerland, which has adopted neutrality and established its credibility by maintaining a formidable military apparatus, a credible ex ante commitment (Fearon 1997).

For the largest and most powerful states, balancing is the most salient policy option. This can be achieved either through the internal redistribution of resources in a bipolar world or through alliances in a multipolar one. In a bipolar world, the poles will balance against each other. Binding might be an option only for certain limited objectives, such as arms control agreements, and then only if verification is possible. In a bipolar world, there is no one for the poles to bandwagon with.

Medium-size states face the most complex set of policy options. Depending on their strategic environment, they can bandwagon, balance, or bind—they can join with a more powerful state, they can attempt to form alliances among themselves that allow them to balance against a dominant power, or they can bind themselves in ways that make them less threatening to their neighbors. By binding or limiting their freedom of action, they might find it easier to elicit cooperation from weaker partners who might otherwise be loath to sacrifice any of their autonomy or relative capability lest they become more vulnerable to the initiatives of an untrammeled great power. Medium-size states may have a range of policy options or their strategic environment might privilege one strategy over another. Binding has been easier for Germany than for Japan because in Europe there were regional partners of moderate strength, comparable economic development, and compatible regime type with whom Germany could develop a symmetric, institutionalized relationship. Japan's options were more constrained.

The distinguishing characteristic of Germany's postwar strategy has been to bind itself externally through mutual economic self-interest and multilateral institutions, notably the EU and NATO. The distinguishing characteristic of the Japanese strategy has been unilateral balancing in the economic arena and bandwagoning with the United States in security affairs; Japan has not effectively engaged in binding.

The United States and the Cold War

Both Germany and Japan benefited from U.S. policies during the cold war. U.S. leaders were intent on strengthening their alliance partners, particularly Germany and Japan. The United States was a wonderful ally and sponsor: it was far away, it was obsessed with the threat of Soviet communism, and it was anxious to build up the capacity of its own alliance structure even at some cost to its own power within that structure (Gowa 1994). The United States offered Germany and Japan resources, technology, and access to its markets in order to strengthen anticommunist forces in Europe and Asia. Thus the emergence and, more important, the success of German and Japanese embedded capitalism not only evolved from historical legacies and institutional developments since the nineteenth century, but were also enabled by U.S. policies both during and after the occupation periods.

In both Germany and Japan, initial U.S. plans called for disarmament, demilitarization, the dismantling of existing economic groups, and purges. In Japan some 200,000 individuals lost their political rights. In Germany, an ambitious program of denazification was initiated. War crimes tribunals were established in both countries. In 1947, General Douglas MacArthur ordered the breakup of the *zaibatsu* (business conglomerates). In Germany, monopolies such as IG Farben were dismantled. By the early months of 1947 the German and Japanese economies were in shambles and both countries were heavily dependent on aid from the United States (Ermath 1993, 10–13; LaFeber 1997, 259, 269–70; Schaller 1997, 11).

With the onset of the cold war, however, the stance of U.S. policymakers changed dramatically. Their primary concern was to promote democracy, capitalism, and stability in Germany and Japan and, above all, to discourage any movements toward communism or the Soviet bloc. For both Germany and Japan, this meant the promotion of economic recovery. And in both countries economic recovery could not take place without using existing institutional arrangements and personnel. Faced with the threat of spreading communism in the early months of 1947, the Harry Truman administration reversed course. There was a consensus in Washington that Germany and Japan had to be rebuilt and that if the *zaibatsu* were dismantled there would be economic chaos in Japan that would open the way for much greater communist influence.

In the summer of 1948 the National Security Council approved NSC 13/2, which declared that economic recovery was the prime objective in Japan. Joseph Dodge, a Detroit banker, was appointed as the economic czar of Japan. The effort to create an independent labor movement, based on the U.S. model, was abandoned in part because U.S. officials feared that labor organizations were becoming radicalized. Unions with a total of more than a million members were forced out of existence. Other labor groups were curbed. These measures facilitated the creation of firm-based labor organizations that became an important component of Japan's embedded capitalism. The government bureaucracy was strengthened. The Ministry of International Trade and Industry (MITI) was reconstituted out of the prewar Munitions Ministry. Only 19 out of the 325 industrial firms that were initially scheduled to be broken up were actually affected (LaFeber 1997, 264–65, 274–78; Schaller 1997, 13–18; Ward 1975, 31–32).

The Korean War accentuated U.S. anxiety about the situation in Japan and also provided a mechanism through which the United States could provide aid and capital. Between 1950 and 1952 the U.S. military accounted for 70 percent of Japan's exports, and during the early 1950s U.S. military purchases paid for 25 percent of Japan's imports. By the time the U.S. occupying authority, the Supreme Commander for the Allied Powers, went out of business in 1952, some 3,000 Japanese firms held military contracts. Toyota, for instance, which made only three hundred trucks a month just before the war broke out, increased its capacity to 2,000 trucks a month as a result of orders from the U.S. military. The Americans agreed that Japanese reparations to other Asian countries would take the form of Japanese exports. U.S. leaders wanted to develop Japanese markets in Asia to assure stability in Japan and they feared Japanese firms would not be able to export to the U.S. market (Hein 1993, 110; LaFeber 1997, 291, 293; Schaller 1997, 48, 55).

After the peace treaty was signed, the United States backed the Shigeru Yoshida government. The CIA funneled money to Yoshida and other conservative politicians. Almost all of the Japanese officials who had been purged in the immediate postwar years regained their political rights. Forty-two percent of the individuals elected to seats in the Lower House of the Diet in the election held after the occupation ended had been purged (LaFeber 1997, 287; Schaller 1997, 38).

Some of the policies introduced during the occupation were enduring, land reform being the most notable example. Yoshida and his allies won lasting support from the many farmers who secured title to their property as a result of policies instituted under U.S. tutelage. But the essential features of Japan's embedded capitalism endured—the strong role of the central bureaucracy, especially MITI, was reestablished and the economy continued to be dominated by large oligopolistic firms.

The situation was very similar in Germany. In the immediate aftermath of the war, U.S. leaders had been intent on creating a new German polity and purging individuals who had been involved in the Nazi regime, but once the cold war set in their primary concern was to establish a Germany that would be firmly anchored in the Western alliance. Initially the Americans pressed for a series of reforms that mirrored New Deal America. Germany would be a federal system. Financial activities would be decentralized. The central banking system would be organized at the level of the *Länder*. The large commercial banks would be broken up; Deutsche Bank, for instance, was divided into ten regional banks for business purposes. Unions would focus on collective bargaining, rather than more general political activities or active involvement with management. There would be extensive purges of individuals who had been associated with the Nazi regime (Fichter 1981, 107–12; Holtfrerich 1995, 408–86).

In winter 1947–48, when it became apparent that the United States and the Soviet Union would be in conflict, the focus of U.S. policies changed. The Americans picked the conservative Ludwig Erhard to serve as the first economic minister of Germany. They supported Konrad Adenauer and his Christian Democrats. Germany was included in Marshall Plan aid. The denazification program was all but abandoned. In 1951, the Bundesrepublik rehabilitated all Nazis who had not been accused of war crimes (Ermarth 1993, 8; Jonas 1984, 286–87, 291–92; T. Schwartz 1993, 37).

As in the case of Japan, some of the reforms introduced by the Americans were enduring; others were not. The industrial structure, as in Japan, reflected some of these initial U.S. reforms. The federal system endured and flourished. However, key elements of Germany's indigenous economic organization persisted, despite being at variance with occupation policies, and provided the foundation for Germany's embedded capitalism. The private banking system was recentralized. Codetermination became a central element in the union movement.

In the international sphere the United States was intent on enmeshing both Germany and Japan in a structure of economic ties that would exclude the Soviet bloc. It was willing, indeed during the early years of the cold war, even happy to accept free riding. The United States supported European integration, the opposite of a divide-and-conquer strategy that might have been expected had there been no Soviet Union. For the United States, the European Economic Community was inevitably trade diverting but strengthened the American-led Western alliance.

Japan became a member of the General Agreement on Tariffs and Trade (GATT) in 1955 as a result of strong support from the United States which, at the same time, accepted protectionism not only against U.S. goods, but also against U.S. foreign direct investment. The Japanese market remained closed. The pattern of Japanese trade, technology transfer, and foreign direct investment was, and continues to be, unique among the advanced industrialized states. The United States began to run a large bilateral trade deficit with Japan in the 1970s, but its initial response was to press for voluntary export restraints (VERs) that generated rents for Japanese corporations—tariffs or some system of bidding for import licenses would have provided additional revenue for the U.S. Treasury rather than for Nippon Steel or Toyota. Only in 1986 did the United States levy countervailing duties against a Japanese export—semiconductors. And only in the later 1980s did the United States begin to press systematically for an opening of the Japanese market. Thus, during much of the cold war the United States encouraged Japanese growth and accepted short-term economic losses as a direct result of that encouragement.[2]

As in the economic arena, the United States was also prepared to make asymmetrical commitments to both Germany and Japan in the security arena. The language of the North Atlantic Treaty sounds deceivingly egalitarian and symmetrical. For instance, article 5 stated that the "Parties agree that an armed attack against one or more of them in Europe or North America shall be considered an attack against them all and . . . if such an armed attack occurs, each of them, in exercise of the right of individual or collective self-defense . . . will assist the Party or Parties so attacked . . . individually and in concert with the other Parties." In practice, however, it was the United States that could provide aid to the European signatories of the North Atlantic Treaty, not the Europeans who could help the Americans. Likewise, the U.S.-Japan Security Treaty was a one-way commitment. The United States pledged to defend Japan. Japan did not commit to defend the United States, nor did Japan have the military capacity to do so. Large numbers of U.S. troops were stationed in both Japan and Germany. NATO provided a nuclear umbrella for Germany, and the bilateral security treaty provided an umbrella for Japan.

The U.S. guarantee was, of course, always tenuous, for the reason that Charles de Gaulle articulated so well: would the United States give up New York for Paris? Extended deterrence was inherently less credible than a policy of deterrence designed to discourage an attack against the United States itself. Nevertheless, relying on the United States was not just the first best option for both Germany and Japan; it was the only option. The United States would not have accepted a unilateral military buildup or independent security policy in either country.

The alliance with the United States not only provided security against

2. One study has estimated that the U.S. Treasury lost more than $11 billion in revenues as a result of limiting Japanese auto exports in the early 1980s through a voluntary export agreement rather than tariffs, almost as much as the estimated consumer loss of $13 billion (see Berry, Levinsohn, and Pakes 1999, 401, 428).

any communist threat, it also made Germany and Japan less threatening to their neighbors. It was reassuring for France, Britain, and Korea to have the largest state in their immediate neighborhood so deeply enmeshed with the far-off United States. Even for China and the Soviet Union, a Japan tied to the United States was better than a Japan entirely on its own.

The reconstitution of embedded capitalism in Germany and Japan after World War II was, obviously, not a direct result of the policies carried out during the occupation period. Nor was it directly related to the security postures adopted by Germany and Japan once they were again recognized as sovereign states. Nevertheless, without the permissive stance adopted by U.S. policymakers, institutional arrangements in Germany and Japan might have been very different. The Soviet Union, in contrast, simply imposed many elements of its own economic and political system on its east European satellites. Had the Americans been less anxious about communism and the Soviet Union, they might have been more draconian during the occupation and less willing to support the general reconstruction of the German and Japanese economies. Had Germany and Japan not been incorporated into the U.S. security system, the Americans might have been less willing to support European unification and the integration of the German economy in Europe and more insistent about opening the Japanese market not only to U.S. goods, which the Japanese initially had difficulty paying for, but also to U.S. direct investment, which would have alleviated Japan's need for hard currency. Had the United States been less willing to accept asymmetrical relations with Germany and Japan, the success of German and Japanese embedded capitalism might have been less striking.

Thus in many ways, the experiences of Germany and Japan in the economic and security spheres were similar. Due to security guarantees and economic support from the United States, both were able to focus on rebuilding their economies in similar, more egalitarian models based on cooperative relationships between business, labor, and government. There were, however, marked differences between Germany and Japan even during the cold war. In its foreign relations, Germany committed itself to a policy of binding, not just bandwagoning with the United States. There was no equivalent initiative for Japan.

Germany

The creation of NATO and the project of European union allowed Germany to embed itself in a multilateral framework rather than choose a more independent strategy for economic growth and defense, as Japan did. NATO and the institutions of European political and economic union made possible an equilibrium strategy, in particular Germany's active participation in multilateral institutions, from which neither Germany nor the other members of the Western alliance have had an incentive to defect. These arrangements have left Germany in a more stable situation, not only with regard to international security but also with regard to international economic opportunities.

It was not obvious at the conclusion of World War II that NATO would provide a mechanism that would allow Germany to bind itself. In the early postwar years, both NATO's form and Germany's membership in this collective security framework were highly uncertain. In fact, the first in a string of treaties that eventually culminated in NATO, the 1947 Treaty of Dunkirk between France and Great Britain, was constructed "solely" to protect against "a possible renewal of German aggression" (Cook 1989, 259). Due to the emerging Soviet threat, evidenced by the breakdown of the Four Power London Foreign Ministers Conference (among Britain, France, the USSR, and the United States) on the German question in November and December 1947 and the violent suppression of the Prague coup in early 1948, the next incarnation, the Brussels Treaty of the Western Union signed in March 1948, expanded its mission to include protection against both Soviet and German aggression (Cook 1989, 122; Ireland 1981, 74–75; Thomas 1997, 11; Varsori 1991, 25–32).[3] Initially, these treaties provided for an alliance between Great Britain and France (and the three Benelux countries, in the case of the 1948 Brussels Treaty), a more-or-less standard balancing act against a regional threat—Germany (Varsori 1991, 31). The United States, ultimately a key figure in NATO, was not a part of this alliance at first; the United States initially intended to provide for European security in a limited, low-budget way with a unilateral security guarantee and was not interested in making a permanent commitment immediately after the war.

However, due to a variety of factors including the increasing threat of communism and the lack of consensus among the four powers over how to resolve the German question, the United States began conducting secret Pentagon talks with Canada and Great Britain in late March 1948 that helped lay the foundation for a greater U.S. role in European security (Cook 1989, 131; Ireland 1981, 74; Varsori 1991, 34). The United States pushed for German membership in this broadened collective security framework. The final result, NATO, resulted from a bargain between France, which demanded greater and more permanent U.S. military protection against possible German aggression, and the United States, which wanted the three western German zones to be consolidated and demanded that western Germany be included in the European Recovery Program. As a result, in April 1949 the Occupation Statute for Germany

3. On the insistence of Benelux countries of Soviet threat, see Varsori (1991, 29).

was finalized and the North Atlantic Treaty was signed. The permanent presence of the U.S. military on west European and particularly German soil was solidified (Ireland 1981, 75, 121, 138). With the signing of the 23 October 1954 Brussels Treaty, West Germany (and Italy) were included as new members of NATO. Produced by this rare combination of circumstances and actors, NATO allowed Germany to tie its hands and thus grow stronger in Europe without threatening its neighbors.

The London nine-power conference at which West Germany gained membership in NATO allowed national forces, including German forces, to remain under national command during peacetime. Command had to be formally transferred during a conflict, indicating that German forces were not fully subordinate to NATO (Fedder 1973, 9).[4] However, despite the fact that Germany's forces, like those in other NATO countries, remained under national command during peacetime and that Germany, like other NATO countries, retained the right to transfer or deny the transfer of that command, Germany's forces were still very much constrained under the cold war NATO framework.

Germany's hands were tied in five ways. First and perhaps most important, in joining NATO, Germany agreed not to reestablish a general staff.[5] As Major General Klaus Reinhardt stated, "For professional as well as political reasons the decisive competence for the command of troops was transferred to NATO at the time of the founding of the Bundeswehr" (speech given 24 April 1991, quoted in Asmus 1995, 37).[6] Without a general staff for its armed forces, it would be quite difficult, if not impossible, for Germany to generate the capability for the large operations necessary

4. Edwin H. Fedder writes that, "The forces assigned to NATO (the forces-in-being) are only nominally assigned. The several members retain all decision-making powers, including command authority over their troops 'assigned' to NATO command. Operational order to national units assigned to NATO must be transmitted through national chains of command. . . . The NATO forces at no time become part of a NATO operational command" (1973, 9). This challenges the notion that German forces were constrained.

5. Don Cook writes that in joining NATO, West Germany agreed that there would be "no re-creation of a German General Staff and . . . all German military forces would be totally integrated under the command and control of the NATO Supreme Allied Commander" (1989, 259). Similarly, Reed writes that West Germany agreed "not to establish a General Staff for its armed forces, and to forgo a military role independent of the Alliance" (*Brussels Treaty of 1954,* Protocol No. III on the Control of Armaments, in Reed 1987, 222–23). Catherine Kelleher also writes that one of the most important changes to the Bundeswehr in the postwar period was the "failure to re-establish a central national military command," which she argued was "unquestionably . . . one of the conditions imposed as a stipulation for rearmament, both by continental allies and by British and American observers." Instead, in the post–World War II period, "German national command was . . . to be controlled by an integrated military commander (eventually SACEUR [Supreme Allied Commander Europe])" (1990, 23–24).

6. "Gedanken zur Persönlichkeit, Amt under Wirken des Generalfeldmarschalls Helmut Graf von Moltke aus heutiger Sicht," delivered before the Moltke-Stiftung in Berlin on the occasion of the commemoration of the one hundredth anniversary of the death of Field Marshall Helmut Graf von Moltke on 24 April 1991.

to wage an independent war, to conduct national operations, and to coordinate troops autonomously (interview with Norbert Stier, military attaché at the German Embassy to the United States, 15 March 1999, Washington, D.C.).[7] Second, Germany's air defense forces and system were under NATO command, the Supreme Allied Commander Europe (SACEUR) in particular, during peacetime and could be ordered into conflict without any transfer of operational command (Stares 1990). Germany could not wage an independent war without these air defense systems.

Third, various NATO restrictions on Germany's production of weapons, on the composition of its naval equipment, and on the size of its armed forces limited Germany's ability to act autonomously, other than in a defensive capacity. The Brussels Treaty of 1954 singled out Germany (not Italy, although it was also a new member) and prohibited it from producing atomic, biological, or chemical weapons and restricted its production of other arms including long-range missiles, guided missiles, mines, warships, and bomber aircraft (*Final Act of the Nine-Power Conference*, London, 3 October 1954, in Stares 1990, 108–9; also in Reed 1987, 222, 226–27).[8] The German navy was restricted to "vessels and formations necessary for the defensive missions assigned to it by the North Atlantic Treaty Organization"; the Paris Agreement of October 1954 limited West Germany to only a 500,000-person peacetime total in its armed forces (*Brussels Treaty of 1954* in Reed 1987, 222; *Protocol No. II on Forces of Western European Union*, art. II, in Reed 1987, 219; Reed 1987, 60; Stares 1990, 14).[9] The NATO agreement thus ensured that Germany's armed forces would only be equipped with defensive weaponry and that they would be limited to a conquerable size.

Fourth, West Germany agreed to have a large number of foreign troops semipermanently stationed on its territory (*Protocol II on Forces of Western*

7. As Thomas-Durell Young writes, the German Federal Ministry of Defense of Bundesministerium der Verteidigung (BMVg) "was organized with the explicit aim of not providing operational command and control over its standing national forces. The Federal Armed Forces (Bundeswehr) was created without the capability to exercise operational command and control over joint national military operations of any size or of any significant duration" (1997a, 135). In addition, Ronald Asmus writes that the cold war Bundeswehr "was specifically designed to defend German territory, and largely lacked the logistics and C3I elements required to give it projection capabilities" (1995, 21).

8. The Protocol III specified that Germany could not manufacture certain armaments "except that if in accordance with the needs of the armed forces a recommendation for an amendment to, or cancellation of, the content of the list of these armaments is made by the competent Supreme Commander of the North Atlantic Treaty Organization, and if the Government of the Federal Republic of Germany submits a request accordingly, such an amendment or cancellation may be made by a resolution of the Council of Western European Union passed by a two-thirds majority" (Reed 1987, 222).

9. This does not include reserves and Home Defense Forces, which is a division of the military not assigned to NATO but specifically trained for territorial defense.

European Union, 23 October 1954, art. VI, in Stares 1990, 115). Fifth, West German forces were divided geographically into four separate corps; Germany's three national corps would be geographically separated by corps from other NATO countries in the case of war.[10] By contrast, the Danish, Dutch, Belgian, British, and U.S. forces would remain geographically unified in case of an attack from the east (Cordesman 1988, 88).[11] The large external force present on German territory and the geographical division of German forces would have further complicated any efforts on the part of the West German forces to act autonomously from NATO.

As a result of the lack of a general staff, the peacetime NATO control over Germany's air defense system, the limitations of German rearmament, the stationing of large numbers of foreign troops on German soil, and the geographical division of German troops, Germany's hands were tied. Any attempt to act outside this multilateral framework would have been a clear signal that Germany's policies were changing. Because the multilateral framework tethered Germany's military, Germany was quite dependent on NATO and its allies to ensure its defense against the looming Soviet threat. Therefore, the multilateral security framework ensured that it was not in Germany's interest to pursue security unilaterally; Germany would be more secure as a committed member of NATO.

In the post–cold war era, Germany's hands continue to be tied, albeit perhaps not quite so tightly. The end of the cold war and German reunification brought a number of changes in Germany's relationship with NATO and a restructuring of the German army that may theoretically allow Germany to act more autonomously but in practice has enabled Germany to strengthen its commitment to NATO and NATO's new missions.

By the late cold war period, some of the earlier restrictions on the German military had been lifted. For instance, the last of the restrictions on Germany's manufacturing of conventional weapons was nullified by the WEU in 1985 (Sloan 1990, 57, 66). Other NATO allies encouraged Germany to accept a greater role in the alliance through increased financial contributions and, eventually, increased military involvement.[12]

With German reunification and the end of the cold war, some of the

10. In addition to these three corps, Germany also participated in two multinational configurations: the German-Danish Jutland Corps, established in 1970, and the German 12th Panzer Division, which included U.S. troops (Seitz 1992, 9).

11. As Anthony Cordesman writes, "The FRG's Corps are divided by other national corps zones. They are denied both cohesion and concentration of force, and the ability to take defence positions with any predictable capacity to exploit the advantage of the defender, a problem which is compounded by the need to give some units poorly defensible wartime deployment positions for political reasons" (1988, 94–96).

12. For further information regarding Germany in the Gulf War and the changing expectations of NATO allies regarding Germany's military contributions, see Asmus (1991, 1992).

earlier restrictions were reinforced or reestablished. For instance, the Two-Plus-Four Treaty, signed in September 1990, and the Treaty on Conventional Forces in Europe, signed in November 1990, specified that Germany could only have 370,000 troops by December 1994, with the army and air force having a maximum of 345,000 combined, and limited the "number of major weapons systems Germany could field" (Linnenkamp 1992, 97).[13] Germany also pledged to "do more disarming in all categories of treaty-limited equipment (TLE) than any other Western country" (Linnenkamp 1992, 96–97). These limitations particularly addressed the security concerns of the USSR, but also of other states that considered a united Germany a security threat. As Karl Kaiser writes, "The reduction of German forces by 40 percent and Germany's commitment to a continued non-nuclear status were meant to create in the eyes of the other powers a reasonable certainty that, even if political circumstances changed, Germany would not be able to reestablish itself as a great military power" (1991, 198).

In line with these treaties, Germany steadily decreased its defense expenditures from DM 68,376 in 1990 to DM 48,876 in 1996 (in 1990 prices, adjusted for inflation) (*NATO Review* 1996). In addition to accepting limitations on its own military, Germany continued to allow foreign troops to be stationed within German borders. By early 1995, there were still almost one-half as many foreign troops stationed on German soil as there were German troops total. In 1995, the United States stationed approximately 100,000 troops in Germany; there were also 38,000 British forces, 10,000 Belgian forces, 3,000 Dutch, and 15,000 French,[14] among others. Perhaps most important, NATO had been restructured since the end of the cold war in ways that further embedded Germany into the multinational framework. In May 1991, the NATO defense ministers decided to replace the eight existing national corps with four binational corps, the Rapid Reaction Corps, and the Eurocorps (Seitz 1992, 5; Young 1997b, 1–2). For Germany, this meant the dissolution of two of its national corps and its membership in four separate multinational corps formations: Corps Landjut, the Dutch-German Binational Corps, the Eurocorps, and the U.S.-German Corps.[15]

In addition to these changes, which have continued to bind Germany in the collective security framework, Germany restructured its military since reunification in ways that might allow it more leeway to pursue its security unilaterally. First, Germany continued to maintain a national corps, IV

13. Together they are called the *Treaty on the Final Settlement with Respect to Germany*.

14. The French troops were mostly part of the Eurocorps and not committed to NATO.

15. In addition, Germany contributes troops to other multinational formations. The German-Danish Corps, Landjut, was established in 1970. France, Germany, Belgium, Spain, and Luxembourg contribute to the Eurocorps.

Korps based in Potsdam, but has not earmarked it for NATO. IV Korps, which incorporates newly trained former East German divisions and makes up approximately 15 percent of German armed forces, may be used for NATO missions in the future but is under national operational command and control and has not been formally committed to NATO (Whitford and Young 1997, 63; interview with Norbert Stier, military attaché at the German Embassy to the United States, 15 March 1999, Washington, D.C.).[16]

Second, the German Supreme Court's July 1994 ruling, which dismantled the constitutional ban on the use of German armed forces beyond German borders, prompted a restructuring of the Bundeswehr to enable it to take on non–article V missions, or missions other than territorial defense, including peacekeeping and crisis management.[17] Most notable among the changes in this restructuring were the creation of the Crisis Reaction Forces (CRF), which have been "designed to consist of combat-ready rapidly available forces for operation in either a NATO, WEU, or UN framework under any and all geographical and climactic conditions," and the Führungszentrum der Bundeswehr, a new national operational command-and-control structure (Asmus 1995, 31, 38). Although both the CRF and the Führungszentrum may better enable Germany to act unilaterally and outside the multilateral security framework, they were actually created to allow Germany to improve its contribution to NATO and the new missions of other multilateral institutions, such as peacekeeping, in the post–cold war security environment. For instance, in practice the Führungszentrum has been used not to act autonomously from the multilateral framework but rather to communicate policy-type recommendations to German troops in multinational formations (e.g., specific instructions that German troops should not plant new land mines) and improve the contribution of German forces to multinational (peacekeeping) formations (Asmus 1995, 38; interview with Norbert Stier, military attaché at the German Embassy to the United States, 15 March 1999, Washington, D.C.).[18]

16. IV Korps is the only remaining national corps in NATO's central region according to Whitford and Young (1997, 63).

17. For more information on the initial interpretation of this constitutional ban, see Asmus (1995, 15–16). The German policy regarding the purpose of the Bundeswehr began to change prior to this 1994 ruling. A February 1992 law "clarified that the Bundeswehr's mission was not limited to the defense of German territory but that it included in-region or what [Defense Minister Volker] Rühe called 'extended defense' within NATO's border—i.e., that the Bundeswehr could be deployed beyond Germany in both combat and non-combat roles" (22). This law was followed by a new Defense Policy Guidance issued by Defense Minister Rühe in November 1992 and the first German White Paper to be released since the 1970s; both emphasized the new roles the Bundeswehr should assume in order to meet its changing security environment (23–24).

18. For more information on the restructuring of NATO, see Seitz (1992).

By embedding its military in NATO, Germany has been able to grow stronger without threatening its neighbors. Neither Germany nor its neighbors has any incentive to deviate from existing strategies. If Germany did alter its security policies, for instance, by abandoning NATO, pursuing its security unilaterally, or reconfiguring its forces to make them more autonomous, this would trigger a response from other states that would leave all of them worse off, assuming German objectives had not changed.

In the economic arena, Germany has constrained its options even more decisively than in the military one. Germany was able to rebuild without threatening its regional neighbors by deeply integrating its economy in regional institutions and opening its economy to market pressures. Like NATO, European economic integration also emerged out of series of decisions taken primarily by U.S., French, and German leaders, pursuing varied objectives during the late 1940s and 1950s. The Americans wanted to strengthen western Europe against the Soviet threat. The French wanted to constrain the Germans. The Germans wanted to reestablish their sovereignty. From those decisions, a framework developed that enabled Germany to enmesh itself in multilateral economic institutions and to tie its hands. However, European economic integration was not the result of a concerted effort on the part of Germany to bind itself.

As discussed previously, the United States played a key role in the economic reconstruction of Europe and in the initial stages of European economic integration. The United States contributed $17.6 billion to the Marshall Plan and insisted on the creation of the Organization for European Economic Cooperation (OEEC) to administer the funds. A weaker United States, or one in which ideological factors (particularly anticommunism) were less salient, might not have been so eager to rebuild Europe and encourage economic cooperation and integration among the countries of western Europe (Duignan and Gann 1994, 40).

When the British occupation of Germany ended, the Americans were also crucial for the 1949 decision to establish an international authority to control the industrial output of the Ruhr. Germany was given only three of fifteen votes, and even these votes were to be cast by the occupying authorities until a government was established. Adenauer supported German participation in the Ruhr authority and the Council of Europe, despite heavy criticism from political opponents who accused him of abandoning German sovereignty over the Ruhr and of joining an organization that might block the reunification of Germany. His position was strengthened by support he received from the United States including permission to increase the Ruhr's shipbuilding capacity, to sign an economic agreement with the United States, and to resume commercial and consular activities with other countries (Jonas 1984, 288).

The European Coal and Steel Community (ECSC), which followed the agreement on the Ruhr, was an early step toward the European Economic Community. The community was not the result of some grand vision for a united Europe, in Germany or elsewhere. For instance, whereas some groups in France hoped that a strong ECSC would lead to a more unified Europe that would allow France to challenge the two superpowers, other groups wanted a weaker agreement. Germany did not support the French foreign minister Robert Schuman's vision of a strong supranational authority but, rather, hoped that some kind of plan would promote the revival of the German coal and steel industries and would end occupation controls. U.S. pressure remained critical for German acceptance of even the relatively weak ECSC; the Americans threatened to impose their own decartelization plan if the European countries failed to reach agreement (Milner 1997, 182–91).

The European Economic Community was also the result of bargaining that involved specific commercial interests as well as commitments to a more unified Europe. By the mid-1950s it was evident that German unification was highly unlikely in the short term; there was no deal to be cut with the Soviet Union. Adenauer wanted to embed Germany in a multilateral security and economic framework. German industry wanted a reduction or elimination of tariffs within Europe, but had to make concessions with regard to agriculture and atomic energy to secure approval of the Treaty of Rome in the French parliament (Moravcsik 1998, chap. 2).

Since the 1960s, Germany has been a consistent supporter of European integration, while still acting in its own commercial interests.[19] It has advocated a stronger role for the European Parliament and has backed qualified majority voting. Germany has been the largest contributor to the European budget, with a four-person German household paying about DM 2,000 for Europe in 1993–94, more than the unification tax (Katzenstein 1997c, 27–28, 32).

The prospect of a reunified Germany strengthened commitments, both in Germany and elsewhere, to European integration. The rest of Europe, and especially France, tied its acceptance of German unification to the strengthening of European unity. François Mitterrand insisted on accelerating the process of monetary union and initiating discussions of political union as a condition for supporting German unification. The Germans were not reluctant participants in these developments.

The creation of the European monetary system is perhaps the most dramatic testimony to German support for European integration and, in this case, promotion of a policy that makes any change of course extremely

---

19. Moravcsik (1998) has argued that the concern for economic interests has been the critical element in explaining the positions taken by all key members of the European Union, not just Germany.

costly. Prior to 1999 the Bundesbank was the de facto central bank for Europe. Germany was the largest economy and the Bundesbank had a high degree of independence. By joining the European Monetary Union, Germany arguably diminished its own national leverage. The Statute of the European System of Central Banks and of the European Central Bank (ECB) does state that its primary purpose is to "maintain price stability" (art. 2), an objective completely consistent with practices of the Bundesbank. Nevertheless, Germany is only one member of the bank. Voting power on the governing council is determined by the population and GDP of the member states. Although Germany does have the largest voice, approximately one-quarter of the votes, it cannot unilaterally determine policy (European Central Bank, Statute of the European System of Central Banks and of the European Central Bank, art. 10).[20] Confronted with resistance from his own constituents, Helmut Kohl argued that monetary union was necessary to assure the peace of Europe. The creation of a single currency for Europe is as close to an irrevocable step as can be taken by its member states, and for Germany's leaders it was a step motivated more by political than by economic considerations, by an explicit recognition of the advantages of binding Germany, especially a unified Germany, within a larger European framework.

Germany's trade has also been integrated with the other European states. Germany has consistently exported a large percentage of its GDP to its European neighbors. Between 1984 and 1994, Germany exported between 14 and 20 percent of its GDP to other Organization for Economic Cooperation and Development (OECD) European countries (see table 2.1). Its trade relations with its European neighbors are symmetrical; German imports from OECD Europe equaled 12–15.6 percent of its GDP.

From cautious beginnings in the ECSC through a series of decisions in the 1990s, Germany and its European neighbors have created and accepted a level of integration at odds with traditional notions of sovereign statehood. The member states of the EU have identifiable territory and are recognized as sovereign persons (they are members of international organizations, send and receive ambassadors, and sign international agreements), but their domestic structures are not autonomous. The rulings of the European Court are directly applicable in their own national legal systems. Some of the decisions of the European Council are taken by qualified majority voting; a member state can be obligated to follow policies it has not accepted.

The European Parliament is a supranational organization that can take decisions in some areas that are binding on the members of the union.

20. The National Central Banks' percentage shares is the key for the capital of the ECB as decided by the ECB Governing Council on 9 June 1998.

Table 2.1 Trade between OECD Europe[a] and Germany (% of German GDP)

	Imports/GDP	Exports/GDP
1984	15.7	18.3
1985	15.6	19.6
1986	13.9	18.6
1987	13.6	18.7
1988	13.9	19.5
1989	14.8	20.8
1990	14.9	18.8
1991	15.5	17.2
1992	14.5	16.3
1993	12.3	14.3
1994	13.0	15.0

Source: International Monetary Fund (1996); OECD (1989, 1995b).
[a] OECD Europe includes Austria, Belgium-Luxembourg, Czech Republic (1993–94 only), Denmark, Finland, France, Germany, Greece, Iceland, Ireland, Italy, Netherlands, Norway, Portugal, Spain, Sweden, Switzerland, Turkey, and the United Kingdom.

The EU itself is also recognized as a sovereign entity distinct from the member states. The community has been a participant in many international conferences including the UN Conference on the Law of the Seas, the Uruguay round of trade negotiations, and the Conference on Cooperation and Security in Europe. The community has been a signatory to international accords that fall within its purview, including the UN Law of the Seas Convention, various international commodity agreements, the Helsinki Final Act, and several environmental conventions. It maintains diplomatic representation in a number of countries (see http://europa.eu.int/comm/worldindex.htm). The member states of the EU have used their international legal sovereignty, their mutually accepted right to enter into international agreements, to create a structure that undermines the domestic autonomy and independence of their national policies and institutions.[21]

Thus, Germany has embedded itself in a set of security, economic, and political relations that constrain its freedom of action. Germany has tied its own hands. By supporting the creation of these international institutions, Germany pursued the strategy of binding—to enmesh itself in multilateral institutions and pursue its economic and strategic goals through these in-

21. For a discussion of various ways the concept of sovereignty has been used, see Krasner (1999, chap. 1).

stitutions. This binding is effective. It is an equilibrium outcome because (at least at the moment) none of the players has an incentive to defect.

It is difficult to imagine that the other European states and the United States would have accepted, in the case of the United States even encouraged, German reunification had Germany not engaged in binding. From a structural perspective, the division of Germany was a constructive outcome of World War II. A smaller Germany was a safer Germany. Unification made Germany again unambiguously the largest power in western Europe. As a result of the consolidation of the German Democratic Republic and the Federal Republic of Germany, the GNP of France, one simple indicator of relative capability, went from 89 percent of Germany's aggregate economic output in 1988 to 68 percent in 1993; the GNP of Britain went from 79 to 55 percent (World Bank 1995). The underlying power configurations in Europe are not so different from those that existed before the two world wars, but the degree of stability in Europe is far greater because the creation of new organizational structures, especially NATO and the EU, has provided Germany and the other states of Europe with policy options that were not available before 1914, 1933, or 1939.

Japan

The security and foreign policy prospects for Japan are more precarious than for Germany. Its security relationship is ensured mainly through a bilateral treaty with the United States that is of questionable durability and for which, in contrast with NATO, there is no obvious replacement. Its economic relations with the United States are more conflictual than those between the United States and the EU, including Germany. Its economic relations with other east Asian states are based on asymmetrical dependence rather than interlocking and symmetrical mutual interests. Japan has striven, so far as it could, to maintain its independence rather than to engage in binding, to expand rather than limit its policy options.

To some extent, especially with regard to security, this reflects the circumstances of Asia with its three major regional powers—Japan, China, and Russia—and very unequal levels of growth. Stable institutional arrangements in this environment would be difficult, probably impossible, regardless of the disposition and strategy of any Japanese government. But in the economic arena, the Japanese government has pursued programs that reduce the country's dependence but, precisely because of this, preclude binding commitments that might be stabilizing.

Japanese policy in the postwar period was guided by the Yoshida Doctrine, which called for economic development, close ties with the United States, and a minimal military establishment. The initial security arrangement between the two countries was established in 1951 and the Treaty of Mutual Cooperation and Security was concluded in 1960. The alliance with the United States has been the key component of Japan's security policy. However, unlike NATO and Germany, the alliance has not put constraints on Japan's military autonomy and has not embedded Japan's military in a multilateral framework, thereby reducing its threat. Although Japan has relied on the alliance, its commitment level is relatively weak. Obligations are asymmetrical; the United States has committed itself to the defense of Japan but not vice versa. This is de facto true for NATO as well, but the formal element of the North Atlantic Treaty does treat all member states in the same way. Since the 1950s there has been tension in the alliance generated by U.S. pressure on Japan to make greater commitments, pressure to which Japan has reluctantly and gradually acceded. The strain in the alliance arises not so much from the U.S. commitment to protect Japan but rather from the U.S. desire for Japan to make a greater contribution to the ambitious policies that have been pursued by the United States in east Asia and beyond. The Japanese in turn fear their country will be drawn into ill-advised conflicts precipitated by U.S. policies.

From the late 1940s, the United States pressured Japan to make greater military contributions, pressures Yoshida and his immediate successors resisted (T. Berger 1996, 140; Schaller 1997, 26–27). Although Japan has reluctantly increased its military involvement with the alliance, the essential ambiguity as to whether Japan could or would support U.S. policies has never been resolved. Prior to 1976, the linkage between U.S. and Japanese policy had not been explicitly stated. In 1976, in response to the Nixon doctrine, which called for a greater Japanese contribution, the Japanese government adopted a program that dismissed the possibility of full-scale aggression against Japan. The military was to be organized as a defensive force that could cope with small-scale aggression. Any larger effort was to take place through U.S.-Japanese security arrangements (Soeya 1998).

New military tasks have been accepted in fits and starts almost always as a result of pressure from the United States. In the early 1980s, Japan agreed to extend its protection of the sea-lanes. The 1992 International Peace Cooperation Law authorized the use of Japanese troops overseas but limited the number of troops to 2,000, prohibited the use of weapons except for self-defense, and required that a cease-fire already be in place; these restrictions reflect a deep reluctance to engage in any military action outside Japan. In 1998 Japan and the United States, prompted primarily by anxiety about North Korea, agreed to undertake joint research on theater missiles. In 1999 new legislation was adopted that would allow Japan to provide greater support to the United States in case of a crisis in Asia involving U.S. troops, such as sending ships to evacuate civilians, supplying fuel and spare parts, making airfields and medical facilities available to

U.S. forces, and conducting rear-area search and rescue missions for U.S. troops. But there was no provision for Japanese forces to fight with the United States and it was unclear whether the new laws would apply if a crisis developed over Taiwan as opposed to Korea (T. Berger 1996, 143; Christensen 1999, 64; *New York Times*, 24 April 1999, p. A5; Soeya 1998, 214). In contrast with Japan's wavering commitment to the U.S.-Japanese security pact, Japan has provided well for its own defense and thereby helped preserve its autonomy. Japan's air force and maritime forces assume primary responsibility for Japan's air defense and maritime commercial lanes, respectively (Hosokawa 1998, 4).

Whereas Germany's military is constrained by the multilateral framework in which it is embedded, Japan's military is constrained by domestic factors, such as article 9 of the constitution and the commitment to keeping military expenditures below 1 percent of GDP.[22] Article 9 of the constitution states that "the Japanese people forever renounce war as a sovereign right of the nation" and has been frequently invoked by pacifist groups that have objected to various efforts to expand military activity. Shortly after 1976, defense expenditures were limited to 1 percent of GNP, a stance that fits comfortably with Japanese attitudes, explicit policy, and the constitution. One percent of Japan's gross national product, however, turned out to be a very big number. Japanese defense expenditures increased approximately 6 percent a year from 1973 into the 1990s, following very high rates of growth in the Japanese economy. In 1986 Prime Minister Yasuhiro Nakasone publicly attempted to breach the 1 percent restriction on defense expenditures. He met with protests and backed away. The restriction was, however, quietly exceeded a year later. By the late 1990s, although Japanese expenditures remained low as a percentage of GDP compared to other industrialized countries, they were second only to the United States in absolute terms. This buildup took place largely in consultation with, and with pressure from, the United States. It was explained to the Japanese public as an effort to appease the United States. Approximately 10 percent of Japan's defense budget is used to support U.S. troops in Japan (T. Berger 1996, 126–28, 141; Soeya 1998, 214).

In the international arena, simply stating a policy does not make it binding. International commitments, such as Germany's, are often more credible than domestic ones, such as Japan's, both because policy changes are more transparent and because external enforcement is considered more credible to outside observers—the neighboring states. Other states ensure that these commitments are prohibitively costly to break. Japan's neigh-

---

22. In fact, Germany is also constrained domestically by constitutional provisions that limit its military activities. This essay argues that the more significant constraint is the international one, however.

bors and potential rivals recognize that the interpretation of article 9 is determined primarily by decisions taken within Japan. Policy could change even if formal constitutional constraints remain intact. For instance, changes in domestic sentiment could change the Japanese leaders' incentives and encourage them to shift to a more aggressive military policy and effectively dismantle the constraint of the constitution. Because Japan is not bound internationally by a transparent multilateral framework, Japan's interlocutors would not know whether to interpret changes in domestic sentiment as a harbinger of policy changes.

Moreover, incremental changes in budgets or force configurations might (or might not) be viewed as a signal of significant deviations from past strategies. The possibilities for misinterpretation of Germany's military policies are decreased both because its NATO commitments make its policy choices more transparent and because its incentives not to deviate from its existing military policy are derived from the international, rather than the domestic, environment. Departures from existing policies, especially unilaterally initiated changes, are more visible and therefore more likely to evoke a response from other states. Because the leaders of both Germany and its partners recognize this, there is less incentive to defect from existing strategies. The greater clarity provided by the web of international institutions within which Germany has bound itself has established a more stable equilibrium than Japan's domestic constraints on its security policies.

Japan's military strategy has not been coherent. Its military expenditures are substantial, although dwarfed by those of the United States. It has little capacity for force projection, but could develop additional capability given its economic and technological resources. Its alliance with the United States has been the subject of criticism by both leading politicians and the Japanese public.[23] Its most important ally has fought two land wars in Asia without the help of Japanese soldiers. The United States has pressed Japan to increase its military contributions, a step that Japanese governments have undertaken only reluctantly and in the face of domestic opposition. Aside from the U.S.-Japan Security Treaty, there are only the most limited institutional arrangements for security in Asia directly involving Japan. There were, for instance, regular visits between officials of the Japanese and Korean defense departments during the 1990s, but the first port of call by a South Korean naval vessel to Japan took place only in 1994 (Soeya 1998, 222–23).

Japan's security environment is dynamic and potentially unstable.

---

23. See, for instance, the article by Morihiro Hosokawa (1998), prime minister from 1992 to 1993, which cites popular dissatisfaction with both the number of U.S. troops stationed in Japan and the cost of maintaining them.

Institutional arrangements are weak. The distribution of power is changing. There are a number of specific conflicts. The Japanese-U.S. alliance, the cornerstone of stability for the regime, could unravel and, if it does, there is nothing to take its place. Situations of dynamic change in underlying capabilities are always problematic. The rules of the game—territorial claims, international regimes, and regional arrangements—are never continuously modified in ways that reflect the ongoing changes in underlying capabilities. As with the tectonic plates on some parts of major fault lines, the pressure keeps building but the relationship between the plates remains the same until the tension is released by a major earthquake.

There are a number of worrisome security issues in Asia. Despite setbacks, the Korean economy has grown rapidly. Unification is a possibility. A united Korea would never be as powerful as Japan, but it would be a formidable middle-size power, and Korea has had much more experience than Japan in security affairs. Relations between Japan and Korea have not been characterized by mutual trust. Korea was a Japanese colony during the first part of the twentieth century. The two major Korean national holidays celebrate freedom and independence from the Japanese. Mutual images are negative. There has been a dispute about the Takeshima Islands, which were placed under Korean physical control in 1952 but over which Japan has also claimed sovereignty. Japan has been concerned about developments in North Korea, including nuclear weapons, missiles, and terrorism. Any unification process in Korea would strain the security balance, particularly if a united Korea were anti-Japanese (Soeya 1998, 202, 206–7). If there were another war on the Korean peninsula, it is not clear what contribution Japan would make to any U.S.-led effort.

In addition, the economic resources of China are growing rapidly. Looking ahead ten or twenty years, China could be a much more formidable military power. A crisis over Taiwan could lead to very uncomfortable choices if the United States asked for Japanese assistance. If the Japanese refused such a request, it could undermine support for the alliance in the United States. If the Japanese acceded to the request, it would alarm China even more than U.S. military action would (Christensen 1999, 67–68).

Chinese officials are much more suspicious of Japan than they are of the United States. According to Thomas Christensen, "Chinese analysts view Japan with much less trust and, in many cases, with a loathing rarely found in their attitudes about the United States" (1999, 52). There is resentment in China about Japan's failure to acknowledge its responsibility for the treatment of China during World War II. Chinese leaders have complained about Japan's treatment of the war in its school textbooks, and they were disquieted by the 1986 visit of the prime minister to Yasukuni Shrine, which commemorates Japan's war dead. There are territorial disputes over island groups in the South China Sea. Japanese investments in China have not lessened the negative sentiments. Japanese businessmen are often viewed with distrust; Japan is now seen as an economic competitor (Christensen 1999, 52–55, 65).

And Russia, the other major power in the area, is at least for the time being, collapsing. There has been little movement toward resolving the dispute over the Northern Territories, which were seized by the Soviet Union at the conclusion of World War II and are claimed by Japan.

In sum, the security of Asia is more unstable than that of Europe—the power of China is rising, Korea could reunify, and Russia is crumbling. Japan's alliance with the United States is a keystone of Asian stability, but critical issues, especially the support Japan would provide for U.S. initiatives, have never been resolved. Given Japan's economic size and technological sophistication, its military capabilities could be rapidly enhanced. In the security arena, Japan has not found an international mechanism by which it could credibly tie its own hands. The constraints on Japanese security policy are domestic, not international. These domestic constraints cannot commit Japan to a nonthreatening path as credibly as Germany's international institutional constraints have.

In the economic sphere Japan has also failed to devise a set of arrangements that could bind it to a specific set of nonexploitative policies. Unlike Germany, Japan is not embedded in a regional structure that is in any way comparable to the EU. Japan has not compromised its Westphalian sovereignty through the creation of supranational institutional structures, although its domestic institutional arrangements have been altered as a result of *gaiatsu* (external initiatives), especially from the United States, that have succeeded because of support from domestic actors in Japan. Japan's concept of comprehensive security, which includes economic as well as security considerations, is designed to limit Japan's external vulnerability by, for instance, diversifying sources of energy supply and maintaining a high level of domestic technical competence. Japan has developed a set of economic ties that enhance rather than constrain its autonomy.

Japan's pattern of interaction with other major industrializing areas is very different than that of either the United States or Germany. The so-called triad of major industrialized areas is not a triad at all, if triad implies relatively symmetrical patterns of interaction and interdependence. A pillar of Japan's embedded capitalism, its distinctive form of economic organization, has been its protection of certain export-oriented industries. Since the 1970s, Japan has often run very large trade surpluses. Japan is more heavily an importer of raw materials and an exporter of manufactured goods than are other major industrialized countries. Moreover, its trade in manufactured goods is more heavily dominated by trade within Japanese firms. Between 1983 and 1992, intrafirm trade accounted for

70 percent of all trade between the United States and Japan, compared with 43 percent between the United States and Europe (Pauly and Reich 1997, 18).

The pattern of foreign direct investment between Japan and other major industrialized countries is also unbalanced. Japan's direct investment in the United States and Europe is much greater than either European or U.S. foreign direct investment in Japan. In the United States, the ratio of Japanese investments in wholesaling to manufacturing is approximately five to one, whereas for Germany investments in these two sectors are approximately equal (Pauly and Reich 1997, 22). Japanese firms have focused more on selling goods they have made elsewhere.

In the 1990s, Japanese trade and investment involving east and southeast Asia has increased rapidly and Japan has become the dominant economic player in this arena. Japanese direct investment in Asia has increased much more rapidly than U.S. investment. In 1977, U.S. and Japanese foreign direct investment in Asia were approximately equal. In 1994, cumulative foreign direct investment for Japan had grown to $74 billion, whereas U.S. foreign direct investment had increased only to $45 billion. In 1994 approximately 7 percent of Thailand's production workers were employed by Japanese firms. Japanese investment in Asia has been concentrated in the manufacturing sector. Investment growth continued during the mid-1990s despite the slowing of the Japanese economy (Hatch and Yamamura 1996, 6–11). This dramatic increase in Japanese trade and investment has solidified Japan's dominance in the region and over its regional neighbors.

Japanese foreign direct investment has been characterized by the same pattern of network connections that are present in Japan—close cooperation between government and business and within the business community. Japanese overseas development assistance has financed the construction of infrastructure in east Asia that has benefited Japanese investors. Japanese corporations are not as transnationally engaged as many of their German or U.S. counterparts are. Despite expansion, they have held fast to their membership in the Japanese structure (Hatch and Yamamura 1996, 15–19). The model of embedded capitalism attributed with such great success in Japan has been consequently adopted by other Asian states.

The east Asian economies are heavily dependent on Japan. For example, the value of manufactured intermediate goods imported from Japan represented 11 percent of Asia's manufacturing GNP. In contrast, parts imported by Japan from all sources were less than 2 percent of Japan's manufacturing GNP. The east Asian economies rely on Japan for 40 percent of their machinery imports (Hatch and Yamamura 1996, 178). Although Japan's embrace has spurred development in these countries, it has also threatened the smaller east Asian economies with the danger of being penetrated both economically and politically by Japanese actors. In general, the east Asian countries are losing bargaining power. The dominant Japanese firm provides its subsidiary in Asia, including Japan, with capital, technology, managerial expertise, and a market and it guides the organization of the subordinate. The subordinate is bound not only by these carrots but also by the sticks—the costs of breaking the relationship. Despite their formal independence, subordinate firms have limited options because many of their assets have been specifically committed to their relationship with their Japanese parent company (Hatch and Yamamura 1996, 30–33, 36–37, 57–59).

Developing a network of dependent relations is not inherently unstable. The subsidiary players might not like their dependence, but it could be their best option. Mexico, for instance, is very heavily dependent on its trade with the United States, especially in the area of manufactured goods. More than 70 percent of Mexico's exports are directed to the United States; less than 10 percent of U.S. exports go to Mexico. The North American Free Trade Agreement (NAFTA) has made Mexico even more dependent than it might otherwise have been, but given the asymmetries of size and economic development between the two countries it was still the best option available to Mexico. Mexican rulers might not be enchanted with their level of dependence, but it is nonetheless a stable outcome.

Japanese relations with east and southeast Asia are more problematic. Whereas the countries of Asia (with the exception of China) are heavily dependent on Japan for technology, capital, and intermediate goods, the United States and Europe are their more important export markets. If North American or European markets closed, the economic organization of Asia, and hence Japan's relationship with east and southeast Asia, might unravel. Without these major external markets there would be much less incentive to stay with the Japanese system.

Perhaps the most striking indicator of Japan's policy of independence is its overall level of international trade. In general, the importance of trade is negatively correlated with size; the larger the country, the more self-contained its economy is. Given the size of the Japanese economy, it is not surprising that its dependence on trade has been less than that of the major European states. But what is surprising is that the percentage of Japanese exports plus imports to GDP is less than that of the United States and, even more surprising, it has not grown over time. Table 2.2 shows the ratio of trade (exports plus imports) to GDP for several countries.

The importance of trade for the United States more than doubled between 1960 and 1997 and increased by approximately 30 percent for the United Kingdom, and 60 percent for France and Germany. It hardly changed at all for Japan. Given the taken-for-granted nature of globaliza-

Table 2.2 International Trade, Exports plus Imports (% of GDP)

	1960	1970	1980	1990	1997
United States	10	11	20	22	25
United Kingdom	44	46	52	57	57
Japan	21	20	28	21	22
Federal Republic of Germany	34	40	58	60	55
France	28	32	46	46	49

Source: World Bank (1983, vol. I, table 3, 506; 1992, country pages; 1999b, tables 4.17, 4.2; see also http://www.worldbank.org/data/wdi/economy.html).

tion, Japan's ability to contain any increase in its aggregate dependence on trade is surprising, if not stunning.

In sum, in contrast with Germany, Japan has pursued, to the extent possible, a policy of independence in the economic arena. It has not constrained itself through regional integration. It has nurtured a set of asymmetrical relations with the smaller states of east and southeast Asia, who have depended heavily on Japan for capital and technology but not for markets. These asymmetrical economic relations with neighboring countries and with the United States reflect Japan's embedded capitalist model. In the security arena, the treaty with the United States has been the key element of Japanese strategy. With the United States present, Japan has less incentive to enhance its military prowess and other Asian countries have less reason to be nervous about Japan. The nature of the security relationship, however, has remained ambiguous in critical areas. Japan is not constrained by the U.S.-Japan Security Treaty and its commitment in the case of an Asian conflict is questionable. It is also not clear whether Japan's domestic commitments, such as article 9, are truly ties that bind. This uncertainty about the degree to which Japan will continue to adhere to its present security policies, the fragility of U.S. military commitments, and the asymmetry of Japan's economic involvement with other states (both industrialized countries and the smaller states of south and east Asia) make Japan's neighbors more cautious about relations with Japan and generate an additional source of stress for Japan's embedded capitalism.

Prospects

The cold war anchored international politics for more than forty years. The United States was deeply involved in both Europe and Asia and provided the foundation for the security systems in both regions. As an occupying power, the United States took a permissive stance toward the reconstitution of embedded capitalism. U.S. leaders were more concerned with enhancing the strength of their alliances in the aggregate than with the U.S. position within those alliances (Gowa 1994).

In the post–cold war world, U.S. tolerance for asymmetrical military and economic commitments is waning. Germany will remain secure in Europe because it has bound itself both economically and militarily. Japan, however, will be less secure internationally because it has left itself unconstrained and will face pressure from the United States to remedy these asymmetrical economic and security relations.

With the end of the cold war, U.S. policy is more uncertain and, as developments in the Balkans and elsewhere have demonstrated, the absence of any assurance regarding superpower intervention can promote, rather than inhibit, the breakdown of order. During the cold war, strategic concerns for the United States trumped economic interests. This is no longer the case.

Even the resources of the world's only superpower, the Unites States, will be strained, and commitments that are not directly related to security or economic interests will be retrenched. Consider the extraordinary range of engagements that have been undertaken by the United States since the end of the cold war. These include expanding NATO to incorporate Hungary, Poland, and the Czech Republic and refusing to place any limits on further enlargement, even the inclusion of the Baltic states despite the anxiety this has caused across the political spectrum in Russia; commitments to discourage the use of force against Taiwan; support for nonproliferation despite the fact that expansive U.S. policies can only make nuclear weapons look more attractive; growing economic and security involvement in central Asia; troops in Bosnia; an air war against Yugoslavia; troops in Kosovo; troops in Macedonia; a commitment to defend Korea; missile strikes against supposed terrorist targets in Afghanistan and the Sudan; an effort to condition Russian and Chinese involvement in international organizations on changes in their domestic political institutions; the invasion of Afghanistan, the displacement of the Taliban, and the subsequent occupation of the country; and a global war against terrorism. Wow!

The relationship between basic U.S. security and economic interests and many of these commitments is far from clear. Public support for expansive goals is weak, as evidenced by the decision of the Bill Clinton administration to publicly reject the use of ground troops in Kosovo even though it would have been strategically advantageous to have left Slobodan Milosovic with a higher level of uncertainty about the military forces that might be used against him.

Given that U.S. commitments are less certain, what does this suggest for German and Japanese foreign policy, for regional stabilities, and for their embedded capitalisms? The situation is more precarious for Japan than for Germany.

First, in terms of regional stabilities, Asia rather than Europe is likely to be the focus of great power conflict in the future. Both the European and the Asian regions will be multipolar. Multipolar systems are more problematic than bipolar ones. Balances do not always form. Germany has been able to pursue a policy of binding that has reassured its allies (who also could have been and have been its adversaries), whereas Japan has pursued a policy of independence that would leave it adrift were the United States to withdraw. Misperceptions of peaceful intentions can also be mitigated by nonstructural factors, including domestic politics and values. Whereas Europe is wholly democratic, Asia's regimes are more heterogeneous, ranging from totalitarian (North Korea and Myanmar), to firmly democratic (Japan, Australia, and New Zealand), to more tenuously democratic (Russia), with some in between such as South Korea, Singapore, Taiwan, and Pakistan. Although there is some shared conception of a European identity, there is no Asian equivalent (Friedberg 1993–94, 7).

Arms spending in Asia has seen a sharp increase since the mid-1980s and in the late 1990s approximated that of Europe, excluding the former Soviet Union. In general, there has been a restructuring from counterinsurgency to high-technology forces. The protection of the sea-lanes requires a power-projection capability that can be provocative because defensive and offensive weaponry often cannot be distinguished (Christensen 1999, 49–50). Smaller countries are worried about the increasing military, especially naval, capabilities of Japan and China (Ball 1993–94). It is not evident that there could be a stable equilibrium without the active engagement of the United States, not so much because the United States is a balancer but because U.S. troops provide assurance that Japan will not take a more active military stance.

Given the potential instability in Asia and the important balancing role the United States plays, a weakening of the U.S.-Japanese agreement could precipitate a spiral of distrust, increased arms expenditures, and escalating tensions. It is not difficult to imagine how this alliance could weaken. Consider, for instance, a crisis or war on the Korean peninsula that results in active U.S. military involvement. Legislation might allow Japan to support U.S. military efforts, but the body bags would be returning to U.S., not to Japanese, military airfields. Not only might domestic politics make it difficult for Japan to commit troops to Korea, but it would hardly be easy for Korea to welcome the presence of Japanese soldiers. An armed conflict over Taiwan could be even more divisive because there could be deep policy differences between the United States and Japan. The United States is far more committed to preventing an armed invasion of Taiwan than is Japan. Not only might U.S. military personnel die in a situation in which there were no Japanese forces, but the government of Japan might not support U.S. action at all.

There is nothing inevitable about a destabilization in Asia. But if the United States did become involved in an armed conflict in Korea or Taiwan and if Japanese troops did not fight side by side with their U.S. counterparts, it would be very difficult for any U.S. leader to support a continued security commitment in Asia and particularly with Japan. Anticommunism provided a domestic rationale for the wars in Korea and Vietnam. There is no equivalent rationale currently available. If the U.S.-Japanese security alliance were actually needed for something other than the defense of Japan itself, it could easily fall apart. Without the U.S. presence, Japan would again face the predicament of being too big but not big enough and security relations in Asia would likely become even further destabilized.

By contrast, consider the consequences of a U.S. pullback or withdrawal in Europe. This need not be anything nearly as exciting as the abandonment of NATO. Would European stability be unhinged if the United States backed away from its current level of commitment? The answer is almost certainly no. Germany and its European partners have established a stable equilibrium by creating institutions that have made it possible for Germany to tie its own hands. Given the configuration of economic interests in Europe, Germany can neither withdraw from nor dominate the EU. A North Atlantic alliance with a decreased role for the United States would continue to allow Germany to embed its military forces in a multilateral structure and multinational formations. Even if NATO collapsed completely, the security and foreign policy pillar of the EU could be expanded. Already Germany and its European partners are discussing plans to reinvigorate the WEU, to make new investments and commitments, not only to establish Europe's independence from NATO in out-of-area operations but also to safeguard the future of Europe.

Europe is not exactly a zone of peace. The disintegration of Yugoslavia has precipitated local conflict and the first use of NATO forces. The position and foreign policy of Russia is far from certain. Greece and Turkey have long-standing conflicts including the unresolved issue of Cyprus. Nevertheless, the situation is more problematic for Japan in Asia than it is for Germany in Europe. Military contingents from France, Germany, Britain, and other European members of NATO are active in the former Yugoslavia, not just ones from the United States. If the body bags were sent, they would arrive in more than one country. Even if NATO were at some point to crumble, there are European institutions that would allow German leaders to constrain their options in ways that would be reassuring to other European states.

The shift in U.S. policy at the end of the cold war also threatens Japan's embedded capitalist model and potentially its regional economic stability more than Germany's. As mentioned earlier, the United States has become increasingly intolerant of economic asymmetries and has pressured Japan to open its economy to goods, services, and investment. This pressure challenges Japan's embedded capitalist model which, unlike Germany's, has maintained high barriers to trade and investment. An economic network centered on externally oriented and protected corporations has been at the core of Japan's embedded capitalism. Although both Germany's and Japan's embedded capitalisms have been under pressure due to market competition, the globalization of finance, technological innovation, and other factors (see the essays by Kozo Yamamura and Gregory Jackson in this volume), Japan's embedded capitalism has faced pressures from other states, most notably the United States, as it tries to remedy its asymmetrical economic relations. Japan's regional economic relationships are also contingent on the United States in a way that Germany's are not. The U.S. market is the major target for manufactured exports from east and southeast Asia, many of which are produced by the formal and informal subsidiaries of Japanese corporations. Were trans-Pacific trade to erode, the costs would be higher for Japan and east and southeast Asia than for the United States. Therefore, U.S. pressure has a salience in Japan that it would not have in Germany, which is much less dependent on the U.S. market and more symmetrically embedded in its regional economic environment.

As the cold war weakened and then ended, U.S. pressure on Japan to decrease asymmetry by changing its economic policies and opening its economy to goods, services, and investment mounted. The United States challenged *keiretsu* ties and links between the private sector and the state. U.S. policymakers have used the Super 301 provision of the 1988 trade act—essentially targeting Japan—as a generalized threat against Asian economies. The United States imposed antidumping duties against Japanese computer chips in 1986, the first such action directed at Japan in the postwar period (a remarkable fact considering how much pressure Japanese corporations had put on their U.S. competitors and how much penetration of the U.S. market there had been). The 1991 semiconductor agreement included a provision for a 20 percent share of the Japanese market for U.S. chips, a figure that was actually reached.

U.S. demands for access to the Japanese market were often inconsistent with Japan's embedded capitalist model. During the 1990s, negotiations between the United States and Japan, notably the Structural Impediments Initiative (SII) and the Market Opening Sector Specific (MOSS) discussions, involved automobiles and automobile parts, telecommunications, insurance, medical equipment, land use, *keiretsu* organization, exclusionary business practices, public works expenditures, and even retail sales laws. Some of these issues are far removed from conventional notions of trade and investment barriers and reach deeply into the domestic institutional arrangements central to Japan's embedded capitalism.

U.S. negotiators have had mixed success. For instance, the United States pressured Japan to increase access for Motorola in the Japanese cellular phone market, declaring that Japan had failed to honor the spirit of a 1989 agreement promising "comparable market access." Although this was ostensibly an agreement between private companies in which the Japanese company (IDO) responsible for the Tokyo market agreed to build 159 new relay stations for Motorola, Motorola had effectively been denied equal access to the Tokyo market until the U.S. government intervened. In contrast, U.S. negotiators made little headway in securing changes in *keiretsu* practices. Leonard Schoppa has argued that the success of U.S. pressure (*gaiatsu*) has depended on the extent to which support has come from groups within Japan. When the Americans were able to expand the range of elite participation, to attract the attention of the Japanese electorate more generally as a result of mass media coverage of an issue, or to mobilize the interests of groups that had been previously excluded from a specific issue area, they were able to alter Japanese policies and even structures (*New York Times*, 15 February 1994, p. 1; 16 February 1994, p. C4; Reuters 1994; Schoppa 1993). *Gaiatsu* has nevertheless resulted in "substantial and probably irreversible changes in Japanese policies and political arrangements" (Katzenstein and Tsujinaka 1995, 90). External trade tensions with the United States have led not only to some adjustments in policies but also to changes in institutional structures. U.S. foreign economic policy, not just technological change and globalization, have put Japan's embedded capitalism under pressure.

Both politically and economically the situation in Europe is more robust than it is in Asia, and the involvement and interests of the United States are more symmetrical. The level of institutionalization is high in both the economic and the security realms. Commitments are symmetrical. Formal barriers to the movement of goods, services, and people have largely disappeared. The European monetary union will not be easily undone. There is a broad base of support for maintaining open economic relations between Europe and the United States. Intrasectoral trade is high, as are flows of foreign direct investment.

Germany might be the biggest economic player in Europe but with its extensive, open, and relatively symmetrical trade and investment flows, with the European monetary union, and with the highly institutionalized structure of the EU, Germany has tied its own hands in a way that makes it very difficult to imagine how the rope could come undone. Other states are not as anxious as they would otherwise be about the prospect of a German-dominated economic Mitteleuropa because the range of policies Germany could deploy to encourage asymmetric ties is limited by its membership in the EU. No German leader will be eager to withdraw from the monetary union lest such a move prompt a reaction from other European states that would leave Germany worse off. It is not in the interest of any of the major states to undo the present deal and there is little chance for changes in the players, the choice set, or their preferences.

Conclusion

Much conventional thinking about international and domestic politics has emphasized the importance of power and freedom of action. That is at least one lesson of the realist position. In some cases it is a lesson that should be embraced. A dominant power can establish a regional and sometimes a global order that suits its economic and security interests. But there are other configurations of power that make an absence of constraints problematic. Throughout the twentieth century both Germany and Japan have been potential regional hegemons—too big but not big enough. They have been large enough to threaten their neighbors but not powerful enough to establish stable regional, much less global orders. Regardless of the nature of domestic political regimes, such a distribution of power is inherently problematic. Other states, concerned with relative not just absolute gains, are tempted to form alliances or to limit their pattern of economic interaction, lest they make themselves even more dependent. Confronted with a potentially hostile environment, a potential regional hegemon may react in ways that increase the insecurity of others. Even a state with peaceful and defensive intentions can be regarded as a threat, prompting a spiral of reactions that each side fears is an indication of aggressive intent. And if the domestic regime of a potential regional hegemon is nationalistic and militaristic, the situation is even worse.

How can such a predicament be resolved? One solution is to engage the active participation of an extraregional power. Such has been the role of the United States since the late 1940s. The configuration of the postwar world hardly emerged full-blown from the ashes of World War II. But U.S. involvement in Asia and Europe provided a balance that made Japan and Germany much less threatening even after their economic recoveries had taken place. The United States was an ideal balancer—distant, concerned with counteracting the Soviet Union, and easily able to constrain Germany or Japan.

Without an external balancer, a potential regional hegemon may be much better off if it can limit rather than expand its range of options. By constraining itself, it may reassure its allies and potential adversaries, and, by reassuring other states, it can make itself more secure than it would otherwise have been. But commitment is an inherent problem in the international system. Guarantees of future behavior and policy are problematic (Fearon 1995). Governments can change. Regimes can be transformed. Attitudes can shift.

By enmeshing itself in a set of economic and security institutions, Germany has been able to tie its own hands. The EU has created interests within Germany—export-oriented industries, lawyers engaged in European jurisprudence, high-technology services—that would oppose an alternative economic strategy. NATO has also provided a device through which Germany can bind itself. Any effort to back away from the EU or NATO would be taken as a clear indicator of a change in German policy. Such a change would prompt a response from other states that would leave them all worse off. The fact that this sequence of events is known by all the parties discourages any efforts to unravel existing institutional arrangements.

Japan finds itself in a more problematic situation. The U.S.-Japanese security alliance provides stability for Asia by reassuring other Asian states about Japanese policy and behavior. But if actual fighting broke out in Korea or the Taiwan Straits, Japanese support for the United States is far from certain, a scenario that could destroy the alliance. Moreover, even if Japan wanted to more fully engage its military forces, something that might be reassuring to the United States, it would be discomforting to other states in Asia. Unlike Europe, Asia does not have a set of more or less equally endowed states that might bind themselves together in ways that would be mutually constraining. China is large and undeveloped. Korea is smaller than Japan and less highly developed. The member countries of the Association of Southeast Asian Nations (ASEAN) are all relatively weak. Economically, Japan has adopted policies designed to maintain its freedom of action—foreign investment from other states has been discouraged, technology flows have been asymmetrical, and trade with the industrialized countries has been inter- rather than intrasectoral. Trade and investment have established relations of asymmetrical interdependence with east and southeast Asia that will be stable only so long as the U.S. market remains open.

It is not evident that Japan could have followed different policies. Given its local environment, its security options were limited. In the economic sphere, Japan's strategy has been both unique and until the 1990s exceptionally successful. But by maintaining its freedom of action in the economic arena and relying on the United States for its security, Japan has left itself in a more precarious position than Germany.

Bosnia and Kosovo are demonstrations of the robustness of west European stability and of Germany's place in Europe. NATO military decisions concerning Kosovo were made not only by the U.S. General Wesley Clark, the SACEUR, but also by the German General Klaus Naumann, who is chairman of the North Atlantic Military Committee. Perhaps in the sorry story of the former Yugoslavia, the fact that a German general speaking in lightly accented English could be one of the major military commanders of a multilateral force acting on behalf of human rights in an area where such rights had been trampled by the Nazi military during World War II is a small illustration that sometimes progress is possible in human affairs. Anything like a Kosovo in Asia would only reveal the brittleness of security arrangements and could potentially undo economic ones as well. There is no Japanese equivalent to Klaus Naumann.

The fundamental shift associated with the end of the cold war is not the U.S. abandonment of international commitments, as some had predicted, but rather its lack of tolerance for asymmetrical relations (e.g., Mearsheimer 1990). Germany is fully committed to NATO and the EU framework and is therefore in a more comfortable position. The constraints of these multilateral institutions reduce its threat, at least for the time being, and resolve the problem of its being too big but not big enough. By contrast, Japan is unconstrained; its commitment to the U.S.-Japanese security arrangement is unproven, and it has continued to reap asymmetrical benefits from economic relations with the United States and its neighbors. As a result, Japan is not only in a more vulnerable international position, its embedded capitalism and the asymmetrical unilateral policies it promotes are also under international assault. Japan's formula for economic success has become a point of international contention.

Regional States: Japan and Asia, Germany in Europe

Peter J. Katzenstein

Since the end of the cold war, the central concept for organizing world politics has not been strategic bipolarity or economic globalism. It has been regionalism. We could think of a world of regions as multipolar; in this view, regions are the poles of power around which international conflict and cooperation are organized. We could think of a world of regions as global markets; from this perspective, corporations and other actors are linked through exchange to a triadic international political economy linking North America, Asia, and Europe. Or we could think of a world of regions (as this chapter does) as the different political connections between national polities and the regions of which they are a part. The character of core polities and of the different connections to their regional environments is consequential for the kind of regionalism that emerges. Specifically, this chapter argues that Germany and Japan are important regional states that are central to the evolution of European and Asian, and thus global, politics.

The comparative political economy of German and Japanese capitalism at the end of the twentieth century was to some extent shaped by the international dismemberment of protective national cocoons. But the pressures of international markets do not simply oppose national forms of capital-

This chapter draws on material previously published in Katzenstein (1993a, 1993b, 1997a, 1997c), Katzenstein and Tsujinaka (1995), and Katzenstein and Shiraishi (1997a), among others. For their criticisms and suggestions I thank Wolfgang Streeck and the participants in the Seattle (10–12 April 1997), Berlin (22–24 January 1998), and Köln (24–26 June 1999) conferences on The Future of Nationally Embedded Capitalism in a Global Economy.

ism. Instead, world politics since the end of the cold war is the blending of national and international elements in distinct world regions across different issues that extend far beyond the field of political economy. For example, international liberalization opens borders for economic exchanges, including the smuggling of drugs and illegal immigrants, that prompt states to reposition police at borders that have been liberalized. Rather than thinking of one prevailing over the other, it is more productive to analyze the recalibration of national and international factors in regional settings that connect both realms. Contemporary regionalism can both strip away and mend the social fabric that embeds patient capitalism.

In contrast to the 1990s, in the 1950s both Germany and Japan were linked much more closely to the United States and the global system than to their regional environments (Lehmkuhl 1999; Schmidt and Doran 1996). Europe and Asia had been destroyed physically and psychologically, and U.S. and Soviet power loomed large in European and Asian affairs. Germany and Japan were clients that depended militarily on the United States for their national security and economically for easy access to international markets. This client status permitted both countries to spend fewer resources on national defense than might otherwise have been the case and to concentrate attention instead on export-led growth.

For the early postwar period, a focus on global military and economic constraints and opportunities emphasizes quite correctly the similarities in Germany's and Japan's positions in the international system and underlines the similarity in their political responses to the novel conditions of the Pax Americana. This analysis can be complemented easily by arguments that focus on the gradual and, by U.S. standards, incomplete democratization of their domestic political institutions and practices.

The first section of this chapter discusses this plausible and parsimonious argument for the first two decades after the end of World War II. The argument is less compelling when applied to subsequent decades because it assumes we can analyze Germany and Japan at different historical break points, for example, 1945, 1970, and 1990, without the political effects that a variety of experiences have had on both countries since the 1970s. These effects have created very different regional and national structures and identities that help explain why Germany and Japan followed different paths in a world of regions in the 1990s. Their anomalous character as militarily incomplete states with formidable economic strengths and politically soft shells is this essay's justification for focusing on Germany and Japan as regional states. For Germany, building a European Union (EU) has become a natural response to both the terrible memories of unilateral power politics and the challenges that global and international changes are creating for all European states. In sharp contrast, Japan seeks to avoid past mistakes and meet current challenges primarily through informal initiatives and arrangements that are typically linked closely to economic transactions in regional and global markets. Are Germany's and Japan's different domestic structures reflected in different policy choices at home and abroad, or are these choices broadly speaking similar? How do Japan and Germany respond to the external pressures and transnational influences to which they are exposed in Asia and Europe? What is at the root of a contemporary regionalism in world politics that is open to global and international developments in both Europe and Asia, but that tends to bilateralism and informality in Asia and multilateralism and formal arrangements in Europe?

The other three sections of this chapter offer answers to these three questions. First, Germany's and Japan's different domestic structures lead to very different policy choices at home and abroad. Japan's developmental state relies more on national means and Germany's welfare state more on international means to achieve national purposes. And in contrast to Germany's industrial democracy, Japan's productivity democracy typically relies on informal ties rather than formal legal rules. Second, Japan yields to external pressures (*gaiatsu*) when Tokyo's game of money politics grinds to a halt and seeks influence abroad through low-key lobbying and a strategy of cultivating a favorable climate of public opinion. By contrast, Germany is open to transnational influences and embraces the world with an institutionalization of what is called societal foreign policy (*gesellschaftliche Aussenpolitik*). Finally, although both Asian and European regionalism are open, the source of their openness differs. The scope of Japan's global economic influence and its heavy dependence on the United States for its national security and for export markets create an accumulation of global and dyadic vulnerabilities that strengthen an open regionalism as well as bilateral and informal policy arrangements in Asia. In the case of Germany, a far-reaching transformation of domestic structures and policies and the process of Europeanization have created domestic conditions for a European regionalism that is open, multilateral, and formal. A brief conclusion underlines the political and analytical importance of regionalism and regional states in contemporary world affairs.

German and Japanese Similarities: Global Constraints and Opportunities

Germany and Japan were relative latecomers to the Industrial Revolution and the game of international power politics. Germany's belated unification and the Meiji Restoration set the stage for a process of delayed rapid industrialization and the growth of militant nationalism. As the first volume of this project (Streeck and Yamamura 2001) illustrates, each country found distinctive responses to large historical challenges such as the domestic incorporation of the working class or international competition in an era of imperialism. In the late nineteenth century, Prussia and Germany served often as an institutional model for Japan (Baring and Sase 1977; Eisenstadt 1996; Kudo 1998; Martin 1987, 1995; Pyle 1984). The military alliance that linked Germany and Japan during World War II thus reflected common historical trajectories in which authoritarian politics prevailed at home over democratic politics and in which power politics dominated abroad over commercial expansion (Japanisch-Deutsches Zentrum Berlin 1992).

In the thirty-year war that marked world politics between 1914 and 1945, Japan and Germany were revisionist powers. In a multipolar international system, their military and fascist regimes adopted autarchic policies, prepared for and waged imperialist wars, and conducted brutally violent campaigns of ethnic cleansing which, in the case of Germany, included genocide. Surprise attack was the military strategy with which both countries hoped to reach their political objectives.

Unconditional surrender in 1945 turned a multipolar into a bipolar international system to which, broadly speaking, Germany and Japan responded similarly. Japanese and German national security depended largely on the protective umbrella that the United States extended for the last half of the twentieth century over the Pacific Rim and western Europe. Both states depended greatly in their security on the U.S. nuclear umbrella and conventional military forces. Neither Germany nor Japan provided fully for its national security. Both relied on the U.S. deterrent as their security guarantee. Among the advanced industrial states, the principle of liberal commercial exchange, rather than national autarchy, organized the international economy. Here too, Germany and Japan reacted similarly. Both became supporters that developed strong interests in maintaining an open international economy (Lake 1988). In brief, during the cold war, Germany and Japan acted like prosperous, civilian powers or trading states that responded similarly to a bipolar system of states and a liberal international economy (Kurth 1989; Maull 1990–91; Rosecrance 1986).

Broad similarities in structural constraints and strategic response offer a plausible explanation of the first two postwar decades (Grieco 1999; Liberman 1998). For subsequent decades, however, this approach leaves empirical anomalies, suggesting the need for an alternative conceptualization that pays more attention to regional factors.

The doctrine of realpolitik, for example, analyzes the balancing of states in the international system. From the perspective of power politics, because they lack independent nuclear deterrents, Germany and Japan are woefully incomplete states. Furthermore, Germany's formidable army remains today fully integrated into the North Atlantic Treaty Organization (NATO), a supranational military security arrangement that leaves the

German government without national control over its armed forces. Japan's long-standing commitment to limiting defense spending to less than 1 percent of GNP, broken only on rare occasions, has left it with military forces inadequately prepared to fully guarantee its security.

The emasculation of Germany's and Japan's military strength after total defeat is not surprising; but the institutionalization of incomplete statehood one-half century after the end of war is. This anomaly prompts T. V. Paul, for example, to explain Germany's and Japan's nonnuclear policies as the result of "the regional dynamics arising out of security interdependence that these states entered into in the aftermath of World War II" (1996, 2). In the case of Germany and Japan, the acquisition of offensive weapons would have destabilized greatly the security of neighboring states to which they were closely linked politically. Regional considerations dictated a policy that sought to minimize the risk of creating regional security dilemmas.

After the failures of the command economies of the 1930s and 1940s and the wartime destruction brought about by the defeat of heavy-handed states, the rise of market-based economies in Germany and Japan came as no surprise. Germany has consistently adhered to a liberal approach in product markets while developing the institutions of its vaunted social market economy in labor markets. Competition in Japanese product markets is tougher than in most other states in the Organization for Economic Cooperation and Development (OECD), and enterprise unionism furthered in the 1960s and 1970s what T. J. Pempel and Keiichi Tsunekawa (1979) have called "Corporatism without Labor." In contrast to Japan, Germany's approach to international liberalization has been much more forthcoming. For an argument that emphasizes similarities, the institutionalization of differently organized political economies rather than similar market-based economies is an anomaly.

Regionalism has much to do with that difference. The U.S.-led drive for international liberalization after 1945 made provisions for customs unions operating under the auspices of the General Agreement on Tariffs and Trade (GATT). In 1957, six west European states, Germany among them, formed this union with strong U.S. support. No such union emerged in Asia, which helps explain the less far-reaching processes of regional market integration in subsequent decades. The U.S. market thus looms large for Japan, the European market for Germany. This difference in regional market integration has left Germany and Japan with different types of soft-shell political economies, open to different forms of external political influence.

The importance of regionalism makes questionable those historical analogies that simply interpolate from 1990 back to 1945 or earlier historical periods and that simply assume away the effects the intervening decades had on Germany, Japan, and their regional environments. At the end of the cold war, authors titled their books on Germany and Japan with the phrases *The New Superpowers* (Bergner 1991) evoking the 1950s, or a *Struggle for Supremacy* (Garten 1992), referring to the 1930s. Pitting the United States against Japan and Germany made for excellent copy. But these books relied on analytical categories that neglected altogether how the exercise and experience of German and Japanese power has been altered in distinctive regional settings during the previous three decades. Thus they overlook the novel ways in which regional states operated at the end of the twentieth century.

Historians are not immune from adopting an ahistorical perspective. With all the appropriate qualifications, historian Arthur Schlesinger made this mistake: "Japan is well on its way to achieving the Greater East Asia Co-Prosperity Sphere for which it fought in vain half a century ago. A united Germany . . . will be the most powerful country in Europe and well on its way to the continental hegemony for which it fought in vain half a century ago" (Schlesinger 1989, A6). Shorn of misleading historical analogies, William Schneider was much closer to the truth when he argued that "the 'natural' inclination of both the FRG [Federal Republic of Germany] and Japanese international interest is regional in character" (1989, 22).

Structural effects are the result of prior choices. The difference between the trilateral relations among the United States, Japan, and Germany in 1991 and their relations in 1945 or 1914 is the result of past policies. After 1945 U.S. diplomacy set in motion processes by which the projection of German or Japanese power across national boundaries has been altered (Herz 1983; Montgomery 1957; Moulton 1944). Neglecting this fact amounts to neglecting change in history. Newtonian metaphors of recurrent equilibria and time-reversible processes of political change are not helpful in understanding the disequilibria and path-dependent processes that have defined Germany and Japan as regional states. How do Germany and Japan's different domestic structures shape their policies at home and abroad in Europe and Asia? How do external pressures and transnational influences shape the domestic politics and foreign affairs of these two states? And how have these regional states become the creatures of different kinds of regions, which in turn they help shape?

Domestic Structures and Political Strategies

Different types of democratic capitalism follow different logics. Applied to Germany and Japan, labels such as corporatist and statist or the Rhine model and the Japanese model (Albert 1993; Katzenstein 1978, 1985) unavoidably conceal complex, evolving relations that blend domestic and foreign elements and state and society. Japan and Germany take different stances toward the international system that I have dubbed elsewhere "Hobbesian" in the case of Japan and "Grotian" in the case of Germany (Katzenstein 1996, 153–54). For Japan, the world beyond is fundamentally hostile, and Japanese actors must cope on their own. Japanese politicians act with a mixture of guile and goodwill in developing long-term, interest-based relations. For Germany, the larger world beyond is a community— European, Atlantic, or global—to which Germany belongs. For German politicians, long-term interest flows from membership in these various communities.

Political and economic asymmetries are, from the Japanese perspective, a source of both power and community. But a clearly defined national sense of self is never in doubt. In the case of Germany, collective identity has a more international cast than in Japan. Germany is part of an international community of states whose conduct is defined by legal rules. And it is that community that helps inform the definition of interests that Germany pursues. As a prominent Krupp executive told Isaac Deutscher in 1946, "now . . . everything depends on whether we are in a position to find the right, great solutions on a European scale. Only a European scale, gentlemen, isn't that so?" (Kramer, quoted in Cronin 1998, 12). This difference between the national and international purposes of the Japanese and German states is central to our understanding of many of Asia's and Europe's most important political problems.

Amy Gurowitz (1998, chap. 2) has developed analytical categories that further specify this distinction. She identifies four dimensions of a state's international identity. First, is the state strongly or weakly committed to the principle of multilateralism, as indicated by both how it pursues its objectives internationally and the extent of its involvement in international institutions and organizations? Second, is the state active or passive in its international activities? Does the government tend to lead in international initiatives and participate in global problem solving or does it tend to lag behind? Third, does the state identify itself, in terms of both material and cultural attributes, and is it viewed by other states as part of the core of a Western international society of states; does it see itself as related to the core but not part of it or does it see itself as marginal? Fourth, how does the state respond to and view its relationship with the dominant state in the system, currently the United States? Is it strongly in favor of the United States, dependent on the United States but not necessarily in the same camp with the United States, or actively resistant to the United States? Germany and Japan vary along these dimensions quite consistently, with Germany tending more toward the international and Japan more toward the national pole along each of these four dimensions (see the essay by Erica Gould and Stepher Krasner in this volume; see also Grieco 1997).

The difference between a primarily national and a primarily international orientation is a matter of degree not kind. For Japan, internationalization was both a process experienced since the 1970s and the subject of a political debate fundamentally shaped by national purposes. And the Europeanization of Germany is intimately linked to the Germanization of Europe (Bouissou 1994; Gloannec 1994; Katzenstein 1997b).

This difference in degree is important for both Japanese and German foreign policy and the nature of Asian and European regionalism. It is illustrated by how these two countries have internationalized domestic sectors and institutions that were central to their domestic political economies. Since the early 1970s, Japan has been affected by internationalization. Until the 1990s, agriculture was the one notable exception. Yet unrestricted trade in agriculture would have done much more to correct the persistent imbalances in international trade than elaborate, complex, and fragile international negotiations on exchange rates because it could have affected profoundly the Japanese prices for food, real estate, and housing. The political realities of Japanese domestic politics, however, prevented the liberalization of agriculture since the 1960s. Only in the early 1990s, during the conclusion to the Uruguay round of tariff negotiations, did Japan make important concessions that will, eventually, have substantial consequences for Japanese agriculture.

In Germany the analogous example is the Europeanization of the Bundesbank. This is an enormously powerful institution in German politics; it enjoys a very strong political position of independence from the federal government. With the possible exception of the Constitutional Court, its prestige overshadows that of all other political institutions. Yet European monetary integration was Germany's preferred form of regional European integration. Germany's international stance is thus in striking contrast to the reluctance with which Japan's government led by the Liberal Democratic Party (LDP) finally made concessions on free trade in agriculture during the latest GATT-sponsored round of tariff cutting.

Beyond the degree and kind of national and international orientation (as the chapters in this volume richly illustrate), Japan and Germany also differ in the structural arrangements of their distinctive types of capitalism. In Japan's developmental state, business plays the central role in what T. J. Pempel has called a system of "creative conservatism" (Pempel 1982, 1998; Gao 1997; Weiss 1998; Woo-Cumings 1999). Business, especially big business, is at the center of the political coalition that sustained the LDP in power for four decades before it was toppled in 1995 by the excesses of money politics that the economic bubble of the late 1980s brought. Despite new electoral rules, the LDP retains its leading position in Japanese politics. Political change in the 1990s led to a dramatic weakening of leftist parties while leaving the LDP in a leading position. After a brief period of explosive growth in the immediate postwar years, Japan's labor movement did not succeed in escaping from the relative political isolation in which the political and economic left in postwar Japan found itself. Ikuo Kume (1998; Knoke et al. 1996) argues, however, that reorganization of the labor movement since the 1970s has given it a stronger voice in influencing some of the issues that matter most.

Government and bureaucracy have been the central actors in the evolution of Japan's postwar society and economy. The network linking the various actors in Japan's political economy is relatively tight. Traditionally, Japan's financial system was based not on autonomous capital markets but on a system of administered credit that accorded the state a prominent role in influencing investment flows in the economy. The chummy relations between government and the financial sector are at the root of the mountain of bad debt that became a serious drag on the economy in the 1990s.

Distinctive of German politics is the relative equality in the distribution of power among different actors. No great disparities exist, by the standards of Japanese politics, between business and labor or between the two major parties. In Germany business and labor are politically so well entrenched that they can accommodate themselves with relative ease to changes in government control by center-right or center-left coalition governments. The organizational strength and institutional presence of both business and labor are variable, although always impressive, by Japanese standards. In Germany's political economy they are, as in Japan, relatively closely linked, but, unlike Japan, at more nodes. The relation between industry and banks is close, based on a system of competitive bargaining rather than of private capital markets or credits administered by the state. Tight links among interest groups, political parties, and state bureaucracies create an inclusionary politics. The Constitutional Court and the Bundesbank act as watchdogs and institutional restraints. Political issues that appear to be too hot for party politicians to handle are left to judges and bankers.

In Japan policy revolves around the interaction between party politicians and the state bureaucracy, which is endowed amply with the instruments and institutions for shaping policy. Government policy relies on information, moral suasion, financial incentives, and political muscle rather than on legal instruments. This generates a symbiotic relation between business and government that puts little store in transparency. Informal connections rather than formal institutional rules are a defining characteristic of Japanese politics. In Germany policy centers on the relations between party politicians, powerful interest groups, the federal and state bureaucracies, and a variety of parapublic institutions. A consensual style of politics prevails and is typically cast in legal terms. In times of rapid political and economic change, the legalization of politics creates rigidities that Germany's way of conducting political business has a difficult time shedding, as developments in the 1990s illustrated.

These thumbnail descriptions of productivity democracy in Japan and industrial democracy in Germany illustrate that we should avoid mistaking the liberal Anglo-American tree for the capitalist forest. In Germany a wide variety of parapublic organizations open the state to group influences while at the same time providing state officials with channels reaching deep into society. Law offers the normative context for the formulation and implementation of public policies. By contrast, in Japan that normative context is defined by informal ties rather than by public law. A large number of formal and informal consultative mechanisms make Japan, even more than Germany, into a structure geared to the creation and re-creation of consensus. The extension of legal rules into Europe and of informal political arrangements into Asia reflect ways of conducting political business that Germany and its European partners and Japan and its Asian partners consider normal.

External Pressures and Transnational Influences

When the outside world impinges on Japanese politics, politicians and bureaucrats experience it as external pressure (*gaiatsu*) at the hands of the United States, the sole occupation power after 1945. In contrast the transnational influences affecting Germany emanate not so much from Washington as from Brussels, reflecting a history of Allied rather than U.S. occupation. Japan and Germany also seek to exercise, in different ways, informal international influence beyond their national borders. Japan typically works through markets, money, and middlemen. Germany relies instead on its societal foreign policy, which, beyond government ministries, accords important roles in foreign affairs to many of Germany's major private and parapublic institutions.

Japan

In the case of Japan, external pressure emanates largely from Washington. In the interest of gaining better access to Japanese markets, U.S. actors tend to pressure directly the Japanese bureaucracy and its ancillary political and social interests (Katzenstein and Tsujinaka 1995; Schoppa 1997). Foreign actors are included either directly or indirectly into domestic policy coalitions in which nationalists and internationalists seek to find compromises acceptable to both as well as to impatient Americans who insist on changes in traditional ways of doing business.

Japan's persistent export surplus and cautious defense policy have been the two issues that have fueled this external pressure. The negotiation of voluntary export restraint agreements since 1955 and the Structural Impediment Initiatives (SII) talks designed in the late 1980s to open the Japanese economy are examples of a repetitive political process that at times takes on ritualistic and predictable forms.

This external pressure has to some extent become institutionalized in Japanese decision making when U.S. interests are activated in the domestic political arena. The U.S. lobby in Japan has a predominantly public character with the embassy, the representatives of thirty-nine U.S. states, and the U.S. military supporting the activities of individual U.S. corporations. Although a substantial amount of lobbying takes place indirectly through what is known as the old-boy network and influential middlemen, the system is fundamentally driven by the political pressure exerted by the U.S. government on the networks linking the Japanese government, state bureaucracy, and business community. U.S. corporations seek to play the political game in Tokyo by Japanese rules, but they rely also on pressure tactics. It is heavy pressure, especially heavy political pressure exerted by the government rather than by U.S. business leaders, that makes the system of external pressure politics function.

The distinctive aspect of *gaiatsu* is that it overcomes the immobilism that inheres in the Japanese policy system with its bottom-up consensus decision-making style (Stockwin et al. 1988). Because self-persuasion is so difficult, *naiatsu* (internal pressure) is a rare commodity in Japan's political system. In the words of John Dower, *gaiatsu*, or "small violence," is often invited by the government or business "to put pressure on the bureaucracy. Or, in certain circumstances, the bureaucracy itself may desire *gaiatsu* to strengthen its case against recalcitrant politicians or rival ministries. Whatever the case, it is apparent that a complex political dance is taking place" (1988, 26). The end of the cold war has changed the nature of that dance. For a variety of reasons, Japan has become less deferential to U.S. trade demands, and the success rate of U.S. pressure politics has declined (Schoppa 1999). In sum, external pressure has become an integral part of the shifting coalition of political forces that has led to the opening of Japanese markets since the 1960s, particularly when it supported a growing domestic coalition favoring a change in existing policy (Calder 1982; Fukai 1992; Woodall 1992).

In contrast to U.S. pressure on Japan, Japanese influence in the United States takes unobtrusive forms. The Japan lobby in the United States is largely private in character with individual corporations, business associations, and the Japan External Trade Organization (JETRO) as central actors. Japan's lobbying in U.S. politics received much attention in the early 1990s and became the subject of a number of studies by U.S. authors who stressed its size, breadth, and effectiveness (Choate 1990; Morse 1989). A knowledgeable and well-known lobbyist himself, Ira Wolf argues that, with the possible exception of Israel, "there is little doubt that the Japan lobby in the United States is the largest and most effective foreign effort to influence legislation, policy making, and public attitudes in this country" (quoted in Pempel 1991, 43). In contrast, an older Japanese literature has pointed to the weaknesses and failures of the Japan lobby in U.S. politics (Howe and Trott 1977).

Japan engages in unobtrusive political activity in the United States. The Japan lobby in the United States has a relatively long history of steady growth. Starting with only one lobbyist in 1951, by 1957 Japan had joined other client states such as West Germany, Taiwan, and Israel, as well as France, in the number of lobbyists it deployed in Washington. By 1962 it had moved into the number one position, a position it has not relinquished since. For historical reasons, Japanese lobbying maintained a low profile for many years and recorded very few successes in the legislative realm. In the words of one well-known lobbyist, William Tanaka, "my office does not lobby either for private companies or the Japanese government. For Japanese corporations simply cannot exert any influence on the process of policy formulation in the federal bureaucracy or legislative debate in Congress" (quoted in Kusano 1992, 123). The Japan lobby gathers instead information and gives advice. It has avoided making any substantial contributions to political action committees. It invests instead in old boys, that is, in well-placed officials, many of them former members of the U.S. government, who enjoy excellent access to key decision makers. This unobtrusive style is in line with the networking and buying of access that is so important in Japanese politics.

This explains why in the early 1990s the Japan lobby spent so much money on a low-profile set of activities, specifically to create a favorable public climate in the United States. Japan's fifteen consulates in the United States, for example, regularly hire local public relations firms to advise them on how to create on a regional basis a favorable public climate for Japan's political objectives (Lee 1988, 142). Furthermore, *Business Week* has estimated that in the late 1980s Japanese corporations spent annually $45 million on public relations, $140 million on corporate philanthropy, and $30 million on academic research grants (Farnsworth 1989, F6).[1] Academic research proved particularly vulnerable to a potential overdependence on Japanese funds. Up to 80 percent of the studies on U.S.-Japanese relations conducted at U.S. universities and research institutes in the late

---

1. At approximately $300 million, Choate's (1990, xviii) estimate is considerably higher. Suzanne Alexander (1991) reports that Japanese philanthropy increased from $30 million in 1986, to $300 million in 1990, and $500 million in 1991.

1980s were estimated to have been financed at least partly by Japanese corporations, foundations, and government agencies (Farnsworth 1989, F6).

In a book written before Ross Perot selected him as his running mate in the 1992 U.S. presidential election, Pat Choate writes that the "Japanese penetration of the American political system is now so deep that its integrity is threatened. In their own country the Japanese call this sort of money politics 'structural corruption.' In this case, it means that so many advocates of Japan's position are involved in decision making that the ultimate outcome is structurally biased in Japan's favor" (1990, xx). This is overstating the case. But the attention to image building and the creation of a favorable public climate is a distinctive feature of Japan's transnational relations with the United States. It reflects the importance attached to the media and the creation of a favorable public climate in Japan's domestic politics.

Germany

In contrast to Japan, Germany experiences external pressure as a less intrusive and more pervasive process of transnational, and especially European, influence. Shaped by the political experience and sensibilities of postwar Germany, it was a German political scientist who in the late 1960s coined the term "transnational relations," subsequently elaborated and more fully developed by U.S. and German scholars of international relations (Risse-Kappen 1995; Kaiser 1970, 1971; Keohane and Nye 1977). The political experience of the FRG made this a natural category of analysis. With its unconditional surrender in May 1945, the German state ceased to exist. It was partitioned and occupied. And it participated in a variety of innovative international institutions designed primarily to constrain a possible resurgence of Germany's autonomous national power.

In the late 1940s and early 1950s, in the form of the European Coal and Steel Community (ECSC), European states put their, and Germany's, coal and steel industries under supranational supervision. This amounted to an internationalization of the economic core of a possibly resurgent military-industrial complex of the FRG. A few years later Euratom sought to accomplish the same for the nuclear industry, as the high-tech industry of the future. These institutions gave expression to an innovative and successful political strategy, a European answer to the continent's traditional German question.

In hindsight we know the direct effects of either of these institutions on Germany's economic potential has not mattered greatly. Much more consequential was the unforeseen indirect influence of a customs union, the European Economic Community (EEC), which matured eventually into the EU. The gradual growth of a European polity with emerging political properties shaped German politics quite profoundly; in the 1990s, German and European scholars talked of a multitiered or multilevel European governance system in which Germany was deeply enmeshed (Katzenstein 1997b).

A growing number of policy issues and many features of German politics are increasingly affected by the process of Europeanization (Risse, Cowles, and Caporaso 2001). At times this process is publicly visible and creates political debates. German subsidies to ailing firms in the former German Democratic Republic (GDR) and the size of Germany's financial contribution to the EU budget were examples in the 1990s. But this is not the core of the Europeanization process. In the EU, the Council, Commission, and Parliament together affect thousands of issues, most of them minute, that touch all aspects of German economic and social life. "External pressure" does not capture the dynamics of this process because Germany is, generally speaking, an active proponent of Europeanization. And when it lags on specific issues in implementing the directives, regulations, and decisions that emanate from a variety of European bodies, the self-understanding of Germany as a European state is an important barrier to the notion, harbored in some political quarters and by groups disadvantaged by specific decisions, that Germany is caving in to external pressure.

The importance of Europeanization is most clearly evident in the politically delicate relations between two core German and European institutions. Since the 1960s, the European Court of Justice has argued successfully that European law supersedes national law. Innovative legal procedures have guaranteed individuals access to the court on specific issues. And they have assured that national and European courts do not work at cross-purpose. Although with some reluctance, Germany's powerful Constitutional Court has, with brief intermissions, acknowledged the primacy of the European Court and European law over the Constitutional Court and German law.

Politically more significant in the 1990s was the creation of the Economic and Monetary Union (EMU). Germany's powerful Bundesbank had run, de facto, Europe's monetary policy since 1979. But at the behest of the German government in the 1990s the Bundesbank was reduced to the status of an important regional bank of the newly created European Central Bank (ECB) that has opened its doors in Frankfurt.

In its policies, the ECB is designed to imitate the Bundesbank. Yet it represents as much a French as a German political victory. Since the 1960s, successive German governments have supported monetary integration as the culmination of a gradual process of political unification that would guarantee the coordination of national economic policies. French governments pushed for monetary integration without political unification. German unification and the stability pact that was part of the EMU provided the political issues that made a compromise between Germany and France finally possible. German public opinion has remained hesitant about relinquishing the deutschmark, perhaps the country's politically most salient source of collective political identity and economic pride. But in the broad center of German politics the surrender of monetary sovereignty from a position of great economic and political strength has received strong support. Outside of Bavaria, running for office on a cautiously anti-European platform proved to be a recipe for failure in the 1990s.

Throughout the cold war, German participation in NATO was also a very important conduit of transnational influence. Germany's controversial rearmament was made palatable to a hostile public and suspicious European neighbors only through a full integration of the armed forces under NATO command. In addition to keeping the Americans in and the Russians out, keeping the Germans down was how Lord Ismay, secretary general of the alliance, described NATO's three main purposes. Things turned out differently. As the first alliance in history with a peacetime, integrated, standing defense force, NATO kept Germany in, not down. Across all of the practical aspects of military policy, including nuclear targeting, German defense officials became partners and eventually were asked to assume leading positions in the Western alliance. Professional contacts between Germany's military and those of its European partners and the United States have created links that, over time, have transformed Europe and the North Atlantic region into a security community, defined by the dependable expectation of peaceful change (Deutsch et al. 1957). Many Germans regarded NATO as a nuisance and an environmental hazard in the 1970s and 1980s. And a significant minority, especially in the early 1980s, objected to both Germany and NATO as dangerous and destabilizing. But because Germany was an integral part of NATO, the public did not perceive NATO influence as external pressure. In the 1990s, this was illustrated by active German support of NATO's enlargement, its bombing campaign in Serbia, and its peacekeeping operation in Kosovo.

Projected abroad, Germany's transnational relations appear in the form of a societal foreign policy. Most of the important institutions in Germany typically engage partner organizations in other countries in conducting their own foreign relations. Created after 1949 to help democratize Germany and attached to each of the major parties, political foundations are the nucleus of this unusual system. With the passing of time and the growth of funding, these foundations have opened up offices all over the world while engaging their ideological allies, from right to left, and initiating projects on a global scale.

Similarly, many of Germany's most important institutions also conduct their own foreign relations: unions, such as IG Metall, the largest industrial union in the world; employer and business associations; scientific organizations and cultural foundations; publicly funded research institutes and think tanks of all ideological stripes; and churches. In contrast to Japan, the visible presence of these institutions engages their partner organizations in other countries. It is Germany's distinctive contribution to the growing importance of transnational relations.

This brief discussion outlines the systematic differences between Germany and Japan. In sharp contrast to Germany's exposure to a pervasive process of Europeanization, Japan's involvement in Asian regional organizations has left hardly a trace. And although there is a substantial amount of journalistic and scholarly debate on the external pressure that has been brought to bear on Japan by the United States, a shelf of books and monographs on the U.S.-German relationship does not contain a single chapter devoted to the same subject (Knapp 1975). With the exception of Marxist writings that interpret the relationship in the language of neoimperialism, the literature focuses on interdependence and transnational relations, not external U.S. pressures on Germany or unobtrusive German influence in the United States. Germany's and Japan's terms of engaging international and regional influences thus differ greatly.

Open Regionalism: Informal Arrangements in Asia and Formal Institutions in Europe

In the 1990s, the weight of regional forces in world politics increased (Ohmae 1995). During the cold war, regional factors had often been overshadowed by superpower confrontation; in the 1990s, they became more visible and consequential. The beginning and the stalling in the peace process in the Middle East, for example, was fueled largely by regional and national pressures, not by the intervention of the United States, Russia, or any other major power. The Russian project of reconstructing a sphere of influence in the near abroad of the Commonwealth of Independent States was driven by regional factors, as was the formation of the North American Free Trade Agreement (NAFTA). And in Latin America a substantial decrease in political tensions and military expenditures cleared the ground for sharp increases in regional economic cooperation. But in all of these instances regionalism has remained linked to the larger international system.

In Europe, for example, developments in international capital markets were decisive in spurring a change in French policy in the mid-1980s that permitted the adoption of the Single European Act in 1987 and the acceleration of the European integration process. The end of the cold war and German unification was important in furthering the acceleration of that process, most visibly in the Treaty of Maastricht and the simultaneous move toward both a deepening and widening of European integration at the beginning of the 1990s. Its most important achievement at the end of the 1990s was the formation of the EMU.

Asia is no exception to the growth of regional forces in world politics. A frequently used measure of regional integration, intra-Asian trade, increased greatly in the 1980s. Japan's backing of South Korean trade minister Kim Chul Su as the Asian candidate, running against a European and a North American candidate, made the selection of the first director general of the new World Trade Organization (WTO) an exercise in interregional politics that reappeared when Mike Moore, former prime minister of New Zealand, and Supachai Panitchpakdj, deputy premier of Thailand, were deadlocked for many months as the WTO sought to find a successor to Director-General Renato Ruggiero. And Japan's financial crisis is linked closely to the financial crisis that has engulfed Thailand, South Korea, and especially Indonesia since 1997.

Global and regional factors are closely intertwined. The increasing globalization and deregulation of markets describe an erosion of national economic control that industrial states in the north seek to compensate for in part through regional integration schemes. Regional integration can occur de jure (as in Europe) or de facto (as in Asia). And it occurs also in subregional groupings within and between states, as for example in southeast Asia and along the south China coast, and in some border-spanning Euroregions. In the words of François Gipouloux: "the integration scheme, in Europe as well as in North America, favors territorial integration, the Asian one emphasizes a kind of integration through networks. Two different sets of logic or conclusions are at work. One is negotiation by intergovernmental agreements (the international approach). The other approach is transnational whereby comparative advantage is more important than national borders. In the American as well as the European cases, approaches are political, led by governments. Integration proceeds in Asia through informal linkages" (1994, 40; see also Dollfus 1994; Pape 1994).

Regionalism thus is not only an attempt to increase economic growth or achieve other objectives. It is also an effort to regain some measure of political control over the processes of globalization that have impinged on national policy. The economic effects of de facto or de jure regionalism can either help or hinder market competition and liberalization. By and large, the existing evidence points to the prevalence of trade creation and open forms of regionalism between the late 1960s and the early 1990s (O'Loughlin and Anselin 1996).

For national governments, regional integration is attractive for a number of reasons. First, neighborhood effects encourage intensive trade and investment relations. Second, economic regionalization processes often do not require the reciprocity that the WTO insists on. Third, at the regional level, efficiency and competitiveness are often strengthened through internationalized forms of deregulation, thus weakening directly the attraction of traditional, global approaches to liberalization while strengthening them indirectly. In addition, the effects of regional economies of scale and savings in transportation costs can create dynamic effects that also accelerate economic growth.

Furthermore, geographic proximity and the functional interdependencies and transborder externalities it creates have favorable implications for regional economic growth. The geographic concentration of production is increasingly driven by the emergence of technology complexes and networks of innovation and production that offer important advantages for regional agglomeration. Technological development paths are contingent on the actions of and interactions among developers, producers, and users who hold different positions and make different choices in the national and global economies. Technological innovation thus is a discontinuous process establishing different trajectories in different parts of the world that cluster both nationally and regionally. The supply base of a national economy, the parts, components, subsystems, materials, and equipment technologies, as well as the interrelation among the firms that make all these available to world markets also cluster regionally (Borrus and Zysman 1992).

In an era of increasing turbulence in global capital markets, monetary and financial integration at a regional level appears to many European governments as a form of protection in an uncertain world. The European Monetary System (EMS) was created in 1979 to reduce European dependence on an unpredictable U.S. monetary policy. With the onset of the global financial crisis in Asia in the summer of 1997, the political commitment to the EMU grew further throughout Europe because the EMU promised to be a shield against the adverse consequences of global liberalization in capital markets that had been a prime objective of U.S. policy in the 1990s.

For a variety of reasons, financial and monetary integration in Asia has not been a political option. When Japan, in August 1997, floated a proposal for the creation of an Asian monetary fund to deal with the consequences of the Asian financial crisis, the U.S. government and the International Monetary Fund (IMF) had little difficulty in brushing that proposal aside. Because the Japanese government had for decades been adamant in refusing an international role for the yen, it simply lacked the political clout and financial resources to offer a compelling rallying point for other Asian states. U.S. officials conceded only a year later that Japan's proposal probably deserved a serious hearing and possibly might have dealt with the crisis more effectively than had the IMF (Kristof 1998, A6).

The openness of Asian regionalism thus has two different, closely inter-twined sources—dyadic and systemic vulnerability. First, Japan is embed-ded in a relationship of dyadic dependence on the United States, in particular, that creates three extraordinary military and economic vulnera-bilities. Japan depends on the U.S. Navy to patrol the sea-lanes through which its exports and imports flow; even after diversifying away from the U.S. market since the 1970s, 30 percent of Japanese exports are still des-tined for the U.S. market; and Japan remains extraordinarily dependent on the import of raw materials. Military, economic, and political depen-dence thus constrain any Japanese inclination to build an inward-looking Asia.

Second, Japan's systemic vulnerability derives from what Kato (1998) calls global-scope interdependence, which also constrains the emergence of an Asian bloc. Along numerous dimensions of trade, aid, investment, and technology transfer, Japan has a more broadly diversified set of eco-nomic and political links to both rich and poor countries, than does, for example, Germany, which lives internationally inside a European cocoon (Lincoln 1993, 135; Wan 1995, 98). The Asian financial crisis illustrates Japan's strong commitment to contributing to the continued functioning of the international system on which its economic prosperity depends so heavily. By September 1998, Japan's level of contribution to the solution of the Asian financial crisis stood at $43 billion, approximately one-third of the total, compared to $12 billion for the United States and $7 billion for European states, even though the exposure of European banks was compa-rable to those of Japanese banks (Kristof 1998, A6). Approximately one-half of the Japanese credit was committed to credit lines to be disbursed under IMF bailout plans over which Japan had little influence (Kato 1998, 2).

Asia

Japan's growing role among the member states of the Association of Southeast Asian Nations (ASEAN) can be easily traced in the areas of trade, aid, investment, and technology transfer. In the two decades pre-ceding the Plaza Accord of 1985, Japan accounted for close to one-half the total aid and foreign direct investment the region received. The dramatic appreciation of the yen after 1985 led to a veritable explosion of Japanese investment, which between 1985 and 1989 was twice as large as between 1951 and 1984. And the flow of aid has continued to be strong as Japan seeks to recycle its trade surplus with the region. All governments in south-east Asia are bidding for Japanese capital, as is illustrated by the massive deregulation of their economies as well as the lucrative incentives they are willing to grant to foreign investors. More important, Japan's developmental state became in the 1970s and 1980s a model emulated in both the public and private sectors. The establishment of private trading companies and a general commitment of governments throughout the region to vigorous policies of export promotion testify to the widespread appeal of the Japanese model.

The massive inflow of Japanese investments in the 1980s and early 1990s created severe bottlenecks in the public-sector infrastructures of countries such as Indonesia and Thailand. And these bottlenecks created serious impediments for the future growth of Japanese investment. Roads and ports were insufficient and needed to be expanded and modernized. The same was true of national systems of communications and public services more generally. The New AID (Asian Industries Development) Plan that Japan revealed in 1987 signaled that Japan had serious long-term interests in the region. The plan addressed the needs of the public sector as they related to Japanese industrial investments and the restructuring of the Japanese economy more generally. Broadly speaking, the program offered investment incentives for selected Japanese industries to relocate to ASEAN countries. It made explicit Japan's hierarchical view of the international division of labor in Southeast Asia. To some extent this was also true of Japan's view of its relations with the newly industrialized countries (NICs) in northeast Asia. Here a takeoff into self-sustaining rapid growth had occurred earlier than in southeast Asia.

The sharp growth in Japan's economic presence in Asia has created widespread unease about the political consequences of intensifying economic relations in an emerging regional political economy. Japan's power is simply too large to be met in the foreseeable future by any coalition of Asian states. With the total GNP of ASEAN amounting to no more than about 15 percent of Japan's GNP, a world of self-contained regions in the northern half of the globe would leave the ASEAN members at the mercy of a Japanese colossus. This fear is palpable also when good economic times turn to bad. Without a sustained solution to Japan's financial crisis, Asia's financial crisis cannot be solved.

In the view of most Asian countries, only the United States and China can act as indispensable counterweights to Japan. A China that does not succumb to financial instabilities would be a welcome counterweight to an economically wobbly Japan. And with the U.S. Navy firmly committed to retaining a strong position in Asia and with the consolidation of U.S.-Japanese security arrangements in the 1980s and 1990s, the United States is likely to remain an Asian power. Furthermore, because virtually all Asian countries run a substantial trade deficit with Japan and a large surplus with the United States, the United States is essential for regional economic integration in Asia. An Asia that includes the United States diffuses the economic and political dependencies of the smaller Asian states away from

Japan. And it provides Japan with the national security that makes unnecessary a major arms buildup, and the hostile political reaction it would engender among Japan's neighbors.

Europe

Regionalism in Europe is institutionally better defined than in Asia. This is mostly due to the presence of the EU. It has developed such a strong political momentum that formerly neutral states such as Sweden, Finland, and Austria joined in the 1990s. And as was true of southern Europe in the late 1970s, the new democracies of central-eastern Europe look to the EU rather than to any individual European state as the political and economic anchor during their difficult period of transition. A united Germany will figure prominently in an integrating Europe. But Germany is unlikely to want to build a Fortress Europe, a concept the Nazis coined that lacks all political and economic appeal in Germany.

Throughout the postwar era, German foreign policy has always sought to avoid having to choose between France and the United States, between the European and the Atlantic option. There is little indication that in the coming years German foreign policy will deviate from this line. Both Germany's economic and security interests are best served by a closer European integration that does not isolate itself from the United States. In economic terms, it would be outright foolishness for one of the largest export economies in the world to favor building economic barriers. The success of U.S. corporations operating in Europe and the European investment strategy of Japanese firms in important industries such as automobiles show that trade protection is no longer an effective instrument for isolating national or regional markets.

Furthermore, the creation of a single European market by 1992 and the Treaty of Maastricht excluded security policy. After the war in Kosovo, the European states commited themselves to building a European security capability for peacekeeping and peace-enforcement operations. Although this was an entirely new departure for EU policy, it could build on the political revival of the West European Union (WEU) and the growing importance of the European pillar in NATO. But German unification also increased French and British resolve to retain a national nuclear option and to keep the United States involved in European affairs, both politically and militarily. Although French and British policy differ in their emphasis, on this basic point they converge with German interests. NATO remains of fundamental importance in Germany's security policy. And so does a U.S. presence in Europe, symbolically with ground forces, strategically with sea- and possibly air-based systems of conventional and nuclear deterrence, and logistically in a variety of ways for dealing with possible ethnic conflicts in the European periphery. The Organization for Security and Cooperation in Europe (OSCE) is in German eyes a useful instrument of diplomacy that supplements NATO and the EU because it avoids a narrow definition of Europe and keeps the United States as well as Canada and Russia involved in European and thus German security affairs.

Germany's weight in Europe and Europe's weight vis-à-vis the United States are, however, likely to increase both economically and politically. This redistribution in power is unlikely to find political articulation in military terms. Instead, it will be fed by the compatibility between the German model of an efficient, capitalist, democratic welfare state and a political milieu of European states organized along similar lines and subscribing to similar political values. The compatibility between the German model and the European milieu is substantial and ranks high as one of the most important German foreign policy objectives. This was very evident in the mid- and late 1970s when Germany took a very active role in trying to shape the process of transition to democracy in southern Europe. The southern enlargement of the European Community (EC) that contributed greatly to the success of that foreign policy provides something of a model for the approach of Germany and its EC partners to the daunting task of assisting the much more difficult process of transition in central and eastern Europe. Similarly, in the 1980s the EMS was a very important instrument for establishing compatibility between Germany and Europe, largely on German terms. The stability of the deutschmark and Germany's low inflation policy, even at the cost of permanently high unemployment rates, became generalized throughout Europe. The early years of implementing the EMU thus are very important. They define the extent of compatibility between Germany and its European milieu.

Summary

European regionalism is differently defined than Asian regionalism, and it is politically more easily recognized. The EU gives a well-institutionalized vision of European regionalism, which is favored by the relative equality between Germany and the other major European powers. In Asia, by contrast, formal regional institutions are relatively weak and of recent origin, and Japan towers over all its neighbors with whom it might want to cooperate in a regional framework. Although they are both open, Asian and European regionalism differ substantially. Summarizing the findings of their edited volume, Jeffrey Frankel and Miles Kahler (1993, 4) talk of Asia's soft regionalism, closely integrated and centered on the Japanese economy, that differs from the hard European regionalism that is based on politically and juridically defined arrangements (see also Beeson and

Jayasuriya 1997; Green 1995, 725–34; Higgott 1995; Kahler 1997, 1–4, 15–24; Stubbs 1998).

Significantly, the United States will be part of both the emerging Asia and the new Europe, in economic terms no less than on security issues. Even more than for Japan, the growth trajectory of many Asian economies relies on free access to U.S. markets. And the economic stake that U.S. corporations have built up over the decades in their European subsidiaries makes the United States a silent beneficiary of the European integration process. In the 1990s, world regions were compatible with an integrating global economy. In security matters the U.S.-Japanese security arrangement is an indispensable instrument for alleviating the worries of Japan's Asian neighbors about Japan's rising power. And in Europe, through NATO, the United States is retaining an important military and political voice that is welcomed by virtually all European states.

This difference is tied to Germany's and Japan's domestic structures. Examples of this difference, reflected in the exercise of power at the regional level, are not difficult to find. Germany's power must be harnessed by law, both domestically and internationally. Law defines in normative terms the conduct of Germany and its partner states. Equally important, it defines Germany's identity as a lawful member of an international community of states. Personalism and informality play a role, but only within a legal and political framework that is the objective of diplomacy. This approach to regional affairs is consistent across issue areas and time and, as in the case of Japan, it is deeply rooted in German domestic politics. Since the mid-1970s, the FRG, for example, has been persistent in trying to create, with the cooperation of a number of its European neighbors, a zone of monetary stability. The EMS and the EMU are the results of that persistence. They generalize Germany's strong antiinflationary preferences to its main trading partners.

Japan's approach to Asian regionalism is also an extension of its distinctive domestic experiences. Power is the exploitation of points of leverage carefully built up in a system of mutual vulnerabilities. Personal contacts, superior information, and quiet middlemen working behind the scene do not confront issues head on but seek to influence them indirectly. This type of politics is embedded in a public climate that needs to be cultivated carefully; without the support of favorable public opinion, Japan's subtle game of politics cannot endure. These features of domestic politics shape Japan's approach to regional and global affairs. For example, the relatively unrestricted trade in textiles and apparel between Japan and its new competitors in the Pacific basin and southeast Asia is in part the result of friendly industry conversations that characterize not only some of the practices of Japanese industries in domestic markets, but also span national borders. Germany and Japan thus project power differently across national borders.

Conclusion

The theoretical perspective informing this chapter is sociological-institutional. It thus differs from the variants of realism and liberalism that typify other studies, including those dealing with the growth of regional forces in international and global politics. Although realist and liberal perspectives capture important elements of the manifold relationships between Japan and Asia and between Germany and Europe, they tend to slight unduly the institutionalization of state power and market relations. To be sure, both of these rationalist perspectives are often complementary in their insights. Liberalism's insights can make up for realism's discounting of the importance of domestic politics, transnational relations, and international institutions. And liberalism's neglect of the distributional consequences and power can be complemented by realist accounts. Yet in a comparative analysis of world regions, neither perspective pays sufficient attention to institutional effects that often counteract relationships marked by great asymmetries in material power and bargaining positions (Katzenstein 1996). This chapter's analytical stance is attuned to the analysis of institutional effects without insisting they must always prevail.

The transformation of Japan and Germany from political and military challengers to trading states and civilian powers supporting the existing international order was a major factor stabilizing world politics in the late twentieth century. The character of Japan and Germany makes it highly improbable that in the foreseeable future the leaders of these two countries will attempt to exchange the coinage of technological and economic power once again for military power, to transform themselves from trading to warfare states. The outcome of World War II and the history of postwar growth leaves both countries with a discrepancy between their economic and military power. With some justification, both have been described, Germany in the 1970s and Japan in the 1980s, as economic giants and political dwarfs. In both countries, state and society have been realigned to conceal or transform state power. Japan relates state strength to market competition; Germany combines state power with semicorporatist arrangements. In both countries, the convergence of political conservatism with economic liberalism characteristic of the United States has taken hold. Both thus cherish the U.S. definition of what Charles Maier (1978) has called the politics of productivity. Both countries project their power onto other societies through economic means, often refusing to acknowledge the new coinage. Since the late 1970s both were pushed, Germany a bit earlier than Japan, toward a more active definition of their role in global politics. In neither case does it appear likely that the power politics of the 1930s will reappear.

Differences in their domestic structures and international connections make Japan and Germany affect Asia and Europe differently. This chapter has argued that these differences are not ephemeral but have deep domestic and international roots and are consequential for European and Asian regionalism.

In different ways Japan and Germany are likely to continue playing the role of supporters of the United States and, more important, of the international order that evolved under U.S. leadership during the last half of the twentieth century. Both are shouldering a growing burden of international responsibilities. But the lessons Germany and Japan learned from 1945, five decades of experience with their neighbors, and the structure of their states make it highly implausible that Japanese and German leaders and mass publics will rally to the task of international action with a forward-looking, can-do attitude. Instead, both states prefer to play an important regional role and assume a relatively low profile in international politics that has a deeply ingrained preference for multilateral rather than unilateral action.

Japan and Germany are increasingly being drawn to new tasks, sometimes against their will. In the area of trade, for example, Germany has played the role of a broker between the various protectionist currents in Europe and the United States. Similarly, the Japanese government tries to take account of U.S. domestic politics and the protectionist lobby in Tokyo in fashioning a diplomatic approach to trade and investment conflicts that maintains the essential pillars of a liberal international economy. In the future, the international coordination of exchange rate policy is unthinkable without the active cooperation of the Bank of Japan and the ECB, with the Bundesbank as a central actor. Japan moved rapidly in the 1980s to become the largest aid donor in the world. And both Germany and Japan have assumed positions of leadership in Europe and Asia that compensate at times for the economic or political weaknesses of the United States. Germany's south European policy in the 1970s was aimed at smoothing the process of transition from authoritarianism to democracy in Spain, Portugal, Greece, and Turkey. In the 1990s, Germany's influence was pervasive as the central and east European democracies moved toward Europe. In the 1980s and 1990s, Japan sought to play an analogous role in the Philippines, Korea, Vietnam, and Cambodia. It remains to be seen whether and how, from a position of declining economic strength, Japan will seek to shape the political consequences of the Asian financial crisis in Indonesia, Malaysia, and throughout southeast and northeast Asia.

Contemporary regionalism takes different forms in different world regions. Regionalism is institutionalized in networks that operate informally in Asian markets largely through corporate, ethnic, and familial networks (Katzenstein and Shiraishi 1997b; Hatch and Yamamura 1996). The elites of many of Asia's developmental states remain deeply suspicious of relinquishing sovereignty to an international bureaucracy not easily held accountable. In contrast, European regionalism takes an explicitly political form in the emergence of distinctive transnational governance structures that are organized around the EU (Katzenstein 1997c). The institutionalization of the relations among different states is Europe's most defining characteristic.

Finally, contemporary regionalism in Asia and Europe is open to developments in the global system. The main reason is the historical legacy of the U.S. empire's worldwide quest for access to society and economy rather than territorial control. This has altered significantly the regional politics of Asia and Europe. Germany and Japan are the centers of a new regionalism in Europe and Asia that is increasingly supplanting the waning system of strategic bipolarity—as long as Europe does not unite militarily and Japan forgoes the technological options it has for becoming a military superpower. This regionalism differs from Hitler's New Order and Japan's Co-Prosperity Sphere in the 1930s and 1940s, as well as from George Orwell's (1949) nightmarish projection of a tripolar world in his novel *Nineteen Eighty-Four*. After suffering total defeat in World War II, Japan and Germany were compelled to adapt their domestic institutions and policies to new international arrangements expressing the worldviews and interests of the United States. As their power grew in subsequent decades, Japan's and Germany's international exercise of power was similarly shaped by interactions with their regional settings in a new global system. In short, what separates Asia and Europe's new regionalism from the old is the difference between autarchy and direct rule, on the one hand, and interdependence and indirect rule, on the other.

Germany and Japan in a New Phase of Capitalism: Confronting the Past and the Future

Kozo Yamamura

This chapter has three goals: to show historically demonstrated relationships between the pace and character of technological change and the performance of industrial economies; to argue that a more market-based capitalism, exemplified by that of the United States, has comparative institutional advantage over a more cooperation-based capitalism, such as those of Germany and Japan, when technology is changing fundamentally and rapidly, while the converse is the case when technological change is adaptive and gradual; and to suggest the importance for Germany and Japan of recognizing these relationships and the need for a new national vision of the future of their political economies and a broad consensus on policies and behavior essential to overcoming the many formidable challenges their variant of capitalism faces.

In pursuit of these goals, this chapter first argues that during the final quarter of the twentieth century the capitalism of advanced economies entered a new phase, unprecedented since the beginning of the Industrial Revolution, in which the following closely intertwined developments took place simultaneously: the digital revolution changed many dimensions of advanced capitalist societies in fundamental ways; the world economy became substantially more interdependent because trade and the cross-border flows of information, technology, and capital are larger than ever; competition grew more intense than ever because of both reduced impediments to trade and a large excess capacity in many markets of manufactured products; and, to maintain or increase competitiveness, the largest

115

firms and financial institutions merged at an accelerating pace within and across national boundaries.

Next, the chapter discusses two analytic observations. One is that a more market-oriented capitalism has institutional advantage over a more cooperation-based capitalism in the new phase of capitalist development. This is because the former is better able to respond to the changes in relative prices of all resources that occur more frequently when new technologies are being adopted and when global interdependence is accelerating and worldwide competition intensifying. The second observation is that a more market-oriented capitalism is able to maintain competitive advantage by imposing higher social costs, manifested in an increasing disparity in income distribution and other evidence of declining equity, on a larger proportion of its citizens than is possible in cooperation-based capitalist economies. This occurs because a sufficiently large majority of the citizens of more market-based economies accept the view that the social costs of responding to market signals are a price that must be paid for increasing over time the living standard of all citizens.

The chapter then turns to the importance of transforming German and Japanese institutions in response to two conflicting realities: that in the new phase of capitalism many of the strengths of the German and Japanese political economies have become serious weaknesses causing economic performance to falter in many ways and that the desire to preserve the strengths of a more cooperation-based capitalism is justified for various reasons. Most important, cooperative institutions can adapt some of the technologies of the new phase more effectively than market-based institutions when the period of digital revolution is succeeded in due course by a period during which adaptive and incremental innovations again become critical for economic performance. The section concludes by suggesting that Germany and Japan can regain economic strength in the latter period that inevitably follows the former period only if each is able to evolve a broadly shared vision of the future and a consensus on policies and behavior essential in a successful pursuit of the vision.

Some caveats are in order. The analysis offered in this chapter focuses on core institutional characteristics, and the comparative analysis of more market-based and more cooperation-based capitalism is therefore limited to broadly stylized differences in their core institutions. Given the primary intent of this chapter, the comparative discussions of German and Japanese institutions and economic performance are confined to a few differences that are especially significant in this analytic context. And, because of space constraints, I am unable to present here the descriptions, data, and technical discussions necessary to better support many of the observations made and analyses offered.

The New Phase

The Unprecedented Beginning of a Technological Paradigm

In continuing to study technological change since the beginning of the Industrial Revolution, I have become persuaded that three major analytic observations can be made[1] concerning the number, phases, and cycles of technological paradigms.

Three Paradigms

Since the 1760s, there have been three readily identifiable technological paradigms—more or less unified bodies of knowledge that most people living in an economy of the time could easily, at least conceptually, recognize as determining the essential technological characteristics of their economy.[2] The first two paradigms prevailed for approximately one century each, and sufficient evidence exists for us to conclude that the advanced capitalist economies have now entered the third paradigm.

The first paradigm, beginning in the 1760s and ending in the 1870s, consisted principally of innovations that harnessed and conveyed steam power on a large scale by many types of machines, thus making possible the rapid growth of the cotton textile, iron and steel, and coal industries, as well as a veritable revolution in transportation (i.e., the swift and steady expansion of rail and transoceanic shipping). The growth of these industries and transportation capabilities and all the developments that occurred directly and indirectly because of them—the oft-told story of the Industrial Revolution—will not be repeated here.

The second paradigm extended from the 1880s to the mid-1970s. Its most significant innovations made available many human-made materials (e.g., cement, chemical dyes, ammonia, and rubber) and made it possible to generate electricity in large amounts and make wide-ranging use of electricity (e.g., light, motors, and home electric appliances). Petroleum played an important part in this paradigm, but the *force majeur* was electricity because it is impossible to conceive of this paradigm without the myriad uses of electricity.[3] The mass-production system that became prevalent for

---

1. The discussion contained in this subsection owes greatly to the late Yasusuke Murakami, who spent countless hours with me discussing the pivotal roles that technological paradigms play in determining the performance of industrial economies. His analytic insights, first presented in Japanese in the early 1980s, are summarized in Murakami (1986).

2. I use the term "technological paradigm" as defined by Thomas Kuhn (1970), a historian of science. The following studies provided analytic bases for, and are useful in better understanding the exposition of, this subsection: Abernathy (1978), Chandler (1977), Dosi (1983), Murakami (1983, 1996), Rosenberg (1976), Touraine (1969).

3. Nuclear energy began to be used during this paradigm, but did not become a part of it.

many products (e.g., automobiles, home electric appliances, and many types of machinery) was also an integral part of this paradigm.

The third paradigm is information technology. It began with the digital revolution, and it depends crucially on precision measured in millionths of seconds or millimeters and on analytic constructs that have no visually comprehensible analogue. Even though rudimentary computers (such as the one hundred-foot-long ENIAC with 18,000 vacuum tubes) were already used experimentally in World War II and the transistor was invented in 1947, a new paradigm began in the 1970s. In this decade, digital technology was adopted rapidly by firms and individuals, as attested by the total output of semiconductors, which soared in the early 1970s (Mowery and Rosenberg 1998, 129). Also, investment increased in both hard- and software, as did output and employment in industries adopting the new technology. Although we cannot yet be certain how significant a role biotechnology will play in shaping the character of the present paradigm, we must also take note here of its striking progress since the 1970s. It is indisputable that by the final quarter of the twentieth century, most people living in advanced economies became increasingly aware that their lives were changing in novel and significant ways because of the products and services associated with the digital revolution.

Phases of Paradigms

Extensive analyses at various levels of disaggregation of data such as GDP growth rates, investment, demand, productivity, employment, real wages, and the pace of diffusion of new technology unmistakably reveal that the first two paradigms each comprised two readily identifiable phases—a breakthrough phase and a maturation phase—each lasting approximately one-half century. In the first paradigm, the breakthrough phase lasted from the 1760s to the 1820s and the maturation phase began in the 1830s and ended in the 1870s. For the second paradigm, the breakthrough phase lasted from the 1880s to the 1910s and the maturation phase was from the 1920s to the 1970s.[4]

In the breakthrough phase of both paradigms, new technologies were adopted only by firms in industries that had little difficulty finding increasing demand for their new products. Thus, because investment and output increased steadily only in a small number of industries, the overall performance of industrial economies (measured in the growth rates of GDP, investment, productivity, employment, etc.) remained lethargic. And, most notably, the growth rate of labor productivity, and thus that of the real

---

4. Note that these breakthrough and maturation phases overlap with Kondratieff's fifty-year wave cycles of the past two hundred years (see Murakami 1996, 118–22).

wage, was either very low or at times negative. As quantitative and case studies show, this was because only a few industries were adopting the new technology because doing so was costly (e.g., in terms of acquiring new skills and learning to use the new technology efficiently) and because most industries, still reliant on the technology of the maturation phase of the past paradigm, were experiencing a decelerating productivity increase. See also Murakami (1996, 166–67, 189–99).

This enables us to better understand why, for example, historians of the British economy long debated the reliability and significance of regional and occupation-specific real wage data, which rose little or even fell in some cases during the first several decades following the robust beginning of the Industrial Revolution in England. The analysis also explains why the industrial economies experienced what economic historians call the Great Climacteric—a prolonged industrial stagnation—during the final quarter of the nineteenth century when a new (the second) technological paradigm was beginning.[5]

In both paradigms, however, overall economic performance improved when the maturation phase arrived for three intertwined principal reasons. The first reason is the increasing pace of normal innovations and the diffusion of these innovations. Normal innovations are made, in innumerable ways, to increase the productive efficiency of resources by adapting or improving the new technologies that have appeared in the breakthrough phase. In the nineteenth-century paradigm, normal innovations included the successful adoption of steam energy for oceangoing ships, innovations that made rail transport faster and less costly, and a large number of significant inventions that transformed the steel, textile, and chemical industries. In the twentieth-century paradigm, normal innovations came even more steadily and often in even more unanticipated ways, yielding constantly improving internal combustion engines, numerous types of more reliable machines performing more functions, automobiles superior in all respects, and an increasing variety of higher-quality home electric appliances, pharmaceutical products, construction materials, and many other products (see Rosenberg 1976; Mowery and Rosenberg 1998).[6] Because of these normal innovations, few living in the 1770s and the 1880s could have envisioned the world in which their grandchildren would live.

The second reason for improved economic performance was steady increases in investment and employment in more and more industries in response to demand, which continued to rise because of the acceleration

---

5. The English case was in 1873–96 (see Elbaum and Lazonick 1986; Floud and McCloskey 1994).

6. The bibliography in Mowery and Rosenberg (1998) is especially useful for those who wish to study these technological developments further.

of normal innovations that reduced costs, thereby lowering prices. This also meant labor productivity was increasing and real wages were rising, motivating more workers to acquire the skills necessary to adopt normal innovations.

The third reason, no less important than the second, was a gradual but continuing increase in the institutional capabilities of firms and markets to accommodate and respond to, as well as promote, normal innovations. That is, had it not been for the well-known developments in the organization and management of firms and in financial markets including laws that more effectively monitored financial transactions, the maturation phase of neither paradigm could have evolved as it did.

Here, let me interpose the following assertion. I believe we will witness in the present paradigm, too, what we see in the histories of many industries in the maturation phase of past paradigms: a steady increase in minor and major normal innovations and a headlong race to introduce new or better products by adapting these innovations.[7] Put very simply, in the new paradigm we can anticipate developments of a sort exemplified in the past paradigm by the appearance of monochrome and then color television sets, in which increasingly advanced capabilities were made possible by over 2,000 minor and major normal innovations (e.g., transistors, diodes, Yagi antennas, trinitron tubes, and the like) entirely unforeseen when the second paradigm based on electricity began (Abramson 1987; Shiers 1977).

Because of the arrival of the maturation phase of the first paradigm, improving economic performance accompanied by steadily rising real wages was observed in England (and in follower countries such as Germany, the United States, and France) during 1830–70. In the maturation phase of the second paradigm (the 1920s and 1950–73), advanced industrial economies maintained high performance as evidenced in real wages that continued to rise, albeit at a slowing rate, and in the unemployment rate that remained low in most advanced economies. (In evaluating economic performance in the 1930s and 1940s, we can reasonably conclude that the underlying growth-promoting effects of the maturation phase were overwhelmed by the effects of the Great Depression and World War II.)

An important addendum concerning the maturation phase is that, in its late stage, more and more of the industries in an economy spearheading a paradigm see their performance falter, especially relative to the same

---

7. "Minor innovations" improve products marginally and are not always patentable; "major innovations" make substantive, patentable improvements, many generating new products not anticipated during the breakthrough phase.

industries in other industrial economies. The most obvious reason for this is large and often excess capacity due to foreign competition and declining domestic demand caused by the ending of a product cycle. This was why England was the first to show signs of entering the Great Climacteric in the early 1870s and why the United States saw more and more of its industries lose market share, both at home and abroad, to followers, especially Germany and Japan, during the 1960s and 1970s. It explains why both England in the maturation phase of the first paradigm and the United States in the same period of the second paradigm experienced longer periods of weak economic performance relative to other large industrial economies (see Elbaum and Lazonick 1986; Floud and McCloskey 1994; Kuznets 1965; Maddison 1964).

Cycles of Paradigms

History repeats itself but never in the same ways, as seen in the following summaries of the similarities and differences between the breakthrough phases of the first two paradigms and that of the new paradigm that began in the 1970s.

Quantitative analyses show that the first decades of the third paradigm have been similar to those of the preceding two paradigms. Total output, investment, and employment in industries adopting the new technologies increased steadily from the 1970s. However, in the final years of the twentieth century, investment and employment as well as output remained relatively small (as a proportion of total investment, employment, and GDP).

In the United States, leading the digital revolution, the total value of products and services of industries adopting new technology (both the "hard" variant, all digital electronic machinery and equipment, including liquid crystals, and the "soft" variant, software and information and communication services using digital electronic technology) rose rapidly after the early 1970s. However, the total value was still small even in the 1990s, much the same as in the leading industries in the breakthrough phase of the two preceding paradigms. In 1996, the most recent year for which all necessary data are available, the total value of both "hard" and "soft" high-tech industries had risen to only $753 billion or 9.9 percent of GDP. Although the same total value is estimated to have risen to more than $1 trillion (11.8 percent of GDP) by the end of the 1990s and to continue to rise into the twenty-first century (to an estimated 13.7 percent of GDP by 2005), the GDP share of these industries remains small, as had been the case for leading industries in preceding paradigms. For Japan the counterpart datum is 7.0 percent of GDP in 1996, estimated to reach 10.4 percent by 2005.[8] The definition of "leading industries" can be debated, but their employment data make it difficult to deny that their GDP share remains relatively small.[9]

Similar also to the past paradigms was the slow increase since 1973 in labor productivity and real wages (although this observation must be qualified by examining the level of overall economic performance as the outcome of underlying technological factors and various short-term factors; see the next section). Because the readily available data, especially on labor productivity, show unambiguously a much lower increase in productivity in contrast to the 1950–73 period (see table 4.1), I summarize here one of many studies demonstrating that the increase in productivity, especially labor productivity, for industries (let alone for economies as a whole) adopting new technology has been low since the mid-1970s.

In an exceptionally carefully crafted econometric study analyzing voluminous amounts of data for manufacturing industries in 1968–86, Ernst Brendt and Catherine Morrison have established that "there is a statistically significant negative relationship between productivity growth [labor and total factor] and the high-tech intensity of the capital stock," measured by a high-tech capital aggregate index constructed for investment made in office high-tech computing and accounting machinery, communications equipment, scientific and engineering instruments, and photocopy and related equipment (1995, 12).[10] Their principal conclusion, reached reluctantly, was that their finding is "a mystery" because their study shows

8. The data are based on an extensive comparative study of the United States and Japan by the Japan Economic Research Center under the leadership of Koichi Nishioka; for data and analyses, see Japan Economic Research Center (1998). Although focused only on investment, an Organization for Economic Cooperation and Development (OECD 1997b) study is useful in showing the still-limited importance of information technology (IT) industries. The study shows that the total investment in IT industries—office, computing, and accounting equipment; radio, TV, and communication equipment; and communication services (i.e., ISCI 3825, 3882, and 72)—as a proportion of total investment in manufacturing industries was 13.27 percent in the United States, 12.23 percent in Japan for 1994, and 8.80 percent in Germany for 1992 (West Germany only).

9. An examination of employment data for IT industries (i.e., those covered in Brendt and Morrison 1995; OECD 1997e) shows that, in the OECD economies in the 1990s, the ratio of employment by these industries over total employment was less than one-half (and even less than one-third in some economies) the ratio of investment made by IT industries over total investment. Even in the least capital-intensive IT industry, the software and computer-related service industry, total employment in 1995 was only 0.9 percent of total U.S. employment (for Japan 0.8 percent). For OECD employment data, see OECD (1996); for employment, investment, and other data relating to the software and computer-related service industry, see OECD (1997e). The latter does not include Germany in the sample.

10. The industries Brendt and Morrison analyzed are those in Bureau of Economic Analysis codes 14, 15, 16, and 26. The authors excluded service industries because their productivity is apparently growing more slowly than that of manufacturing industries and also because the productivity of service industries cannot be measured accurately enough for use in a rigorous econometric analysis (Brendt and Morrison 1995, 38–40).

Table 4.1 Productivity in the Business Sector (% change at annual rates)

	United States	Japan	Germany[a]
Total factor productivity[b]			
1960–73[c]	2.5	5.4	2.6
1973–79	0.2	1.1	1.8
1979–95[d]	0.5	1.2	0.4
Labor productivity[e]			
1960–73	2.6	8.4	4.5
1973–79	0.4	2.8	3.1
1979–95	0.8	2.2	0.9
Capital productivity			
1960–73[c]	2.3	−3.3	−1.4
1973–79	−0.2	−3.7	−1.0
1979–95[d]	−0.2	−2.1	−0.6

Source: OECD (1996, A68).
[a] The first two averages concern West Germany. The percentage change for the period 1979–95 is calculated as the weighted average of West German productivity growth between 1979 and 1991 and total German productivity growth between 1991 and the latest year available.
[b] TFP growth is equal to a weighted average of the growth in labor productivity and capital productivity. The sample-period averages for capital and labor shares are used as weights.
[c] Or the earliest year available; 1962 for Japan.
[d] Or the latest year available; 1993 for Germany, 1994 for Japan.
[e] Output per employee.

that "like lemmings gone to sea, US manufacturing firms have irrationally overinvested in high-tech office and information technology capital" (37). Of course, had they been familiar with the history of the breakthrough phase of earlier technological paradigms, they would have known that this was not "a mystery" but an expected outcome in a breakthrough phase of a new technological paradigm.

It is important to be reminded that labor productivity in the United States appears to have risen at an increasing rate approaching 2 percent per year during the 1997–2000 period, based on provisional data gathered under various assumptions. Note that such an estimated rate is still much lower than the increase in labor productivity achieved (ranging from 5 to 9 percent) by the manufacturing industries of several industrial economies during the maturation phase (1960s and 1970s) of the previous technological paradigm.

Along with these similarities in the slow increase in the GDP share of the leading industries and negative or meager effects on labor productivity of investment, there are, however, two very significant differences between the breakthrough phases of the past two paradigms and the present one. These differences have important implications for how we perceive the challenges facing Germany and Japan and for how demanding the collective task will be of achieving a sufficiently broad consensus regarding the future of their economies.

The first difference is that, for firms in a score of important industries of the second paradigm, adapting the breakthrough technology of the digital revolution is distinctively easier than that experienced by firms in earlier breakthrough phases. We need only to envision the difficulties of steam-powered cotton textile mills, machine shops, and iron works in the maturation phase of the first paradigm as they attempted during 1880–1920 to adopt the new technology of the breakthrough phase of the second paradigm, which was based on modern chemistry, electricity, and mass production and which required new scientific knowledge and skills as well as significantly larger amounts of capital than nineteenth-century firms were accustomed to raising. This was why none of the established firms of the first paradigm became a successful large firm in a leading industry of the second paradigm. The easier transition to the technology of the third paradigm reflects the fact that the preceding, electricity-based paradigm provided many firms in advanced industrial economies with the human capital (scientists, engineers, and workers whose skills could be upgraded) and the social infrastructure (education, laws, and capital market) necessary to adopt the technologies of the digital revolution and produce hybrid products that assimilate specific technologies of the new paradigm. Such products include automobiles, airplanes, many types of machinery, home and office electronic appliances and equipment, telephones, and even toys that have very significantly changed in quality and function because of the assimilation of digital technology. The ease of assimilating the new technology is why most major producers of hybrid products were also the leading producers in the previous paradigm. The assimilated technologies of these hybrid products result in descriptions such as: "The new Mercedes S-class has electronic air suspension, radar-guided cruise control and gadgets that respond to spoken orders" ("World in 1999" 1999, 9).

The second difference between the present breakthrough phase and its predecessors is that the time required for economies as a whole to see a steady and significant increase in productivity and real wages will most likely be longer. In order to make truly productive use of the new technology, new institutional capabilities have to be developed. These will include creating flexible and constantly evolving organizations of firms, managerial and employment practices, new and adaptable methods of production, and novel and increasingly cross-national interfirm relations; devising and upgrading educational systems; and developing new concepts of private property rights and finding effective ways to enforce them. Using steam energy or mass-producing automobiles also required many profound changes in numerous aspects of society; however, it seems self-evident that the institutional changes required cannot but take more time than did similar efforts in past paradigms because of the multifarious complexities of the digital technology itself and the large-scale infrastructural requirements that will undoubtedly continue to become more global.

Increasing Global Interdependence and Competition

Let me now summarize developments directly or indirectly linked to the arrival of the current breakthrough phase. Most significantly, the economies of the world, and especially the most advanced among them, became more interdependent than ever during the last few decades of the twentieth century. This is evident when we examine, for example, data for total global trade; range of products traded, especially in intraindustry trade; cross-border capital flow for various types of arbitrage and for both direct and portfolio investments; and international joint ventures in research and development (R&D) and technology transfer, including those embodied in capital goods and made under royalty and licensing agreements. By the 1990s, information flowed in massive and accelerating amounts via cyberspace. As often noted, this development has made possible in all but a few closed economies around the world virtually instantaneous responses by governments, investors, and financial institutions to changes in interest rates and stock-price fluctuations. Daily international capital flow, mostly via cyberspace, were by the mid-1990s well in excess of $1 trillion.

In such a world, competition in all markets, and particularly in those for manufactured products, cannot but grow more intense. This, of course, is an outcome of closely linked developments such as the end of the cold war, the continued postwar reductions in tariffs and nontariff barriers of many types, and the sharply increasing ability of developing economies to produce more and more competitive manufactured products. Competition has intensified visibly in markets such as automobiles, steel, semiconductors, a wide range of machines and tools, ever-proliferating kinds of consumer and office electric appliances and electronics products, and pharmaceutical and chemical products. Numerous econometric studies since the 1970s, such as those analyzing the pace and magnitude of the pass-through rate to consumers of gains realized by producers because of changes in exchange rates and the dissipation of oligopoly rent due to international trade, show that our own daily perception and mass media reports of steadily growing competitiveness are indeed accurate (Bresnahan and Reiss 1991; Kozmetsky and Yue 1997; Marston 1991).[11]

11. These sources are examples of the numerous econometric studies dealing with the subjects. The bibliography in Marston (1991) cites fifteen econometric and economic-theoretical studies published during the 1980s on issues relating to pass through involving U.S., Japanese, and German firms. Bresnahan and Reiss (1991) and Kozmetsky and Yue (1997) provide useful theoretical analyses and rich empirical findings.

Competition became much more intense also because of the increasing excess capacity in many markets even in the peaks of business cycles. The most familiar and significant example of this is the motor vehicle industry (passenger cars, trucks, and other types of automobiles), which in 2000 had a world total productive capacity of 78 million automobiles and total sales of 55 million units. Because experts forecast the total demand to stagnate at approximately 50 million units in the coming several years, the industry is more than likely to remain saddled with a very large excess capacity of no fewer than 20 million units into the near future ("Car Industry" 2001).

Similar data and observations could be added to demonstrate that a large and often growing excess productive capacity existed in the 1990s in many markets that faced strong downward pressures on prices, such as auto parts, commercial airplanes, copper, lead, polyester, polyvinyl chloride (PVC), dynamic random access memory (DRAM) and most other types of readily mass-produced semiconductors, many types of steel products, and numerous kinds of electronic machines and tools, including personal and office computer hardware.[12] Also significant is the fact that when excess capacity is analyzed for these markets, it is often not only growing but has also become more chronic; even when demand is high, as seen at the peak of a business cycle, productive capacity remains significantly larger than demand. Were it not for this fact, it simply would not be possible to explain why the capacity utilization rate of U.S. manufacturing industries did not exceed 80 percent during the final quarter of 1998, when the economy was growing at a sizzling real rate of 5.6 percent (U.S. Department of Commerce 1999, 1–6). Important reasons for chronic excess capacity are the strong motivations of firms in many industries to participate in the investment race (discussed later) and their ability to increase their productive capacity rapidly due to expanding engineering and infrastructural capabilities and steadily increasing technology transfer accompanying rapidly growing foreign direct investment.[13]

Such sharply rising competitive pressure is the major cause in most markets of the fast-increasing number of mergers and acquisitions (M&A), especially since the late 1990s. As reported by the mass media literally daily, the pace of both domestic and international mergers continues to

12. For several of the major products (e.g., auto parts, commercial airplanes, DRAMS, and personal computers), the correlation between excess capacity and downward price pressures can be readily confirmed by examining sales (or shipments), capacity, and price data for the 1970s–1990s. There are also numerous anecdotal descriptions of the correlation.

13. Noted also that reducing productive capacity has grown significantly more difficult (costly) because of the increasingly highly specialized nature of machines, equipment, and facilities.

accelerate. Although the total annual M&A around the globe increased from 11,300 in 1990 to almost 30,000 by 2000, the total value of post-merger assets rose during the same period even more rapidly from $500 billion to $3.5 trillion, an amount almost double that seen in 1997. Although mergers among U.S. firms accounted for a lion's share of all mergers ($1.5 trillion in 2000)[14] (*Economist* 9 January 1999, p. 22; Okumura 1998) mergers among European firms and between European and non-European (especially U.S.) firms accelerated as well (from a total of $600 billion in 1998 to $1.4 trillion in 2000) ("Europe's New Capitalism" 2000). And, as the 1990s progressed, even large Japanese firms, long known for their aversion to M&A, except in cases of business difficulties or failures, began to merge or be acquired in increasing numbers, and more and more of their partners were foreign firms and financial institutions.[15] By 2000, M&A activities rose to a level few in Japan would have believed possible only a few years earlier: foreign firms acquired 101 Japanese firms and financial institutions at a total cost of approximately $34 billion (Okumura 2001).[16] Given the quickening pace of M&A activities, especially for international megamergers, no one can doubt that the trends seen in these data will continue.

M&A enable the parties involved to better respond to looming competitive pressure. They enable firms and financial institutions to make more efficient use of resources in production, R&D, and marketing, and they help them gain the market share necessary to remain competitive. Not to be forgotten is that in many more industries, including important ones such as telecommunications and pharmaceuticals, cross-border mergers are the most efficient or only means to gain access to the foreign markets crucial for surviving and prospering in ever-more-competitive global markets.

Here the following microeconomic exposition is useful as an analytic summary of the foregoing observations relating to the increasing global interdependence and competition we have seen since the mid-1970s in the new phase of capitalism. The developments have been more visible and rapid fundamentally because this new phase of capitalism provides opportunities to realize gains of increasing returns for firms assimilating new technology to produce hybrid products or adopting the new technology of the digital revolution as their principal business strategy.

14. In 1998, there were 2,200 M&As involving German firms. The total post-M&A asset size of these M&As reached DM 300 billion ("Kontrolle" 1999, 33).

15. This explains developments such as Japan amending its Antimonopoly Act in 1998 to permit holding companies (i.e., to facilitate M&A) and the president of Bundeskartellamt, Dieter Wolf, expressing serious Europewide concern about possible negative effects on competition. For the former, see Yamamura (1997); for the latter, see "Kartellamt" (1999).

16. U.S. firms accounted for approximately 60 percent of these acquisitions (*Asahi shinbun* 1999).

Increasing returns are efficiency gains that owe to the adoption of new technology (i.e., moving to a new long-term cost curve), economies of scale and scope, or learning by doing (in the broadest sense of each of these terms to include gains realized in production, R&D, and sales). Faced with opportunities of this kind, firms are strongly motivated to increase their output or the variety of products they produce. Because all firms in an industry are similarly motivated, an investment race occurs in which each firm tries to be the first to reduce costs and gain a larger market share. This motivation has become stronger because of the seemingly ever-shorter life cycle of many hybrid and new products in the new phase of capitalism. These are the basic reasons for the growing excess capacity that has become chronic, for the more frequent forward pricing (selling below current marginal cost) to gain a larger market share, and for increasing M&A activities. Freer trade and massive cross-border capital flows since the 1970s are both causes and effects of these developments.

Because of the investment race and the global competition intensified by it, the pursuit of increasing returns has failed to bring high returns to most investors or rising real wages to most employees. This is a familiar story. The investment race requires a goodly portion of profits to be plowed back into expanding capacity, R&D, depreciation, and amortizing debt, and intense competition, often forcing firms to sell their products and services at low prices, if not to engage in forward pricing, cuts sharply into profits. Wage earners do not fare well, except for a minority who possess the skills desired by the firms producing hybrid products or products of the new paradigm. In addition to the slow increase in labor productivity expected in a breakthrough phase of a new technological paradigm, the reasons for stagnant real wages include increasing international competition, especially from the developing economies; management's need to offer competitive returns to investors lest they divest in search of higher returns at home and abroad, and to do all that is possible to remain in the investment race; and active M&A activities that reduce employment.[17] This summary is important for the later discussion of the challenges faced by Germany and Japan today as they seek to forge a vision of the future and attempt to build a sufficiently broad national consensus that is indispensable if the vision is to be pursued successfully.

The preceding analysis and observations relating to the new phase of capitalism explain why since the 1980s more and more neoclassical eco-

---

17. Although macroeconomic analysis is beyond the scope of this chapter, note that this investment race, along with its effects on prices and wages, was one of the important causes of disinflation in the 1990s.

nomic theorists have realized the need to remedy the increasingly apparent inadequacy of their theory. It is beyond the scope of this chapter to enter into an extended discussion of these theoretical developments; let me instead illustrate the efforts made to respond to this need with a very brief discussion of two examples—one specific and the other broadly stated—of utmost significance in the context of this chapter.

One of the most important responses to the need for theoretical progress has been to endogenize technological change. Beginning in the late 1980s, theorists tried to explain why and how technological change occurs to determine the long-term economic growth rate, instead of dealing with it as an exogenous variable outside analytical purview. This attempt to advance a new growth theory—a theory of economic growth focused on technological change as the most crucial variable determining the growth performance of an economy—has produced rapidly proliferating versions of the theory first proposed in 1986 by Romer (1986, 1987, 1990).

By 1999, articles and monographs on the new growth theory showed that the theory had been significantly improved in various ways. For example, the later versions no longer suffered from the two most widely criticized shortcomings of the pioneering versions: scale effects (the size or scale of an economy determines the long-term equilibrium growth rate; i.e., a doubling of the population and resources devoted to R&D will increase the growth rate proportionately, or government expenditures as a pure public good generating growth-promoting externalities increase with the size of the economy) and razor's edge growth (to generate an equilibrium of ongoing growth, all production functions must exhibit constant returns to scale in the accumulated factors of production; i.e., slightly increasing or decreasing returns to scale will produce explosive growth or extinction of growth). Also, whereas earlier versions found little empirical support for the theoretically deduced growth performance of an economy over time or for economies at a given time, the later versions of the theory are better supported (or, more accurately, less contradicted) by various long-term national and cross-national data relating to economic growth.

But, the later versions still cannot escape two closely linked serious criticisms: the theory is exceedingly abstract, primarily because of numerous strong assumptions made to maintain the analytic and mathematical tractability of variables and parameters, and, as acknowledged by the theorists themselves, it is of little practical value to policymakers. Thus, the only objective assessment we can make of the collective efforts of neoclassical theorists to endogenize technological change is that they have succeeded in taking the first few very significant steps toward building a useful theory, but we cannot foretell if or when a credible theory, able to aid policymakers, will come forth.[18]

No less important are the efforts of a much larger number of economists since the 1980s to bring institutions back into their analyses. More and more economists have become aware that they have paid a very high price by assuming away institutions in developing neoclassical theory, the most rigorous among all social scientific theories. Assuming away institutions—all formal and informal constraints imposed on behavior including laws, policies, customs, accepted norms, and values—made their theory universalistic (i.e., attached little import to institutional differences across national boundaries) and short-term (because economic behavior and outcomes are determined by markets and not shaped by institutions with their long-term effects on economic behavior and outcomes).

The efforts to bring institutions back are too numerous to summarize. The most significant in the context of this chapter are neoinstitutional analysis and comparative institutional analysis, which recognize the primary importance of various institutions in shaping the behavior and determining the performance of individuals and firms and thus economies; strategic trade theory and similar attempts to place analytic emphasis on an oligopolistic market (which is prevalent in manufacturing industries) and on the many roles that institutions, especially governments, can play in affecting the trade performance of firms (particularly their ability to adopt new technology); and the new theories of the firm and of industrial organization that revise accepted theories in very fundamental ways by recognizing that long-term cooperative relationships maintained between firms by dedicated investment (i.e., for exclusive purposes of a specific interfirm relationship) and evolving mutual trust can substantively enhance productivity and profits.[19]

The essential fact is that we do not have a theory that enables us to explain many of developments in the new phase of capitalism and to predict the future of the advanced capitalist economies. This fact is denied or

18. For excellent critical analyses of strong assumptions made (e.g., regarding the behavior and motivations of firms, and for mathematical tractability), and the ad hoc character and unnecessary implausibilities and complexities of Romer's and others' endogenous growth theory models, see, for example, Amable, Boyer, and Lordon (1996), Gries, Wigger, and Hentschel (1994), Solow (1994), and Weder and Grubel (1993). For an excellent, succinct review of the endogenous growth models appearing in the 1990s and an example of a later, more generalized, nonscale model, see Eicher and Turnovsky (1999).

19. Among the very large number of theoretical works attempting to bring back institutions, North (1990) is a readable summary of neoinstitutional analysis and Aoki (1988, 1995) and Aoki and Okuno (1996) provide the essential bases of more rigorous, game-theory-based comparative institutional analysis (Aoki 2000 is a translation of Aoki 1995). Those interested in the new theory of firm and industrial organization, based essentially on transaction cost analysis and in strategic trade theory, are referred to the sources discussed and fully cited in chapter 3 of Hatch and Yamamura (1996, 43–61).

disregarded by those who are fixated, for reasons of self-interest or ideology, on the sharply contrasting performances of the more market-driven U.S. capitalism and the more cooperation-based German and Japanese capitalism. Selectively invoking a textbook version of assumption-laden neoclassical analysis, they declare that the more market-driven U.S. capitalism is thus a superior model to be emulated by all other countries, especially Germany and Japan. As described in the following section, the number of converts to this view has been increasing since the beginning of the 1990s in both Germany and Japan, which are struggling to confront their pasts and futures.

Two Capitalisms in the New Phase

The High Performance of U.S. Capitalism

The institutional comparative advantage that the more market-based U.S. capitalism has in the new phase of capitalism is best seen in the price responsiveness of its labor and capital markets. Others have provided us with extensive analyses of this responsiveness from comparative perspectives (concerning Germany and Japan, see the essays by Sigurt Vitols, Gregory Jackson, and Steven Vogel in this volume); here a brief summary description of the advantage will suffice.

Significantly less shackled by legal, negotiated, and socially embedded constraints, U.S. firms can pay more market-determined wages and terminate employment much more easily than can German and Japanese firms. Put simply, the market responsiveness of U.S. employment practices reflects the fact that in the United States long-term employment or lifetime employment is not a part of the social contract as it is in both Germany and Japan. Much quantitative evidence has been accumulated by specialists to demonstrate the market responsiveness of U.S. employment practices. For example, compared to Germany and Japan, in the United States total employment by industry and sector changes more quickly, the average tenure of employment is shorter, differences in wage levels within firms and across industries are significantly larger, and the rates of employment and unemployment are substantially more responsive to the economic performance of firms.

The responsiveness of the U.S. capital market and the character of U.S. corporate governance shaping and shaped by the U.S. capital market can be readily seen in the following facts. In sharp contrast to Germany and Japan where capital is patient (i.e., committed for the long term mainly via *Hausbanks* or main banks), in the United States capital responds more quickly to immediate market signals. For example, this means that new entrants can obtain capital more readily than can their counterparts in Germany and Japan. Although venture capital became a little easier to obtain in both Germany and Japan during the 1990s, raising capital by initial public offering of shares is still far easier in the United States for various institutional reasons.

A significant distinguishing characteristic of the U.S. capital market accompanying this market-responsive fluidity of capital is the relative strength of market discipline because it is exercised by shareholders who are much better able than their counterparts in Germany and Japan to demand market-responsive share values and to control management. As seen in the incidence of takeovers and M&A, firms' decisions regarding maintaining share value versus making long-term investment and determining total wage costs demonstrates that market discipline is much more effective in the United States than in Germany and Japan in forcing the swift allocation of capital to the firms and industries that promise the highest returns.

This responsiveness of labor and capital markets only typifies the broader institutional advantage of U.S. capitalism in a breakthrough phase. In comparison to the economies of Germany and Japan, the U.S. economy is much less regulated, especially because of the deregulation measures it adopted in the 1980s. The U.S. decision-making process in both government and boardrooms is significantly more transparent (especially in contrast to Japan), thus providing more information necessary for assessing risk and reducing many types of rent-seeking activities. U.S. capitalism is more accepting of the large rewards reaped by winner-take-all innovative entrepreneurial ventures as just laurels awarded for the risk-taking that is essential for a vibrant capitalism. These and other characteristics of U.S. capitalism, along with the price-responsiveness in its factor markets, give the U.S. economy the comparative advantage that enables it to lead in innovating and adopting new technology.

Often neglected, or even intentionally dismissed, in the ongoing policy debate in Germany and Japan is that this U.S. advantage is underlying, in the sense that it enables the U.S. economy to achieve high performance as long as no adverse short-term factors interfere. In the 1970s and 1980s, even after the new phase of capitalism had begun and the underlying comparative advantages of U.S. capitalism were becoming increasingly more salient, the performance of the U.S. economy was in the doldrums and lagged behind that of Germany and Japan for several reasons: the breakthrough phase of the third paradigm had just begun, the investment and output of the leading industries adopting new technology were still small, and the productivity of the overall economy was still low. Also the still-significant U.S. industries in the maturation phase of the second paradigm were losing market share, both at home and abroad, to German and

Japanese firms enjoying comparative institutional advantages in producing hybrid products. Of course, the macroeconomic policy of the Ronald Reagan years, which increased the value of the dollar, was an important reason for the deteriorating performance of U.S. firms in most of the 1980s. Thus during these two decades the U.S. economy continued to deindustrialize while Germany and Japan were able to maintain their performance, aided substantially by their comparative advantage in producing hybrid products.

However, from the early 1990s on, the U.S. economy began to enjoy sustained high performance for two mutually reinforcing reasons: U.S. firms exploited their comparative advantage in the breakthrough phase to adopt the new technology of the digital revolution and a combination of such serendipitous developments as the end of the cold war (enabling the United States to reduce defense expenditures and thus the fiscal deficit); a continuous large inflow of capital from Japan, Europe, and elsewhere; and price stability maintained because of the strength of the dollar (due mostly to the inflow of capital, the declining economic performance of many trading partners, and the wise course of monetary policy that was relatively easy to chart in the noninflationary prosperous U.S. economy of the 1990s).

The point is that more market-based capitalism, such as that of the United States, cannot and thus does not achieve high performance at all times. It can attain high performance only when two conditions are met: the technological paradigm is in its breakthrough phase and no short-term factors, policy-induced or otherwise, are sufficiently strong to negate the underlying strength of the comparative institutional advantage such an economy possesses in a breakthrough phase. Thus, to believe that emulating U.S. capitalism assures high economic performance at all times is to disregard both what occurred in the U.S. economy in the 1970s and 1980s and the possibility of the same thing recurring at any time in the near future for any number of easily conceivable domestic or international short-term reasons.

The market-responsiveness of the U.S. economy comes at high social costs. This is because it requires that the economy satisfy a third condition: there is a distinctively higher disparity in the distribution of income—with its manifold consequences—than in Germany and Japan. The increasing disparity in income distribution and its consequences since the mid-1970s have been analyzed and documented extensively. Alan Greenspan stated in 1997 in congressional testimony that "there has been, as we know and discussed over the years, a significant opening up of income spreads, largely as a function of technology and education. The whole spread goes right through the basic system. It is a development I feel uncomfortable with" (quoted in Galbraith 1998, n.p.). Although there is no shortage of quanti-

Table 4.2 Distribution of Disposable Income, 1995[a]

	Lowest Three Deciles	Middle Four Deciles	Top Three Deciles
United States	11.5	35.0	53.5
	(−1.2)	(−1.4)	(2.6)
Germany	14.8	36.1	49.1
	(−1.1)	(−0.1)	(1.2)
Japan	15.7	36.5	47.8
	(−0.6)	(−0.2)	(0.8)

Source: Burniaux et al. (1998).
[a] In percentage of national total disposable income (TDI); numbers in parentheses are change—in points—from 1974 to 1995.

tative evidence attesting to this "uncomfortable" fact, space permits me to present only the following from among those most credible.

In a recent authoritative study by the Organization for Economic Cooperation and Development (OECD), a group of specialists made the utmost effort to make their findings on income distribution internationally comparable. They established that, as shown in table 4.2, the distribution of total disposable income (TDI)—total posttax income adjusted for transfer payments—was distinctly more unequally distributed in 1974 in the United States than in Germany and Japan in the same year and that the distribution of TDI grew significantly more unequal during 1974–95 in the United States than in either Germany or Japan. Major reasons for this increasing disparity over time were that the TDI of the three top deciles rose much more rapidly in the United States, from their already high 1974 level, than in Germany and Japan and that the TDI of both the four middle deciles and the three lowest deciles in the United States declined more than in Germany and Japan.[20]

The "uncomfortable" fact can also be made evident in other ways. In the United States, a significantly larger proportion of citizens suffer poverty and they remain in poverty considerably longer than in all other major industrial economies. A most revealing demonstration of this is made in a major study in which "poverty" is defined, as it is by most specialists making international comparisons of income distributions, as having a postgovernment income (disposable income net of taxes and transfers) that is less than one-half the median income of an economy. For 1985–94, the proportion of Americans in poverty at least one year of the ten-year period was 18 percent; the proportion in poverty during the entire ten-year period

20. Several other studies also present various measures of income distribution, for example, the Gini, Theil, and Atkinson coefficients, that confirm the findings (Burniaux et al. 1998).

was 13 percent. Comparable figures for Germany were 8 percent and 5.8 percent (and for the Netherlands, 5.5 percent and 0.5 percent) (Goodin et al. 1999, apps. A1–A3). For Japan, I know of no study using the same method of analysis; however, many similar studies of income distribution and unemployment suggest that comparable figures for Japan fall between those for Germany and the Netherlands.[21] As many specialists have noted, a major reason for the relatively high proportion of Americans in poverty is the larger number of working poor, an outcome reflecting the significantly larger dispersion in wages paid to employees in the United States than in all other OECD nations (OECD 1996, 61–62).[22] Most working poor, approximately 15 percent of the total labor force, earn the legal minimum hourly wage, which in 1999 remained in real terms below that of 1975 despite increases.

Few would claim direct causality between such data and the various serious manifestations of social malaise and bleak public health seen in the United States compared to all other OECD economies. But, at the same time, few would deny that the increasing disparity in income and the sizable proportion of the population who have remained poor over a long period in the United States are major reasons for these conditions. Among the readily obtainable comparable data are the following. In the 1990s, the U.S. homicide rate averaged approximately 9.5 per 100,000 and the incarceration rate hovered between 360 and 390 per 100,000. Both rates are approximately ten times those in Germany and Japan, and the incarceration rate of black males in the United States in 1996 was quadruple that in apartheid-era South Africa. In the United States, where 48 million of its citizens had no health insurance in 2002, the infant mortality rate in the 1990s was approximately 8 per 1,000, twice that in Japan and 50 percent higher than in Germany (Statistics Bureau, General Affairs Agency, 1990–2000).[23] These data and much other quantitative evidence strongly suggest that the distribution of income, especially the existence of a long-term, low-income underclass in U.S. society, is probably a predominant reason for these unpleasant comparative realities of U.S. life.

The costs of the U.S. institutional comparative advantage are real and high. However, owing greatly to the underlying advantage it possesses in the breakthrough phase of a new technological paradigm, the U.S. economy enjoyed its longest ever period of peacetime prosperity in the

---

21. The best overall analysis of income distribution in Japan is Tachibanaki (1998), available only in Japanese. In English, Tachibanaki (1989, 1992, 1996) are most useful in providing the analyses and data for comparative assessments.

22. The same source also contains other useful comparative data and discussions (OECD 1996, annex 3A, 100–103).

23. The comparative data in this publication are drawn from those gathered by the World Bank, OECD, and the World Health Organization.

1990s and continues to outperform the sluggish German economy and the recession-ridden Japanese economy in the first years of the twenty-first century. It is a serious mistake not to acknowledge fully this substantial and tangible advantage; it is no less serious an error to believe that the U.S. economy will continue to outperform the German and Japanese economies well into the future or to argue, as some did vociferously and misguidedly until the bursting of the dot-com bubble and visible slackening of the U.S. growth rate, that the U.S. economy has become recession-proof. The maturation phase of the new paradigm will inevitably come, as it did in past paradigms, and, as also noted, U.S. prosperity could end with little warning for any number of short-term factors.

German and Japanese Capitalism in Search of a Consensus for the Future

As the new phase of capitalism began (in the 1970s and 1980s), issues relating to the comparative institutional disadvantage of Germany and Japan were debated increasingly by political and business leaders, scholars, and others. They did not, however, become preponderant in politics and in public discourse in these decades. The principal reason for this was the performance of the two economies.

Germany was still outperforming the United States in its growth rate and in most other indicators of economic performance. Even the unemployment rate was lower than in the United States until the mid-1980s. Similarly Japan, recovering rapidly from the oil crisis of 1973–74, maintained a higher economic performance than the United States in the second half of the 1970s and, by the end of the decade, many in Japan were beginning to refer to their nation as "an economic superpower." By virtually all indicators, Japanese performance bested that of the United States and Germany during the first half of the 1980s to make Japan the largest net creditor in the world in 1986. Japan's economic performance rose even more after 1986 and remained stellar until 1991 because of the bubble.

In the 1990s, however, politics and public discourse changed with a vengeance. Germans and Japanese could now see, much more compellingly than in the preceding two decades, the competitive disadvantage of their version of capitalism which was able to achieve only a visibly diminished performance in sharp contrast to the high and sustained performance of U.S. capitalism.

For Germany, the unification-induced boomlet ended by 1993 and the unemployment rate rose from 4.6 percent in 1992 to 5.7 percent in 1993 and then rose at times beyond 10 percent. Although the high rate was in part due to unification with the former East Germany, which had almost double the rate of the former West Germany, it was now seen as the central indicator of the shortcomings of German economic institutions. For critics of German capitalism, both within and without, it became much easier to diagnose its weaknesses and compile a long list of their manifestations.

By the early 1990s, it was evident that the German model had lost much of its undisputed leadership in quality markets. German firms, accustomed to evading price competition, had neglected innovation to meet the challenge of the quickening pace of product turnover. They were also slow to adopt process innovation, especially the lean production methods of Japanese automobile firms (see the essay by Ulrich Jürgens in this volume). As competitiveness eroded for these and other reasons, especially vis-à-vis U.S. and Japanese firms, high unemployment became endemic. Neither worktime reduction nor early retirement helped prevent a further increase in unemployment. With deteriorating competitiveness in global markets, it became apparent that "improved product innovations alone would not win back a sufficiently large market share" because "labor market, training, and working time policies had reached their financial, social and other limits" and "effective cost reduction was achievable only by deregulation returning allocation decisions to market forces" (Streeck 1998, 85).

And Germany's capital market and banking system, which had long prided themselves on being prudential and patient providers of capital and managerial oversight, were now confronted with the harsh reality of a new phase of capitalism in which their virtues had become shackles seriously restricting the market-responsive flow of capital (see the essay by Sigurt Vitols in this volume). The long accustomed modus operandi of German financial institutions was now seen as a major culprit responsible for the lack of vigorous U.S.-style discipline needed in the capital market. It was also seen as the reason for a lack of venture capital, fettering the entrepreneurial vigor necessary in the global market of the new phase of capitalism.

In postbubble Japan, criticism of its institutions, both from within and from abroad, continued to intensify as the economy remained ensnared in a prolonged severe recession. Increasingly more acerbic criticisms of Japanese capitalism became all too familiar.

In the 1990s, criticism grew much harsher against the rigidity of the labor market, the long-standing financial ties maintained between the main banks and their *keiretsu* firms, intra-*keiretsu* and intraindustry cooperation of many types, close government-business relations, and excessive regulation. Put differently, as I have discussed at length elsewhere (Yamamura 1997), Japanese capitalism came in for reproof far more trenchant than ever of its long-maintained cooperative institutions because during the decade many became persuaded that cooperation—once the growth-promoting institutional advantage—had become rent-seeking exclusionary collusion, evinced in the prevalent behavior of politicians, firms, financial institutions, and bureaucrats.

As in Germany, more and more conservative politicians, business leaders, and probusiness pundits came to take active and vocal roles in berating their national version of capitalism. Self-servingly but understandably, the principal targets of their criticisms were excessive regulation of the economy and the high costs of labor (due chiefly to permanent employment and seniority-based wages) that, they argued, made large Japanese firms incapable of being as market responsive as their U.S. counterparts. As global competition continued to intensify and the Japanese economy failed to grow, their demand for fundamental changes in long accustomed practices, especially in labor markets, seemed increasingly persuasive because they could now point to the fact that Japanese firms were losing international competitiveness because of the inability of their institutions to be market-responsive.

And, we cannot but note, both in Germany and Japan, more and more of those calling for a de facto Americanization of their capitalism became more willing to draw on those parts of neoclassical economic analysis that they believed support their demand. To be sure, in enlisting the aid of selected parts of neoclassical theory, they invariably stressed their awareness of the shortcomings of the theory. However, in seeking theoretical support for their demands, they had no choice but to ignore that U.S. capitalism was able to maintain its high performance principally because industrial economies were in the breakthrough phase of a new technological paradigm, that the high U.S. performance was maintained at the cost of disparity in income and wealth distribution, and that even their preferred elements of neoclassical theory, which was now undergoing significant revision, were unable to help demonstrate an inherent, long-term superiority of more market-driven capitalism over more cooperation-based capitalism.

As the demand for making the German and Japanese economies more market-responsive grew, the forces resisting this demand remained strong in both economies. These forces are well known. Labor did its utmost to minimize the risks for income and employment; capital—investors and management—did its best to preserve various laws and practices limiting competition; and all were unwilling to see reductions in any of their institutionally embedded entitlements (e.g., subsides, pensions, and welfare payments). And in both Germany and Japan, but especially in the latter, bureaucracy only grudgingly yielded its vested rights—the turf and power that had become bloated in the cooperative capitalism of the two economies.

Another counterforce was the confidence of many Germans and Japanese in the demonstrated comparative strengths of their institutions in achieving high performance in the production of hybrid and numerous other products. Despite all the manifestations of the comparative advantage of the U.S. economy, many Germans and Japanese were aware of the indisputable global presence of the products of their automobile, machinery, electronics products, and a score of other industries. They also knew this global success was due in substantive ways to their cooperative institutions. That is, for them it was hardly necessary to examine trade data to demonstrate the still substantial strengths of many of their industries. Germans knew they had DaimlerChrysler, not ChryslerDaimler, and many Japanese were very much aware that Sony's products were in virtually every U.S. household, whereas no U.S. producer of electronics products could claim to enjoy anywhere near the same hospitality in Japanese homes.

Put differently, a large number of business and labor leaders in both economies were aware that, despite the increasingly criticized shortcomings of their institutions, not all the various efficiency-promoting capabilities of their institutions—capabilities that a very large number of scholars, pundits, and business people not only from Germany and Japan but also from the United States and elsewhere had acclaimed until the late 1980s— had abruptly become efficiency-depriving institutions in need of immediate Americanization. This was especially the case because many knew that short-term factors such as German unification and the postbubble crisis of financial institutions in Japan were responsible, to a very significant extent, for the current poor performance of their respective economies.

Still other forces resisting the fundamental transmutation of socially embedded capitalism were social contracts and social preferences that valued equity, such as that manifested in a more equal distribution of income and the minimization of risks to income and employment of wage earners. Because the contracts and preferences are deeply embedded in their respective societies, institutions in Germany and Japan that help maintain equity are highly resistant to change. Indeed, citizens in the two countries had long demonstrated their predilection toward conservativism in politics and ideology. And, we should also remember that, as in all societies, institutions in Germany and Japan are both complementary and path dependent; thus it is difficult to alter any one of them selectively or to transform their character completely within a short period.

The paths traveled by Germany and Japan since the 1980s and especially in the 1990s have been reactive, i.e., reacting to looming political-economic realities without a coherent national vision of the future, supported by a broad consensus with respect to the policies and behavior necessary to realize the vision. This, I believe, is evident in the policies that were adopted and in the changes that were seen in the behavior of industries, firms, and individuals in the German and Japanese economies.

In the 1980s, the center-right government of Helmut Kohl believed the economy, which was performing better than those of the United States and most OECD nations, required no major renovation of its institutions. The fiscal policies the government adopted to trim the increasing fiscal deficit showed it was not willing to tighten its fiscal belt to any significant extent. The other policies pursued, for example with respect to promoting innovative activities, made it clear the government was opting for palliative measures in order to offend neither business, the electoral base of the Christian Democratic Union (CDU), nor wage-earners whose votes the CDU needed.

In the 1990s, the Kohl government became preoccupied and distracted. It was preoccupied with the socioeconomic issues created by unification, the visible signs of deteriorating competitiveness of German industries (as seen in the debate on *Standort Deutschland* that began early in the decade), the need to reduce the budget deficit and adopt various harmonization measures in preparation for further integration of the EU and the introduction of the euro, and, in the final years, the necessity of coping with an electorate that seemed ready to spurn Kohl's desire to remain in office for another term.

The preoccupied government did not come to grips with the fact that capitalism had entered a new phase that required the government to take leadership in articulating a new vision and adopting policies based on it. Thus, the policies it pursued were stop-gap and expedient. For example, the tax policy of the decade can only be characterized as a series of improvised and incompatible compromises between the need to aid industries and attempts to prevent the defection of middle-income taxpayers to opposition parties in the approaching election. Various deregulation measures were adopted (e.g., in the communication and rail industries), but the government, which did not appoint its Deregulation Commission until 1987, was either slow or reluctant to adopt the recommendations of the commission. Thus, at the end of the decade, the German economy remained significantly more regulated than the Anglo-American economies.

And, as many have observed, the employment practices of firms and unions too reacted to the increasing trend of unemployment in an ad hoc fashion or, as Germans put it, by internalization of flexibility—individual employers and works councils were allowed to implement more flexibility in working hours. That is, as in the tax and deregulation policies, employment practices too were altered case by case in reaction to imminent crises—firms facing sharply increased competition and employees threatened by a high risk of unemployment (see Smith 1994).[24]

24. Few of the commission's recommendations had been implemented by the time the change in the government occurred.

Coming to power at the end of the unemployment-plagued 1990s, the government of Gerhard Schröder appeared more aware of the institutional exhaustion of German capitalism than its predecessor, as reflected in the new chancellor's frequent references to the *Neue Mitte* (new center) and by those parts of the sixty-three-page Social Democratic Party (SPD)–Green Coalition agreement that contain a lengthy list of long-term policy goals.[25]

Although it managed to enact a few laws benefiting wage earners (a modest tax cut for those earning below the median income, increased family allowances, and restoration of a few employee benefits lost under the Kohl government) within a few months of coming to power, the new coalition government quickly discovered that it was impossible to pursue a *Neue Mitte* policy course that was more mindful of the needs of business while at the same time satisfying the left wing of the SPD (which demanded a Keynesian policy of a significant wage hike to boost demand in order to reduce unemployment) and the Greens (which advocated higher taxes on petroleum, electricity, and gas as well as eliminating the nuclear energy industry in Germany as soon as possible).

At the beginning of the twenty-first century, the *Neue Mitte* has not yet been found. On one hand, the Schröder government, appointing pragmatic Hans Eichel to replace Oskar Lafontaine (its initial finance minister who pushed the agenda of the left wing of the SPD), pursued a course of fiscal policy that differed considerably from the pro-wage-earner and antibusiness policy that was anticipated from some of the SPD's campaign oratories. The budget for 2001, proposed by the finance minister and successfully enacted, contained an ambitious parcel of budget cuts enabling the government to propose tax cuts on both personal income and corporations. In short, the government seemed willing to downsize itself in the interests of letting business invest more for the sake of international competitiveness.

On the other hand, what the German chancellor does is determined (or limited) by the realities of brittle coalition politics and a fractious SPD and by the necessity of his keeping firmly in mind what he believes the voters—especially the median voters (see the essay by Herbert Kitschelt in this volume)—wish him to do. Thus, he felt obliged to step in to rescue Holzmann, a large construction firm facing financial difficulties, in order to save jobs, and he also expressed, although to no avail, strong displeasure at Vodafone's hostile takeover bid of Mannesmann.

In Japan, few substantive changes occurred in the 1980s in the policies

25. The coalition agreement is "Aufbruch und Erneuerrung—Deutschlands Weg ins 21 Jahrhundert. Koalitionsvereinbarung zwischen der Sozialdemocratischen Partei Deutschlands und Bündnis 90/die Grünen," Bonn, 20 October 1998.

adopted or in the behavior of firms. The changes that were made (e.g., the 1980 law liberalizing capital markets and the 1985 equal opportunity employment law) were more cosmetic or were designed to benefit industry instead of helping remold the entrenched character of the economy (the equal opportunity law did not have enforcement provisions). And, as the bubble began in 1987, the voices calling for fundamental changes in the institutions of postwar catch-up capitalism found few attentive listeners.

Not surprisingly, in the 1990s the policies adopted and the changes in the behavior of firms were reactive, as could be expected in an economy facing its most serious economic crisis since 1945—the consequence of suffering simultaneously both the institutional exhaustion of its model of capitalism that became all too apparent after the bubble had burst and the decade-long postbubble stagnation. The government, dominated by the Liberal Democratic Party (LDP), floundered in both fiscal and monetary policies. It wavered during most of the 1990s between fiscal reconstruction (to prevent further accumulation of national debt) by raising taxes and trimming expenditures and fiscal stimulation, an increasingly obvious need to adopt debt-financed measures to revive the economy. In coping with the growth-halting crisis of financial institutions, the government hesitated far too long before injecting public funds for fear of incurring the wrath of voters. The discount rate was sharply reduced and taxes were cut belatedly only after 1997, following a most ill-advised hike in the consumption tax. A decision to inject public money to bail out prostrated banks was not made until 1998. With the fresh memory of the punishing electoral loss suffered in the Upper House election in 1998, the LDP could not but be most cautious in steering its progrowth (probusiness) policy.

As in Germany, many firms were caught between the social contract to minimize risks to the employment and income of their employees and the evident necessity in the 1990s of being more market-responsive. However, in that decade, more and more firms chose the course of reducing employment (as seen in the rising unemployment rate) and keeping wages from rising or even reducing them. The most important reasons for such developments are the declining power of the unions due to the prolonged recession, a trend of falling membership, and the political decision in the mid-1980s of a large majority of unions to form Rengō, a new federation of unions aligning with conservative parties rather than with their traditional allies, the leftist parties. This development differs significantly from that in Germany where major unions could effectively flex their muscles in demanding wage hikes, as was amply demonstrated by the IG Metall in February 1999.

Despite these developments in Japan in the 1990s, the observation that firms struggled to find ways to preserve the social contract and survive in the highly competitive markets still stands. To be sure, firms reduced employment, granted few wage increases, and reduced wage costs in many other ways (e.g., introducing more productivity-based wage scales to replace seniority-based ones and rehiring near-retirement employees at reduced wage levels), but, at the same time, they were endeavoring to retain as many of their employees as possible (as seen in the low rate of interfirm mobility of employees despite the ongoing serious recession). In short, just as German firms were forced to, Japanese firms too sought ways to react to the dictates of unforgiving market forces while preserving the essential terms of the social contract.

When many other ongoing significant changes in corporate governance, the relationships between banks and firms and among firms, and the roles of the bureaucracy are added to these developments, it becomes apparent that Japan was struggling to remold itself by reacting to the harsh realities of the exhausted institutions and an economy suffering from a serious long slump. The struggle continued without the benefit of a shared vision or a broad consensus on the policies to be adopted. In summer 2001, what the mass media calls the Koizumi revolution came. Jun'ichirō Koizumi, a maverick LDP Diet member who called for a thorough reform of the Japanese political economy, was unexpectedly chosen to become the new prime minister on the strength of the support of the rank and file of the party, which in turn reflected a broad and unusually enthusiastic support of a public deeply disillusioned by the LDP policy of the recent years that had been pursued by prime ministers handpicked by faction leaders of the party.[26] Koizumi's bold proposals included the following, which by his own admission will impose significant short-run pains of increased bankruptcies among small and medium-size firms, more unemployment, and reductions in many types of subsidies and benefits: the reconstruction of national finance by severely limiting deficit spending; the reduction or reallocation of government expenditures without sanctuaries; the privatization of postal saving and numerous other public enterprises, thus reestablishing sound financial institutions by accelerating the elimination of nonperforming debts; and the thorough reform of the pension systems, national health programs, and education in order to limit expenditure and to introduce the principle of competition.

It remains to be seen how, or even whether, some or all of these proposals will be carried out, overcoming the overt and covert opposition of many in the LDP itself, the bureaucracy, and many interest groups. Given

26. Koizumi was elected the leader of the LDP in an intraparty election because he garnered a very large majority of votes from the prefectural party organs, which cast three votes each, and a minority of the elected LDP members of the Lower and the Upper houses, each of whom cast a vote. Because the LDP led a three-party coalition in power, the leader of the LDP automatically became the prime minister.

the opposition and the forces resisting changes in the core institutions of Japanese cooperation-based capitalism, it is premature indeed to speculate on the possible direct and indirect effects a success of any degree of the Koizumi revolution would have on the core institutions. The most that can be said is that Japan has finally begun an earnest search for a vision of the future.[27]

The foregoing characterizations of developments in Germany and Japan can be criticized as being one of the many possible characterizations possible, based only on very limited observations. However, what is important is not how many differing characterizations of developments in Germany and Japan are possible. Rather, no one can deny that, despite the ongoing intensive debate on how each nation can or should best remold its institutions, the policies and practices adopted by Germany and Japan since the 1970s have predominantly been makeshift and expedient reactions attempting to respond to imminent exigencies—lagging economic performance and the manifest challenges faced by their version of capitalism in the new phase of capitalism.

This is to be expected because neither Germany nor Japan has reached a broad consensus among its citizens about changes to be made in the core institutions of their capitalism, which involve difficult trade-offs between entrenched interests and the likelihood of high economic performance in the future. Such a consensus will not resolve the conflicts of interest and ideology, but it will enable both economies to adopt more of the intelligent and farsighted policies necessary to avoid costly short-term expediencies and to find a path leading to sustained high economic performance while compromising their respective national preferences as minimally as possible.

We can readily envision two sharply contrasting outcomes if Germany or Japan fails to achieve a broad consensus, based on a shared vision for the future, on necessary changes in policy and behavior. One outcome is that their capitalism in the coming decades will increasingly resemble that of the United States. In this outcome, the economy will be better able to realize the gains of more market-driven uses of resources and of enhanced societal capability to make breakthough (as opposed to normal) innovations. The costs of achieving these gains will be the forfeiting of much of the long-term strengths of their more cooperative capitalism and the effective abrogation of the enduring social contract. The gains realized will be significantly diminished when the breakthrough phase of the new techno-

27. Of many sources on the most recent developments in Japan, one of the most useful is a special issue on various aspects of the Koizumi revolution in *Ekonomisuto* (3 July 2001, pp. 22–35, 72–88).

logical paradigm comes to its inevitable end, and the costs will loom even larger when the maturation phase of the new technological paradigm arrives, as it did in the preceding two technological paradigms.

The other possible outcome resulting from a failure of Germany or Japan to reach a broad consensus is that, except for superficial or makeshift changes, the core institutions of their economies will remain essentially unchanged. In this case, in the ongoing breakthrough phase of the new technological paradigm (the phase that has a high likelihood of lasting longer than in the preceding paradigms), the two economies will see their current economic performance, much less robust than that achieved today in the United States, continue in the decades to come. This is because in this scenario the economy can only suffer the irreparable deterioration of its capabilities to achieve a high performance when the maturation phase of the new technological paradigm arrives. And the lessened prospect of high and sustained economic performance means a diminished capability to preserve the social contract.

However, we are not likely to see either of these outcomes in Germany or Japan. The Americanization of German and Japanese capitalism will not occur because the core institutions of the two economies are deeply embedded and path dependent and because the confidence in their long-term strengths, albeit severely challenged, has not been lost. These institutions will not remain unchanged because the costs of not responding to the hurricane of market forces unleashed by globalization of the economy and the digital revolution are extremely high. Nor will we observe the ideal outcome of expeditiously changing policies and behavior to remold the core institutions with a support of a large majority of citizens in pursuit of a widely shared vision of the future. Instead, we will see both Germany and Japan continuing to struggle, as expected of democracies with kinetic party politics, in search of a compromise—a modus vivendi feasible in domestic politics and possible for a government whose sovereignty has been much reduced by increased global competition and the World Trade Organization (WTO) and other international regimes (including the EU for Germany).

We cannot predict what this modus vivendi will involve. It may steadily edge toward a consensus and a vision of the future or reveal an inability to make such progress (thus bringing forth one of the possible contrasting two outcomes). We will be able to assess it only ex post (i.e., sometime in the future) by reviewing the footprints it has left—the policies and practices Germany and Japan have adopted.

Neither a more market-driven capitalism nor a more cooperative capitalism is superior at all times because the former excels in the breakthrough phase of a technological paradigm, but the latter flourishes in its maturation phase. Thus, the best possible modus vivendi can be achieved when decisions to alter policies and practices are made by critically assessing how the long-term strengths of cooperation-based capitalism can be best preserved. This means that decisions must be made unaffected either by the din of the triumphalism of U.S. capitalism or by the braggadocio of the recent converts to the phantasm of the new economy promising perpetual prosperity.

The Embedded Innovation Systems of Germany and Japan: Distinctive Features and Futures

Robert Boyer

As far back as the 1960s, U.S. and British scholars saw "miracles" everywhere outside the United States and United Kingdom and were eager to capture the distinctive features that enabled European countries and Japan to achieve impressive macroeconomic performances. The picture was reversed in the 1990s when U.S. scholars saw economic failures everywhere in the world except North America. The density of coordinating mechanisms that provide alternatives to market adjustment was seen as an obstacle to the fast reactions required in an uncertain world and to the quick implementation of innovations associated with a new productive paradigm. Then, the bursting of the Internet bubble in the United States in the early 2000s again challenged received wisdom. Such an abrupt and radical reversal deserves explanation.

The theoretical issues involved relate to the theory of economic and social systems and especially to the nature, variety, and evolution of capitalism. Is there a single best capitalism? If so, why should national economies differ? Do globalization and information-related technologies make for the superiority of a specific brand of capitalism? The questions, however, cannot be resolved at this level of generality. This analysis therefore focuses on a specific problem: whether the impressive economic comeback in the 1990s of the United States is related to the superiority of its technological and scientific organization. If it is, should other countries, such as Japan and Germany, try to emulate its institutions, including the organization of universities, patenting, risk capital, and research and development policy?

Given the primacy attributed to innovation in contemporary discussions

147

about competitiveness and growth, it is promising to compare the characteristics of scientific and technological systems in Germany and Japan to those of other major developed countries. Generally speaking, the success of neo-Schumpeterian ideas has popularized the view that macroeconomic performances—growth, employment, external trade, and even low inflation—are closely related to the ability of national systems to convert scientific and technological advances into sources of competitiveness.

Economists have built a new framework for analyzing growth, suggesting that innovation is endogenous and responds to research and development's (R&D's) being relatively profitable, compared to the production of standard goods, because it delivers new goods or new techniques. Basically, this replaces the linear model, which moves from science to technology to economic performance, with an interactive configuration, in which innovation reacts quickly to changing relative prices and expected demand. There is a large spectrum of such endogenous growth models that focus on a single causal factor, be it quality improvements, radical innovation, human capital, or even public infrastructures. By contrast, the analysis in this chapter adopts a more eclectic view according to which innovation may have various sources. It may result from a pure division of labor effect à la Adam Smith, incrementally from the initiative of skilled and committed workers, or from radically new inventions by scientists and engineers. In such a framework, Japan and Germany clearly display different social systems of innovation, and this is why these countries showed contrasting patterns of evolution during the last quarter of the twentieth century.

But this is not the final explanation. Macroeconomic performance is not related exclusively to the quality of the social innovation system, but also to the coherence of a *régulation* mode and its relevance given the new trends of the world economy. It is thus important to analyze the similarities and differences between Germany and Japan in terms of institutional architecture. The main findings of a series of international comparisons are used here to check and interpret the results derived from the theoretical model developed by *régulation*ist research. The opposition between market and organized capitalism, or alternatively between disembedded and embedded capitalism, is shown to be too simple because it does not capture some basic differences displayed by the statistical and institutional analysis.

Another important analytical point is why and how a successful institutional architecture may trigger a slow process that finally destabilizes the previous economic virtuous circle. This dialectic is particularly enlightening for the comparison between Germany and Japan. The actual sources of structural crisis are different in each country; Germany and Japan do not suffer solely from not being typical market-led capitalist systems, such as the United States. Given this diagnosis, economic policies may be contemplated that are largely idiosyncratic to each country. Thus it is not at all necessary to develop carbon copies of the U.S. institutions supposedly at the origin of the impressive success of the country's social systems of innovation and growth performance. Rather it is possible to design incremental reforms for each country, in innovation and general economic policy, to promote competitiveness and faster growth. Such a strategy is perfectly compatible with international competition between distinctive socioeconomic systems, which means that institutional convergence is not at all a logical outcome of globalization. A short conclusion sums up the main findings in terms of economic theory, institutional design, and innovation policy, as well as with respect to general economic reform.

From Science and Technology to Macroeconomic Performance: Japan and Germany Compared

The diversity of categories and dimension, and the scattered distribution of countries on them, make a synthesis desirable to address the core issue of the basic institutions of capitalism. This is the aim of *régulation* theory. Although first designed to understand the long-term transformation of U.S. capitalism, it can also be used to compare various contemporary economies (Aglietta 1982; Barou and Keizer 1984; Baslé, Mazier, and Vidal 1999; Boyer 1990; Boyer and Saillard 2001). Five institutional arrangements determine how social and economic relationships are structured: the monetary regime, the wage-labor nexus, the form of competition, the character of citizen-state relations, and the nexus to the world economy. The issue is whether the different institutions, which result from past social and political conflicts and structural crises, coalesce into a coherent *régulation* mode in the short term and into a stable accumulation regime, or growth pattern, in the long term.

Neoclassical growth theories once considered scientific advance and technical change as pure public goods, freely available, with no adoption costs. Thus the potential for growth was basically similar as soon as the same investment strategy was followed. By contrast, neo-Schumpeterian and neoinstitutionalist economists think the dynamism and direction of innovation is governed by certain basic institutions and institutional incentives. Growth patterns are thus not purely technologically but also institutionally driven. By implication, the concept of a production function, shifted according to total factor productivity increases, is replaced by that of a productivity regime (Boyer 1988), which consists of relevant factors determining the size of increasing returns to scale, the intensity of capital formation, the efforts in R&D expenditures, or the competence of workers.

Neoclassical reasoning suggests there is a single optimum method for organizing innovation and production. Since the 1980s, however, it has been recognized that science- and technology-related activities are organized differently in different institutional settings across nations and regions. Christopher Freeman (1987) was among the first to analyze the specificity of the Japanese innovation system and its relation to the catching-up process. Since then, various comparative analyses of national systems of innovation have provided additional results (Lundvall 1988, 1992; Nelson 1988, 1993; Nelson and Rosenberg 1993; Organization for Economic Cooperation and Development [OECD] 1997a, 1997c, 1997d). The present chapter builds on two previous works that suggest an interpretation of the major social systems of innovation and their contribution to macroeconomic performance during the 1990s (Amable, Barré, and Boyer 1997; Boyer and Didier 1998).

Skill-Induced Innovations in Different Institutional Settings

It has frequently been argued that U.S. mass production techniques required a strong polarization of skills. On the one hand, highly educated workers organize firms, make strategic decisions, and define very precisely the task content of jobs. On the other hand, less or poorly educated workers are hired to comply with the rules set by foremen, technicians, and managers. This was the objective of Taylorism and then Fordism (Boyer and Durand 1997).

Most European countries and Japan have, however, not followed the same industrialization pattern, and the erosion or destruction of the competence of blue-collar workers has nowhere gone as far as in the United States. This is confirmed by many comparative studies between France and Germany and between France and Japan (Lanciano, Nohara, and Verdier 1998). Japan and Germany share the same concern for upgrading the skills of rank-and-file workers, and this plays a significant role in the nature of innovation and the growth process.

But do German and Japanese institutions governing the skill-labor nexus exhibit the same configuration? A comparison of educational systems, training schemes (Caroli 1994), industrial relations, and the internal organization of firms suggests that the two systems rely on different mechanisms and labor mobility systems. This is the outcome of a long historical process in each country (Thelen and Kume 2001).

In Japan, the educational system delivers a high level of general knowledge that is more equally distributed than in most other countries. Firms hire young people according to their school achievements and then promote on-the-job training by task rotation, internal career paths, and high employment stability. Innovations proposed by workers are as a result largely specific to each firm or even factory. Wage systems are designed to deliver incentives for the continuous improvement of skills (Koike 1987).

In the German system, firms belonging to the same industry participate in a dual training system, which combines the creation of theoretical competencies with practical apprenticeship. This system produces skills that can be used by different firms, and workers with the same training get the same wage because collective bargaining is organized so as to promote homogeneity across firms. Portable skills go along with sectoral wage negotiations and the absence of a seniority wage. Wage disparity is limited in Germany compared to Japan, and external mobility is not an obstacle to skill formation.

This brief summary of previous research (Boyer 2000a; Boyer and Caroli 1993) raises an interesting question for comparative institutional analysis. Are identical institutions required for given macroeconomic consequences or may similar outcomes be produced by different arrangements? The question is especially relevant to the issue at hand. Given that the Japanese and German economies share many features, and thus are significantly different from the U.S. and British economies, why do their growth patterns differ?

Distinct Long-Term Growth Trajectories

Both economies were latecomers to industrialization, which took place later in Germany than in Britain and later still in Japan, where the end of World War II triggered an unprecedented transformation of industrial and social organization. Still, a careful comparison suggests many differences between the two countries, as seen in table 5.1.

First, science and technology have a far longer legacy in Germany than in Japan, where authorities have been eager to import the relevant scientific and technological advances from abroad since the Meiji period (1868–1912). By contrast, Germany has long been a world leader in basic research, achieving radical innovations and market penetration of new products. At the end of the nineteenth century, the basic chemical industry made significant advances in the research laboratories of large German companies, in close connection with public policy (Lenoir 1998). Interestingly, the quality of the link between public research and private firms may have declined in the second half of the twentieth century, and this seems to have had adverse consequences for German economic performance (OECD 1998).

A second difference relates to engineering. Germany has benefited from a century of indigenous achievements, whereas Japan used reverse engineering to reach the technological frontier by the end of the 1970s. A study of industrial structures suggests that Germany's specialization was

Table 5.1 Structural Changes and Catching Up in Japan and Germany

	Germany	Japan
Contribution of science to growth	Invented research by universities and institutes, directed toward economic activity	Small during the catching-up period
Contribution of technology	In most sectors, technology domestically generated and located at the technological frontier for decades	Permanent process of learning by importing foreign technologies; technological frontier not reached until 1980s
Intensity of structural change	Large stability in the distribution of competitive advantage across industries	Very rapid from 1950s until mid-1980s, a shift of leading sectors
Nature of foreign trade	Highly diversified industrial structure and exports	Concentration of exports in a restricted number of industries and large firms
Intensity of foreign trade	Very high exports per capita; search for competitiveness permeates most national organizations	Moderate exports per capita, domestic demand important except during specific periods (oil shocks, etc.)
Nature of growth regime	Based on servicing and quality of differentiated goods with significant oligopolistic power in world markets	Based on increasing returns to scale and pricing to market

stable for nearly a century, whereas Japan quickly evolved from one leading sector to another during the twentieth century (Ifo Institut für Wirtschaftsforschung and Sakura Institute of Research 1997).

The role of foreign trade has been important for both countries in the postwar decades, but the leading role of exports and competitiveness is much more permanent and significant for Germany than for Japan. Exports per capita are far higher for Germany, and export-led growth was not central for Japanese long-term growth, except in the 1970s and 1980s (Uemura 2000). Furthermore, the domestic market is traditionally much more open in Germany than in Japan. Another important difference is that Japanese exports are concentrated in three major sectors (cars, consumer electronics, and electronic and mechanical equipment goods), whereas German trade is highly diversified, with the direct participation of many small and medium-size firms.

It should be no surprise, then, that the growth regimes of the two countries are dissimilar: efforts to catch up quickly and a strong role for increasing returns to scale for the Japanese manufacturing sector (Kumon and Rosovsky 1992) compare with a permanent search for differentiated, high-quality market niches for German manufacturing (Keck 1993). As a result,

price formation is different: whereas German firms have adopted oligopolistic pricing to preserve high and stable profits (Aglietta, Orléan, and
Oudiz 1980), Japanese firms pursue a strategy of pricing to the market,
offering competitive prices in each national market in order to increase
market share (Ito 1992).

The Patterns of Innovation and Growth

The contribution of the alternative innovation systems to growth can be
assessed by a formal model (Boyer and Caroli 1993, 50–58). In the eclectic
approach of this model, innovation is associated with three sources: increasing returns to scale brought about by an extended division of labor,
incremental innovations proposed by rank-and-file workers, and more radical innovations developed by researchers and implemented by engineers.
The growth pattern observed is then related to the efficiency of the training system, the ability to pay for this training, the degree of cooperation
between managers and blue-collar workers, and the growth trend in world
markets and the size of increasing returns to scale.

How Do Japan and Germany Differ?

To investigate whether the Japanese and German economies display similar characteristics, let us consider in turn the magnitude of the increase in
returns to scale, the contribution of skilled workers to productivity, and the
innovations generated by engineers and scientists. To highlight both similarities and differences between Germany and Japan, the United States,
France, and Great Britain are used for comparison.

Returns to Scale

The renewed interest of economists in growth and endogenous technical change (Barro and Sala-I-Martin 1995) has placed new emphasis on the
issue of the size of scale economies. Generally speaking, they are supposed
to be important enough to propel endogenous growth, in contrast to the
view expressed by Robert Solow (1956) in a seminal study. But little rigorous research has been done to investigate the empirical relevance of
increasing returns to scale and the importance of mechanisms associated
with patenting, higher education, and static and dynamic increasing
returns. In many cases, econometric studies do not confirm the core
hypotheses of the new endogenous growth theory (Boyer and Juillard
1991; Amable and Juillard 1995), and many other mechanisms seem to
have more explanatory power (Sala-I-Martin 1997). One reason for these

Table 5.2 Estimates of Returns to Scale for Five Countries[a]

	Germany	Japan	United States	France	United Kingdom
Manufacturing					
Short run	0.14	0.72*	0.17*	0.46*	0.37*
	(1.3)	(9.2)	(2.1)	(9.5)	(4.2)
Long run	0.07	0.63*	0.33*	0.37*	0.69*
	(0.3)	(4.9)	(2.1)	(5.1)	(4.3)
Whole economy					
Short run	0.16	0.50*	0.19	0.40*	0.50*
	(1.4)	(5.0)	(1.9)	(3.6)	(6.0)
Long run	0.38	n.a.	0.48	0.58	0.31
	(1.5)		(1.8)	(4.4)	(1.2)

Source: Derived from Amable (1989).

[a] * indicates significance at 5 percent threshold; n.a., not available. Short run means annual variations from 1960 to 1986; long run means variations over complete cycles that have been detected for each national economy. The estimates presented in this table are parameter a in the equation $g = a\dot{D} + b$ where g is the rate of growth of total factor productivity and $\dot{D}$ the rate of growth of output. Numbers in parentheses are t-values. For a complete discussion of the theoretical and empirical background for this equation, see Boyer and Petit (1991).

disappointing results might be that cross-national econometric studies assume the same parameters for all economies, although these mechanisms appear to be quite different from one country to another.

Whereas Japan, and to a lesser extent France and the United Kingdom, exhibit the largest increasing returns to scale for the manufacturing sector (table 5.2),[1] Germany is a complete exception. For both the manufacturing sector and the whole economy, there is no increasing returns-to-scale effect, neither in the short nor the medium term (i.e., over a complete business cycle). This major difference is confirmed by econometric studies on Japan (Uemura 2000; Uni 2000), analyses of the organization of the Japanese firm (Aoki 1994b), and general studies about the sources of Japanese growth (Imai and Komiya 1994; Odagiri 1992); no econometric study has been able to reveal significant increasing returns to scale for Germany, which is consistent with the nature of German specialization on the production of differentiated quality goods (Streeck 1997c).

Worker Training

Fordist industrial relations display a very specific pattern—the frequency of training once employees have been hired increases with the

1. These effects still exist at the level of the whole economy with a coefficient of approximately 0.5, i.e., typically the value expected according to a Kaldor-Verdoorn law linking productivity to growth (Boyer and Petit 1991; Kaldor 1966).

educational level attained by individuals before they first enter the labor market (OECD 1991, 159). The United States and France are very good examples of this—more educated individuals get more lifelong training; others get less. This is strong evidence that managers, engineers, and technicians have a major role in technological change and not just in management tasks (Boyer 2000a).

German industrial relations, by contrast, are typically different. The less educated workers get more training than the most educated. This fits the basic hypothesis that in this country rank-and-file workers have a say in work organization and innovation because the dual system gives them knowledge about the content of their work; if they do not have that knowledge, the firm provides extra training. Clearly, the production of differentiated quality goods calls for the high and widely distributed competence of the whole workforce.

The Japanese employment system exhibits hybrid features. On one hand, the general level of training is very high and this is compatible with the findings of many comparative international studies (Koike 1987) that a high employment stability of core workers induces substantial on-the-job training and the formation of firm-specific knowledge. On the other hand, in contrast to Germany, workers with higher educational levels get still more training from the firm, which demonstrates some similarity to the U.S. configuration. This is why the Japanese configuration may be labeled a hybrid (Boyer et al. 1998). Statistical investigations about lifelong training confirm that such features were still present during the 1990s (OECD 1999c).

Innovation by Engineers

If we assume that efforts in R&D and engineering can be captured by the share of scientists, engineers, and R&D personnel in total employment (European Commission 1997), it is surprising that the density of R&D personnel is nearly the same for each of the countries compared here, except the United Kingdom. This may imply that similar definitions have been used across OECD countries, in spite of different institutional configurations. As seen in table 5.3, Japan displays some typical features that are important for the dynamism of innovation. In this country, more than 93 percent of total R&D personnel work for private firms, the highest rate among OECD countries. Econometric studies confirm that the rate of return on privately funded and operated R&D investment is higher than for research with public funding or in public institutes (Amable and Boyer 1992). This gives an advantage to the Japanese innovation system, which is clearly more market-oriented than the British one.

Table 5.3 Direction and Intensity of Efforts in Scientific and Technological Systems (%)

	Total Effort		Business Orientation Index		Business-Oriented Effort	
	R&D Personnel/ Total Employment	Scientists and Engineers/ Total Employment	R&D Personnel in Firms/ Total R&D Personnel	Scientists and Engineers in Firms/Total Scientists and Engineers	R&D Personnel in Firms/ Employment Total	Scientists and Engineers in Firms/ Employment Total
Germany	1.32	0.64	85.0	56.1	1.12	0.36
Japan	1.28	0.86	93.2	69.6	1.19	0.60
United States[a]	n.a.	0.81	n.a.	79.4	n.a.	0.64
France	1.43	0.68	78.4	44.7	1.12	0.30
United Kingdom	1.09	0.57	87.6	57.0	0.95	0.32

Source: Computed from European Commission (1997, S-25, S-27, S-29, S-33, S-35).
[a] n.a., not applicable.

Japan also has the highest proportion of scientists and engineers, a little above the United States, which leads in basic science and in the exploration of frontier technologies in many sectors. But this does not necessarily mean the Japanese innovation system is stronger than the U.S. one. We see why not if we compare the relative productivity of both basic science and applied research in OECD countries (table 5.4). Of course it is not easy to measure the productivity of R&D personnel, and this is still more difficult for academic research. The incentive to patent is related to the ability and interest in codifying advances in knowledge, a factor that varies widely among innovation systems. If we assume, however, that this incentive is similar for all countries, both Japan and Germany exhibit good patenting performance, whereas France and the United Kingdom are lagging (unfortunately, the variable cannot be computed for the United States).

The picture is different for academic research because the publication performance of Japan is far inferior to that of Germany, and the gap is still wider in terms of citations. Here the British and U.S. systems seem to be more productive, and the position of France and Germany is in between. The recurrent worries of Japanese authorities about the management of universities and research institutes in their country are confirmed (Hirasawa 1998; Koyama 1994; Okubo 1996; Sato 1998). But it must be remembered that strength in basic research is only partially and indirectly linked to economic performance because it concerns only sectors in which innovation is directly science-pushed.

Table 5.4 R&D Personnel Compared to Scientists and Engineers (1993–95)

| | Research and Development | | | Science and Technology | | |
| | | Productivity | | | Productivity | |
	Number of R&D Personnel	U.S. Patents/ 1,000 R&D Personnel	European Patents/ 1,000 R&D Personnel	Number of Scientists and Engineers	Number of Publications/ 1,000 Scientists and Engineers	Number of Quotations/ 1,000 Scientists and Engineers
Germany	475,016	12.9	30.9	229,837	200	782
Japan	826,656	26.1	14.0	551,990	95	296
United States[a]	n.a.	n.a.	n.a.	962,700	210	1,137
France	315,159	8.3	18.7	149,193	245	899
United Kingdom	277,000	8.0	20.6	145,752	373	1,543

Source: Computed from European Commission (1997, A3.1, A3.5, A5.1, A5.3, A6.2, A6.5).
[a] n.a., not applicable.

The Japanese Growth Slow-Down: Fordist and Post-Fordist Sources of Technical Change

Even though a complete quantitative evaluation of the parameters is not always possible, previous institutional analyses and statistical indicators (Caroli 1994) have shown that the configuration of the Japanese economy is distinctive. First, its manufacturing sector features, as previously noted, the highest level of increasing returns to scale. This is the major difference between Japan and Germany and may explain why the Japanese economy grew faster after World War II.

Second, microcorporatism and companyism (Yamada 2000) are associated with more cooperative industrial relations, a positive factor for the acceptance of innovations originating from blue-collar workers. Also, given the stability of employment, large firms are willing to finance on-the-job training as well as professional training. Because decisions are made at the firm level, we observe in Japan a good match between efforts to upgrade skills and the requirements of firms. And, given the diffusion and quality of general education, shop-floor workers are able to make many suggestions for marginal but continuous improvements. The Japanese potential for this kind of technical change is better than that of the United States and France, which rely mainly on the expansion of markets and on innovations by engineers.

Third, the productivity of Japanese engineers and R&D personnel is good. This feature was important during the 1970s and 1980s because it allowed the Japanese manufacturing sector to combine scale and scope economies and product and process innovations (Nonaka 1994). Japanese firms even developed original approaches to the design of complex systems, mixing many competencies and sectors (Kodama 1995). But in the 1990s, the relative weakness of basic research may have hindered further growth, especially to the extent that a new productive paradigm based on scientific advances came to dominate.

Given the relative intensity of these three mechanisms, it turns out that before 1973, Japanese growth was achieved mainly through quasi-Fordist mechanisms, with a limited contribution from other sources of technical change. This implies that a slowdown in growth is especially detrimental for the Japanese economy, which is best at achieving the largest productivity increases when growth is rapid and when it is aided by growth of the world economy—that is, when it can best benefit from Fordist effects as well as from fast technical change originating in the skill-labor nexus. This is why Japan was able to achieve a very high average real growth rate of 9.3 percent per year during the 1950–73 period. This was not merely a catching-up effect; for instance, the United Kingdom was unable in the same period to speed up technical change in its effort to converge toward U.S. productivity standards. Clearly, the configuration of the skill-labor nexus matters.

The strong dependence of Japan on the growth of the world economy is a major drawback. After the two oil shocks of the 1970s, the growth rate of the Japanese economy decelerated to 3.9 percent for 1973–89. Technical change induced by the skill-labor nexus remains important, but it is not sufficient to counterbalance the negative impact of the crisis of the international regime. Although both countries benefit from good training systems, this Fordist feature distinguishes Japan from Germany, which has built its growth mainly on the quality and differentiation of manufactured goods. That is, whereas Japan's growth performance depended on the volume and cost of standardized goods, for Germany the slowdown in the volume of world trade had fewer detrimental effects, but intensifying competition focused more and more on quality and innovation. Whereas the high-growth period revealed some similarities between Germany and Japan, the post-1973 period and still more the 1990s exacerbated their differences. Therefore they will not necessarily experience the same future.

Two *Régulation* Modes and Distinctive Crises

Any prospective analysis calls for a clear understanding of the logic of the systems under review. Thus, let us examine the various conclusions

Table 5.5 Germany and Japan Compared: The Five Institutional Forms[a]

	GERMANY		JAPAN
Skill-labor nexus			
Skills	High skills at the shop-floor level		
Work organization	Relative autonomy of workers		
Labor mobility	Internal and external	⟷	Internal and organized
Wage formation	Sectorally negotiated, with a concern for competitiveness	⟷	Synchronized, but at the firm level
Welfare	Large, universal, and institutionalized	⟷	Small, unequal, and company-based
Form of competition			
Internal	Organized competition		
External	A significant degree of price control	⟷	Pricing to the market, in order to increase market shares
Monetary regime			
Status	Independent with the objective of low inflation	⟷	Strong influence of Ministry of Finance, a concern for growth and stability
Exchange-rate policy	From under- to overvaluation		
	Deutschmark, a strong currency	⟷	Yen, a pragmatic approach
State and the economy	State required for long-term structural decisions		
Volume of redistribution	Large and institutionalized	⟷	Small, few entitlements
Nature of state intervention	Extended regulation organizing the balance of relative power of actors	⟷	Administrative guidance, via regulation and ad hoc interventions
Insertion into the world economy	Competitiveness important for macroeconomic evolution		
Degree of openness	Significant but balanced by European integration	⟷	Rather low, but low institutionalization of Asian links

[a] The grey area indicates similarity of institutional forms; the arrows indicate differences.

about the diversity of capitalism, the variety of scientific and technological systems, the heterogeneity of the basic institutional forms, and the existence of different growth patterns.

Common Functional Features, but Different Architectures

Germany and Japan display both converging patterns and clear differences across five institutional forms, as summarized in table 5.5: the skill-labor nexus, the form of competition, the monetary regime, the state-economy relationship, and the link between the domestic economy and the world economy.

The skill-labor nexus in the two countries deviates from typical Fordism because the deskilling of blue-collar workers and the implementation of strong hierarchies are mitigated by the influence of efficient education and training systems. Nevertheless, the precise mechanisms governing labor mobility and wage formation are quite different. External mobility seems to be more important in Germany; seniority wages are more significant in Japan, welfare is company-based in Japan, but universal and state-based in Germany; and the structure of wage bargaining is different, even if the common outcome is synchronized wage hikes. The difference in the skill-labor nexus between the two countries plays an important role in short-term adjustments—there is more labor hoarding in Japan and more open unemployment in Germany.

In both Germany and Japan, competition is more organized (i.e., more limited) than in the Anglo-American economies because large firms, business associations, and public regulation influence price formation and market dynamics. The banking system used to have a monitoring role in the management of industrial firms, with limited influence of the stock markets; these became very strong in the United States and United Kingdom during the 1990s. But the degree of external competition is quite different. In the mid-1980s, unlike Japanese manufacturing firms, which adopted a pricing to market strategy, German manufacturing firms benefited from significant oligopolistic rents in relation to the quality of goods and related services.

The monetary regimes differ too. In Germany, the Bundesbank was independent from the Ministry of Finance and has built its credibility on the ideal of price stability, even though it was only partially fulfilled, especially after unification. The Bank of Japan, conversely, has long been subject to the influence of the Ministry of Finance and seems to have a more eclectic approach to monetary policy in that growth, credit, and the stability of the financial system appear to be objectives of monetary policy.

The relationships between state and economy show both similarities and differences. In Germany and Japan, the state does not limit itself to enforcing property rights and minimal preconditions for market relations, but it provides structural conditions for long-term growth. After World War II, the Japanese government adopted a developmentalist strategy; in Germany, a balanced organization of economic, social, and political interests promoted stability by creating the condition for the adoption of long-term strategies by private agents. The accords between state and citizen, however, are different. Whereas Germany has built an exemplary welfare state and quasi-universal social security, Japan still provides social welfare highly differentiated by the size of firms, a system that can be labeled industrial welfare (Hanada and Hirano 2000, 87–103). The aging of the populations of the two countries might be a common challenge, but the institutional reforms undertaken are different.

The link between the home economy and the rest of the world is essential in both countries because competitiveness is seen as a key factor that shapes the organization of firms as well as macroeconomic evolution. Nevertheless, the external context is significantly different because the degree of openness of the two economies differs—high and increasing for Germany, modest and more uneven for Japan. Thus the external relations of the German economy are increasingly governed by the rules of the European Single Market. Under these rules, each national economy tends to become one region inserted into an embryonic federal state, at present visible only in the common European monetary policy and, to a lesser extent, the joint competition policy enforced by Brussels (Boyer 2000b). By contrast, the Asian environment of Japan is mainly shaped by the strategy of large Japanese corporations organizing a division of labor within the region in reaction to the evolution of production costs, the dynamism of various national markets, and the variation of exchange rates (Y. Inoue 2000).

Two *Régulation* Modes and Growth Regimes

The preceding analyses lead us to conclude that capitalism in Germany and capitalism in Japan are far from identical in their institutional architectures. In Germany, the *régulation* mode is a mix of social democratic features based on frequent and explicit negotiations among social partners with strong public intervention at two levels (federal and *Länder;* Streeck 1997c). In the Japanese system, the state is less a leader than a catalyst and lubricant of the initiatives of large corporations, which tend to organize not only economic life but also the very socialization process and in some cases political governance itself. This architecture has been called companyist (Yamada 2000). Such a corporate-led *régulation* mode has very different properties than a social or public one; exposed to the same external shock—for instance, an exogenous appraisal of the exchange rate—the reaction of key macroeconomic variables is very different.

Consequently, crises in the two *régulation* modes differ. An appraisal of the German and Japanese currencies against the dollar does not trigger the same reaction in manufacturing activity because the formation of export prices is not identical. German firms used to be price makers, but their oligopolistic power has eroded, which exacerbates the unemployment problem caused by job loss in the manufacturing sector. In contrast, the pricing-to-market strategy of Japanese firms enables them to moderate the effects of export slowdowns. Japanese firms can adopt this strategy because their control over their domestic market can contain the erosion of profit margins on their exports.

Also, the wage-labor nexus and related labor-market institutions are distinctive, which introduces an important difference in macroeconomic dynamics. Slow European growth as well as the characteristics of its wage-labor nexus explain rising unemployment in Germany, first after the two oil shocks and still more during the 1990s. High unemployment, in turn, strains the financing of welfare and public budgets. By contrast, just before the financial bubble burst in Japan in the early 1990s, manufacturing firms experienced labor scarcity because fewer young workers were ready to accept the stress and strain inherent in the Japanese wage-labor nexus.

Most important, the growth regimes themselves are different. The German regime is built on the search for a quality premium for differentiated goods, well tuned to the demand of each segment of the market. The Japanese growth regime, by comparison, was much more dynamic because it relies on increasing returns to scale. The evolution of the world economy does therefore not have identical consequences for each country.

Here a specific feature of *régulation* theory needs to be underscored. Most other approaches look at different countries as unequal approximations or imperfections of a single model, which should ideally apply to any country. This is strongly challenged both by careful qualitative examination and by quantitative studies. Even in the era of globalization, or more rigorously in the context of new and extended interdependency, national trajectories remain distinctive. They are the direct expression of the fact that history matters, in terms of polity, economy, and society.

Structural Crises with Different Origins

It is therefore not very enlightening to argue, as many scholars do, that contemporary Germany and Japan suffer from an inability of their institutional arrangements to converge toward market-led forms. The many differences in their institutional forms call for different explanations for the destabilization and seemingly slow reform of the institutional architecture in both countries.

The skill-labor nexus is subjected to different pressures. In Germany the role of unions is so deeply embedded in a web of institutions and rules of the game that workers still have strong bargaining power, in spite of rising unemployment. However, a structural weakness has resulted from unification and the related overvaluation of the deutschmark. Unsuccessful attempts to find alternative compromises suggest that the crisis of the German skill-labor nexus is now fully developed. In Japan, a continuous decline in union density and the fact that unions are organized at the firm level explain why adjustments to the oil shocks, to the development of the exchange rate, and even to the drastic growth slowdown were compatible with near-stability of the companyist compromise (Boyer and Juillard 2000). This is in spite of the frequent dramatic statements found in the mass media about its irreversible collapse or obsolescence.

Both countries suffer from a shift in the form of competition at the world level, but differently. German manufacturing is adversely affected by the evolution of the international economy as a result of a declining demand for capital goods, a traditional German strength. But there are also internal sources of erosion. Combining mechanics and electronics turned out to be difficult because the electronic sector is weak in Germany. Thus Japanese manufacturers have challenged the position of German firms not only in the car industry but also in capital goods. For Japan, the basic change is the slowdown in the world market, reinforced, of course, by the appreciation of the yen and the catching up of Japanese manufacturing wages. Also, pressure from the United States, and to some extent from Europe, to open the Japanese domestic market has weakened the counterweighting mechanisms that used to prevail between domestic and export prices.

The monetary regimes have also followed different trajectories. Japan's economic policy was probably the most Keynesian among OECD countries during the 1990s. No fewer than eight deficit-financed expansionary budgets were adopted, and interest rates were drastically reduced toward zero by the end of the decade. Authorities perceived a possible financial meltdown and subsequent depression caused by deepening deflation as the main danger. Unfortunately, the stimulus provided by a huge increase in public debt has not delivered the expected outcomes. In the same period, the Bundesbank stressed the danger of inflation, especially after German unification. This brought extensive restructuring that generated public deficits. To comply with the Maastricht Treaty, German authorities followed a rather restrictive policy in the second half of the 1990s, which allowed the launching of the euro in 1999. Thus the monetary regimes of the two countries have become dissimilar—Germany has lost its domestic basis in favor of a common, quasi-federal monetary approach (Boyer 1999a), whereas the yen is still an independent currency.

The financial regimes of the two countries have undergone significant structural transformations since the 1980s. A common feature is the internationalization of the adjustment of saving and investment, which was enhanced by financial innovation, deregulation, and globalization of individual markets. Both Germany and Japan experienced a net outflow of investment, but for different reasons. Given current costs, regulations, and long-term prospects for growth in Europe, many large German firms go abroad or seek joint ventures in order to capture new markets by producing outside Germany at competitive prices. Since the mid-1980s, Japanese firms have also opened factories abroad to lower production costs, benefit from new domestic markets protected by national authorities, and organize a new international division of labor, especially among Asian countries. But the fragility of the Japanese financial system and the very low rate of return at home have caused large net capital outflows, whereas such a concern is not apparent in Germany. The major difference relates to the process of financial deregulation—careful and slow in Germany, bold and hasty in Japan. The German financial system therefore experienced no debt crisis, whereas Japan at the end of the 1990s was still trying to overcome the financial losses caused by the bursting of the bubble of the 1980s.

The respective crises of state and political coalitions are also different. In Germany, the system of political parties has been only marginally disturbed by the influence of the Greens, and the 1998 shift from the Christian Democratic Union to the Social Democratic Party has not drastically altered economic policy. The primary issue is about restructuring state intervention to bring back some dynamism in job creation without downsizing the welfare system; this dilemma is still to be overcome. The Japanese development involved first the breaking down of post–World War II political stability and then frequent changes of prime minister, whereas the objectives and tools of economic policy have remained essentially unchanged; they are still controlled by the various ministries, especially the Ministry of Finance. The aging of the population does not seem to have the same impact on public spending as in Germany, and the differences in welfare systems have become very apparent.

Finally, the international relations of the two countries remain different. Traditionally, Germany used to set the tune for monetary policy in Europe and its neighbors had to adjust, by sticking to the deutschmark or accepting a devaluation of their currencies. Since 1999, this asymmetry has theoretically been removed by the creation of the European Central Bank, which considers only aggregate European indexes for inflation, growth, and unemployment (European Central Bank 1999). For Japan, by comparison, the two biggest issues involve its asymmetrical relations with the United States and Asia. It is therefore quite unlikely that both countries could follow the same paths under the impact of financial globalization.

This institutional analysis confirms previous findings derived from a more focused study of the scientific and technological systems of innovation. Given these long-lasting differences and contrasting responses to the challenges of the 1990s, their convergence toward market-led capitalism is unlikely.

Japanese and German Trajectories in the Early Twenty-First Century

The 1990s seem to have brought a paradigm shift in production methods. The U.S. system is again a reference for many other OECD countries; however, the feature to be emulated is no longer mass production but instead a science-based wave of innovation, creating a cluster of sunrise industries. Are the German and Japanese innovation systems able to cope with this challenge? Should they marginally reform their *régulation* modes, or do they need to adopt U.S. institutions? If that is impossible, should they at least try to generate functional equivalents in accordance with their historical legacy?

These are difficult questions. They could be addressed by systematic comparison of science and technology policies in order to assess whether they are converging or, on the contrary, displaying strengths that cannot be easily emulated by other countries—if so, no single best way exists for technology and innovation (Benz 1998; Bruce 1998; Georghiou 1998; Rodney 1998).

This section summarizes the argument, describes the forces at work, and then extends the previous analysis to the early twenty-first century, taking into account four major factors that seem to govern the transformation of innovation systems and growth regimes.

Endogenous Structural Transformations, External Pressures and Opportunities, and the Political Ability to Work Out New Compromises

Analyses of scientific and technological advances usually imply a causality that runs from innovation to the organization of firms, then to economic performance, and finally to political institutions. Each step is assumed to be governed by an implicit economic optimizing behavior. The present approach uses a much more interactive analysis, in accordance with the meaning and objectives of the social system of innovation studies.

First of all, globalization is not a purely economic and deterministic process but is partly a matter of choice for domestic communities. For instance, the varying frequency of financial instability suggests that different regulations can be adopted that affect the emergence, or nonemergence, of structural imbalances (World Bank 1999a). Therefore, there is a link between the evolution of the national presence in the international economic system and the strategies open to domestic policy. Even given the same international environment and nearly identical economic specialization, two governments may select quite different policies. This is an important factor contributing to national differences, although of course the scope for choice may vary from one historical period to another.

A second implication of such a framework is that there is no economic determinism with respect to the future of German and Japanese capitalism. The way the political process is organized within existing institutions shapes the available options and thus makes some outcomes more likely than others. Therefore, the ability of political leaders to identify the relevant issues is more essential than ever, and the future of *régulation* modes is closely related to the intricacy of the interactions between the international arena, the domestic endogenous evolution, and finally the development of domestic political groups. For instance, small or medium-size countries, with no international ambition, may consider the rules of the game in the international arena to be given, whereas larger countries may play a role in shaping these rules. Clearly the United States belongs to the second category; the role of Japan has varied over time and is now modest. The German case is more ambiguous—by shaping the nature of the Central European Bank, the stability and growth pact governing budgetary policy at the national level, and extending the subsidiarity principle, German authorities have hoped to protect their domestic institutions even in the context of deepening European integration. Conversely, with different levels of success, French, Italian, and Spanish governments have used European monetary integration to restructure their national institutions, which had become obsolete. Such restructuring would have been much more difficult in the absence of strong external constraints.

If we adopt such an analytical framework, what prognoses can we propose for Germany and Japan? Japan and Germany can still rely on the quality of their manufacturing workforces and on marginal innovations cumulating in and generating, in the long run, high macroeconomic performance. But the contribution that increasing returns to scale can make to this is at best debatable.

For some analysts, product differentiation is at the heart of modern competition and scale effects are no longer relevant (Piore and Sabel 1984). Others point out that scope and scale effects can be and are combined. Japan was very good at this game until the 1980s (Yoshikawa 1996). If new markets for differentiated products were emerging at the world level and would stimulate growth, then the Japanese economy would be in a good position to recover its dynamism, provided that these markets were only marginally different from those already mastered by Japanese firms.

Given this context, two alternative analyses can be made of the contemporary Japanese system. On the one hand, if many sectors require extensive coordination among producers, a sharing of information and technology, rapid diffusion of innovation, and the development of common standards, then the cooperative learning typical of the Japanese governance structure may prosper (Okada 1998). On the other hand, the legacy of the bubble economy seems to have been detrimental to the compatibility between product differentiation and increasing returns to scale. More generally, some experts consider that the technological system that was so efficient for catching up became largely irrelevant in the 1990s (Katz 1998). For instance, the productivity of capital in Japan has declined, whereas it has recovered in the United States. Thus it would be desirable for Japan to look for new sources of innovation related to science and technology so as to overcome the fatigue of an aging system and make better investment decisions. But again, two conflicting mechanisms are at work.

As seen in table 5.6, Japan and Germany noticeably increased the number of R&D personnel between 1980 and 1995, at a higher rate than other large industrialized economies. Simultaneously, the ratio of patents to R&D personnel also increased during the 1990s for Japan in comparison to both the United States and Europe. The case of Germany is more difficult to assess because the efficiency of its R&D seems to have declined drastically in the highly competitive U.S. patent market while remaining the same or even rising somewhat in the European patent market. If the technological paradigm continues to be governed by marginal innovations generated by applied research, the outlook for Japan might be hopeful, but the future of Germany will be more uncertain.

However, it should be noted that in some new sectors in which spillover from basic or academic research is increasingly important, Germany is likely to outperform Japan, not so much because the number of its scientists and engineers has grown faster—this might be due to German unification—but because the productivity of German scientists and engineers in terms of publications seems significantly higher. At the same time, Germany and Japan both lag behind the United States and the United Kingdom in basic research. Thus, if growth were totally science-led in the twenty-first century, both countries would face a substantial challenge in their efforts to renew their competitive advantage.

Growth, however, is never entirely science-led. In a stable international regime, alternative sources of innovation can be drawn on by different national systems and may coexist in the long run to the extent that they are largely complementary (Amable, Barré, and Boyer 1997). A simpler argument is that it is highly unlikely anyway that all innovation will derive from basic science. In the early 1900s it was speculated that basic science would account for all innovation; this has largely been proven wrong, although science-pushed innovations may have increased in share and impact since then. In sum, diminished economic performance for Japan and, to a lesser extent, for Germany could be expected if the next productive paradigm were totally governed by basic science—but such a scenario is unlikely.

Table 5.6 Inventiveness of R&D Personnel and Scientists

	Technology (R&D Personnel)			
	Total Number	Average Annual Rate[a]	U.S. Patents[b]	European Patents[b]
Japan				
1985	669,115		23.0	8.4
1990	794,327		28.4	14.9
1995	826,656	+2.1%	26.1	14.0
Germany				
1985	390,938		18.4	20.6
1990	431,000		15.9	27.5
1995	475,016	+1.9%	12.9	30.9
France				
1985	273,014		10.1	11.1
1990	292,964		10.8	16.5
1995	315,159	+1.4%	8.3	18.7
United Kingdom				
1985	289,000		8.6	9.7
1990	275,000		8.2	14.1
1995	277,000	−0.4%	8.0	20.6

	Science (Scientists and Engineers)			
	Total Number	Average Annual Rate[a]	Publications/ Scientists and Engineers (thousands)	Quotations/ Scientists and Engineers (thousands)
Japan				
1980	298,974		90	244
1985	380,761		88	234
1990	477,866		86	284
1995	551,990	+3.8%	95	296
Germany				
1985	147,418		200	693
1990	241,869		135	571
1995	229,837	+4.5%	200	782
United States				
1980	651,200		236	1,003
1985	801,900		212	920
1990	960,500		193	988
1995	962,700	+1.8%	210	1,137
France				
1985	105,253		229	726
1990	123,938		221	824
1995	149,193	+3.9%	245	899
United Kingdom				
1985	131,000		332	1,138
1990	133,000		341	1,383
1995	147,752	+1.1%	373	1,543

Source: Computed from European Commission (1997, S-25, S-27, S-29, S-33, S-35).
[a] 1985–95.
[b] Number per R&D personnel (thousands).

Another scenario starts out with the fact that Germany and Japan are good examples of social systems of innovation with a strong spatial localization within the domestic space. But the United Kingdom, or smaller countries such as the Netherlands, Switzerland, and Denmark, are highly visible in the international flow of researchers, patents, and high-tech trade. Therefore there is an alternative to the persistence of nationally based innovation systems coherent with domestic productive systems. Large corporations could locate their research labs near the most dynamic universities, whatever their nationality, and the science sector could become as internationalized as the car or oil market is today. Thus, Japanese and German weaknesses in science-led sunrise sectors could be overcome. Science would become global, but not necessarily the production and applied research systems, which might remain largely national or regional. Empirical evidence suggests that such a process has been taking place since the mid-1980s, both for Japan (many corporations have bought small innovative firms in North America) and for Germany (there has been an impressive number of mergers with U.S. firms since the mid-1990s).

From the 1990s to the Twenty-First Century

Analysts and economists commonly imagine that future long-term trends will be similar to the most recent developments. With such a vision, it is assumed that the U.S. innovation system will continue to dominate all others by the dynamism of the virtuous circle that associates macroeconomic booms with buoyant expectations and a rise in R&D expenditures. A closer look suggests the existence of at least four countervailing factors that give the German and Japanese innovation system a chance.

Transitory Turbulence or Permanent Radical Innovations?

Since the early 1970s, a series of largely unexpected macroeconomic shocks have negatively affected *régulation* modes that used to privilege the synergy between dynamic efficiency and the reduction of social inequalities. By contrast, market-led capitalism has prospered in the face of a significant volatility of exchange rates, as well as of many other macroeconomic variables (Boyer 1999b). Furthermore, some innovation systems, such as in Germany and Japan, are good at marginal innovations, whereas others prosper in the domain of radical innovations. Thus, economies such as the United States experienced improved macroeconomic performance in a period featuring both a paradigm shift in production models and increased financial and economic uncertainty.

Table 5.7 Emerging Paradigms and Competitiveness of Social Systems of Innovation (% of GDP)

	Paradigm and Innovation System		
	Fordist—Physical Investment (1995)	Information-Led—Spending on Information (1997)	Knowledge-based—Public Education and Software (1995)
Japan	22.9	7.5	6.5
Germany	21.5	5.6	7.1
United States	19.2	7.8	8.0
France	18.1	6.4	10.2
United Kingdom	16.4	7.6	8.4

Source: OECD (1999b, 9, 21).

The early twenty-first century may, however, reverse these two changes. On the one hand, a new general production paradigm may finally emerge, led by information and communication technology (ICT) and ultimately leading to a knowledge-based economy (KBE). In this context, both the German and Japanese systems may find their plan. For instance, in the biological sector, German manufacturers may provide highly competitive instruments and machine tools, in accordance with their long-term specialization (Casper, Lehrer, and Soskice 1999). Also, Japanese and German firms might again show their potential competitiveness as the macroeconomic environment becomes more predictable. This can be concluded from a previous comparison of U.S. and Japanese firms, when the variability of the environment was increasing (Aoki 1986b). Similarly, a highly hierarchical organization of firms and innovation systems may be quite efficient when radical, although not permanent, innovations are the rule, France being a good example.

Consequently, it could be forecast that as soon as a new method of production has emerged and the international financial system has stabilized, Japan and Germany, as well as France, may prosper again. This is the prognosis offered by Kozo Yamamura (see his essay in this volume).

But what will be the contours of the emerging new productive paradigm(s)? In light of the previous analysis, several trajectories seem possible and they may differ significantly from one country to another (table 5.7). If the future belongs to increased mass production of differentiated goods along the line that prevailed under Fordism, Japan will be in a good position, given its high investment in physical capital. But it is far from evident that this scenario will dominate in the early twenty-first century, because new goods and sectors have emerged that call for a radically different organization.

The role of ICT in growth performance has been stressed by many, and the increasing importance of ICT has significantly affected the structural changes of the 1980s and 1990s. Statistical data gathered by the OECD (1999b) suggest that the United States and United Kingdom are in good position to be part of this technological revolution and that Japan will be less lagging than usually perceived. By contrast, both France and Germany seem to experience difficulties in coping with the implementation of ICT. This gap has fed the idea that the new economy is a U.S. invention and exclusive feature (*Economic Report to the President* 1999).

The late 1990s, however, suggest a more refined analysis. The diffusion of ICT seems to be only the first step in a broader industrial revolution linked to the implementation of a KBE (Soete 1999). OECD (1999b, 21) estimates suggest that both Germany and Japan are spending relatively little on public education and software. Although these are actually rather crude measures for the knowledge content and efforts of modern economies (table 5.7, third column), the OECD data yield a striking result—the ranking of national economies is different in each vision of the next productive paradigm. Provided that statistical measures capture real features, this is a second message for both Germany and Japan—we imagine that their innovation system will evolve and specialize according to their initial endowment.

Hybridizing Innovation Systems in Germany and Japan

If there is not a single best way for innovation systems and if contemporary systems are quite complex, new perspectives open for the transformation of each national economy. Instead of measuring the proximity to a model innovation system with strong complementarities among its components, most systems may be recomposed by marginally reforming specific parts, that is, by adding new elements to get a new system that combines old and new features. Such a process has been observed in many industrial sectors, such as the car industry (Boyer et al. 1998; Freyssenet et al. 1998).

Marginal reforms to each national system are highly likely given the diversity of specialization among countries. For instance, in the early twenty-first century, Japan might continue to specialize in electronic hardware associated with ICT or KBE, whereas the United States might reinforce its leading position in software and basic science. Furthermore, Germany could be part of this emerging international division of innovation by specializing in mechanical engineering and the production of instruments associated with ICT and KBE. But the diffusion of features from one innovation system to another may well result in a new system, possibly superior to the preceding ones. This is nothing other than the process of hybridization, which has been observed in all previous technological revolutions. Again this opens some freedom for science and technology policy in both Germany and Japan. Paradoxically enough, trying strictly to imitate the successful U.S. configuration may be an inferior strategy compared to marginal recomposition and tinkering.

Complementarities among National Systems of Innovation

The previous arguments may sound abstract and linked too closely to the historical trajectories followed by individual countries. Is not the contemporary phase of globalization creating a radically new environment, promoting in the long run convergence to a series of best practices? Previous research has already shown that such convergence is the exception, whereas the rule seems to be an increasing specialization of national or regional systems (Amable, Barré, and Boyer 1997, 231–63).

A study by Bob Hancké (1999) confirms the trend toward increasing specialization. First, it is striking to note that the German distribution of patents in the early 1980s was the mirror image of the U.S. distribution— whereas Germany was strong in civil engineering, agricultural machines, mechanical equipment engines, and machine tools, the United States was weak in all these. At the same time, the U.S. economy was highly successful in information technologies, semiconductors, biotechnologies, and new materials—all areas in which Germany displayed a relative weakness. In other words, the German and U.S. innovation systems were largely complementary in 1983–84.

Second, although we might think the drastic changes since then have altered the picture and eroded the correspondence between the weaknesses and strengths of the two economies, Hancké (1999) presents evidence to the contrary, showing that complementary specializations were reinforced between 1983–84 and 1993–94, with only a few instances of erosion. But this is not really a surprise because the surge of internationalization, including that of R&D centers, has increased the importance of previous institutional and technological endowments. This is no more than a consequence in international relations of the social construction of competitive advantage (OECD 1991) and its strong path and past dependency (David 1988).

To sum up, the weaknesses evidenced during the 1990s by the German and Japanese innovation systems may not continue forever. Nor do they require an irreversible convergence toward the U.S. configuration.

How Will Asian and European Growth Evolve?

Much empirical evidence suggests that long-term growth performance is determined not only by innovation (Boyer and Didier 1998), but also by the dynamism of demand requiring a mutual adjustment of capacity formation and the emergence of new needs. From a theoretical standpoint, Schumpeterian mechanisms have to be combined with Keynesian ones, and this is especially important in the medium and long term. On the one hand, the emergence of new processes and products creates an incentive for firms to invest, hire new workers, and thereby generate additional income. This is the conventional mechanism emphasized by specialists of technical change, who observe a correlation between productivity increases, market shares, employment creation, and intensity of innovation, such as R&D expenditures and number of patents. This is a medium- and long-term phenomenon that runs from innovation to growth. On the other hand, a second mechanism has to be taken into account, namely, the generation of demand, with respect to both volume and distribution across old and new industries. The concept of a demand regime captures the impact of a given pattern of technical change on the consumption of households and the investment of firms. This is the precise meaning of accumulation and growth regimes proposed by *régulation* theory (Boyer 1988).

Therefore, the success of an innovation system depends on its compatibility with the demand regime associated with the prevailing *régulation* mode. More precisely, a Schumpeterian growth pattern cannot emerge in the absence of a concurrent transformation of the demand regime. This is especially important for the future of the German and Japanese systems.

When the economy is booming and expectations are high, whatever the configuration of the national system of innovation, firms become more optimistic about the future and tend to invest more in R&D.[2] Conversely, during recession or stagnation periods, especially when they are as long as the one observed in Japan beginning in 1992, innovation-pushed strategies are hindered by the long-term pessimism of firms, and rampant uncertainty about the future may induce a shift from consumption to saving and a strong preference for liquidity. Then, it is no longer the absence of dynamic innovation that limits growth but a lack of coherence and credibility of government economic policy (Boyer and Yamada 2000). Similarly, the direction of innovation may be governed by inertia with respect to the demand of the previous period, which introduces a possible industrial mismatch between the evolving expectations and needs of consumers and the supply offered by firms because it generally takes from five to ten years for R&D expenditures to produce a marketable product. Consequently, macroeconomic demand management is important for the viability of any

2. A high correlation between R&D expenditures and macroeconomic performance is supported by 1970–96 data on the OECD economies (see OECD 1997a; Boyer and Didier 1998, 89).

innovation strategy, and this also creates strong differences among the United States, Europe, and Japan.

The U.S. Boom Makes Innovation Easier, but It Cannot Be Assumed to Continue Forever

From 1992 to 2000, the U.S. economy experienced a macroeconomic boom that was a direct benefit of the success of the new innovation strategy pursued by large U.S. firms, which managed to recover a large part of their lost structural competitiveness (*Economic Report to the President* 1999). It would therefore not be sufficient for a country to import only the institutions governing science and technology in order to reap the same benefits from innovation as the U.S. economy (Boyer and Didier 1998). The fine-tuning of monetary and budgetary policies played a significant role, too, as did simultaneous transformations of competition policy and labor markets. But the changing macroeconomic and financial context of the early 2000s made clear this two-sided causality between innovation dynamism and macroeconomic environment.

Will European Integration Promote Growth?

Until 1997, the German economy muddled through the difficult processes of unification and preparation for the euro. German austerity policies spread all over Europe and made innovation both more necessary and more difficult. Large productivity increases were observed in Germany in the second half of the 1990s, but they were achieved by the rationalization of organizational structures and reduction of employment, not a surge of new products. The decision to launch the euro in May 1998 at first generated optimistic expectations, but the first half of 1999 brought a more sober view of the prospects for German growth, which seem to be below average European performance (OECD 1999a).

Transforming Innovation Systems and Macroeconomic Performance

During the 1990s in Japan, the negative impact of the bubble years caused a long slow-growth period and made economic policy orientations more uncertain than ever. Firms were constrained by the macroeconomic environment to rationalize their R&D organizations (Goto and Odagiri 1997; National Institute for Science, Technology and Economic Policy [NISTEP] 1998; Odagiri and Goto 1993) and they did not increase their R&D expenditures as much as might have been expected. The transformation of the Japanese innovation system is indirectly but rather closely related to the success or failure of general macroeconomic policy.

Generally, the viability of any innovation system, the Japanese and German systems included, cannot be assessed independently from the macroeconomic dynamism of the domestic economy and its international environment. This causes special concerns for Japan because the country is largely dependent on an emerging division of labor among Asian countries. They, however, are currently experiencing a period of drastic transformation after the severe depression caused by the 1997 financial crisis (Sakakibara 2000). The trajectory to be followed by Germany is more open—everything depends on the introduction of the euro and the related learning process of the actors involved in the new policy mix (Boyer 1999a, 2000b). More generally, the evolution of regionalism (see the essays by Peter Katzenstein and by Erica Gould and Stephen Krasner in this volume), both in Europe and Asia, may play a crucial role in the reconfiguration of the German and Japanese innovation systems.

Can Institutional Change Overcome the Current Structural Crises?

Clearly the 1990s marked the end of an epoch, and all governments need to reform their national economies in order to adjust to the major changes in the international arena, the new conditions for competition, and the emerging social needs in the next century. Many analysts agree with this vision. Nevertheless, the present chapter challenges conventional wisdom about the current Japanese and German situation. Both economies seem to be experiencing the same difficulties as a result of having reached the end of the easy part of the catching-up process, related to the implementation of U.S. production methods and basic science advances (Katz 1998). If this were the only component of the crisis experienced by the two countries, then clearly the task of the authorities in charge of science and technology policies would be to import, adapt, and hybridize those institutions at the root of the U.S. and, to a lesser extent, British successes. However, insights gained from the *régulation*ist analyses show that this strategy captures only part of the problems the two economies face (figure 5.1).

Germany needs to promote a new dynamism in its very specific growth regime, led by the production of differentiated and quality goods. The oligopolistic power of German firms in the world market has eroded. In some industries, this was due to the dynamism of Japanese manufacturers. Furthermore, the erosion of German competitiveness was exacerbated both by the unexpectedly large costs of German unification, which slowed innovation significantly, and by the overvaluation of the deutschmark

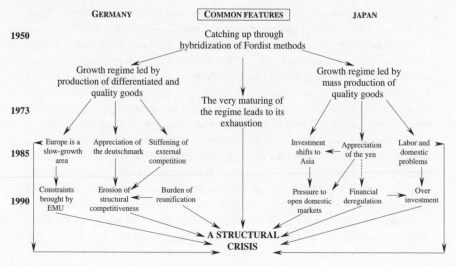

Figure 5.1 Two Structural Crises

against the dollar during the 1990s. The viability of the German innovation system depends on whether these two major structural problems can be overcome and on an adequate exchange rate for the euro (Boyer 1999a). Of course, some U.S. institutions, such as risk capital for innovation, were introduced at the end of the 1990s. It will, however, not be possible to find a way out of the crisis using this strategy alone. Many other structural reforms are required: welfare, taxation, labor institutions, and so on.

Japanese manufacturing firms will recover their competitiveness if the general macroeconomic uncertainty produced by accumulated bad debts, the credit crunch, and the diffusion of pessimistic expectations among households can be reversed by a new and vigorous economic policy. Innovation can solve many of the current economic, ecological, and social problems of Japan. But a reconfiguration of the Japanese innovation system would be easier if the pace and character of institutional change became easier to anticipate and the macroeconomic recovery were more vigorous. Of course, it might be wise to introduce some new institutions organizing closer links among universities, research institutes, and the R&D laboratories of large firms, but the results would not be felt for one or two decades. In any case, such strategies do not provide a direct solution to the impediments to economic recovery in the early 2000s. Science and technology policies do indeed forge the future of a nation, but they are not sufficient to pull an economy out of a recession caused by the excesses of the bubble economy and the subsequent financial fragility.

Fortuna and Virtú

Before any conclusion can be presented, it is important to list some methodological consequences of the analytic approach of this chapter, which lies somewhere between two alternative visions: (1) the typical neoclassical view that there is a single best policy that will be adopted by all those who are fully rational and that the success of the policy will be built on coherent and stable interaction between policymaking and the economy and (2) the vision of the economist of the Austrian school that the contemporary world is so complex that nobody can master it intellectually, still less practically. A neo-Schumpeterian would add that a successful strategy is the unexpected outcome of a series of reactions to a series of events that cannot be forecast; success depends on selection and learning mechanisms that are far from deterministic. The view advanced here is that real historical trajectories, operating between the two visions, result from a complex set of interdependent factors that combines internal coherence with external relevance, that is, the quality and the compatibility of the strategies followed by private and public agents (*virtú*) and a form of serendipity given the intrinsic uncertainty of market economies and democratic systems (*fortuna*).

The success of the Japanese manufacturing sector after World War II is a good example. Firms and public authorities aimed to implement typical U.S. mass-production methods, but failed because of the limited size of the domestic market, the paucity of credit and natural resources, and turbulent industrial relations. Therefore firms learned to produce differentiated goods in low quantities, and ultimately firms improved quality in order to export to world markets. The resulting Japanese production system that finally emerged by the end of the 1970s was different from the U.S. system. Its surprising success was due to the follower doing better than the leader—the coming together of two seemingly unrelated events: a powerful domestic strategy of modernization and a new phase in the history of the world economy that put a premium on the production of quality and differentiated goods, given the intrinsic lack of capacity of Fordism with respect to delivering this combination.

This explains why this unexpectedly successful synchronization of domestic and international factors could not last forever. Through the bubble years, the rapid *endaka* (the appreciation of the yen against the dollar) put severe strains on the Japanese production system while, in response to unprecedented speculation in financial and land markets, land prices skyrocketed. All this together finally triggered the reversal of Japanese performance during the 1990s. Furthermore, U.S. and European manufacturing sectors, challenged by their Japanese competitors, progressively learned to restructure and reorganize by modernizing their mass-production methods and developing new sectors built on the marriage of telecommunications and computer science. Finally, the globalization of finance caused new shocks to the world system, such as the 1997 Asian crisis, which especially affected Japan. The world centers of financial intermediation are Wall Street and the City of London rather than Tokyo, which is due to a deep inertia in social systems of production and innovation. We could say that Japanese *virtú* and *fortuna* have both been reversed.

Although the picture is rather different, similar concepts can be used when considering the German trajectory. First, the transformation of the German production base was less spectacular because specialization and organization seemed stable and no significant breakthrough in new sectors occurred. Second, we could have imagined that a quick and successful transformation of the Soviet Union into a market-based economy and democratic society would trigger a large demand for goods typically produced by German manufacturers: highly competitive and efficient capital goods on the one side, income-elastic consumer goods on the other. Similarly the eastern *Länder* would become a new industrial Eldorado. Unfortunately, the great transformation of the Russian economy has largely failed. Therefore, from the point of view of traditional German specialization, the period after the mid-1980s had an adverse effect, but for reasons different from those that have shaped the Japanese trajectory. Bad *fortuna* and less *virtú* than expected explain the erosion of German macroeconomic performance: slow growth, high and rising unemployment, a less-than-robust trade performance, and a negative foreign investment balance. The large transfers to eastern *Länder* partially explain this outcome.

The future of German capitalism thus remains uncertain. The Helmut Kohl government was unable to pass urgent social and fiscal reforms, and the first years of the Gerhard Schröder government experienced similar difficulties. The synchronization and compatibility of political reforms with the strategies of the big corporation raise major problems. Merely reproducing the configuration that led to the German miracle will not solve the issue of growth and job creation, whereas a bold adoption of shareholder value and U.S.-style governance modes may violate citizens' expectations and ultimately damage social cohesion (Jackson 2001; Thelen and Kume 2001). The twenty-first century clearly calls for renewed *virtú*.

Conclusion

Japan and Germany are not market-led U.S.- or British-style capitalism, and they share many features: a rapid catching up with U.S. technology and productivity level, a strong emphasis on high-level skills, and the key role of international competitiveness in contemporary national arrangements. The two economies also experienced many difficulties in coping with the new circumstances of the 1990s. Nevertheless, much institutional and statistical evidence suggests they have not followed the same growth regime. Japan has caught up by adapting mass-production methods to a specific context and then emphasizing product differentiation. On the other hand, Germany has relied on the production of differentiated quality goods.

Short-term macroeconomic adjustment also displays different features. The Japanese economy is corporate-led, whereas the German economy combines features of social democratic countries with strong public intervention at national and regional levels. Both economies are clearly concerned about competitiveness, via the quality of workers, but educational and training institutions differ—significant internal mobility in Japan contrasts with a much more active labor market for professional competence in Germany.

Contrary to many neoclassical models that focus only on a single factor to explain endogenous technical change, this chapter argues that at least three mechanisms impel innovation. First, the division of labor is extended along with the growth of the market, according to the old idea proposed by Adam Smith. Second, skilled workers may contribute to incremental innovations accumulating through time and contributing significantly to productivity. Third, engineers and scientists may initiate radical breakthroughs, enabling firms to realize the productivity gains that result from learning by doing. Convergent estimates tend to suggest that the Japanese manufacturing sector was very strong in capturing both increasing returns to scale and competence-induced innovations, but weaker in converting basic science to profitable industries and products. By contrast, the German manufacturing sector has never played the game of increasing returns to scale but has built its growth on a highly polyvalent workforce and moderate use of basic science.

Therefore, when international trade problems and financial globalization led to significantly slower growth in the 1990s, Japan was more severely affected than Germany because its main source of dynamism—the growth of domestic and world markets—was exhausted. Germany, by comparison, relied on product differentiation and quality enhancement and suffered less from the new economic context. Unification has, however, imposed unexpectedly high costs and induced a slowdown in innovation.

For many analysts, the current problems experienced by both countries may be blamed on their structural weaknesses, in failing to derive useful and profitable innovations from scientific advances. A social system of innovation analysis tends to downplay such an argument.

In Japan, the links between market and technology are strong and make for good economic performance of firms because a large fraction of R&D

expenditure comes from firms rather than public authorities. But the other side of the coin is that the contribution of Japanese science to the advancement of knowledge and economic activity seems, for the time being, quite modest, in spite of efforts during the 1990s to increase the number of researchers and improve their working conditions. In any case, the contribution of radical innovations based on advances in basic science should not be overstated. Even in the United States, when more and more scientists are working for private firms, institutions, and universities, total factor productivity has not recovered to match the growth rates of the 1960s, even during the long boom of the 1990s.

In the nineteenth century, Germany was good at using academic research in emerging new sectors, such as chemicals and equipment goods. There is a strong tradition of basic research, but the bulk of twenti-eth-century German competitiveness is no longer associated with it; instead it is based on a series of incremental innovations in well-established sectors. Therefore, no sunrise sector has clearly emerged, and the feedback from academic research to economic activity is far from satisfactory. Furthermore, the behavior of the banking sector and large firms has been quite conservative with respect to possible breakthrough and radical innovations. The reforms of the 1990s—creating, for instance, risk capital—have been decided, but of course their possible benefits will only be reaped in the long run.

Will the twenty-first century be shaped by a productive paradigm built on basic science? If so, Japan will suffer from some rather severe structural weaknesses. On the one hand, public authorities clearly perceive this challenge and have undertaken a series of reforms. They have created incentives for research within universities, promoted links between research and the activities of firms, attempted to internationalize the Japanese research system, and so on. But on the other hand, the contribution of science to growth remains rather modest, science is not highly appreciated by the public (NISTEP 1998), and a smaller proportion of students follow scientific and technological courses (NISTEP 1990). Japan is still importing more high-tech products from the United States and even Europe than it exports to them, and Asia is the destination of the most technologically advanced Japanese products (NISTEP 1997). Germany does not look specialized in high-tech products in terms of the R&D behind them, but the picture is more sanguine if the level of skills involved is taken into account. Nevertheless, German unification seems to have destabilized the dynamism of innovation, partially by diverting large resources toward the restructuring of the eastern *Länder* universities and allocating savings to the building of basic infrastructures. Furthermore, public authorities are not satisfied by the quality of the links between academic and applied research. The much-admired German training system suffers from competition with universities and other options attracting the younger generations in search of general training. Thus, the system is in flux and will probably be reformed.

If the globalization phase implied a convergence toward a standard innovation system, then drastic reforms would be required in order to adapt the educational system, on-the-job training, and wage hierarchy in science-related jobs. But such a conclusion would be extreme because globalization is especially acute for finance and science but less so for technology, which is largely built on tacit knowledge and not just patenting. Furthermore, at least four distinctive innovation systems coexisted in the mid-1990s and were specialized in different industries (Amable, Barré, and Boyer 1997). Market-led systems, U.S.- or British-style, are strong in science-related innovations but relatively weak in updating mass production in line with the need for quality and product differentiation. Conversely, the Japanese system is strong in the very same branches in which the United States is weak. This structural complementarity could bring a rather optimistic message about the future of both systems. They would probably not converge to a single best way but, in fact, could prosper from their differences.

This scenario assumes that all relevant reforms are successfully undertaken. Japanese society requires the reconstruction of a sound and efficient domestic financial system and all the related transformations in state interventions, the wage-labor nexus, and insertion into the world economy. Germany has to reassess the legitimacy and efficiency of many of its core institutions concerning the welfare system, taxation, the relationship between general education and training, and links between the academic world and firms. Furthermore, European monetary policy will no longer be tuned to the requirements of Germany but rather to the average situation of the old continent, and this will call for change in some German institutions and arrangements.

In any case, there are two visions of the future that seem unlikely: the rapid and irreversible convergence of Germany and Japan toward a market-led U.S.-style capitalism and the strict conservation of the current institutional architecture in the twenty-first century. Between these two extremes, however, it is difficult to make any prognosis about the complex interactions between political reforms and economic trends triggered by financial liberalization and regional integration.

Nevertheless, we may venture a possible scenario. The analysis suggests that innovation systems do not exhibit the strong and complete complementarities put forward by the proponents of any future and emblematic configuration, be it a modernization of post–World War II mass production (Womack, Jones, and Roos 1990), the leading role of ICT, or alternatively a KBE (OECD 1999b; Boyer 2000c). Thus there is room for tinkering and marginal adaptation in the existing systems in order to enhance their fit to contemporary forms for competition. This process has taken place previously and seems to be enhanced by the current phase of globalization. Within this framework, the Japanese innovation system could be redeployed in order to exploit the fact that Japanese companyism is quite beneficial for building and accumulating the tacit knowledge so crucial in the manufacturing of sophisticated goods, the result of a vast array of competence and practical knowledge. Similarly, the strength of the German configuration is different from both the Japanese and the U.S. trumps—the German economy displays a clear competitive advantage in highly differentiated products in response to precisely defined needs and the search for high quality. Market-led capitalism, such as in the United States and United Kingdom, on the contrary, specializes in more radical innovations, covered by patenting and resulting from a fast and efficient use of advances in basic, including scientific, knowledge.

This optimistic scenario assumes that stable and legitimized rules of the game can be found and implemented in order to govern a globalized world, the instability of which would be detrimental to the recovery of both the German and Japanese systems. It is not really surprising that the issue of innovation and intellectual property rights received heightened attention in the Millennium Round of the World Trade Organization, raised some conflicting positions in Seattle, and was reexamined in the Doha conference. The future of most institutional and technological systems is crucially dependent on the outcome of this uncertain process.

The Future of Nationally Embedded Capitalism: Industrial Relations in Germany and Japan

Kathleen Thelen and Ikuo Kume

In the 1980s, the German and Japanese systems of industrial relations were held up as models of efficiency and productivity. The German system—featuring centralized bargaining through powerful but responsible industrial unions and plant-based negotiations with strong works councils—was seen as an important institutional support for the kind of up-market ("high everything") strategies that German firms had pursued so successfully in a wide range of manufacturing industries (Streeck 1992). Japanese industrial relations were similarly heralded as embodying just the right mix of flexible rigidities to support firm strategies based on constant innovation and high productivity (Dore 1986). As a matter of fact, Japanese management techniques such as lifetime employment guarantees, internal promotion ladders, and flexible job design became export items in themselves.

The late 1990s saw the emergence of new tensions in industrial relations in both countries. Scholars and practitioners alike have begun arguing that institutions and practices previously regarded as vital sources of flexibility now constitute debilitating rigidities. In Germany, centralized collective bargaining has traditionally rested on a relatively high degree of

We wish to thank the participants in the project, Germany and Japan: The Future of Nationally Embedded Capitalism in a Global Economy, and particularly the project directors, Wolfgang Streeck and Kozo Yamamura, for useful comments and suggestions. This chapter is a slightly revised version of Kathleen Thelen and Ikuo Kume, "The Effects of Globalization on Labor Revisited: Lessons from Germany and Japan," in *Politics and Society* (Vol. 27, No. 4), pp. 477–505, copyright © 1999 by Sage Publications Inc. Reprinted by Permission of Sage Publications, Inc.

organization both among workers and—especially—among employers. Social partnership there is premised on the need by employers to accommodate a labor movement that enjoys strength at the national as well as plant level. More recently, however, centralized collective bargaining has come under pressure from employers demanding a retreat from rigid industry-wide regulations in favor of more flexible bargaining arrangements to accommodate the varying needs of individual companies and plants.

In Japan, by contrast, union influence derives more from labor's indispensable cooperation in production at the plant level, in the context of the stakeholder position of enterprise unions within the firm. In Japan, too, however, traditional managerial practices such as lifetime employment and seniority wages—once praised as excellent mechanisms for motivating workers and encouraging investment in skills—are increasingly seen as costly and unsustainable drags on efficiency and productivity. Despite their different starting points (Thelen and Kume 1999)—coordinated industry-wide bargaining in Germany and strong internal labor markets in Japan—we find employers and policymakers in both countries calling for reforms, employing rhetoric that is strongly deregulatory, and invoking the Anglo-Saxon model of vibrant external labor markets and more decentralized, even individualized bargaining.

This chapter explores developments in the Japanese and German industrial relations systems. We argue that the sometimes radical rhetoric of deregulation obscures important sources of resiliency in traditional industrial relations practices, a resiliency that goes back in large part to employers' own continuing stake in them. Although acknowledging new tensions, we argue further that the nature of the crisis of industrial relations in both countries is in many ways quite different from that painted in much of the contemporary labor literature. By recasting what the crisis is about, we are better able to understand the distinctive pattern of continuity and change that has come to characterize labor relations in both Germany and Japan.

We begin by providing a sketch of developments in the two countries that documents significant changes and also important continuities in industrial relations institutions. The existing literature tends to focus on the destabilizing trends and sees the crisis of industrial relations as stemming from a neoliberal offensive against traditional institutional rigidities. The argument is that globalization—understood mostly in terms of capital mobility or the threat of exit—has shifted the balance of power decisively toward employers (Kapstein 1996; Kurzer 1993; Ross and Martin 1999). Unions are typically seen as the main defenders of traditional practices, but their power to resist decentralization and deregulation is sapped by ongoing struggles with employers and, in many countries, also undermined by high unemployment. Less attention has been devoted to explaining institutional stability. To the extent that it is addressed, the observed resiliency of traditional arrangements is frequently chalked up to successful union defense (but how long can labor hold out?) or simply to institutional inertia.

Our analysis takes issue with this set of arguments and indeed with many of the premises on which they are based. First of all, there is another face to globalization that the existing literature has largely neglected, having to do with employers' heightened dependence on stable and predictable relations with labor at the plant level, in the context of tightly coupled production networks and the demands of producing at high quality on a just-in-time basis (but see Streeck 1987 for an exception). Focusing on this aspect provides insights into the resiliency of traditional bargaining arrangements; in both countries employers themselves are, if anything, more dependent than ever on the shop-floor peace and predictability that these institutions have traditionally generated. We argue that current strains in Germany and Japan emanate less from an all-out frontal attack on the part of employers against the traditional system than its partial and declining coverage. We find a substantial core of workers (Japan) and firms (Germany) for whom traditional industrial relations arrangements apply and indeed where, if anything, employers seek to intensify their cooperation with labor within the prevailing structure. However, the intensification of cooperation within that stable core in both cases has been closely linked to the exclusion of a growing number of firms and workers from traditional protections. The question for the future is whether these systems can survive in partial form; we close the essay with some thoughts on that issue.

Patterns of Resiliency and Change in German and Japanese Industrial Relations

A large number of empirical studies have richly documented new pressures on traditional industrial relations institutions in both Germany and Japan. Although acknowledging significant new strains, we find that these systems are much more resilient than many accounts have portrayed them. Most analyses focus on the factors that are allegedly pulling these systems apart, not those holding them together. Observed stability is frequently attributed to institutional stickiness or to successful union defense, but, either way, the long-term staying power of traditional institutions is seen as seriously in doubt. By contrast, we find evidence that employers' own continuing attachment to—and interest in—traditional institutions plays a more important role in their survival.

Germany

The overall structure of Germany's dual system of industrial relations is known well enough to forgo a detailed description here (see, e.g., Markovits 1986). Briefly, this system juxtaposes relatively centralized collective bargaining through multiindustry unions with a statutory system for labor representation at the plant level through works councils that are formally autonomous from the unions. Collective bargaining is conducted on an industrywide basis, with a degree of national coordination achieved through the pattern-setting role played by the powerful Metalworkers' Union (IG Metall). Collectively bargained contracts have very broad coverage, less as a result of high unionization levels than as a consequence of a traditionally very high degree of organization on the employer side.[1] Collective bargaining at the industry level in Germany is complemented by labor representation at the plant level through works councils possessed of strong statutory rights on issues relating to personnel and employment policies.

Contemporary strains in German industrial relations emanate from employers' increasingly vocal demands for greater flexibility—calls, in other words, for a move away from uniform industrywide regulation toward more plant-oriented negotiations. Discontent with the current system is particularly strong among small and medium-size firms (Germany's sizable *Mittelstand*), which have roundly criticized their industry associations for catering to the interests of large firms at their expense.[2] Small and medium-size firms were particularly vehement in condemning a series of deals in the 1980s that reduced the regular working week because, for them, the costs of negotiated working-time reductions were not easily offset by the compensating enhanced opportunities for working-time flexibility (see Silvia 1999).[3]

1. Union density in Germany has been fairly constant at between 30 and 35 percent throughout most of the postwar period, except for a sharp, although also short-lived, increase immediately after unification. By contrast, organization among employers has traditionally been higher, with over 80 percent of all companies organized by the German Federation of Employers before the Wall came down (Katzenstein 1987, 25). Organization rates always varied by industry, with some industry associations (such as chemicals and mining) organizing close to 100 percent of firms in the sector. Others associations, such as that for the metalworking industry (Gesamtmetall), organized fewer firms before unification (42 percent), but these accounted for a large majority of workers (72 percent) in the sector (Zagelmeyer 1998).

2. On the complaints by small firms about large-firm dominance of collective bargaining policy, see Schnabel and Wagner (1996).

3. Pattern-setting contracts in the metalworking industry (in 1984, 1987, and 1990) resulted in overall reductions in weekly working times, in exchange for which employers won new flexibilities in scheduling work. Large firms were able to make up for lost working time by expanding shift work or by devising complicated and highly differentiated working-time

These small firms have in the meantime emerged as vocal proponents of bargaining decentralization. Their interests are represented by such groups as the Arbeitsgemeinschaft Selbständiger Unternehmer (Working Group of Independent Entrepreneurs, or ASU) and the Verband Mittelständiger Unternehmer (Association for Small and Medium-Size Enterprises, VMU). These organizations have proposed a number of changes in existing bargaining arrangements, all of them in one way or another aimed at allowing more local bargaining over wages and benefits. Proposals have ranged from a separate clause in central agreements specifically tailored for small and medium-size firms (*Mittelstandsklausel*) to central contracts that set only the parameters for wage increases (e.g., 1–5 percent) and/or establish a menu of benefits from which local bargainers can pick and choose to the insertion in all contracts of an opening clause allowing firms in hardship cases to negotiate subcontractual rates (see especially Silvia 1996, 41–42; also *Süddeutsche Zeitung*, 25–26 February 1995).

The strains on centralized bargaining intensified with unification as a result of enormous gaps in productivity between firms in the east and west and the precarious state of most eastern companies. The disruptive effects of unification on coordinated industrywide bargaining have taken two forms. First, unification set in motion a hemorrhaging of membership in some key employer associations, above all and most consequentially in the employer association for the metalworking industries (Gesamtmetall). After the Wall came down, firms held by the agency charged with privatizing East German industry (Treuhandanstalt) were also members of the relevant employer association. But as soon as these firms were privatized, the new (refounded) companies often opted not to join in order to avoid having to pay the collectively bargained wage. A 1997 survey indicates that overall only 25.7 percent of firms in the east (accounting for 43.9 percent of employees) belong to their employer associations and are thus subject to the terms of the industrywide bargains these associations negotiate with unions (Kohaut and Schnabel 1998).[4] Metalworking has been especially hard hit by this trend; by some accounts, membership in the eastern branches of Gesamtmetall fell from 57.4 percent of firms in 1992 to 35 percent in 1994 (Silvia 1996, 46), although other analysts' figures indicate this still covered between 55 and 65 percent of employees (Schroeder 1996, 25–34).

arrangements, but smaller companies—often without a personnel department, sometimes family-owned and operated—were less able to exploit the potential for more flexible working times.

4. This is down from 27 percent of companies (accounting for 64 percent of employees) two years earlier (Schnabel and Wagner 1996, 294). However, it must be kept in mind that some of these companies have concluded separate agreements with the union, which is to say that employer membership is not identical to collective bargaining coverage.

Employers remain overall better organized in the west, but the declining membership has spilled over and become a problem there as well. The same 1997 survey shows a general (all-industries) drop in membership in the west between 1995 and 1997, from 51.8 percent of firms (accounting for approximately 70 percent of employment) to 49.0 percent (covering 65.3 percent of workers). Again, focusing on the crucial metalworking industry, we find that employer association density in the west had dropped from a preunification high in 1984 of 75 percent (by employment) to 65 percent in 1994 (Silvia 1996, 38).

The effects of these formal defections from the system of industrywide bargaining are exacerbated by a second trend, namely, a growing tendency on the part of member firms to undercut informally the terms of the central agreement. In such cases, works councils—fearing layoffs—either agree to subcontractual wages or they simply close one eye when management violates the contract. As with declining membership, this problem is more severe in the east, but it has become a growing problem in the west as well. A survey conducted by a labor-oriented research institute (Wirtschaft- und Sozialwissenschaftliches Institut, WSI) finds that approximately 15.6 percent of western German and 29.8 percent of eastern German companies with works councils breach valid collective agreements (Schulten and Zagelmeyer 1998; see also *Mitbestimmung* [1996, 35]). Another study, based on a 1996 survey, indicates that, overall, 41 percent of eastern German enterprises (accounting for 23 percent of employment) were paying wages below the level set down in the industry contract ("Erosion of Employers' Associations" 1997).

These trends are smiled upon by neoliberal radicals such as Hans-Olaf Henkel, the former president of the Federation of German Industries and the country's most outspoken advocate of deregulation. Henkel has praised deviations from uniform collective agreements in the east as exemplary and hopes the west too can learn from this example (*Handelsblatt*, 27 January 1998, p. 4; *Spiegel*, 12 January 1998). He has called on employer associations to loosen their hold on firms and free them from the "yoke" of collective bargaining contracts and has praised regional associations such as those in Saxony that have made it easier for member firms to leave the association to escape the terms of industrywide contracts (*Handelsblatt*, 1 February 1999; *Frankfurter Rundschau*, 10 February 1999; *Kölner Stadt-Anzeiger*, 20 February 1999). Henkel's views resonate with those of other prominent employers, for example, representatives of the business association for the machine-tool industry (Verein Deutscher Maschinen und Anlagenbauer, VDMA), who have voiced support for changing the Works Constitution Act to allow works councils to regulate matters that are currently reserved for unions (*Handelsblatt*, 19 January 1998, p. 1).

These features represent the familiar face of the crisis of German industrial relations—aggressive employers, inflammatory neoliberal rhetoric, widespread defections, unions fighting for their organizational lives under adverse economic and political conditions. Much of this appears to fit the prevailing view of an employer offensive against labor that derives considerable momentum from capital mobility and high unemployment. Whereas capital mobility empowers employers, unemployment weakens labor, and in combination the two promote wildcat cooperation on the part of local workforces with overall corrosive effects on national bargaining institutions. Emphasizing the centrifugal forces at work, a good bit of this literature suggests a system teetering on the brink of collapse (especially Mahnkopf 1991; Fichter 1997; Flecker and Schulten 1999).

But the system has not collapsed, and its surprising resiliency in the face of these intense, literally unprecedented strains has received relatively scant attention in the literature (but see Streeck 1997d). An exception is Lowell Turner (1998), who by and large embraces the dominant characterization of the crisis—a neoliberal offensive of employers against labor—while putting a rather different spin on some of the numbers. The following examples are among those Turner points out:

1. Unionization is down from its inflated postunification high, but at approximately 30–35 percent, it has just dropped back to its normal preunification level (Turner 1998, 108).[5]
2. Membership in employer associations is indeed down (e.g., in the metalworking industry), but the decline (in the west, from an average of 72 percent in 1970–89 to the current 65 percent of workers covered) hardly constitutes a free fall.[6]
3. Association density in the east is lower (e.g., in metalworking, 35 percent of companies), but many firms nonetheless conclude separate contracts with the union, so that collective bargaining

5. We might also mention the results of works council elections in 1998, which show the DGB (Deutscher Gewerkschaftsbund) unions still in command of a large majority of works council seats (61.9 percent) and chairmanships (73.2 percent). Those analysts who emphasize instability can point to a dramatic increase in nonunion works councillors since 1975 (from 17.5 to 33.3 percent) and of works council chairmen (from 1.5 to 21.9 percent), but it turns out that this has been more the result of the almost complete collapse of DGB competitors such as the DAG (Deutsche Angestellten Gewerkschaft).

6. The numbers (for metalworking) for the east are 43 percent of firms, accounting for 65 percent of employees in 1994 (see Jacobi, Keller, and Müller-Jentsch 1998). Other industries, such as chemicals, still organize the vast majority of firms in both east and west, and overall (all industries), a large majority (70 percent) of private-sector firms belong to the industry associations of the Bundesvereinigung der Deutschen Arbeitgeberverbände (205, 1995 data).

coverage is higher than association density figures suggest.[7] Some of the firm-level contracts have less generous provisions than the industry contract, but others are *Anerkennungstarifverträge* (recognition contracts in which an individual firm agrees to abide by the terms of the industry agreement). Of the firms surveyed, 38.4 percent report that they have no contract at all, but these account for only 16.9 percent of employees (Kohaut and Bellmann 1997).

4. Firms that leave the employer association often find themselves using the industry agreement as an orientation point for their own wage levels anyway.[8]

Beyond the numbers, and maybe even more to the point, employers have simply been unwilling to part with industrywide pattern bargaining. Calls for a decentralization of wage negotiations have not led to an assault on centralized bargaining institutions, and in fact several bargaining rounds in the 1990s strongly suggested that employers still prefer to negotiate collectively with the unions than face them alone. This is certainly the case in the chemical industry, in which employers and unions renewed their commitment to social partnership and to branch-level collective bargaining (see, e.g., *FAZ,* 22 September 1997, p. 23; "IG BCE" 1999).[9] But an even more striking example was the 1996 conflict in the metalworking industry (where decentralization pressures have been most intense), in which it became clear that employers wanted nothing to do with plant-level negotiations over the very hot issue of sick-pay reduction and clamored instead for a collective solution (discussed later). Calls for a revision of the Works Constitution Act to open the door to wage bargaining by works councils, likewise, have failed to generate much momentum, and a large majority of employers still oppose the idea (*FAZ,* 27 January 1998, p. 11).

Perhaps most striking, radicals such as Henkel are not always celebrated as heroes; rather, the heads of the most powerful employer associations in the past viewed many of Henkel's interventions as unhelpful interference

7. For the west, for example, a 1995 survey shows that whereas only 53.4 percent of firms are parties to the industry contract, another 8.2 percent of firms have concluded a firm-level contract with the union, so that in fact 62 percent of firms are subject to a collective contract, and this accounts for fully 83 percent of employees (Kohaut and Bellmann 1997, 317–34).

8. Surveys of eastern German firms show that nearly one-half (42.8 percent) of companies outside the associations nonetheless pay the same wages as the industry agreement (Hassel and Schulten 1998, 506). In addition, informal deviations from contracts apparently apply less to wages than to various fringe benefits such as the Christmas bonus (*Mitbestimmung* 1996, 34).

9. Even in the east, the chemical industry organizes 75 percent of firms accounting for over 95 percent of employment (*Mitbestimmung* 1996).

(*Die Welt*, 23 February 1999; *Spiegel*, 19 January 1998, p. 88; *Handelsblatt*, 19 January 1998, p. 4). The president of the German Confederation of Employers (Bundesvereinigung der Deutschen Arbeitgeberverbände, BDA), Dieter Hundt, has publicly distanced himself from Henkel (*Handelsblatt*, 19 January 1998; 12 April 1999). The general manager of the German Steel Employers Association has likewise condemned Henkel's call for contract violations, arguing that this would lead to chaos (*Spiegel*, 12 January 1998). A member of the board of directors of BMW was quoted as saying that Henkel had become "unbearable" (*Spiegel*, 12 January 1998).

In contrast to Henkel's neoliberal rhetoric, the former head of the German Chamber of Industry and Trade, Hans-Peter Stihl, could be heard defending comprehensive collective bargaining as "correct and sensible" (*Süddeutsche Zeitung*, 22 January 1998, p. 5) and Werner Stumpfe (head of the Metal Employer Association) was advocating for a "new partnership" with labor (*Offenbach-Post*, 12 October 1998; Gesamtmetall 1999, especially 71–73). In line with their preferences, the overall trend in Germany has not been toward breakdown or neoliberalism but rather a sustained attempt to achieve greater flexibility in plant outcomes while staying within industrywide bargaining structures. Despite the often vociferous complaining, employers have actually proved very reluctant to abandon traditional bargaining institutions, and indeed most seem committed to working for reform within the existing structures.

The reluctance of employers themselves to part with traditional institutions does not figure prominently in most analyses of the crisis of German industrial relations. That literature, rather, is organized around debates among scholars who subscribe to the same view of the problem—a neoliberal employer offensive—but disagree in their assessments of labor's capacity to defend the system (e.g., see the debate between Mahnkopf 1991 and Turner 1998). In order to cut through this debate and to understand the sources of resiliency and change in German industrial relations, it will be necessary to break entirely with the characterization of the crisis and its solution on which both positions rest.

Japan

Whereas the German industrial relations system involves a relatively high degree of coordination among firms within and across sectors, the traditional Japanese system is premised more firmly on strong plant-based labor markets.[10] The two most remarked-on features of Japanese managerial practice are seniority wages and lifetime employment guarantees.

10. We have explored elsewhere some aspects of the historical origins of this difference (Thelen and Kume 1999).

Despite some popular (mis)conceptions, seniority wages never actually guaranteed workers automatic raises based solely on age. Nor, for that matter, did lifetime employment ever mean no dismissals were possible, only that management would take other steps (e.g., reduce overtime, cut part-time workers, freeze recruitment, reduce board members' remuneration, or call for voluntary retirement) in order to keep regular workers before resorting to layoffs.

In fact, since the 1960s the Japanese system has been premised not purely on seniority wages, but on job capability and skill-based wages (Koike 1993; Kume 1998). Because skills in Japan are acquired through on-the-job training, wage development reflected the accumulation of experience by a worker over the course of his or her career in the firm. Lifetime employment was an important part of the deal because it reduced the credible commitment problems associated with firm-based private-sector training. That is, together, seniority wages and lifetime employment provided incentives for workers to invest in firm-specific skills and to stay with the company that trained them, which in turn made it safe for the firm to commit significant resources to training without fear of workers absconding with these skills to other firms.

As in Germany, however, these traditional arrangements have increasingly been called into question. The critique of Japanese managerial practices typically focuses on three trends. First, with baby boomers reaching middle age, the number of older workers has increased. This demographic trend has made it difficult to generate the kind of opportunities for advancement within firms that in the past justified seniority-based wage increases. The problem has become even more acute in the 1990s, which have been marked by corporate retrenchment, not expansion.

Second, traditional mechanisms for avoiding workforce reductions seem to have reached their limits. Since the 1970s, Japanese companies have pursued a strategy of diversifying and innovating their product lines as an alternative to layoffs. Declining industries such as shipbuilding, iron and steel, and textiles regained their competitive edge in the world market in the mid-1990s through wholehearted diversification efforts (Nishioka and Nagaoka 1998, 73–75). As a result, Japanese shipbuilding companies are selling environment-related equipment and running plant-engineering businesses. Similarly, one large textile company, Asahi Kasei Co., dramatically expanded its business from housing to high-tech materials. However, in the context of Japan's ongoing economic crisis, economists have criticized large manufacturing companies for pursuing an ineffective one-set principle, by which they mean the companies try to produce all the products in their industry—for example, in the electrical machinery industry, everything from washing machines to nuclear power plants. They argue that in a world of megacompetition, Japanese companies should specialize in products in which they enjoy a comparative advantage. Whereas in the past Japanese companies tried to transfer redundant workers out of low-growth sections to the high-growth sections within their companies, these economists now argue that it is more efficient from the perspective of the national economy as well as that of individual companies to move redundant workers across companies, out of low-growth sectors and into the high-growth ones (Takeuchi 1998; Yashiro 1997; "Ōiso-Koiso," *Nikkei shinbun* [hereafter *Nikkei*], 22 May 1998).

Third, rapid technological change in industry has called into question the effectiveness of on-the-job training, which as we have seen was a linchpin in the entire system. The demands of new technologies, it turns out, are not well met through an experience-based system of skill formation (Takanashi 1994). Increasing competition in product markets requires breakthrough innovations more than incremental adjustments in product developments. The incremental adjustments, which have been regarded as a competitive advantage for Japan's manufacturing industries, are consistent with on-the-job training, whereas the breakthrough innovations are compatible with more flexible personnel policies based on external labor markets.

A number of much-publicized cases have led many observers to predict the imminent demise of the entire Japanese employment system. Hitachi, for example, has significantly diminished its lifetime employment guarantees in conjunction with the company's abandonment of the one-set principle. Thus, in 1998, Hitachi spun off its air conditioner and refrigerator plants into a separate company in order to specialize in more profitable production areas; by transferring Hitachi workers into new companies, the firm gave up the promise that its regular workers' employment was protected until their retirement age under the umbrella of the same company. Another industrial giant, Matsushita Electric Industrial Company, has pioneered changes in the traditional wage system. The company now allows workers to take their retirement bonus early (paid out in their monthly paychecks), a change widely interpreted as a move away from the lifetime employment practice. The computer and information technology products maker Fujitsu also abolished its seniority wage system and introduced a performance-based wage system. Similar moves are reported in many companies, such as Takeda Chemical, Yokokawa Electronics, and the trading company Mitsui. In fact, according to a 1993 survey of 123 large (employment over 3,000) firms conducted by Recruit, 67.5 percent of companies adopted a management-by-objective (MBO) practice, one form of a performance-based wage system.

As in Germany, these changes have been associated with heightened appeals to the virtues of flexible markets and shareholder value. For example, a 1998 report by the Economic Strategy Council of Prime

Minister Keizo Obuchi called for more labor mobility to increase Japan's economic vitality (Keizai Senryaku Kaigi 1998). The president of Takeda Chemical also argues for change: "What our company should do now is lay off. The company should not assume any responsibility for retaining workers. It is the government not the company that should care about employment. The company is the shareholders' property, and what it should pursue is profit for the shareholders. In order to increase profits, we should introduce a performance-based wage system, which would motivate workers" (*Nikkei*, 9 December 1998).

However, and again as in Germany, the continuities in traditional Japanese industrial relations practices are in some ways as striking as the changes. Based on a multifactor analysis of data from 1,618 firms, Motohiro Morishima (1995) identifies three types of company attitudes toward employment system reform. One group of firms is trying to change their wage system from seniority-based to performance-based and, at the same time, attempting to use increasingly an external labor market in recruiting workers. This group represents the much-publicized trend away from traditional Japanese employment practices, but in fact it constitutes only 10.8 percent of the sample. The majority of firms in the survey (56.8 percent) belong to another of Morishima's three groups, in which firms have retained the traditional employment system and thus constitute a bastion of continuity within the Japanese industrial relations system. A middle group (32.4 percent) presents a mixed picture; this group consists of firms that are reforming the wage system while at the same time maintaining long-term employment practices. Taken together, these data highlight the striking resiliency of traditional practices, as well as some important changes.

A 1997 survey of 380 large companies reveals a similar pattern—only 18.7 percent of these companies had introduced an annual salary system, a performance-based alternative to the traditional seniority-based wage system (*Nikkei*, 2 March 1998; survey conducted by the Socio-Economic Productivity Center). Although this constitutes a big jump over the previous year (from 9.8 to 18.7 percent), the numbers do not show a free fall into neoliberalism. Moreover, evidence from the same survey suggests that even when new systems have been introduced, they do not depart radically from the old system. For starters, the vast majority of firms adopting the annual salary system (87 percent) have applied it solely to managers, not production workers (Ministry of Labor 1995). In addition, when performance-based pay has been introduced, it has mostly been applied only to the annual bonus, which introduces only 10–15 percent variance in annual salaries among workers of the same tenure (Yashiro 1997, 110).

Thus, contrary to the impression conveyed by the popular and business press (which heaps attention on firms that depart from traditional practices), the trend away from seniority-based wages and lifetime employment practices appears to be, overall, rather slow and cautious. For every high-profile case of change there are equally notable counterexamples. Toyota, for example, has tenaciously defended traditional practices as the only way to secure and retain reliable and skilled workers (*Nikkei sangyō shinbun* [hereafter *Nikkei sangyō*], 1 October 1998). A member of the firm's board of directors said, "Matushita baldly abolished impediments for labor mobility, [but] we cannot go that far" because automakers need more skilled and experienced workers than do firms in the electric appliance and computer industries (*Nikkei sangyō*, 1 October 1998).[11]

Moreover, the putative trend away from lifetime employment guarantees is in some ways even more ambiguous than the trend to reform wage systems. Matsushita, which, as we have seen, is at the forefront of changes in salary structures, remains committed to long-term employment. In fact, the company is currently planning to extend the compulsory retirement age from 60 to 65 in an effort to retain highly skilled workers. A Nikkeiren survey of 255 companies in 1998 revealed that only 8.3 percent of firms actively sought to increase labor mobility (although 67.9 percent felt it would increase whether they like it or not). The companies surveyed predicted that the percentage of long-term employees (or core regular workers) within their workforces would decrease from 84.0 to 72.7 percent in the future. This would certainly represent a change of some significance, but what is equally impressive is the expectation on the part of managers themselves that over two-thirds of their workers will continue to enjoy long tenure. Taken together, then, these figures do not suggest an all-out transformation of the Japanese employment system (Nikkeiren 1998).

In sum, as in the case of Germany we have a mixed picture of significant change and also resiliency and important continuities. In Japan, too, scholars emphasizing continuity versus those stressing change do not disagree so much on the definition of the problem—employers' rejection of traditional practices and heightened demands for more flexibility in personnel policy—as they do on how to interpret the evidence: Is the glass half empty or half full?

Recasting the Nature of the Crisis

One reason most of the existing literature has not been able to account for the mix of stability and change we find in Germany and Japan is that it is premised on a somewhat one-sided characterization of what the crisis of

---

11. Toyota appears unfazed by predictions that its commitment to long-term employment will hinder its competitiveness, reflected, for example, in the downgrading of the company's long-term debt to AA1 from AAA by Moody's Investors Service.

industrial relations is actually about. A large literature tells us that globalization has given capital new power (capital mobility and exit options) at the same time that high unemployment has weakened labor (e.g., Kapstein 1996; Kurzer 1993). The labor scholarship tends to characterize the contemporary period as one in which employers have been able to use their newfound strength to force unions to agree to a restructuring of labor relations on terms more favorable, and above all more flexible, for employers (e.g., Katz and Darbishire 1999). The familiar face of the crisis of industrial relations in the advanced industrial countries features footloose firms shopping for the least restrictive labor regime and aggressive employers wielding the exit threat to secure concessions from unions in what is seen as a neoliberal race to the bottom.

But there is another face to globalization, the full implications of which remain underexplored in the existing literature. In a context in which competition has become more intense, and in fact increasingly so between high-end Japanese and German competitors—as in the automobile industry—and when success in the market increasingly depends on tightly coupled production networks (just-in-time production and highly coordinated supplier links), many employers find themselves more dependent than ever on a high degree of predictability on the shop floor and on the active cooperation of their workforces to produce at high quality and on a just-in-time basis (see, e.g., Streeck 1997d).[12] This alternative angle on globalization gives us a way of understanding aspects of the crisis of industrial relations that the alternative perspective blends out. In particular, employers in both Germany and Japan have actively sought to intensify cooperation with core workers at the plant level, and precisely these efforts have frequently had quite destabilizing effects on the system as a whole. Rather than an all-out frontal attack on the part of employers against the system, we are looking—in both countries—at a trend toward an intensification of traditional protections for some that has, in turn, been intimately linked to the growing exclusion of others.

Germany

Arguably the most destabilizing force in German industrial relations in the 1990s was not aggressive employers preying on unions paralyzed and enfeebled by high unemployment, but rather the breakdown of employer solidarity and the obsolescence of their most effective weapon, the lockout. Dominant characterizations of the crisis of German industrial relations—by both scholars emphasizing stability and those stressing change—

12. Elvander (1997) and Kjellberg (1998) have addressed these issues in the Swedish context.

are unified in their characterization of the crisis as one of unions struggling in the face of an employer attack on industrywide regulation and its replacement with more flexible, decentralized negotiations. They differ only in their assessment of labor's capacity to fight back. But events in Germany simply do not fit this picture; what the existing literature has studiously ignored is the fact that some of the most important collective bargaining rounds of the 1990s saw unions prevail over increasingly disorganized and fragmented employer associations.

Take, for example, a strike in 1995 by the IG Metall in Bavaria, a region characterized by relatively weak union organization and an employer association dominated by hard-line small and medium-size businesses—in other words, just the kind of firms that have been the most vocal in calling for industrial-relations reform. The IG Metall opened the 1995 bargaining round with a demand for a real wage increase, and Gesamtmetall countered by insisting that the union would have to make concessions on flexibility before it would even think about wages. A classic confrontation was expected along just the lines that the employer offensive thesis predicts. In the event, however, the conflict followed a radically different script, one the union itself might well have written.

As soon as the strike began, the employers' unified stand completely collapsed as Bavarian firms broke ranks and began denouncing Gesamtmetall's hard-line position and pushing instead for a speedy settlement. Employers affected by the strike worried openly about the effects of the conflict on the cooperative relations they had developed with labor in their own plants and that they saw as crucial to their competitive success. The strike featured an extraordinary outbreak of wildcat cooperation— but on the employers' side—including threats by individual firms to negotiate separate deals with the union if their national association remained intransigent. Gesamtmetall answered the strike with its usual threat of a lockout, but in the face of growing resistance from its member firms, the association did not follow through. Instead of expanding the conflict, Gesamtmetall settled, dropping its demands for flexibility and conceding wage gains that were widely viewed as an unalloyed victory for the union.[13] The terms of the deal were adopted in other bargaining districts throughout Germany without further conflict, and heads rolled at Gesamtmetall headquarters as the organization's hawks were summarily removed from office.

Bavaria was not an isolated incident. The next year, the stage was set for employers to capitalize on an opportunity to secure new flexibilities denied them under existing central bargains. In response to intense lobbying by employer associations such as Gesamtmetall, the conservative govern-

13. The strike is recounted and analyzed in some detail in Thelen (1999b).

ment had passed legislation reducing sick-pay compensation to 80 percent, down from the 100 percent stipulated by the metal industry contract. Gesamtmetall encouraged its member firms to take advantage of the new law to reduce costs, arguing that the legislation superseded the collective agreement. Daimler took the lead in announcing the reduction—provoking tremendous unrest among the workforce—but retreated when virtually no other firms followed suit. BMW dramatically refused, arguing that, with its order books full, it could not afford the conflict. Once again, employer solidarity completely collapsed in the face of plant-level conflict, and employers (including Daimler) quickly began demanding central negotiations to settle the issue. The 1996 bargaining round in the metalworking industry was pushed forward to deal with this issue. The result was a new industry agreement that reestablished 100 percent sick-pay compensation for the industry.[14]

Against conventional understandings, we thus find that German employers, not unions, are the ones suffering the greatest strategic and organizational disarray. These episodes provide vivid proof of a dramatic new development in German industrial relations, namely, that employers are now (as one employer representative put it) "deathly afraid" (haben höllische Angst) of industrial conflict and can no longer muster the solidarity it takes to answer a strike by the union with even the plausible threat of a lockout (interview, 1998). Moreover, this turns out to be true even where we least expect it to be, in the east, where unions are presumably at their weakest. In 1998, the threat of a strike in the eastern steel industry brought about a rapid disintegration of solidarity among employers. In the face of a looming conflict with the union, leading eastern German steel companies "started to put pressure on their employers' association and demanded new negotiations to avoid a strike at the last moment" (Schulten 1998, 2). One leading firm, Preussag-Walzwerk Ilsenburg (Sachsen-Anhalt), agreed to accept the union's demand for an adoption by eastern firms of the collective agreement in effect for the western German steel industry. Eko Stahl GmbH (Eisenhüttenstadt), which is the largest eastern German steel company, said it could not afford a strike and also threatened to abandon the employer association by concluding a separate agreement with the union along these lines. Prominent defections such as these were sufficient to bring about an agreement, amidst cries of union blackmail by the president of the steel employer association (Arbeitgeberverband Stahl), Josef Fidelis Senn (Schulten 1998).

Needless to say, developments such as these do not fit well with the

---

14. The union did, however, agree to modest wage increases that year, as well as the exclusion of extras such as Christmas and overtime pay from the base wage on which sick pay is calculated.

framework on which much of the conventional literature is premised. That literature features blackmail of a very different sort—employers wresting concessions out of local labor representatives against a threat to locate production elsewhere. We would simply never know from the existing literature that German employers, not unions, are the ones who most fear—and who are most paralyzed by—industrial conflict. The fact is that German employers are worried sick about the possibility of prolonged conflict on the shop floor, and this is painfully clear to the officers of key employer associations such as Gesamtmetall who can be heard publicly bemoaning a lack of parity—in labor's favor!—in industrial conflicts.[15]

By abandoning the standard assumptions and instead focusing attention on these developments, we begin to develop a clearer picture of the centripetal and centrifugal forces at work in the German system. The deep reluctance of German employers to abandon traditional bargaining institutions is rooted in their continuing—even enhanced—stake in arrangements that deliver a high degree of predictability and peace at the plant level. Centralized bargaining guarantees a degree of predictability by concentrating industrial conflict and providing a uniform timetable for negotiations that protects individual companies from isolated disruptive wage disputes, something that has, if anything, become more dear to firms in an era of just-in-time production (Streeck 1997d; interview with Dieter Kirchner, former managing director of Gesamtmetall, 1998).

Moreover, in the context of Germany's dual system, full decentralization would empower works councils in ways that employers are loathe to contemplate. The litany of worries they themselves recite includes (1) the threat of an expansion of works councils' codetermination right to wages and all other material conditions of work; (2) the threat of greater legislative interference (because there is no constitutional guarantee of plant autonomy analogous to Germany's hallowed principle of collective bargaining autonomy); (3) the threat of even higher wage settlements (especially in economic good times); (4) threats to cooperative relations with works councils; (5) the disadvantage of having conflicts over wages settled by outsiders in conciliation procedures; (6) the likelihood that the prohibition against strikes by works councils would become untenable; (7) the threat that drawn-out legal battles would interfere with a firm's capacity for long-term strategic planning; (8) the threat of enhanced union influence in the plant; and (9) a weakening of solidarity among employers,

15. This is what lies behind Gesamtmetall's interest in engaging the IG Metall in negotiations over new dispute resolution procedures. The employer association made a proposal that calls for ongoing dialogue on collective bargaining issues at the central and regional levels, for a third-party consulting committee to accompany negotiations, and for obligatory dispute resolution procedures if negotiations fail after an agreement has expired (Zagelmeyer 1998).

which could contribute as well to higher wage deals with the proliferation of individual company agreements (Bundesvereinigung der Deutschen Arbeitgeberverbände [BDA] 1996, 3–4).

The resiliency of the German model of industrial relations is frequently attributed to union strength, and scholars who subscribe to this view cite the conflicts we have described here as instances of organized labor's successful defense of traditional arrangements (see, e.g., Turner 1998). However, as we have seen, employer interest, not just union strength, accounts for the stability of the system so far. Moreover, quite to the contrary of the labor strength thesis, union victories such as in the 1995 strike, far from shoring up the system, may have heightened the crisis by further fragmenting the employer association and in some cases encouraging firms to opt out of the system altogether (Silvia 1996, 56). The head of the IG Metall acknowledged this in a very telling statement in the wake of the Bavarian conflict. He argued that although the union gained members as a result of the victory while Gesamtmetall lost members, this was no cause for rejoicing. "For me the [current] situation is not cause for . . . *Schadenfreude* [taking pleasure in another's misfortune] but rather for worry," and he emphasized that "collective bargaining autonomy requires strong bargaining partners" (*FAZ*, 6 April 1995).

Here we come full circle, back to the most important sources of strain on the German system we have cited, namely, declining membership in the employer associations and with that the shrinking coverage of collective contracts. The most rapidly growing divide in Germany is not, as commonly announced, between labor and capital but rather between those companies—many but by no means all of them large companies—that remain heavily invested in traditional practices because they depend crucially on a high degree of social peace and labor cooperation and that are willing to pay almost any price to preserve these and a growing number of companies whose situation in the market renders them unable to pay the premium and for whom defecting from the system appears to offer relief.

Research on which kinds of firms are currently in- and outside the traditional collective bargaining system may provide some initial clues regarding the economic and institutional logic of defection. The most comprehensive study (limited, unfortunately, to the west) is based on a 1995 survey of 4,100 firms across industries (Kohaut and Bellmann 1997). The study distinguishes between firms that negotiate a collective bargain with the union (at either the industry or the company level) and those that are not subject to any collective contract. Susanne Kohaut and Lutz Bellmann find that collective bargaining coverage is strongly correlated with plant size and with the existence of a works council. Workers in small plants, in other words, are much less likely to be covered by a contract than those in larger plants, and plants with works councils (also correlated with firm size) are more likely to be included than those that lack plant representation. These results are confirmed by a somewhat more detailed 1994 study of 900 firms in one western state (Lower Saxony); this study underscores as well the importance of union organization in a firm's tendency to join the employer association (Schnabel and Wagner 1996).[16] The evidence suggests that the probability of a firm's being in the association rises with increasing size of the establishment, with increasing union density, with increasing risk of industrial disputes, and for companies that are subsidiaries of larger firms rather than independent companies.[17]

Firm size—which, again, is itself strongly associated with higher unionization and works council presence—appears to be the single most important factor determining the clubbability of firms in the east as well. In fact, large firms in the east are even somewhat more likely to be covered by an industry agreement than western firms of the same size. Coverage in the east rises steadily with firm size, from 18.9 percent of the smallest eastern firms (1–4 employees) to 77.7 percent of the largest (1,000 or more employees). The comparable figures for the west are 35.7 percent for the smallest and 75.8 percent for the largest (Zagelmeyer 1999, drawing on Kohaut and Schnabel 1998).

These studies provide a basis for some inferences concerning the incentives that individual companies face that may affect their propensity to join or stay in the employer association. Larger firms (heavily unionized, typically, and certainly with a strong works-council presence) may stay in the association because they would probably wind up anyway with a firm-level contract that matches (or might even be more generous than) the industry deal (Schnabel and Wagner 1996). Conversely, smaller firms that are poorly organized and may not even have a works council are more likely to try to escape regulation by industrywide contracts because the weak labor representation makes it likely that management can push through a more flexible and inexpensive deal by going it alone. In general, then, it appears that the firms that are most likely to defect are those that do not face much threat from the union, either because they are too small for the union to worry about or because organized labor's presence is so weak

16. Unlike the larger survey, which distinguished between collective bargaining coverage or not, at issue in this survey is membership in the employer association. As previously pointed out, some firms conclude separate contracts with the union; that is, they may be outside the employer association but have a collective agreement nonetheless. Some of these *Haus-* or *Firmentarifverträge* have better conditions than the industry contract (like Volkswagen); more probably have worse conditions. But all are negotiated with the relevant union.

17. Both studies also found that older firms are more likely to be members of the relevant employer association than recently founded companies—an indication that the taken-for-grantedness of association membership may be on the decline.

that the union cannot realistically mobilize to force the firm back into the association.[18]

The heterogeneity of the metalworking industry along these key dimensions (firm size and union presence) has made for stronger centrifugal pressures in Gesamtmetall than, for example, the employer association for the chemical industry (which is dominated by a few big firms and, as we thus expect, remains highly organized). The splits within Gesamtmetall reflect the different market and political conditions across its membership. The collective bargaining system continues to hold onto, and indeed work well for, a significant (although shrinking) core of (especially large) firms, some of whom may have exercised their exit options already, relocating abroad those elements of production that do not rely for their success on the German infrastructure. By contrast, other companies that are for one reason or another less mobile—for example, by virtue of a family-based employment structure—cannot keep up in terms of the costs of collective contracts that increasingly exhaust the ability of large firms to pay.[19] These smaller firms traditionally benefited more than large firms from the information and consulting services the associations offer; however, those benefits are now largely outweighed by the increasingly expensive terms of the industry contracts (Schnabel and Wagner 1996, 298). As long as they can stay out of the union spotlight, opting out of the formal collective bargaining system offers the best of both worlds: relief from the terms of the contract and the ability to take a free ride on the collective benefits that the system continues to generate (most notably, skills and shop-floor peace and predictability).

Japan

In Japan, as in Germany, there have been substantial changes, but here too the popular conception of a straightforward managerial assault on traditional institutions and practices may obscure more than it illuminates. A closer look reveals considerable cooperation between employers and unions at the plant level to maintain employment security for core workers. Moves to reform the wage structure—although typically coded as part of the same managerial offensive that has put long-term employment at risk—are in fact frequently part of a strategy to preserve long-term employ-

18. Schnabel and Wagner's simulations show that, holding firm size constant, an increase in the union organization level increases the probability of a firm being in the association (Schnabel and Wagner 1996, 304). A similar effect comes into play across industries, based on the risk of industrial disputes.

19. It appears that the gap between wages paid by small and large firms narrowed in the late 1990s because wage drift in the large firms declined (Hassel and Schulten 1998, 503–4).

ment. As in Germany, patterns of resiliency and change are closely interwoven.

We have seen that technological changes reveal some of the limits of traditional practices based on seniority wages and on-the-job training. The premise of the traditional system was that workers would become ever more valuable to the company as they acquired experience on the job, and this is what justified their steadily increasing wages. But technological developments in the 1990s outstripped the skills of experienced workers, and the need to fill in the gap has unleashed fierce competition among firms for promising young workers, not so much because of their relatively lower wages but because of their adaptability to new technology.

Not a neoliberal offensive but, rather, this competition for younger workers is what lies behind many of the most important changes in traditional Japanese managerial practices. The seniority wage system has always been based on relatively low entry-level wages; otherwise, upward wage adjustments over time would be too expensive to sustain. But this poses problems for firms competing with one another for these promising entry-level workers, problems that firms have addressed through departures from the seniority wage system. The reforms introduced by Matsushita, for example—allowing employees to take their retirement bonuses early—were specifically designed to attract young skilled workers.

In other words, abolishing seniority wages appears to be less a neoliberal strategy against labor than it is a mechanism for achieving advantage against other firms in competition for the best new recruits. Firms want to pay workers more not less, and young workers are especially happy to oblige. At Matsushita, 44 percent of the newly hired graduates (844 workers) opted for the no-retirement bonus track, whereas only 1.8 percent of workers with more than two years tenure chose this option (*Nikkei*, 3 July 1998). Moreover, and important for our argument, these changes in the company's wage system were introduced at the same time that the firm renewed its commitment to long-term employment.

If reforms of the wage system have in part been motivated by the attempt to achieve advantage in the competition with other firms over the most desirable young workers, the reforms have also reflected a desire to make it less costly for firms to retain older workers. In other words, such reforms are seen as necessary in order to maintain the stability of long-term employment. This is why many specialists on the Japanese wage system predict that even if seniority wages wither away, long-term employment practices will continue. They argue that the introduction of new performance-based wages will help management to retain younger but highly skilled workers with higher wages (*Nikkei*, 25 March 1998). Toyota management, for instance, says that even in the auto industry, in which experience on the job is still important for skill formation, new information technologies have created some gaps between workers' experience and actual performance. The company justifies the changes to its wage system to accommodate this new situation as a way to maintain long-term employment by giving potentially more mobile, young skilled workers better wages (*Nikkei sangyō*, 28 September 1998).

Several successful companies have already introduced performance-based wage systems while at the same time committing themselves to secure employment. Canon makes it a policy to retain workers in hard times, but is famous for its performance-based pay system. In this system, a worker's wage is determined by his or her performance, irrespective of seniority, and wage differences among workers at the age of fifty with the same tenure are large by Japan's standards—as much as 1 to 1.7. Companies such as Nihon Densan, Yokokawa Denki, and Terumo are holding to their commitment to employment security while at the same time shifting to pay systems based on the performance of individual workers (*Nikkei*, 29 November 1998). In these companies, too, reforms of the wage system have been undertaken in part to maintain secure employment.

These data and observations show that contemporary changes in Japanese industrial relations, although significant, do not amount to an all-out transformation of traditional managerial practices but rather are adjustments designed to reduce inflated costs and to enlarge the benefits of the employment and wage system in a new market context. This kind of adjustment is by no means without precedent in Japan. We remember that the Japanese management system was criticized as an impediment to economic efficiency in the early 1970s after the first oil crisis, and many observers predicted that Japanese companies would need to abandon their traditional employment practices in order to survive. However, Tetsuji Okazaki's analysis of thirty-three steelmakers in Japan shows that firms that undertook fewer cuts in employment after the first oil crisis have done better in business indices such as profit increase and productivity increase than those that undertook massive employment adjustment (*Nikkei*, 29 November 1998). The successful companies implemented various rationalization programs, such as flexible job assignments, while rejecting large-scale dismissals of workers. Similarly, in the late 1990s, many companies carefully searched for solutions to maintain traditional strengths in a new globalized world market.

It is also important to note that Japanese unions are not antagonistic toward reforming the wage system, and indeed many of them endorse such reforms as necessary. The Union of Electrical, Electronic, and Information Workers (Denki Rengō) has formulated a new action policy, the New Japanese Employment and Compensation System, which advocates the introduction of performance-based wage systems to maintain employment. Its purpose is to take the initiative in the process of employment-system reform in order to protect its members' interests (interview with Denki Rengō leader, 17 January 1999, Yokosuka City). Denki Rengō is planning to abandon seniority-based wage demands and instead pursue an increase in the minimum wage level for each job category in the upcoming wage round (*Nikkei*, 9 July 1998). This move is very important, because Denki Rengō is one of the largest industry-level union federations, organizing almost all the large electric appliance producers, which are the backbone of Japanese international competitiveness.

Of course, not all unions are so supportive of these reforms. The president of the Japanese Confederation of Shipbuilding and Engineering Workers' Unions speaks for many when he asserts that "management may introduce some arrangements to recruit excellent workers from outside, but we unions should care about average workers" (*Nikkei sangyō*, 1 October 1998). His concern is for the situation of those workers who may be worse off in the new wage system. However, what is interesting in this case is that management in this industry has been more cautious in introducing reforms than in other industries, and so the difference between union and management on the wage issue is not so large. For example, Mitsubishi Engineering bases 50 percent of a worker's wage on job capability, with the other 50 percent based on seniority. The company's vice president/director argues that the firm will not introduce a performance-based principle because it is almost impossible to evaluate an individual worker's performance given the very interdependent nature of production (*Nikkei sangyō*, 1 October 1998).

The distinction drawn here between a job-capability wage and a performance-based wage is subtle, but very important. Performance-based wages are determined according to the job a given worker is actually performing, whereas capability-based wages are based on a worker's skill level and are thus closer to a seniority wage to the extent that workers' skill level increases with their tenure. The same careful attitude toward reforms is present in the case of Fujitsu, whose president argues, "Although the average wage in Japan is now among the highest in the world, we are not paying the highest skilled workers enough. We should reward those workers fairly and maintain them, by introducing a wage system based on workers' *capability*" (*Nikkei*, 9 July 1998; emphasis added).

In the job-capability wage accord, management pays the same wage to workers in the same skill level, whether or not they are fully using their skill in their actual job assignment. Although more costly for management, capability-based wages (like seniority wages) ensure that workers are motivated to develop their skills, because they are compensated for their skill level rather than assigned job. For management, this has the advantage of promoting a large pool of skilled workers readily available for flexible production. For workers, it is more egalitarian than performance-based wages because more workers are paid the same wage despite their actual job assignments. The incentives, in other words, resemble those of seniority-based wages and as such contribute to maintaining the high-skill equilibrium that has been a strength for most Japanese manufacturing industries (Miyamoto 1998).

Thus, when it comes to the reform of traditional seniority wages, we see a picture of significant but in many ways also quite cautious change. The current economic crisis combined with an aging workforce, on the one hand, and decreasing benefits due to such factors as technological changes, on the other hand, have called the traditional system into question. The ongoing economic downturn is so long and serious that management cannot easily count on the long-term benefit of the traditional systems. But, at the same time, management does not want to demoralize workers. The most critical issue in the new wage system is evidently how to measure performance objectively. The president of the Japan Automobile Workers' Unions admits that the wage system should be reformed to take the performance and skills of workers into greater account. But at the same time he insists that they need a fair evaluation system (*Nikkei sangyō*, 28 September 1998). Denki Rengō unions concur on this point too.

It is not just unions who have voiced such concerns. In a survey of 380 large companies, 81.8 percent of those firms that chose not to reform their wage systems argued that it would be too hard to convince workers of the fairness of such a system and they did not want to lower their workers' motivation. Management is thus faced with a difficult trade-off: whether to motivate selected highly skilled workers with performance-based wages or to motivate a wider range of workers with job-capability wages. Drawing distinctions between core and peripheral workers within a plant or company could itself threaten plant peace because such distinctions are at least as much political as they are technical. It could well be that the move toward capability-based pay reflects an effort on the part of some firms to negotiate this difficult terrain without upsetting the moral economy of the company.

As for long-term employment, unions are unanimously eager to protect the job security of their members, and all of them continue to support long-term employment practices. Even the most reformist union leader, the president of Denki Rengō, argues that employment should be protected, and one way to do this is through the introduction of a flexible wage system. A Nikkeiren (1998) survey of 255 firms shows that most firms believe labor mobility would bring benefits for them: 69.7 percent of firms answer that one advantage of labor mobility is enabling rationalization of the wage system, and 59.4 percent answer that workers can be evaluated according to their market value. But at the same time they are fully aware of the disadvantages, which include the loss of workers' loyalty to the company, a loss of organizational integrity of firms, instability of workers' lives, and reduced motivation for skill development within firms (Nikkeiren 1998). In other words, this survey suggests that management is not eager to abandon long-term employment per se, but wants to use some labor mobility as a catalyst to reform the wage system. In light of continuing support for long-term employment by both unions and managers, the reform of the wage system in many companies is best interpreted as an adjustment effort to protect this bottom line, that is, long-term secure employment. Reform efforts, moreover, do not necessarily pit management against labor, and indeed, many of them are founded on labor and management cooperation.

However, it is also true that traditional practices such as lifetime employment apply to ever fewer workers and, again, the logic of the selection process is closely related to the new terms of competition in the market and its implications for employer strategies and employment structures. For instance, faced with a serious business downturn in which its sales decreased by almost 50 percent, Hino Motors (which produces trucks) announced a restructuring plan that calls for voluntary retirement, after 50 percent cuts in company board members' bonuses and various restructuring efforts. The president furthermore announced that if there were not enough workers opting for early retirement, management would have to dismiss workers in order to save Hino Motors, a very radical move in the context of Japanese industrial relations (*Nikkei sangyō*, 3 March 1999). Naturally, the Hino union fiercely opposed this dismissal option and succeeded in forcing management to cancel it (*Nikkei*, 21 April 1999). The union did not, however, oppose the voluntary early retirement scheme. At issue was not whether there would be workforce reductions, only how these would be accomplished—through forced layoffs or through a less radical voluntary scheme. Both sides, in other words, saw a reduction of core workers through the company's rationalization plan as a part of defending the jobs of a (now smaller) core.

Company initiatives to revise traditional arrangements (seniority wages and lifetime employment) often represent efforts to selectively apply these arrangements (i.e., to single out certain workers to be covered), and modifications in traditional practices frequently represent efforts to give (particular, usually skilled) workers more benefits (not fewer) than allowed under traditional arrangements. In particular, high competition among firms for young skilled workers has prompted many firms to abandon seniority wages in an effort to enhance their potential to recruit and motivate these workers. At the other end, retirement, companies are reneging on lifetime employment guarantees in the case of some workers while at the same time making every effort to reinforce some kind of lifetime commitment among others. The overall trend, then, seems to be toward a (shrinking) core of (mostly skilled) workers within individual firms, who continue to enjoy lifetime employment guarantees, combined with an even more generous wage system (Chikuma 1999).

Future Trends

Overall trends in Germany and Japan are thus quite similar, with traditional arrangements proving in many ways rather resilient but covering a shrinking core of workers. Whereas in Germany the divide between those who are and are not covered runs roughly along lines of company size within key industries (such as metalworking) as well as across industries, in Japan it runs more along skill and age lines within companies. The question in both cases is whether the coverage of traditional arrangements—whether at the industry level as in Germany or at the company level as in Japan—can simply continue to shrink down to cover a smaller number of firms (Germany) or workers (Japan) without this destabilizing relations outside this core.

This question poses itself with some urgency because in both Germany and Japan elements of stability and change are intimately linked; that is, the observed trend toward an intensification of cooperation with the traditional framework is one of the forces driving the trend toward narrower coverage. In Germany, as we have seen, the most pressing problem is the defection of firms from industry contracts, a problem fueled in part by strong aversion to conflict on the part of large firms and declining solidarity among employers more generally in the context of industrial strife.[20] Dieter Kirchner (former managing director of Gesamtmetall) argues that in the past the lockout served two important purposes simultaneously: enforcing discipline in relations with the union and generating solidarity among employers (interview January 1998, Köln; see also Schnabel and Wagner 1996, 298). The threat (or in many cases the reality) of a lockout made it possible for the IG Metall to swallow moderate wage gains and sell them as "the best deal under the circumstances" to a highly diverse membership. These settlements typically did not exhaust the capacity of the large firms to pay, but these companies could let wages drift up at the plant level (thus allowing them to recruit the best workers).

It appears that since the late 1990s, this form of flexibility has been greatly reduced; in other words, high union wage increases relative to eco-

---

20. Of course, another pressing issue in Germany is unemployment. This problem overlaps with and is exacerbated by the trends cited here to the extent that the cleavages within the industrial relations system reinforce the gap in Germany between those who enjoy stable, protected employment, on the one hand, and the long-term unemployed and holders of various irregular employment contracts, on the other.

nomic conditions have reduced the room for wage drift, which means that smaller firms are now forced to pay wages much closer than before to those of the large companies (Hassel and Schulten 1998, 503–4).[21] These effects follow naturally from the developments discussed here, which document employers' surprising weakness in industrial conflicts. These developments complicate internal union politics to the extent that a strong opponent is often quite useful for unions needing to forge an internal consensus across workers of different skill levels and employed in firms experiencing quite different economic pressures. This is why, historically, unions needed fights with strong employer associations, which had the mutually beneficial effect of sustaining solidarity within camps.

The German case shows that declining solidarity on the employer side feeds back in ways that destabilize the system further. The more that wage negotiations are geared toward a declining core of overall larger and more dynamic firms, the more the weaker firms are likely to opt out; it does appear to be more common than ever before for firms to protest against overexpensive or overrestrictive contracts by simply leaving the employer association (*DL Nachrichten*, 26 February 1999). Perversely, this has become Gesamtmetall's most potent weapon in conflicts with the union—the threat that hangs in the air now during industrial disputes is not that the employer association will lock out but rather that it will fall apart.[22] The worrisome possibility is that the traditional framework of industrial relations remains intact but over time comes to be inhabited by a smaller core of firms that are willing—and able—to pay almost any price for social peace. Such a trend destabilizes labor relations to the extent that, with time, industrywide bargains will no longer be encompassing enough to generate many of the collective benefits on which the defectors so far have been able to continue to take a free ride. The prospect here is that the system at some point would just tip.[23]

The key to the survival of the German model appears to hinge rather crucially on the continuing strength of the unions. But labor power comes back in a way unanticipated in the conventional literature, in which its role is to beat back the neoliberal employer offensive. There will be some of

21. This appears to be one reason why, against the trend in most other advanced industrial countries, wage inequality in Germany has been declining, not increasing. We thank Jim Mosher for suggesting this to us.

22. We are grateful to Rainer Hank for emphasizing this to us.

23. Some observers, including Dieter Kirchner himself, think that the system could in fact survive—at least for a time—in a "shrunken down" version. He could imagine a situation in which encompassing collective contracts cover fewer firms (although still the largest firms, and thus still a very large number of workers), with other firms outside the central bargain but orienting their own plant-level deals to the industry contract. "There has to be something to deviate *from*," as he puts it, and so the industry contract would serve as the reference point, even for firms outside the bargain (interview, June 1999, Köln).

that, but the more pressing task facing unions turns out to be something more like the opposite, namely, to combat the flagging solidarity of employers and to shore up the embattled employer organizations. Union leaders understand this very well, which is why they have launched regional campaigns (sometimes hand in hand with regional employer associations) to pressure defectors to reassociate with the employer associations or, failing that, to hold them to the same standards as specified in the industry contract. This image of labor strength—not against employers but precisely in the service of shoring up solidarity among them—clashes with the conventional understanding of the challenges labor faces in an era of globalization. But it is crucial to explaining why, in a period touted as one of extreme labor weakness, unions in Germany (quite correctly) view employers' lack of solidarity as labor's number one problem.

The same kinds of issues present themselves in the Japanese case, although in a somewhat different form. Here the question is whether a growing gap between core and peripheral workers with very different career possibilities within the firm is sustainable over the long run. Management's intention in the reform is to motivate high-skill workers with better benefits and to force semiskilled workers to work harder by introducing performance-based wages (Shimada and Ota 1997, 104–6). Management worries that the job-capability or seniority-wage system may sometimes enable workers with less skill to receive better benefits because it is difficult for management to measure their skill level given new technological developments and the uncertain business climate. In other words, management wants to prevent the emergence of incentive problems on the side of workers (i.e., low-performance workers receiving the same wage as high-performance workers). One solution is to use performance-based wages more selectively in compensating workers. Evidence from some firms, however, suggests that selective benefits for privileged, usually skilled, workers make it hard for management to motivate the large number of semiskilled workers who are excluded. Although not perhaps in as much demand as skilled workers, semiskilled employees are nonetheless central to the continued smooth operation of production. Japanese manufacturers' competitiveness traditionally has been based on quality mass production, and the success of this kind of quality-based competition depends very much on semiskilled workers or reduced X-inefficiency of the Japanese work organization (cf. Leibenstein 1976). To the extent that this advantage continues to be crucial for Japanese producers, semiskilled employees are no less central to the companies than more highly skilled employees.

Furthermore, the abandonment by some firms of the job-capability (skill-based) wage system in favor of performance-based wages could reduce the investment that firms make in training, and an overall reduction in the pool of skilled labor in Japan would surely weaken manufacturing industries there. This may be a road to a low-skill, low-wage workforce. As long as management wants to maintain the strength of Japanese manufacturing industries, there is ample room for labor to negotiate on the issue of new management systems. For instance, within Matsushita, the union is demanding an extension of the compulsory retirement age for all workers, whereas management wants some selection mechanism. It is evident that the union's plan would cost the firm more, but management has difficulty in flatly rejecting the demand. This is because management worries that such a selection might demoralize workers as a whole.

This point leads us to a more political aspect. Although large Japanese firms have been employing peripheral workers, such as part-time workers, for a long time, there has been a high degree of egalitarianism among core regular male workers within Japanese unions. Employer strategies of selective benefits for privileged workers will undoubtedly create severe contradictions and tensions for company-based unions that organize all regular workers in a plant irrespective of skill. To the extent that the performance-based portion of a worker's wage grows (thus sparking competition among workers for better jobs), this could unleash potentially disruptive political struggles within the unions over which jobs should be better rewarded and who should occupy those jobs. This prospect brings to mind the U.S. system of job control, something that—if their U.S.-based operations are any indication—Japanese managers certainly want to avoid. Management has to maintain fairness within the firm as long as it wants to motivate workers, and this consideration constrains management attempts to reform traditional practices in ways that introduce new forms of differentiation and divisions among workers.

In sum, in both Germany and Japan, we find significant and surprising resiliency in traditional bargaining arrangements in the face of new global market pressures. Whereas much existing scholarship focuses on a neoliberal offensive and sees stability as a residual outcome (i.e., a lack of change, despite new strains), our analysis sees continuity and change in both systems as intimately and causally linked in important ways. In both Germany and Japan, the most destabilizing forces go back to the intensification of cooperation within a shrinking core that has in turn driven a narrowing of the coverage these systems have traditionally supported.

Transformation and Interaction: Japanese, U.S., and German Production Models in the 1990s

Ulrich Jürgens

In Germany the 1990s began with a massive restructuring of production models, inspired by Japanese lean production, in almost all industries. The German model, however, retained its essential characteristics because the luster of the Japanese model faded as the Japanese economy faltered in the 1990s. In the United States, in contrast, the long-established model of mass production had been transformed in the 1980s by adopting or adapting elements of the Japanese model from companies in Japan and from Japanese transplants in the United States, as well as by downsizing and restructuring. This transformation, necessary to regain competitiveness in U.S. industries, was nearly complete by 1990.

At the end of the decade, however, the direction of change seemed less certain than at its beginning. Future development can no longer be seen as a process of catching up with a superior production model. Still, competitive pressures and new challenges fuel dynamic capability building and the search for new approaches. To what extent these will be nation-specific or differ by industry or company remains an open question.

The debate about national models of production started in the late 1970s in an attempt to explain the different performances of national economies following the three shocks of that decade: the dissolution of the Bretton Woods system; the oil crises, one at the beginning and one at the end of the decade; and—in Western countries—a wave of active and passive labor protests. Sweden, Germany, and Japan were viewed as countries that coped particularly successfully with these shocks, each with a distinctive production approach. During the 1980s, studies of these cases comparing them to less successful industrial economies suggested new perspectives for national economies. In one view, different paths of develop-ment seemed possible, with "space for political vision and choice—and for a diversity of choices—[being] open and wide" (S. Berger 1996, 25). In an-other perspective, nation-specific institutions were seen as the basis for dis-tinct national production models (Sorge and Streeck 1988; Streeck 1989) or as constraining the adoption of new best-practice concepts (Tüselmann 1998). And a third view suggests that specific national characteristics may allow nations to excel in certain types of production but not in others; thus, nations should specialize in their specific strengths (Boyer 1996; Soskice 1996).

As in the debate about national models, the automotive industry plays a paradigmatic role in this chapter, which focuses on the core configuration of country-specific characteristics of production and work organization. The central questions are the extent of transformation in these character-istics in the three dominant automobile producing countries—the United States, Germany, and Japan—and whether, in the changing economic cir-cumstances of today, previous strengths may have turned into weaknesses or vice versa.

Dimensions of National Production Models

A "production model," as it is used here, synthesizes elements from three lines of discussion: Michael Burawoy's (1985) work on factory re-gimes, which is concerned with different forms of social integration and control at the plant level; the concept of industrial models developed by Groupe d'Etude de Recherche Permanent sur l'Industrie et les Salaries de l'Automobile (GERPISA), the French-based international research net-work, which studied the complementarities and interlinkages that explain specific company trajectories (Boyer and Freyssenet 1995; Freyssenet et al. 1998); and the debate on the influence of national institutional settings and societal effects as explanatory factors for economic success or failure (Berger and Dore 1996; Maurice, Sellier, and Silvestre 1986; Sorge and Streeck 1988).

Obviously, there is no set of norms and regulations at the national level that determines how production is organized at the company level. Yet it seems highly plausible that differences in education and vocational train-ing, industrial relations, and labor law, together with other more general historically and culturally rooted societal factors, have an impact on how production in a country is typically organized, socially structured, and controlled.

National production models can be analyzed on three levels: nation-specific inputs of policies, regulations, institutions, social values, and norms, and the specific endowments of productive resources; empirical observation of actual work practices; and distinct outcome patterns, for instance with regard to economic growth and national competitiveness, employment, welfare, quality of work, and environmental impact. Although these levels are closely interrelated, the exact nature of the interrelationship is unclear. Actual work practices cannot be derived from policies, institutional regulations, values, or norms because the influence of these factors may be slight or incoherent and contradictory. Outcomes such as growth and competitiveness also are only indirectly linked to characteristics of the national production model. Three possible relations among the different levels are of particular interest:

1. A country may have only a few policies and regulations and weak institutions to influence the organization of production processes; this represents a specific national approach of noninterference. The paradigmatic case is the United States.
2. National institutions or social norms and values aim to influence the patterns and characteristics of production. Germany and Japan are typical cases.
3. The patterns and characteristics of production change due to the adoption of best practices from other countries, eclipsing nation-specific institutions and traditions. In view of the broad debate about lean production, the trend in the 1990s seems to have headed in this direction. The convergence of actual work practices may render the notion of national production models increasingly meaningless.

In later debates, the issue of convergence under the impact of Japanese best practice has played a prominent role (Berger and Dore 1996; Boyer et al. 1998; Elger and Smith 1994; Jürgens 1998; Kenney and Florida 1993; Liker, Fruin, and Adler 1999). From this perspective, the transformation of national production models is seen as the result of external pressure. This chapter, however, emphasizes the internal dynamics of change in national production systems, which are seen not just as configurations of more or less complementary elements, but as systems evolving and transforming themselves following an inherent logic. As Sorge and Streeck (1988) have shown, national systems develop an evolutionary dynamism based on complementarities and mutual reinforcement among their elements, which can trigger virtuous as well as vicious circles. At certain stages of development, logics can be reversed, virtuous circles change into vicious circles, and strengths may turn into weaknesses.

The following analysis focuses on the patterns and characteristics of the actual practices of production organization and work regulation. The assumption is that changes in approach at strategic levels of the company or regulatory institutions determine these practices. National models are discussed along five dimensions: process design (the organization of production flow), job design (the composition of individual tasks and areas of responsibilities), the involvement of rank-and-file employees in improvement activities, employment security, and worker interest representation and conflict resolution. Whereas the first two dimensions relate to process engineering and industrial engineering, the last two are aspects of social integration. The third dimension connects industrial engineering and social integration. Issues of corporate governance, supplier relations and supply-chain organization, and the relations of production with other corporate functions are not taken up in the analysis in a systematic way.

The Development of Production Characteristics during the 1970s

Until the 1970s, national differences in production models received little attention. In the early 1970s, the dissolution of the Bretton Woods system, labor unrest, and the oil crisis of 1973 came as severe shocks. National economies responded in different ways and with different degrees of success, as became apparent in the second half of the 1970s. Also in this period, reform movements to modernize or humanize production systems occurred in many countries and the superiority of the Japanese system became an issue. To describe the logics of the production models of the United States, Germany, and Japan, the central characteristics of each are reviewed briefly across the five dimensions.

United States

The U.S. model was shaped by principles of mass production that evolved in the United States in the nineteenth century. The system relied on a virtuous circle linking process layout principles with labor market characteristics and a particular division of labor (figure 7.1).

Process organization was in line with the principles of mass production, aiming at the highest possible output at each stage of the production process. Performance regulation took place through expert-centered Taylorist standard setting and direct control of shop-floor workers by supervisors who had no specific technical training.

Job design was centered on individual jobs and followed the principle of narrowly defined tasks and low responsibility of workers. In

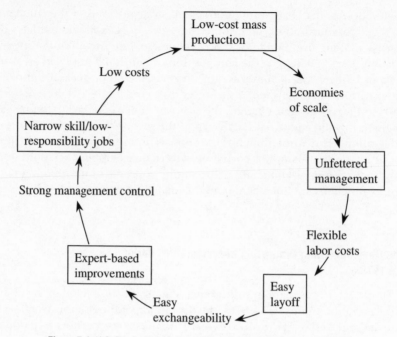

Figure 7.1 U.S. Production Model of Mass Production: The Virtuous Circle

response to the management-initiated division of labor and segmentation of internal labor markets, rules of protective seniority
and job demarcation became established by labor union demand.

Process improvement and process innovation were the exclusive tasks
of experts without the participation or involvement of workers.
Technology was regarded as the major source of improvement and
the panacea to problems of all sorts, including labor relations.
There was no protection against the rationalization effects of improvement activities.

Human resource policy was predicated on a hire-and-fire orientation.
Employees were recruited and then laid off in response to short-
term job requirements rather than developing human resources
in view of a long-term employment relationship. Corresponding to
narrow task definitions, skill formation took place almost exclusively through on-the-job training. Also, there was little selectivity in
hiring, and dismissals were restricted only by seniority rules.

Labor relations were marked by distrust and antagonism. Management's main concern was the defense of its right to manage rather
than seeking consensus with worker representatives.

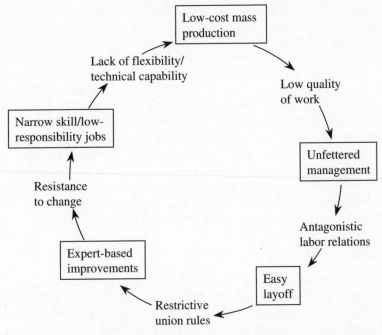

Figure 7.2 U.S. Production Regime in the 1970s and Early 1980s: The Vicious Circle

In short, this model relied on experts, direct supervisory control, and technology as the main sources of performance and improvement and in principle paid little attention to questions of social cohesion.

During the 1970s the U.S. production model was in full-blown crisis because by then it had lost most of its Taylorist-Fordist rationality, and there was no consensus on a new production model or on the direction of reforms. The main reason the U.S. model became caught in a vicious circle was that the market demanded more flexibility but the social system of production was still oriented on mass-production principles (figure 7.2). A long tradition of antagonistic labor relations and the hire-and-fire stance of management had led to an increasingly Byzantine system of regulating internal mobility and of layoffs on the basis of seniority rules. In the face of declining competitiveness in the second half of the 1970s, the negative effects of this system on flexibility and productivity were widely perceived. At the same time, workers and local unions, under the threat of extensive workforce reductions, clung to the model. Flexibility was therefore sought primarily in the deployment of technology. The training system, however, did not provide the skills necessary for this; frequent breakdowns and the associated output losses increased pressure on workers, which in turn worsened labor relations.

Most important among the institutions and agencies regulating work were the company- or plant-level industrial relations systems. With the exception perhaps of the Occupational Safety and Health Administration (OSHA), few institutions existed at the industry level to influence the production model. Semipublic institutions, such as the Work In America Institute, which propagated new forms of work, were closed in the late 1970s. The sharp decline of apprenticeship training in the United States continued, and efforts to revitalize the model failed (Gospel 1994).

Under these conditions, the labor unions were the most important external influence. In addition to pay, they focused on employment security, health and safety, and performance regulation, without trying to influence the way production operations were organized and run.

Germany

Germany took a different course from the United States. Although in the period between 1975 and 1985 the German production model was still oriented toward mass production, a range of labor reforms and production modernization programs were developed in close cooperation among employer associations, unions, and the government. Many of the new concepts were inspired by Swedish work experiments, but because of the specific skill base in Germany, different solutions were sought. Centered on the *Facharbeiter*, the new approaches sought a future-oriented paradigm of work with a high degree of autonomy, the right to determine work hours, and high responsibility of shop-floor workers.

> *Process organization* was based on the same mass-production principles as in the United States; however, concern for economies of scale was less marked in Germany due to smaller company size and production runs. As in the United States, performance was regulated by Taylorist standard-setting methods coupled with incentive pay schemes on the basis of rules and procedures codetermined by the union and the works councils. Shop-floor supervision was exerted via the distinct German *Meister* (first-line supervisors) system, which combined elements of performance control with engineering expertise.
>
> *Job design* was centered on individual jobs as in the United States. This became a focus of work reforms in the 1970s in response to the European debate on sociotechnical system design and the program of the German government for the humanization of work. New job designs were introduced that aimed at job enlargement and enrich-

ment and the decoupling of work from the immediate pressure of machinery or assembly lines.

Process improvement and process innovation were the realm of experts, production planners, and industrial engineers. Technology was regarded as the main driver. Collective agreements on the introduction of new technology protected individual workers against the rationalization effects of such improvement in terms of employment and wage levels.

Human resource policies centered on long-term employment and vocational training. Training took place on the basis of temporary contracts offered by companies to school leavers for the time of their apprenticeship. Unskilled and semiskilled job categories were regarded as obsolete. Production departments increasingly hired *Facharbeiter* and assigned them to ordinary production jobs while the vocational training system introduced new curricula for skilled workers carrying out production jobs with new technology. Skilled workers were regarded as the "winners of rationalization" (Kern and Schumann 1989, 94).

Labor relations were founded on social cohesion and consensus as major sources of productivity. Here, a system of interrelated institutions, internal and external to the company, had developed, based on mutual responsibilities—employers accepted responsibilities in areas such as training, ergonomics, and quality of work; unions accepted the need for flexibility and cost efficiency; and the state accepted responsibilities in areas such as vocational training and labor market policy.

The contrast to the U.S. production model is evident. A major difference was a national emphasis on vocational skill formation. In the German model, raising the skills of blue- and white-collar workers was regarded as a central goal of public policy. The dual system of private and public apprenticeship training provided foundational skills and, because most workers in higher-level positions in the career structure—the *Meister*, technicians, and engineers—had gone through a *Facharbeiter* apprenticeship, a common background of skills and experience existed among blue- and white-collar employees that fostered companywide cooperation.

The classical reason, of course, for promoting apprenticeship training was to support labor-market mobility and reduce the dependence of workers on individual employers and industries. With the diffusion of mass production in Germany, the argument gained ground that a skilled workforce would allow for alternative forms of work in mass production and thereby help avoid some of the negative effects of the U.S. model. The expectation was that preserving skills in areas such as assembly-line work would even-

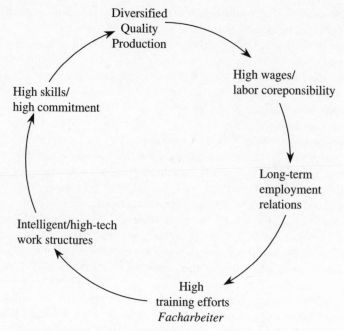

Figure 7.3 German Production Model in the Early 1980s: The Virtuous Circle

tually enable companies to use new technologies more efficiently than in other countries.

In view of the technological development in microelectronics, actors at different levels came to a number of agreements in the second half of the 1970s. On the whole, these can be regarded as a national pact between capital and labor. In exchange for increased flexibility and the acceptance of new technology, labor gained employment protection, an increase in apprenticeship training, and increased works council participation in work design. The national government supported this pact with various programs relating to codetermination, the labor market, and social welfare.

These emerging characteristics of the German production model seemed to usher in a golden age characterized by a virtuous circle that enabled Germany to make best use of its skill potential (figure 7.3). A result were intelligent work structures capable of diversified quality production (DQP), which met new customer expectations and therefore could carry a price premium, which, in turn, enabled companies to pay the comparatively higher German wages.

This virtuous circle, first articulated by Sorge and Streeck (1988), was widely viewed as the principal reason for Germany's comparatively successful economic performance in the 1980s. Indeed, there can be no doubt

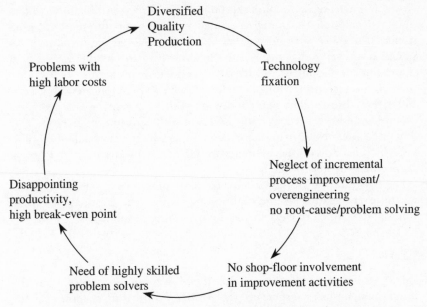

Figure 7.4 German Production Model in the Late 1980s: The Vicious Circle

that German companies during the decade pursued a strategy of DQP, and many continued to do so in the 1990s. As comparative research has shown, German companies tend to produce higher-quality products that they sell at higher prices, not only in the well-known cases of the automobile and machine tool industries, but also in industries such as textiles, precision engineering, and food processing (see Broadberry and Wagner 1996). At the same time, however, it must be noted that, although concepts of intelligent work were widely discussed, reality lagged far behind. This was especially true in the introduction of teamwork, cross-functional project organization, and supplier and customer integration. Second, the high value of the U.S. dollar during the first half of the 1980s made German high-priced products price-competitive, particularly in the United States, creating a bubble situation in support of the DQP strategy. A third fact that became obvious in the course of the 1980s was the ability of the Japanese production model to produce quality and diversity at much lower costs than the German model.

By the end of the 1980s it was obvious that the German model had begun to turn into a vicious circle (figure 7.4). The concentration on DQP gave rise to a trend toward excessively complicated, overengineered products. It also promoted an expert orientation on quality control, causing quality to be inspected in instead of built in. There were few bottom-up improvement activities to exploit the potential of skilled production workers and to develop skills among unskilled workers, who often were immigrants. Also, there were no systematic efforts, either in the form of incremental improvement activities on the shop floor or in the early stages of product development, to alleviate production problems. As a consequence, the technology introduced was much too complicated and, even under the advantageous skill conditions of the German model, problems abounded and productivity gains were not sufficient to reduce costs. This generated pressure to trim labor costs, especially for semiskilled employees, which reinforced the tendency to neglect them as a source of potential productivity improvement.

The frustration with the virtuous circle turning into a vicious circle was an important reason for the enthusiasm for the lean production revolution that developed in Germany at the beginning of the 1990s.

Japan

The Model Japan debate of the 1980s drew on examples from the automobile industry, especially the Toyota production system, and the electronics industry, especially Fujitsu. Here is the typical profile of the Japanese system across the five dimensions.

Process organization, especially in work flow and operations management, marked a break with mass-production principles. The Japanese approach involved buffer minimization and quality assurance. The zero-buffer/zero-defect/single-work-piece flow principle (see Monden 1983) entails strict requirements with respect to work discipline, vertical and horizontal cooperation, and constant improvement activities. Technology is not regarded as the main solution of production, and labor problems play a subordinate role.

Job design stressed flexibility to enhance vertical and horizontal cooperation, and performance regulation and task allocation referred to teams rather than to individual jobs. At the same time, the classical assembly-line structure with short-cycled, line-paced work remained the backbone of work organization in large-scale assembly operations. A different approach was taken in subassembly and machining areas in which production cells (U-shaped lines) with multimachine tending operations were installed as early as the 1970s.

Process improvement and process innovation were not seen as the domain of experts but as part of the ordinary job responsibility of all workers. Rationalization measures did not reduce employment security, due to company commitments to long-term employment, as distinguished from collective agreements.

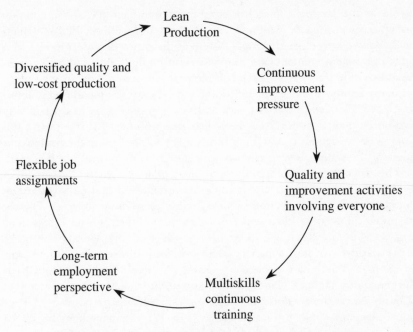

Figure 7.5 Japanese Production Model of the 1980s: The Virtuous Circle

Human resource policies focused on a core group of employees with long-term employment security. Skill formation was on the job and emphasized the broadening of skills. Production and nonproduction workers had the same basic education and in principle there were no pay differences between them. Together with seniority, personnel appraisal systems controlled pay differentiation and promotion in extremely fine-tuned ways (Nomura and Jürgens 1995).

Labor relations were based on institutions at the company level and aimed at consensus and effective control of deviant behavior. Management and worker interest representation were not clearly separated. Strong emphasis was placed on social integration, loyalty, and commitment to the company. Employees had a strong position; shareholders, the local community, and other external stakeholders were of little relevance (Thomas and Waring 1999).

The worldwide attraction of the Japanese production model came from the virtuous circle consisting of lean production and its implications for job design, human resource development, and work organization (figure 7.5). The interdependencies among the various elements of the Japanese production model have often been stressed in debates on its transferability. Here the Japanese model became the prime example of the complementarities approach (Milgrom and Roberts 1994; Boyer 1998a), which sees the strength of the Japanese system as the effect of supermodularities in which system elements are mutually reinforcing and the whole is more than the sum of its parts. These complementarities may explain the failure of many attempts to transfer individual elements of the Japanese model to the West. However, the complementarities approach fails to explain why system elements reinforce or destabilize one another. To understand the source of the system dynamics, it is necessary to determine the underlying logic of the system. There are two opposing interpretations in this regard.

The Toyotism interpretation sees the dynamic core of the Japanese system in the zero-buffer and zero-defect orientation that pulls other elements such as teamwork, multiskilling, and improvement activities. This interpretation is rooted in the accounts given by Taiichi Ohno (1988) and Shigeo Shingo (1981), with their strong industrial engineering emphasis. In this approach, performance, teamwork, and improvement orientation are enforced mainly by process pressures. This leads Knuth Dohse, Ulrich Jürgens, and Thomas Malsch to the conclusion that this system was "not a basic alternative to Fordism" and "regressive from the point of view of more developed labor unions" (1985, 141–42). "Management by stress" was the critical term introduced by Michael Parker and Jane Slaughter (1988), and it became emblematic for the critique that the system with its zero-buffer and zero-defect principles, by removing all slack in the process, exerts a constant pressure on workers. The critique was brought forward in particular by the new direction movement, a group of members of the U.S. United Auto Workers (UAW), which opposed the transfer of Japanese production principles to U.S. plants.

By contrast, the Fujitsuism interpretation of Martin Kenney and Richard Florida (1988) emphasizes human resources, skill formation, promotion, continuous learning, and improvement orientation. The emphasis here is not on industrial engineering but on qualification, continuous improvement, and organizational learning pushing an innovation dynamic that is seen as the major strength of the system (see also Imai 1986; Koike and Inoki 1990; Nonaka 1990).

These two interpretations were often held to contradict one another (Kato and Steven 1993); however, it seems more fruitful to acknowledge that both are necessary to explain the specific strengths of the Japanese model. On the one hand, Toyotism could not explain the degree of commitment to improvement activities and the obvious attraction the system of human resource management and knowledge creation had for the core workforce (Nonaka 1990). On the other hand, Fujitsuism could not explain the opposition to the Japanese model based on the 3K critique of industrial work—work that is dirty (*kitanai*), hard (*kitsui*), and dangerous (*kiken*)—and other labor concerns that emerged in the time of tight labor markets during the bubble period.

In contrast to the German model, the Japanese production system evolved mostly through company experiences without a highly differentiated system of institutions on the national and industry level. Critical impulses shaping the model came from the occupation forces after World War II and from U.S. advisers, including W. Edwards Deming. Institutions such as the Japan Productivity Center (JPC) and the Japan Management Association (JMA) played a role when it came to the diffusion of best practices, especially in the early 1980s when the Toyota production system began to diffuse across industries. Union influence at the company level should also not be underestimated (Nomura and Jürgens 1995), although it was largely restricted to personnel practices. In the larger companies with supplier *keiretsu*, the unions helped in differentiating pay and in regulating labor mobility. Of much greater importance in defining the character of the Japanese model, however, are indirect institutional effects such as the system of general education and sociocultural values that underlie the unique combination of teamwork and competitive orientation of individual employees in Japan, a combination fostered by company policies in particular since the 1970s (Kumazawa 1996).

To summarize, the U.S. production model with its roots in the 1910s and 1920s was clearly in a state of decay by the 1975–85 period and was seen as the *bête noire* of the three models. During the same period, the German model underwent a process of modernization that led to renewed social consensus, new production concepts, and a new market strategy, which seemed to add up to a successful national model. Weaknesses were, for the time being, masked by favorable economic conditions. The Japanese model was in the process of rapid diffusion inside Japan as well as worldwide. It thrived with the success of Japanese export industries, in particular the automotive industry. And, during the bubble in the second half of the 1980s, this success reached its zenith.

Transformation and Mutual Interaction

I now turn to the question of the extent to which national production models in the three countries were transformed during the 1990s due to the changed economic environment and to organizational restructuring.

Japan

Since the late 1980s, the Japanese economy has gone through a period of extreme and opposite pressures. The bubble economy with its tight labor markets fueled dissatisfaction with industrial working conditions (such as the 3Ks). During the bubble boom, a debate about a paradigm shift toward a post-Toyotist/postlean production system started and companies experimented with new approaches. This movement lost its momentum when the recession began. The reactions of Japanese car manufacturers to the recession followed a well-known pattern: campaigns for improvement in product quality and productive efficiency and for cost cutting, demands for cost reduction from suppliers, and a further shortening of product-development times. The principles of the production model itself were not questioned. Christian Berggren and Masami Nomura (1997) conclude that the most remarkable feature of this period was the resilience of the Japanese production system. This seems to hold true even after the most dramatic developments that culminated when the second major car manufacturer of Japan, Nissan, was on the verge of bankruptcy and was taken over by Renault in 1999. A review of the changes in the actual practices of work regulation confirms the resilience of the system.

Process organization still has its traditional principles firmly in place. Despite some changes in the application of the just-in-time principle related to computerization, modifications in process layout, in particular of assembly operations, follow an evolutionary incremental path (Fujimoto 1999).

Job design receives more attention. The prime example again is Toyota, in which new concepts of job design emphasize more holistic tasks, ergonomics, and a strengthening of teamwork by introducing small buffer areas between group areas (Fujimoto 1999; Shimizu 1998). Still, short cycle times and narrow task definitions remain characteristic of assembly-line work, although in other manufacturing areas U-shaped lines and cellular production with long multitask manual work cycles have become more widespread.

Process improvement activities are now more expert-led, a tendency that was already visible by the end of the 1980s. Nevertheless, the expectation is to involve all workers in improvement activities, and the linkage between employment security and rationalization effects has maintained its credibility despite the decade-long recession.

Human resource policy allowed employment guarantees for a core group of employees to be maintained and defended by most companies even in difficult situations. However, opposition to lifetime employment security and seniority has become more open, and some companies have announced they will abolish these practices. Also because of the recession and the uncertainty of the future, companies have increased the proportion of part-timers, thus extending their flexibility to hire and fire. In the area of skill formation, a growing emphasis on specialization can be observed, and the policy of relying mostly on internal capability building is changing in favor of a tendency to recruit specialists who already have job experience.

Labor relations were mixed. Although the Japan Automobile Workers' Union (JAW) was exceptionally outspoken in its opposition to working conditions during the bubble era, it has returned to its previous policy of close support for management.

A source of learning by mutual interaction with foreign production models could have been the Japanese transplant experience in North America and Europe. However, few examples of such feedback can be cited (Boyer et al. 1998; Liker, Fruin, and Adler 1999).

The resilience of the Japanese production model may not be surprising; it is still regarded as a benchmark by many Western companies. Nevertheless, as noted, companies sought new directions in the second half of the 1980s when strong opposition to the production system arose and problems of recruitment, motivation, and turnover began to multiply. One new direction was technology-oriented—many companies experimented with high-tech production approaches. As in Germany and the United States, this failed and was abandoned in most cases. The other new direction was in job design and it emphasized holistic tasks, a limited degree of decoupling work from process pressures, and the introduction of human-fitting automation (Fujimoto 1997), showing that work planners had learned a lesson from the sociotechnical design school. In its newest plant in Kyushu, Toyota in particular went far in the direction of a human-motivating production approach characterized by Takahiro Fujimoto as the "hybridisation of the traditional Toyota system and certain elements from European factories" (1997, 233).

There can be no doubt, however, that the recession of the 1990s reinforced the established Toyotist approach. This approach was also newly adopted by companies that had to react to the adverse business conditions of the decade. For instance, companies in the electronic industries, including Sony, have begun to implement the principles of the Toyota production system.

Little can be said about the effects of the long recession on the values and expectations of employers and employees with regard to past commitments to lifetime employment and continuous improvement. Withdrawing either of these linchpins of the virtuous circle could turn it vicious. In any case, the huge wave of outward foreign direct investment since the 1980s deprived Japanese companies of the growth prospects to which the industry had become accustomed.

Thus the 1990s could turn out to be a watershed in the development of the Japanese model. At the same time, central elements of this model were adopted in the course of the decade by Western companies, and industry gurus and academics proclaimed it as a universal model. The very influential MIT study *The Machine That Changed the World* forcefully concludes with this message: "In the end, we believe, lean production will supplant both mass production and the remaining outposts of craft production in all areas of industrial endeavor to become the standard global production system of the twenty-first century" (Womack, Jones, and Roos 1990, 278).

Germany

In contrast to their Japanese counterparts, German companies in the 1990s were ready for a deep rethinking and restructuring of their production model. Compared to the United States and to other European countries, however, this readiness for change came comparatively late because the German economy had fared well throughout the 1980s. Complacency prevailed because German companies, not having Japanese transplants in their country, did not have the same catalyst of change as U.S. and British companies during these years.

The lean production model propagated by the 1990 MIT study (Womack, Jones, and Roos 1990) came just in time for German companies seeking to reorganize their model in their efforts to retain international competitiveness. What occurred in Germany in the course of the 1990s can be summarized as follows.

  Process organization using the central concepts of the lean production model was adopted by a majority of companies, although in many cases only with hesitation and gradually, in search of a compromise with existing practices that were to be integrated into the new approach.

  Job design now emphasized teamwork and moved away from the traditional separation of production, quality inspection, and repair work, which had caused high costs in the older system. Although the new forms of work developed in various humanization-of-work projects entailed a high degree of time sovereignty and self-regulation within work groups, mostly structurally conservative (Kuhlmann and Schumann 1997) solutions now prevailed, with short work cycles and narrow job definitions. As a result, most long-cycle work operations introduced in the 1980s were scrapped, and the same happened to high-technology equipment installed in assembly areas in that decade (Jürgens 1997). In view of this reconventionalization of production concepts, the rationality of hoarding skilled workers in production areas was now also called in question.

Process improvement activities involving the workforce beyond traditional suggestion schemes also formed part of the new management arsenal. However, the dominant position of experts remained.
A more cautious and incremental approach to technology was
adopted. Protection of employment against the rationalization
effects of improvements was reconfirmed by agreements on work
sharing and collective agreements ruling out plant closures.
However, the credibility of the critical linkage between rationalization and job protection declined due to growing uncertainties
related to globalization, mergers, and the rising shareholder-value
orientation of company management.

Human resource policies, despite continuous pressures for rationalization, showed that employer commitment to long-term employment
remained strong. Due to early retirement and working time reduction to 35 hours per week (and even less in some companies, such
as Volkswagen, with 28.8 hours), mass redundancies and dismissals
were usually avoided.

Labor relations, at the same time, showed that companies and employer associations did take advantage of labor's weakened position
and asked for concessions in return. Though difficult to prove,
the share of employees on lease or with time-limited contracts
increased.

Changes in the German model were clearly inspired by concepts of
non-German origin. In most cases, Japanese companies or Japanese transplants were the benchmark (on Porsche, see Womack and Jones 1996,
189–218). Direct interaction with Japanese companies or consultants
nevertheless remained the exception. U.S. influence was considerable.
First, U.S. multinationals were at the forefront of introducing new practices, such as those at Opel's assembly plant in Eisenach. Also influential
was the experience of German supplier companies interacting with
Japanese transplants in the United States and the United Kingdom. A
third influence were consulting companies, most of which were based in
the United States. During the 1990s, German firms were particularly eager
for their services. Given these influences, we should not be surprised to
find increasing skepticism of such distinctively German institutions as
codetermination, the *Facharbeiter*, and the apprenticeship training system,
even though many see them as strengths of the German model that should
be preserved (Roth 1997).

Against this backdrop, what is remarkable is the continuity of consensus
in industrial relations. In view of increased international competition, collective agreements between unions and employer associations supported
more flexible forms of production, and, at the company level, works

councils and management usually even agreed on far-reaching change programs, often in the framework of location protection agreements.

On the whole, changes in the German production model were conceived in most cases as common projects of management and works councils. This was supported by collective agreements between unions and employer associations, which allowed for more flexibility, especially in the length of the workweek. Established institutions of collective bargaining demonstrated their ability to adapt and innovate, although at times painfully (Turner 1997). This held true also for the process of integrating the former socialist areas in East Germany after unification. Transformation in the case of these new areas had a very different meaning than in western Germany. Under the new conditions, it was easier to introduce new practices in a sort of clean-sheet approach. In view of the huge difficulties in establishing a competitive industrial structure in the east, the transfer of West German institutions and practices increasingly became a matter of controversy and contention in the course of the 1990s. Thus many companies opted to stay out of collective bargaining, and works councils were able to establish themselves in fewer companies than in western Germany. Also, companies showed far less engagement in apprenticeship training, demonstrating that they were obviously accepting this not as a social responsibility but rather as a cost burden.

In view of these changes, is it justified to speak of a transformation of the German production model? On the one hand, new principles of process organization and job design were adopted. This is especially the case for factory reorganization adapting Japanese-style lean production. On the other hand, the institutions of collective bargaining and codetermination remained largely unchanged despite continuous pressure from increased international competition. But controversies and diverging approaches, particularly in East Germany, can also be interpreted as signs of erosion.

United States

During the 1980s the U.S. production model underwent three parallel changes. The first was the restructuring of existing production systems. This was a gradual process that had begun in the 1970s with the quality-of-work-life and employee-involvement programs. In the 1980s, learning from Japanese companies played an increasing role. In terms of concepts and methods, the focus was on process organization and control. The second was the massive wave of Japanese direct investment that brought core production methods, human resource management, and supplier relations systems used by Japanese parent companies (Abo 1994; Florida, Jenkins, and Smith 1998). This enabled U.S. companies to study Japanese practices closely and learn through direct interaction. The third development were new homegrown production systems, the most prominent of which was Saturn, the General Motors (GM) affiliate established to create a new synthesis of best practices from Japan, the United States, and Europe. Although the production layout at Saturn closely follows the Japanese model, the involvement of union representatives at all levels of management was a departure from U.S. practices in the direction of the German model (Pil and Rubinstein 1998). Despite its success in customer and labor relations, the Saturn model remained isolated and by the end of the 1990s what was distinctive about this new synthesis seemed to be on the way out because of the forces of inertia within GM and the UAW.

As a result of these parallel developments, production approaches in the United States became more diversified, making it inaccurate to say that the United States had just one production model. The following review of our five dimensions takes into account some of the new diversity.

Process organization changed as Japanese transplants—which by the end of the 1990s accounted for almost one-third of U.S. passenger car output—established their operations largely based on the Japanese model and U.S. manufacturers adopted major elements of that model, with a focus on its process control characteristics (Florida, Jenkins, and Smith 1998). Few U.S. plants, however, installed the process-driven performance-improvement linkage that is part of the Japanese model, symbolized by the system of line stops. Supplier relations were transformed by the adoption of just-in-time practices and attempts to overcome the previous arm's-length approach.

Job design in many U.S. plants was now based on team principles, job flexibility, and some worker responsibility for quality and efficiency (Applebaum and Batt 1994; Florida, Jenkins, and Smith 1998). Due to a revision of most local collective agreements, many of the rigidities of narrow job descriptions and job demarcations were abolished. There were no efforts to decouple work from process pressure, not even in the modified forms introduced by Toyota in some of its plants, including its main U.S. transplant.

Process improvement is less changed. The role of experts clearly remains dominant in indigenous plants, and, even in the transplants, process improvement relies more on experts than in Japan. Although some of the transplants have made some form of commitment to employment security, none of the Big Three automakers has. Thus the traditional perception of a negative relationship between improvement activities and employment security, at least for those not protected by seniority, still prevails.

Human resource policies have caused both old and new plants to have a highly selected workforce, achieved through downsizing and structured by seniority and also by rigorous screening at the hiring stage. The workforce of the Big Three, however, has aged; in 1999 the average age was 49 years, and the time has come to recruit young workers. When new workers were recruited by the Big Three or by the transplants, training, mostly still on the job, received more attention than in the past. Special training for higher white-collar skills was increased considerably.

Labor relations shows the greatest variation. Most new plants were set up in a nonunion environment. Labor relations in existing unionized plants have changed from adversarial to what can be characterized as tenuously consensual.

Obviously changes in the United States were strongly influenced by Model Japan. Even though there was a debate on the merits of the German production model, focusing specifically on the training system (cf. Dertouzos et al. 1989) and works councils, initiatives to adapt elements of the German model at the national level led to nothing. At a subnational level, however, some remarkable developments can be observed, especially in the field of training (e.g., see Lewis 1997).

A major point of contention with regard to the U.S. production model is the role of unions. Here a dual structure has evolved: most new plants in the South are union free, and most northern plants of the Big Three remain unionized. Whether the new production concepts necessarily work better without a union remains an open question. Although the examples of New United Motor Manufacturing Incorporated (NUMMI, the Toyota-GM joint venture plant in Fremont, California), Saturn, and a number of Big Three plants have shown that the union is in principle not an obstacle to achieving world-class performance or implementing new production systems, Japanese and German transplants have mostly opted for a union-free environment.

In any case, the cooperation and compliance of union and workforce in making production more efficient and improving product quality contributed considerably to the revitalization of the U.S. automotive industry in the 1990s. This revitalization seems mainly a result of a change of union attitudes because during the 1990s investment in new process equipment was low and changes in most aspects of production were only incremental.

Compared with the situation in the 1970s and most of the 1980s, the development in the 1990s is often described as a turnaround. It is doubtful, however, that this really was the result of improved production practices in U.S. companies. The commercial success of the U.S. auto industry in the 1990s was mostly due to the fact that consumers flocked into the new market segment of light trucks, which was protected by tariffs against foreign competition and exempt from safety and emissions regulations. By the end of the 1990s, the light-truck segment made up almost one-half of total passenger-car sales. Although Japanese companies continued to gain market shares in the passenger-car segment, the Big Three thrived by producing cars in the very profitable and highly protected light-truck segment.

Convergence or Divergence?

The 1980s were marked by sharply contrasting performances of the various national production regimes, with dramatic superiority of the Japanese system. This was reflected by the MIT study (Womack, Jones, and Roos 1990), and its data on performance differences among the Japanese, North American, and West European production systems caused shock waves in Western countries. In the late 1980s, the adoption of Japanese concepts intensified and the understanding of the complementarities among the elements of the Japanese production model improved. Survey research on the diffusion of its elements, including just-in-time delivery, total quality control, efforts to improve product and work efficiency, and teamwork, shows little difference between Western and Japanese companies. In fact on some dimensions Western companies seem to have "outjapanesed" the Japanese (Florida, Jenkins, and Smith 1998).

There can be little doubt these changes contributed to the fact that Western companies became better able to master the cost-plus-quality-plus-flexibility relationship, which is key to Japanese production excellence. In addition to outsourcing more parts, process equipment and services were restructured and process chains were newly defined. Although this restructuring process has not yet been completed, the gap in productive efficiency between Japanese and Western autoworkers has narrowed (see the results of the second MIT study, Fine et al. 1996). Western production models have become more competitive and their vulnerability, measured for instance by the break-even point, has declined. Another result is that companies have broadened their capabilities to opt for different product-market strategies. As previously described, the German model in the 1980s thrived on the strategy of product upgrading and profited from the price premium German firms could charge. But, as quality statistics such as the J. D. Powers index show, the quality gap has become very small among companies in general, and German companies are far from being always ahead in the league tables of quality performance (Oliver 1994). At the same time, they have caught up in cost competitiveness, often with the help of production networks developed with low-cost production sites in eastern Europe and on the basis of concession bargaining.

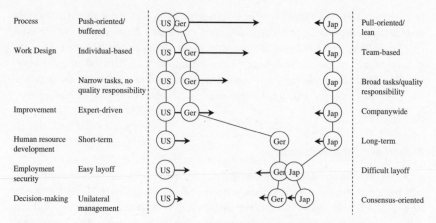

Figure 7.6 Changing Profiles of the U.S., Japanese, and German Production Regimes (1980–1990s) (Lead companies/Core workforce)

All this seems to indicate that convergence among the three national production models progressed due to a shift of the German and U.S. models toward the Japanese model, whereas the latter shows little sign of emulating the U.S. or German models. A closer look, however, reveals a somewhat more differentiated picture.

As shown in figure 7.6, a move toward Japanese-inspired lean production clearly has taken place. There can be no doubt that the central principles of process control—just-in-time, total quality management, and continuous improvement—are now regarded as universal production standards. This is confirmed by the introduction of standard production systems by a number of Western car makers. This movement was led by Chrysler with the introduction of its Chrysler Operating System (COS) in the mid-1990s. The COS was modeled explicitly on the Toyota production system—evidenced by the central role played in the COS by just-in-time supply and buffer minimization, team organization, and quality responsibility of line workers. A few years later, Daimler-Benz introduced the Daimler-Benz production system, which is a copy of the COS. Standard production systems were also introduced by Audi and Volkswagen. The interest in standardizing production systems at the company level, a correlate of the globalization process, was thus one factor driving production-system design in the direction of the Japanese model.

Convergence tendencies also prevail in the area of job design, as witnessed by the fact that many companies scrapped production systems that had been introduced under the influence of Swedish work concepts or the automation euphoria of the 1980s. Thus the assembly line with short work cycles and standardized job operations returned as the dominant element of modern best-practice production. Japanese influence can be observed also in the emphasis on the standardization of operations, on decentralizing quality responsibility, and on continuous improvement. Meanwhile, in Japanese companies modifications to emulate Western practices were taking place in process design, holistic task definitions, and ergonomics.

A further element central to lean production, which is also often described as a central characteristic of the Japanese production system, is teamwork. Teamwork has now become a standard feature of Western production systems, although there are wide differences in its substance and organizational characteristics. We might therefore question whether teamwork as practiced in Sweden and Germany resembles that found in the Japanese production model (Nomura and Jürgens 1995; Sey 1998). This is because behind the notion of teamwork there are widely different forms of work organization and performance regulation, and differences are still very much related to national contexts, as shown by research carried out in the mid-1990s (Durand, Stewart, and Castillo 1999).

The experience with teamwork indicates that the broad diffusion of elements central to the Japanese system by no means implies a convergence of national production models. Neither the German nor the U.S. production model has changed its basic orientations in these areas which, according to the Fujitsuist interpretation, constitute the cornerstone of the dynamic capabilities of the Japanese system. Long-term employment security may be eroding in Japan, but improvement activities of rank-and-file employees continue, and possible redundancies do not seem to dampen employee motivation.

Although many practices of the Japanese model have been transferred to Western companies, they add to, but do not replace, previous practices. Process improvement remains mostly the responsibility of experts, particularly in Germany. Similarly, in human resource development, skill formation, and labor relations, there is little indication of a trend toward convergence among the three production models. Skill formation still focuses on technically specialized front-loaded (*fachliche*) skills in Germany and continues to be restricted to narrow tasks in the U.S. model. Japanese personnel practices—the typical complex of skill formation, career structure, job rotation, and personnel evaluation—were implemented neither in Germany nor in the United States. There is also no rapprochement with regard to labor relations and collective bargaining, including the German system of interest representation via works councils.

To sum up, despite the fact that elements of the Japanese production model were adopted formally by German and U.S. companies, these companies still retain many of their traditional core practices. The diffusion of practices and concepts in themselves cannot, therefore, be interpreted as an indication of convergence of whole production models. Convergence in the sense of a development toward similar systemic dynamics, comparable to the virtuous and vicious circles of the three national models presented earlier in this chapter, is still rare and limited mostly to transplants. In any case, what we see was mostly a unidirectional transfer of elements of the Japanese model to the two others and not mutuality of influence among all three models.

The transformation of national production models may thus more appropriately be characterized as a continuous hybridization in an open process with a wide variety of trajectories (Boyer 1998a, 50–52). The adoption of concepts and practices from foreign production models in Germany and the United States took place because of obvious weaknesses in the traditional national systems, which were trapped in vicious circles. Introducing Japanese-inspired practices in a more systematic way than in the early 1980s proved successful in many cases. New challenges, however, have forced change on all production models including that of Japan, the success model of the late twentieth century. Hybridization must be seen in the twenty-first century as the process that shapes the future of all production models.

Strengths Turning into Weaknesses? Challenges of the Future

The 1990s, as we have seen, was a decade of increased pressure for change for the national production models in all three countries. Although there was a considerable degree of change in the sense of hybridization processes, particularly in the United States and Germany, there was also a high level of resilience. In all three cases there was little change in the institutional settings. In view of the gradual and hybridized—mixing old and new principles and practices—character of the change process, there is little evidence of a clear-cut shift of strengths turning into weaknesses such as the switch that took place in the transition from mass production systems to more flexible systems, a transition that has meanwhile been achieved in all three cases for better or worse.

What about the future? Five aspects appear to be of central significance for the future transformation of production capabilities.

Technological development. The lesson from Japan was that processes have to be simplified and made robust before seeking technical solutions, which then should also be as simple and robust as possible. Companies followed this lesson in the 1990s. The ambitions of full automation and the vision of computer-integrated manufacturing were dropped after many painful experiences. In the meantime, however, technological development has not stood still. Thus, for instance, with the advance of computer systems, the possibilities for computer-integrated manufacturing have considerably improved, as have the possibilities for computer-aided planning and simulation to debug production processes in the planning stages. In the future, it can be expected that automation will play an increasing role again. Due to simplification and standardization efforts, however, the composition of technical skills required in production plants will shift. On the one hand, the numbers of specialists and professionals with university educations will increase. Although in the medium-skill range (*Facharbeiter* and *Meister*) specialists with deep skills (Wever 1995) will still be needed, their number will be smaller due to the more robust technical solutions installed. And a total-quality orientation involving all skill levels will remain important. This suggests that to be competitive, each model must be capable of continuous technical improvement.

Time-based competition. With shorter cycles from the order to delivery of new products, communication and cooperation within companies have to be intensified to support agile business strategies (Goldman, Nagel, and Preiss 1995). Of particular importance is the ability to anticipate production requirements in early stages of product development. Thus, production representatives, including in many cases shop-floor workers, must be increasingly involved in early development activities. All of these are related to the Achilles heel of many companies—the difficulties faced with respect to the increasingly important rapid and smooth launching of volume production of new products. In the past, production workforces in the West were confronted with new production layouts and products at a late stage. Production preparation took place in separate buildings and only a few representatives of the production plant were involved in pilot build activities. This was in stark contrast with Japanese companies at which the new product was tried and tested by the production plant much earlier (Clark and Fujimoto 1991). The activities of debugging, improving the process, design changes, cooperation with suppliers, and participation in the setup of new machinery require new and additional capabilities, in particular the ability to cooperate cross-functionally in project groups and to communicate with product and process engineers as well as with supplier representatives. In regard to the requirements of time-based competition, the German production model seems to be at a disadvantage, especially in comparison with new U.S. approaches. This is because the shift toward more process-oriented, cross-functional, and project-based work has been made much more reluctantly by German companies than by their U.S. and, to a lesser degree, Japanese counterparts (Jürgens and Lippert 1997). The strong functional orientation in Germany, which is closely linked to the strong disciplinary orientation of engineers, tends to be a competitive disadvantage. Whereas German companies often adopt structurally conservative solutions, U.S. companies seem more prepared to choose radically new approaches.

Supplier relations. With the increased outsourcing of production and service functions, the management of external relations has become an increasingly complex task. Due especially to new supply concepts, the new roles of modular or systems suppliers' value chains have to be restructured and actors have to adapt to new roles. In all three national systems, a new balance has to be found between cooperation and competition among the actors of the automotive sector. This requires the bridging of conflicting targets, as in the case of attempts by car makers to link competitive bidding with simultaneous engineering. On the one hand, they want to reduce costs through competitive bidding; on the other, they are looking for innovative suppliers providing their technological know-how as partners in product development. The challenges here seem to be greatest in the Japanese context, in which existing *keiretsu* relationships will be affected. Breaking up long-standing trust-based relations in view of requirements related to product innovation or to the company's globalization strategy could prove difficult. The former strength of the Japanese model could turn into a weakness. There is evidence for this in some later developments in Japan.

Globalization. Because globalization necessitates increased efforts to standardize production systems at all locations of a company, national variations in production models tend to be seen as a source of friction that the world's leading companies must attempt to reduce or eliminate. At the same time, all companies do their best to diffuse innovations in their plants located in many parts of the world. The challenge for all companies is to make progress in the standardization of production while preserving the motivation to innovate locally.

Labor relations. Labor-related issues were less troublesome in the 1990s than in preceding decades. As a result, systems of consensus-seeking, via formal negotiation as in Germany or through informal problem anticipation as in Japan, seem to have become less important for the stability of production models. Given high unemployment, deflationary pressures, and globalization, some believe that the interests of labor, as one of the major parameters of each production model, have fundamentally changed. But this view may be seriously flawed. As the chief economist of Morgan Stanley warned, the aging of the workforce and the possibility of a worker backlash will keep labor and industrial relations issues on the agenda (Roach 1997). The strike wave at GM in the United States in 1998 shows the vulnerability of a system relying on just-in-time processes adopted by a company that still has adversarial industrial relations.

As all advanced industrial economies move into an uncertain future, the question of the strengths and weaknesses of existing production models can only be answered in general terms. What is certain is that the orientation toward current benchmark production models will not suffice because new challenges will require new hybrid models. We should also note a divergence that is likely to develop between two types of production systems: those aiming to become specialists in certain operations and serving different end producers as job-shops or turnkey manufacturers (Sturgeon 1997) and those becoming more integrated in new product development and customer service activities. Whatever the choice of individual companies, nation-specific conditions are likely to be a major factor shaping the outcome.

The German and U.S. production models have regained competitive strength and are no longer lagging behind Japan. But the Japanese model still seems the leader among near equals. At the same time, production is not the only determinant of competitiveness, as the example of Nissan demonstrates. As experience has shown, the productivity advantage gained in years of improvement activities can be destroyed by sudden shifts in currency value. And it is important to recall that despite the weakness of the U.S. model in the 1980s, U.S. producers remained successful because of their product strategy and the arrival of a new market regime. How production models evolve and what other developments, such as product strategy, exchange rates, and macroeconomic conditions, affect their performance continue to be vital concerns for industrial economies. This is especially the case as we traverse the uncharted seas of ever more interdependent economies and the ongoing digital revolution.

From Banks to Markets: The Political Economy of Liberalization of the German and Japanese Financial Systems

Sigurt Vitols

One of the key features of both the German and Japanese postwar political economies is a bank-based financial system (Zysman 1983). Bank-based systems are distinguishable from market-based systems not only by a much higher proportion of bank deposits and loans in total domestic financial assets and liabilities, but also by ownership and managerial links between banks and large industrial companies. In the 1980s, bank-based systems were widely perceived to be superior to market-based systems in their ability to provide long-term patient capital to industry, and many researchers and policymakers in the United States and the United Kingdom advocated the adoption of these systems as a remedy to industrial decline (Jacobs 1991; Porter 1992).[1]

Since the early 1990s, however, the bank-based financial systems in Japan and Germany have faced serious challenges. First, a general structural trend since the 1970s, the shift of major domestic customers such as nonfinancial companies, households, and the state to market-based forms of finance, appears to have accelerated in the 1990s. Second, macroeconomic developments, including slower worldwide growth and policy-induced demand shocks, have contributed to a bad debt problem; this problem is

I thank Gregory Jackson, T. J. Pempel, Wolfgang Streeck, and Kozo Yamamura for important comments on and suggestions for improvement of earlier drafts of this essay.

1. The precise impact of these features on real economic outcomes is a matter of controversy. However, on balance, the evidence seems to show that bank-based systems contributed to the remarkable success of capital-intensive, export-oriented industry in Japan and Germany by allowing more rapid growth (particularly during reconstruction) and by supporting companies during liquidity and demand crises.

particularly severe in Japan but is also apparent in Germany. Third, a variety of actors, including some major banks, the U.S. government, and segments of the German and Japanese state apparatus, are actively pursuing financial reform aimed at dismantling key institutions supporting the bank-based systems. As reflected in the debate on convergence to a U.S./U.K.-style market-based financial system, these challenges are so fundamental as to call into question the future viability of bank-based systems (Gardener and Molyneux 1993; Rybczynski 1988).

This chapter assesses the potential paths of development for these bank-based systems and argues that change in the two countries is poorly captured by the convergence-divergence dichotomy. Instead, path dependency, functional equivalence, and hybridization are more useful tools for understanding the complexity and contingency of processes that rarely (if ever) end in the concrete realization of ideal-typical models. The first point made is that an examination of changes in financial systems should start with an analysis of what are here called the societal foundations of bank-based systems. Bank-based systems rest not just on a set of financial regulatory practices, but also on the institutions and behavior of the household, corporate, and public sectors as savers and investors. A review of these major sectors shows that some but not all have shifted preferences to a market-based system. Although Germany and Japan have similar societal foundations, support for a bank-based system has eroded to a somewhat greater degree in Germany.

The second point made in this chapter is that, although public policy choices are often presented in terms of a stark dichotomy between liberal and nonliberal modes of regulation (the former associated with market-based systems, the latter with bank-based systems), in fact both Germany and Japan are struggling to find a successful combination or hybrid of the two types of financial regulation. Despite the popular image that market-based systems can simply be created through deregulation, in fact the regulation of financial markets in the United States (the benchmark case for liberal systems) is based on an extensive set of rules strictly enforced by a large administrative apparatus with the backing of a strong judicial system. This means that institutions and norms need to be created, not just destroyed, in order to support stable financial markets. Conflicts with existing institutions and their sponsoring interest groups are preprogrammed when liberal institutions are introduced. Although the nonliberal regulatory systems in the two countries were in many ways functionally equivalent (e.g., in suppressing capital markets), German corporatist institutions seem better able to coexist with liberal modes of regulation than does the Japanese practice of administrative guidance. Not surprisingly, regulatory change has taken the form of a Big Bang in Japan versus an obscure (to the general public) set of financial market promotion laws in Germany.

The third and final point is that banks play important (if diminished) roles even in market-based systems. In the United States, banks are still the most important providers of financial services to small businesses and lower-income households; furthermore, they provide liquidity insurance in the form of backup lines of credit to large companies. Thus, the ultimate form that the coexistence of banks and markets will take in Japan and Germany depends in large part on the creativity and efforts of policy-makers and the banks themselves. Those interested in institutional design should focus on how to preserve a viable banking system for small and medium-size enterprises (SMEs) and the household sector while simultaneously promoting stable capital markets for larger companies and high-tech start-ups.

Societal Foundations of Bank-based Systems

Most accounts of change in financial systems focus on financial regulatory reform narrowly defined. Here, however, I argue that the characteristics of financial systems are a product of both narrow financial regulation and what I call societal regulation. According to this approach, the financial system is viewed as a set of institutions and organizations at the center of the monetary economy that mediate the flow of savings and investment between nonfinancial sectors of the economy (i.e., the household, nonfinancial company, and state sectors). Banks and markets thus compete with one another as alternatives for mediating the flow of these funds.

Financial regulations can (and usually do) give an advantage to one alternative over another and therefore play a role in determining which one dominates the financial system. However, nonfinancial sectors also have a set of demand-and-supply preferences with regard to the basic characteristics of different types of financial assets (i.e., bank products versus marketable securities). A stable equilibrium is best produced when the bias of the financial regulations for either banks or markets is matched by the weight of preferences of the nonfinancial sectors. The most important characteristics of financial assets are liquidity, risk, and return, which are (as a broadly drawn generalization) higher for market-based than for bank-based forms of finance.

> *Liquidity* is the ease with which investors can buy or sell a financial asset at its current value. Marketable securities are in principle designed with standardized characteristics in order to have high degrees of liquidity. Securities exchanges are endowed with institutional features in order to promote this liquidity, such as specialized securities houses obligated to accept buy and sell orders in order to

Table 8.1 Preferences of Nonfinancial Sectors for Bank- versus Market-based Finance[a]

Nonfinancial Sector	Subsector	Preference for	
		Banks	Markets
Company sector	SMEs (traditional)	+	
	SMEs (high-tech)		+
	Large firms (high debt)	+	
	Large firms (low debt)		+
Household sector	High income		+
	Middle income	+	
	Low income	+	
Pension policy	Pay-as-you-go	+	
	Company reserves	+	
	Capitalized systems		+

[a] SMEs, small and medium-size enterprises.

assure orderly markets. Bank loans, on the other hand, have little or no liquidity in the limiting case of a loan or long-term deposit contract between one bank and one customer. These contracts can be prematurely terminated or assigned to another party only through negotiation between the two parties to the contract.

Risk is the probability that the stream of income expected from a financial asset will not be realized, due to either the lower profitability of a firm or, in the limiting case, bankruptcy. Company and bankruptcy law defines a hierarchy in the order in which the claims of different kinds of investors should be met in the case of insufficient funds. Stockholders enjoy the last (or residual) claims on income and assets; thus, holders of marketable shares face higher risk than bank lenders.

Return is the expected increase in the value of the original investment made over a specific period. Investors as a rule demand higher returns on riskier investments to compensate for extra risk; thus marketable securities must offer a higher return in order to compensate for higher risk.

It is possible to draw up the following generalized preference schedule for the different nonfinancial sectors with regard to bank- versus market-based finance (see table 8.1).

Company sector. The nonfinancial company sector is typically the largest net debtor sector (i.e., largest source of demand for finance) in industrialized economies. The demand for different kinds of finance varies greatly by type of firm. Due to the large fixed

costs of underwriting new securities, market-based finance is much
more costly or inaccessible to SMEs than bank loans. One reason
for this is that high fixed costs are involved in new securities issues,
which become proportionately larger the smaller the amount of
financing involved. A second reason is that large-portfolio investors
may avoid investing in companies below a certain size because the
costs of information-gathering and monitoring are also fixed and
thus render small investments unprofitable. Large firms with high
levels of debt also tend to prefer bank-based finance because
market-based investors see these firms as too risky for further investment; banks with significant loans to these firms may be forced to
make new loans to stave off default on existing loans. Large firms
with low levels of debt, in contrast, prefer market-based systems
because of the higher returns they can get by investing in market
securities rather than bank deposits. A bank-based system is thus
best supported by economies with high proportions of SMEs and of
high-debt large firms.

Household sector. The distribution of income and wealth in a society has
an impact on the structure of financial systems because different
income groups have varying preferences for financial assets (Vitols
1996). High-income households prefer market-based finance
because of the higher expected return and because of their greater
ability to absorb short-term market risk. Low-income households
have little capacity to save, and what they do goes mainly into short-
term bank deposits. Middle-income groups have a greater ability to
save than low-income groups, but prefer less risky (lower-return)
assets than high-income groups; long-term bank deposits and bank
bonds have such low-risk moderate-return characteristics. Bank-
based systems will therefore be best supported by societies with low
levels of inequality (and thus a relatively large middle-income
group).

State sector. Government bonds are the easiest type of asset on which
financial markets can be built. Government debt is particularly
liquid because it is highly standardized and issued on a regular
schedule according to the budget cycle. Furthermore, the probability of repayment is higher than in the case of private companies
due to the power to tax. Because a government debt-securities
market is thus potentially a great competitor to banks, a low level of
public debt is thus more supportive of bank-based systems than a
high level of public debt.

Pension Policy. Although not a sector per se, it is particularly important
to examine the characteristics of pension policy because the provision for old-age pensions can potentially involve the accumulation

of a huge amount of financial assets. The large pension funds typical of prefunded pension systems are one of the biggest sources of demand for capital-market securities. Thus pension systems that emphasize full funding on an individual basis are most supportive of market-based systems. In contrast, pay-as-you-go state systems (which involve little accumulation of financial assets) and company pension systems that reinvest money within the company rather than in financial markets (a book reserve system) are most supportive of bank-based systems. State pension funds that invest mainly in bank bonds or nonsecuritized assets also support bank-based systems (Jackson and Vitols 1998).

Postwar Germany and Japan share many characteristics with regard to the societal foundations of bank-based systems. Both countries have an industrial structure with a focus on manufacturing and a high concentration of SMEs. For example, companies with fewer than 500 employees account for 65 and 70 percent of manufacturing employment in Germany and Japan, respectively, as opposed to approximately one-third of employment in the United States and the United Kingdom (Acs and Audretsch 1993). In order to jump-start their economies in the reconstruction period, key industries were financed through levels of bank debt that could not be provided through capital markets (Calder 1993; Pohl 1973). Both countries have low levels of inequality and high saving levels in comparative terms, including in comparison with the United States (Atkinson, Rainwater, and Smeeding 1995; Avery and Elliehausen 1986). In the first postwar decades, both countries had low budget deficits or even surpluses, thus the issuance of government debt was low and the market for such debt insignificant. Finally, pension policy has allowed companies to provide for supplementary pensions through the accumulation of company reserves. Germany has a pay-as-you-go state pension system; Japan's pension system is only partially capitalized and invests to a great extent in the debentures of long-term credit banks and state agencies.

The societal foundations of bank-based systems in both countries have faced similar pressures, although somewhat different in terms of timing and intensity. The pattern of financing for large firms in both countries started to shift in the 1970s as growth slowed; the demand for external finance overall started to decrease, and large firms were also best able to tap cheaper sources of finance than bank loans, such as euromarket bond issues (Campbell and Hamao 1994; Deutsche Bundesbank 1992). Thus, large firms that have succeeded in reducing their debt levels have turned into major supporters of market-based finance. High-debt companies, in contrast, need the continued support of banks in order to roll over finance; it appears there are somewhat more of these companies in Japan than in Germany. SMEs in contrast have become even more dependent on bank finance because greater competition has eroded profit margins and thus the ability to self-finance investment. High-tech SMEs, which are potentially interested in market finance through an initial public offering (IPO) of new securities (when a company becomes listed for the first time on a stock market), account for a relatively small portion of the company sector in both countries.

A second important change is the shift in patterns of public finance. Whereas public indebtedness in the postwar period was low and could be handled mainly through the banking system, governments in both countries in the 1990s issued huge amounts of debt. Japan started issuing considerable debt in the mid-1970s in order to provide fiscal stimulus through deficit spending during the oil crisis. Debt issuance increased in the 1990s to try to stimulate the postbubble economy. Germany's public finances held up well through the 1980s, but the government started issuing massive amounts of debt in the 1990s in order to help finance unification. The role of the government debt market in undermining control of the banking sector in Japan is well documented (Hamada and Horiuchi 1987). The German case is not as well documented, but the market for German federal government securities now constitutes the largest single European securities market.

Less change can be seen in the household sector. Increases in inequality and thus in the balance among sectors have remained modest in cross-national comparison. It should be noted, however, that there appears to be a slow shift among the middle-income sectors away from fixed-interest products (such as long-term deposits and bank bonds) and toward investment funds. This shift is more pronounced in Germany, where there is a greater availability of investment funds (Deutsche Bundesbank 1995),[2] and represents an indirect support for markets because these investment funds mainly invest in securitized assets such as stocks and bonds. A sharper movement toward inequality could potentially accelerate this trend of indirect support of markets.

The greatest outstanding public policy issue in both countries at this point is the problem of pension policy. It is increasingly acknowledged that the aging population and the greater flexibility of labor markets are increasingly straining the existing pension systems (pay-as-you-go state pensions in Germany, incompletely capitalized public pensions in Japan, and supplementary pension provision through company reserves in both countries). The considerable problems involved in introducing a fully capitalized system, such as the greater costs involved in the short-term and

---

2. In Japan there appears to have been a slight reversal of this trend during the financial crisis of 1997–98.

tax implications, have blocked a move toward such a fully capitalized system. Such a move could potentially represent a major step in the creation of U.S.-style pension funds, which have become the greatest support for the U.S. market-based financial system.

In summary, the biggest shift in preferences toward market-based finance in both countries has occurred among large firms and the public sector; support for bank-based finance among SMEs and households, in contrast, remains high. Within these broad trends, support for market-based finance appears to be slightly higher in Germany than in Japan due to the lower number of highly indebted large firms and the somewhat greater shift toward investment funds among the household sector in Germany.

Freer Markets—and More Rules? The Development of Hybrid Regulatory Forms

In the previous section I identified a slight shift in the societal foundations in favor of market systems. In order to assess the degree of change in financial systems, it is also necessary to analyze the extent to which financial regulation itself has changed.

Rationale for Financial Market Regulation

A common view of the liberalization process, largely inspired by neoclassical microeconomic models, equates deregulation with the creation of efficient markets. However, a substantial body of literature has emerged to establish that the process is considerably more complex than this, particularly in situations when the standard neoclassical assumptions (i.e., perfect and costless information and a multitude of small price-taking actors) are not realized (Vogel 1996). In such situations new forms of regulation (or reregulation) are needed in order to avoid the (re)emergence of the dysfunctions that the original regulatory systems were designed to address.

One of the strongest cases of deviation from neoclassical assumptions that illustrates the need for reregulation is the financial system (Dewatripont and Tirole 1994). First, the dependence of asset values on expectations of the future development of a multitude of factors makes it extremely difficult to determine the fair value of these assets; changes in expectations can thus lead to radical shifts in asset prices. Second, the financial system is characterized by extreme differences between insiders and outsiders in the quality and speed of access to price-sensitive information. Third, even markets with thousands of investors are typically domi-

Table 8.2 Key Characteristics of Alternative Financial Regulatory Regimes

Regime Characteristics	Liberal Market-based Regimes	Nonliberal Bank-based Regimes
Most favored sector of financial system	Capital markets	Banks
Constraints on large investors	Rule-based	Incentives for responsible behavior
Advantages for smaller investors	Transparency	Stability
Orientation of financial institutions	Predominantly for-profit	Mix of for-profit and nonprofit
Monetary policy	Stability-oriented to avoid asset inflation	Potential for pursuit of developmentalist goals

nated (at least in the short run) by a small number of large actors. Fourth, the problem of moral hazard is particularly great due to the long-term nature of many investments and thus the ability to hide its true performance for substantial periods. As a result of these four factors, unregulated financial markets are particularly subject to market manipulation and to large swings between speculative bubbles and crashes.

Precapitalist societies typically imposed a series of constraints on financial activities such as usury (lending) restrictions and the prohibition of the limited liability corporate form. The lifting of these restrictions in the nineteenth century through the introduction of a laissez-faire attitude to such activity by the state was important for the development of financial markets. This development, however, was accompanied by increasingly severe financial disorders, culminating in the Great Depression in the 1930s. The depth of the financial crisis was one of the main factors catalyzing the replacement of laissez faire with more interventionist regulatory regimes in the 1930s and 1940s (Forsyth and Notermans 1997; Vitols 2001).

Broadly speaking there have been two major alternatives for the establishment of financial regulatory regimes: a liberal regime favoring capital markets and a nonliberal regime favoring banks. The main features of these systems are summarized in table 8.2. The guiding philosophy of liberal regimes is that investors in capital markets should be free to enter financial contracts and to accept the risks and obligations this entails. The main role of regulation is therefore to reduce information asymmetries and to enable the enforcement of contractual obligations. A level playing field for investors should be created through a set of strictly enforced rules requiring high levels of transparency and constraining market manipulation and fraud. Banks, however, should be more strictly regulated because small depositors are less sophisticated and because bank crises are more dangerous for the real economy due to the role of banks in facilitating payment for goods and services. Finally, monetary policy must be oriented to

Table 8.3 Key Characteristics of the Postwar German and Japanese Nonliberal Financial Regulatory Regimes

	Germany	Japan
Variant of nonliberal regulatory form	Corporatism	Administrative guidance
Discriminatory restrictions and rationed access to capital markets	Bond committee	Bond committee
Not-for-profit financial institutions	Public savings and regional banks Credit cooperatives	Special-purpose public banks Cooperative banks
Goal of public institutions	Support of social market economy	Developmentalism
Primary monetary policy goal	Low deutschmark exchange rate	Low interest rates

price stability in order to reduce the potential of rapid asset inflation or deflation that often plagues markets with free price setting.

The second alternative, nonliberal regulation, in contrast sees capital markets as the greatest danger to financial system stability (see table 8.2). It therefore imposes a variety of discriminatory restrictions on these markets, particularly on the use of more speculative financial assets (derivatives such as options and futures) and on the practice of short selling.[3] Stability in the banking system is fostered by creating incentives for responsible behavior by the leading banks. The main benefit of this regime for smaller investors is supposed to be the avoidance of financial loss caused by panics or crashes. A significant proportion of total financial assets is controlled by public or private nonprofit (e.g., cooperative) financial institutions. Finally, the ability to suppress inflationary and speculative tendencies through regulation opens up the potential for orienting monetary policy to goals other than price stability, such as low interest rates or low exchange rates to promote rapid economic growth.

Although both the German and Japanese regulatory regimes can be characterized as nonliberal according to this generic classification, the specific features of both regimes vary broadly (see table 8.3). These differences have significant consequences for the process of transition to a more liberal regime. Before discussing these differences, however, it is useful to analyze the United States, the benchmark for liberal financial regulation.

3. Through the creation of a leverage effect, derivatives allow investors to profit disproportionately from price changes, but conversely to increase the potential of total loss and thus system-threatening bankruptcies on the part of major investors. Short selling involves the selling of borrowed securities with the hope that a price decline will allow for the (profitable) repurchase of these securities at lower cost. It is widely believed that short selling has initiated or exacerbated stock market crashes.

Liberal Financial Regulation in the United States

The United States, which is widely held to have the most developed capital markets, also has the strongest liberal regulatory system (Seligman 1995). The foundations of this system were laid in the 1930s. The weak system of national banking regulation was substantially strengthened through the 1933 and 1934 Banking Acts. National bank regulators, including the Federal Reserve Board, the Comptroller of the Currency, and the newly established Federal Deposit Insurance Corporation (FDIC), were given stronger regulatory and enforcement powers. Portions of the 1933 Banking Act (the Glass-Steagall provisions) also forbid commercial banks from participating in most capital-market activities.

In contrast with the conservative regulation of the banking sector, which aimed to promote stability, capital-market regulation emphasized transparency and prevention of market manipulation. The most significant pieces of legislation here were the Securities Act of 1933 and the Securities Exchange Act of 1934. The first regulated the issuance of new securities by establishing a Securities and Exchange Commission (SEC) to oversee markets. It also defined an obligation to disclose truthfully information in prospectuses for new securities offerings. The second authorized the SEC to develop rules for trading in secondary markets. In line with the adversarial legalistic pattern of state regulation (Kagan 1991), the SEC has developed an extensive set of rules and practices regarding conditions under which securities can be issued, minimum information requirements, fair determination of market prices, exercise of shareholder voting rights and communication with management, abuse of dominant market position and insider information, and takeover rules.

The Federal Reserve Board (the Fed) has long been seen as one of the most independent central banks. Although key members of the board are appointed by the president (with the approval of the Senate), there are no ex officio members of government on the board nor is the government authorized to send observers to board meetings. The Fed has jealously guarded its rights of independent policymaking on interest rates and (with the exception of the 1970s) has put its primary emphasis on price stability.

Corporatist Regulation of the German Universal Bank System

The German financial system regulation prior to the 1930s can be described as laissez faire (Born 1967). In response to the banking crisis of 1931, which was part of the worldwide reaction to the post-1929 stock market crash difficulties in the United States, a number of large banks were effectively nationalized and a corporatist regulatory regime established.[4] Key features of this corporatist regime survived the wartime economy or were reestablished in the reconstruction period after World War II. These included the corporatist regulation of interest rates on deposits and fees on basic services, the authorization of capital adequacy and liquidity requirements to be developed in consultation with the bank associations, the definition of auditing responsibilities by associations of public savings banks and cooperatives, and constraints on entry.[5] Due to fears of increasing long-term interest rates, a corporatist bond committee dominated by the leading securities issuers (joint-stock banks and the national banks for the credit cooperative and municipal savings bank sector) was established in the reconstruction period to control access to capital markets (Büschgen 1983).

Although the postwar government of Konrad Adenauer had a nominal commitment to liberal capital markets, in fact public policy discouraged their development as a source of long-term capital for industry. The tax system favored public bonds (particularly for housing and infrastructure) over industrial bonds. The corporatist bond committee also gave clear priority to public and bank bonds over industrial bonds in the queue for access to capital markets (Rosen 1997). Double taxation of equities (corporation tax plus individual income tax) stunted the development of equities markets. As a result, external finance for industry was almost entirely provided by bank loans rather than equity or bond issues.

A further defining characteristic of German financial regulation is the degree to which the financial system is composed of not-for-profit institutions (Deeg 1992). The public banking sector, composed of municipal savings banks on the city and county levels and regional banks at the *Länder* level, accounts for approximately one-half of all banking system assets. By law these banks are charged with helping lower-income groups save and with promoting regional development. Somewhat less than 20 percent of banking-system assets are accounted for by the credit cooperative sector, whose goal is to support small businesses and professionals. A final characteristic of the postwar German financial system was the orientation of monetary policy toward a low exchange rate to promote exports.

With the exception of monetary policy, which shifted to a price-stability orientation in the early 1970s, this financial regulatory regime survived intact into the 1990s. A number of smaller reforms with a deregulatory

---

4. Corporatism involves self-regulation through associations. In contrast to voluntary regulation, however, the state provides a variety of incentives for association membership and also recognizes association decisions as binding (Schmitter and Streeck 1985).

5. For example, new credit cooperatives had to receive approval from the appropriate regional cooperative association before starting business.

thrust undertaken by the conservative-liberal government in the 1980s had minor effects. These included removing the securities transaction tax, creating an over-the-counter (OTC) stock market segment, and authorizing a junior joint-stock-company legal form with looser transparency requirements. Pressure from the United States to establish a German equivalent of the SEC was resisted.

In the 1990s, however, this pattern of minor changes was reversed and a number of important financial reforms were introduced (Lütz 1996). The most important reason for this change was a shift in the interests of the large private banks (*Großbanken*). Despite their formal designation as universal banks, the dominant self-image of large private banks throughout the postwar period was that of deposit takers and credit providers (Gall et al. 1995). Significantly, people in top management positions generally came from corporate lending departments. These banks, particularly the Deutsche Bank and Dresdner Bank, began to model themselves after top U.S. investment banks and started the difficult process of shifting their focus away from commercial banking activities. Shortly before his murder by the Red Army Faction in 1990, Alfred Herrhausen, head of Deutsche Bank, stated that his bank had a ten-year window of opportunity to change or perish. In the 1990s, activities by German banks in the major international financial centers were expanded, in large part through acquiring British and U.S. investment banks. These banks also saw the need to have a strong domestic base in order to become global players in investment banking. Reform of the domestic financial system along U.S. lines was seen as a crucial step to strengthening this base.

True to the corporatist pattern, the national association of private banks (Bundesverband deutscher Banken) took the lead in making policy proposals. The government's role was mainly one of structuring the legislative process (including preliminary expert hearings, coalition working groups, and parliamentary hearings), leading the negotiating process, and the technical formulation of drafts and final versions of various laws. The most important of these in the 1990s were the Second and Third Financial Markets Promotion Laws and the Law on Transparency and Control in Corporations.

The Second Financial Markets Promotion Law (1994) has been the most important step toward establishing U.S.-style regulation of capital markets. It established an independent regulatory agency (Bundesaufsichtsamt für Wertpapierhandel) for policing financial markets, modeled on the U.S. SEC. It also defined a set of rules for dealing with insider information with potential impact on securities prices. Significantly, the United States had been pressing for the passage of such legislation for over ten years without effect (Lütz 1996). The changed attitude of the large banks toward such regulation (instead of the traditional corporatist policing of responsible behavior) is a key factor explaining the passage of this legislation. This act also authorized money-market funds after the Bundesbank dropped its long-standing opposition and broadened the available legal forms for venture-capital funds.

The Third Financial Markets Promotion Law (1997) increased the permissible form of mutual funds, including the establishment of a special private retirement savings option (*Pensionssondervermögen*), which can be organized as a mutual fund. The large banks were especially keen on increasing their mutual-fund activities, a lucrative new area of business in Germany. An important change between the initial draft and final versions of this legislation was the striking of tax benefits for the private retirement savings plans. This provision was struck out due to the opposition of the life insurance companies (who feared the loss of business to bank-affiliated or independent mutual funds) and the budget division of the Finance Ministry. This act also eased listing and reporting requirements for companies and made some changes regarding venture capital.

Although not falling under the narrow definition of financial regulation, the Law on Control and Transparency in Corporations (KonTraG) of 1998 was important for the development of financial markets (Ziegler 2000). Unlike the Financial Markets Promotion Laws, KonTraG was primarily an initiative of the governing coalition. The coalition felt obligated to do something in response to a number of spectacular failures of control through supervisory boards (e.g., the failure of Metallgesellschaft, Bremer Vulkan, and Balsam, plus the Deutsche Bank's large loan exposure to the bankrupt Schneider property development group). The most significant provisions of KonTraG, however, which authorize stock option plans and the buyback of shares, were inserted at the suggestion of a coalition of the industry and banking associations. KonTraG was held up for approximately one year because unions opposed a provision reducing the size of supervisory boards (and thus the number of union representatives). The relatively small Christian Democratic unions were particularly opposed to this. Local and regional governments also opposed provisions that would reduce their influence over companies partially in their ownership (e.g., abolition of multiple voting rights on certain categories of stock). KonTraG was passed when these provisions were changed and thus opposition was dropped.

Although these changes have been important, Germany is still far removed from a U.S.-style adversarial legalistic regulatory system. First, the policymaking process remains highly corporatistic and consensual. The banking associations remain central to the process of policymaking and a major association can block change. Second, the associations retain their role in monitoring and the enforcement of rules. Third, the new securities regulatory agency has proven extremely weak in the absence of the juridical system needed to support a rule-based system.[6] The financial regulatory system evolving in Germany is a hybrid of traditional corporatist elements and U.S.-style liberal regulatory institutions.

Japan: State-Driven Change or the Rise and Fall of Administrative Guidance?

As in the United States and Germany, the financial regulatory system in Japan prior to the 1930s can be characterized as laissez faire (Ueda 1994). In the context of the Banking Crisis of 1927, a deepening of the financial crisis in the 1930s, and the mobilization for war, a regulatory system emphasizing stability and the channeling of finance for the achievement of public goals was built up. Despite efforts by the postwar U.S. occupation authorities to democratize the Japanese financial system, many features of this regulatory system survived the reconstruction period or were reestablished in the late 1940s (see table 8.3).

At the core of this regime was a regulatory relationship between state and financial institutions characterized as administrative guidance. The power basis of administrative guidance is the requirement that permission be obtained from the state in the form of licenses in order to undertake a wide variety of activities. State bureaucrats enjoy significant discretionary power because the criteria for granting these licenses are quite vague and regulated parties are dependent on further licenses in the future to stay in business (Sohn 1998).

In the financial system, the basis of administrative guidance was created by the Banking Act of 1927, which was passed in response to the banking crisis of 1927 and granted sweeping but vague regulatory powers to the state (Adams 1964; Nakamura 1998). However, these powers were first used to a great extent in conjunction with military mobilization in the mid-1930s when an effective system of close bank regulation under the Ministry of Finance (MOF) was built up. The establishment of an extensive licensing system reinforced government influence by controlling entry to the

---

6. One example that illustrates the continued occurrence of market manipulation in Germany that would be unthinkable in the United States is the second round of issuance of shares to the public by Deutsche Telekom, the German public telecommunications company. The pricing of this second round was to be determined by the closing price of the shares already circulating on the Friday prior to the Monday issuance of these new shares. A consortia of two dozen banks had agreed to take over a major portion of this second round of shares for later sale to the general investing public. In the last half hour of trading on the Friday, many of the consortia banks put unlimited sell orders for the shares on the market, which had the effect of depressing the share price by 13 percent. As a result of this action the proceeds for the government of the second round were approximately DM 2 billion less than planned. Government regulators claimed they lacked the legal tools needed to prosecute such a brazen example of market manipulation.

financial system and by making existing institutions dependent on government approval for many actions, such as the establishment of new branches. The encouragement of oligopolization in the 1930s also helped support administrative guidance by reducing the number of subjects of regulation. After World War II, administrative guidance developed into an extensive system of informal relations between regulators and financial institutions, often involving unwritten instructions on bank lending and branching policy, the acquisition of smaller financial institutions, and many other aspects of financial policy. Administrative guidance was the glue of the convoy system, by which all ships (in this case financial institutions) move at the same pace.

In addition to the informal regulatory powers created by administrative guidance, there were a number of formal restrictions and informal practices aimed at stunting capital-market growth. One was stringent restrictions on the issuance of corporate bonds, such as strict collateral requirements. Another was the practice of issuing new shares at par value rather than market value. This practice discourages using secondary issues (i.e., issuance of additional shares) for raising capital because the proceeds of new issues are limited for companies whose shares have appreciated quite substantially above the original par value. Finally, a bond committee composed of representatives of the state and leading financial institutions regulated access to capital markets through the approval of the size and timing of new bond issues. As a result of all of these restrictions, capital markets proved to be a rarely used financing mechanism for industry and almost all external finance during the high-growth era was raised in the form of bank loans.

Flanking administrative guidance was an extensive set of nonprofit financial institutions established in order to achieve a variety of public goals. The most famous of these is the Postal Savings System, which due to the convenience of an extensive set of branches and tax advantages is the preferred savings vehicle for many households (Calder 1993). Through various types of deposits and insurance policies, the Postal Savings System controls a huge amount of financial assets. These savings are channeled into the real economy through the Fiscal Investment and Loan Program (FILP) and through buying up the debentures of long-term credit banks. In addition to other specialized public financial institutions (e.g., for housing finance), an extensive set of nonprofit credit cooperatives supports the needs of smaller businesses and agriculture.

Due to the various mechanisms available to control the expansion and allocation of credit (administrative guidance and direct control over public financial institutions), monetary policy was to a great extent free of the constraint of controlling price inflation. Throughout the high-growth period, the Bank of Japan (BOJ; under the guidance of MOF) set an artificially low interest rate to encourage industrial investment. Although the efficacy of targeting is still controversial, there is general agreement that the low-interest-rate policy facilitated a massive transfer of capital from the household to the corporate sector (Hamada and Horiuchi 1987).

In contrast to the German case, the first element of the nonliberal regulatory system to weaken was conservative fiscal policy. In response to the 1973 oil shock, the government initiated heavy deficit spending and had to massively increase its issuance of bonds. The increase in bonds was so great that the normal sales channel (purchase by banks) was overloaded and a market had to be created to absorb these securities. In contrast with the stock market, in which shares could be placed largely with friendly *keiretsu* members, this government debt market slowly began to function as a true market in terms of liquidity, price-setting, and return in order to induce purchase of government bonds (Yamamura 1985).

A second part of the postwar system that had to be dismantled was the system of regulated and artificially low interest rates. One reason for this was the previously mentioned creation of the government bond market. The availability of higher interest rates on this market led to a draining of assets from portions of the financial system in which rates were controlled. This was a major incentive for the gradual deregulation of interest rates on bank deposits. A second reason for this shift in interest-rate policy was the need to orient monetary policy toward influencing the exchange rate after the move from fixed to floating interest rates. Japan had rapidly shifted from net debtor to net creditor status, and this was increasing strain on the exchange rate.

Another significant move toward deregulation was taken with a package of financial system reforms passed in 1992. These reforms, which modified sixteen distinct laws, took a major step toward loosening the system of strict segmentation among commercial banking, securities, and trust activities. Financial institutions in one of these segments were allowed to enter other segments through establishing new subsidiaries or purchasing existing (in practice mainly troubled) firms (Rosenbluth 1989).

Although these steps—the creation of a liquid government bond market, interest-rate deregulation, and the weakening of segmentation requirements—represented significant deregulatory moves, the basic structure of administrative guidance remained intact through the first half of the 1990s. Although administrative guidance had been weakened somewhat through interest-rate deregulation and the abolition of window guidance[7] at the BOJ, the 1992 package of reforms in fact strengthened

---

7. Window guidance was the Bank of Japan's practice of influencing the volume of credit made available to the entire economy by controlling the amount of funds it made available to commercial banks.

the powers of MOF over the financial system. Under the rationale of controlling the pace of change in the financial system, financial institutions had to obtain a license from MOF in order to enter a new financial segment. This created a new and powerful means of influence reinforcing administrative guidance. Although a regulatory agency (the Securities and Exchange Surveillance Commission, SESC) was established to police capital markets—ostensibly on the model of the U.S. SEC—in fact this agency was effectively put under the control of MOF (e.g., it had no independent powers to prosecute violations of securities laws).

The system of administrative guidance itself was fundamentally challenged for the first time in 1996 by Prime Minister Ryūtarō Hashimoto's announcement of wide-ranging reforms in government practices and in financial regulation (the latter characterized as the Big Bang). A series of scandals implicating MOF, which turned out to be quite costly for taxpayers, helped create public support for fundamental change. The unfolding of the Asian financial crisis in 1997 and 1998, which brought already-weak Japanese banks to the brink of insolvency due to their heavy lending exposure to east Asian countries, further created an atmosphere of support for fundamental reform.

The Big Bang reforms encompassed a series of important deregulatory measures, including the deregulation of brokerage commissions and the authorization of financial holding companies to further facilitate mutual entry of market segments. Probably the most fundamental change, however, was the attempt to establish a set of regulatory agencies truly independent of MOF and operating in a transparent, rule-based manner. If successful, the creation of such strong and effective independent regulatory agencies would represent a major step in establishing a liberal financial regulatory regime in Japan.

One such move was the transformation of the Bank of Japan from a dependent arm of MOF to an independent central bank. The new BOJ law modified the composition of the monetary policy board by excluding ex officio government members.[8] The policy board is also required under the new law to publish the transcripts of its meetings to improve the transparency of its decision making. The new independence of the BOJ can be seen in public defiance of MOF pressure; against MOF's wishes, the BOJ refused to directly purchase government bonds to fund fiscal stimulus packages, to sterilize exchange rate interventions in late 1999 and early 2000, or to continue the zero-interest-rate policy by increasing interest rates in August 2000.

---

8. Although these government members formally had no voting rights, in fact they were held to exercise considerable influence over board decisions.

A second major step toward creating a liberal regulatory regime was the establishment of the Financial Services Agency (FSA) for the regulation of banks and brokers. The criticism leading to this measure was that MOF had too much conflict of interest as both the coach and umpire of financial institutions. Instead, these functions were to be clearly separated between a MOF with reduced powers and a truly independent FSA. Similar to the case of the 1992 creation of the SESC, MOF attempted to subvert this intention of establishing independence by controlling the staffing of the FSA and seeing that the new agency was provided with inadequate resources. Insufficient resources and permanent rotation of staff between MOF and FSA would substantially weaken the effective independence of the FSA. In part due to public pressure, however, the Liberal Democratic Party (LDP) blocked this attempt by stipulating that FSA staff were not allowed to return to MOF.[9]

A third important liberal measure was the introduction of clear rules and improved transparency for the financial system. One aspect of this was the replacement of the licensing system with a registration requirement for the establishment of subsidiaries in new financial segments. The definition of a set of requirements that granted a right to entry once fulfilled would substantially reduce the arbitrary decision-making power of MOF. A second aspect was the introduction of prompt corrective action (PCA), which automatically triggered intervention by the regulatory agency when the capital of a specific bank fell below the level of 8 percent of total assets. The intensity of intervention was determined by how far the bank capital had been eroded. The replacement of mark-to-cost with mark-to-market accounting was also intended to give a truer picture of a bank's actual financial situation because the value of assets such as stocks may vary substantially from purchase price.

The severity of the banking system's bad-loan situation, however, has undermined an already difficult process of transition to a liberal regulatory regime. The effective bankruptcy of all the city banks except for the Bank of Tokyo-Mitsubishi necessitated the injection of huge amounts of public funds in order to recapitalize these banks. The technical expertise and power of MOF was needed in order to accomplish this de facto nationalization of most of the largest banks and to help develop realistic restructuring plans for restoring profitability. The strict implementation of PCA according to the original intentions would also effectively shut down other segments of the banking system, and the government has admitted that a rule-based approach to regulation must be modified and watered down in

---

9. As anecdotal evidence in support of the independence of the FSA, interview partners indicated that whereas MOF officials exchanged business cards with bank managers at meetings, FSA officials pointed to their official badges.

order to avoid a major disruption in the financial system. The difficulties in solving the bad-loan situation and in restoring profitability to the banking system are thus likely to continue the current uneasy coexistence of the traditional system of administrative regulation and the nascent liberal regulatory system for the foreseeable future.

Comparison of Reform in Germany and Japan

When comparing financial reform in Germany and Japan, we are struck by the differences in the drivers of change and by the greater compatibility of corporatism than administrative guidance with a liberal regulatory regime. In Germany, reform has been driven for the most part by the large banks, which desire to create a home base supportive of global-player investment banks on the U.S. model. Although some Japanese banks have also been interested in entry into other domestic segments, such as securities underwriting, their enthusiasm for reform has been tempered by concerns about international competitiveness and the bad-loan situation. These concerns are likely to continue and thus moderate support for a liberal regime from an important potential supporter of liberal reform, which is especially important given the vagaries of political parties.

Second, an important part of corporatism in the German financial system was the determination of clear rules, such as quantitative banking standards for liquidity and capital adequacy. A gradual and partial shift of regulatory authority to liberal agencies is thus easier to conceive in the case of Germany's corporatism than in Japan's administrative regulation. Not surprisingly, attempts at financial reform in Japan have taken the form of a Big Bang package of changes receiving widespread popular attention, whereas financial form in Germany has been implemented through a series of legislative acts scarcely noticed by the public at large.

On the Future of Bank-Based Systems

In both Germany and Japan, the importance of financial markets increased at the expense of banks in the 1990s. The main contributors to this process were structural trends, particularly the large-scale issuance of government debt and the decreasing demand of large firms for bank loans and regulatory changes in the form of both deregulation and the creation of liberal regulatory institutions. The key questions are: How far will these processes go, and what role will banks play in the future in these two countries? Particularly important is the issue of whether banks will be capable of supporting their natural constituents—the SMEs and low- and middle-income households.

Because it is difficult (if not impossible) to imagine turning back the institutional clock to the heyday of bank-based systems in the 1950s and 1960s, two major scenarios are conceivable. The first involves convergence to the U.S. market-based model. The structural prerequisites for this scenario—in order to reduce the importance of the natural customers of banks—are a major shrinkage of the SME sector, a serious increase in inequality, maintenance of high public budget deficits, and the introduction of a capitalized pension system. The regulatory prerequisites are a major strengthening of the new liberal regulatory agencies and a corresponding weakening of corporatist institutions in Germany and administrative guidance in Japan. Privatization of the public savings banks in Germany and a major consolidation in the banking sectors in both countries are also an important support for this process.

A more likely outcome of the process, however, is a growing dichotomy between the domestically and internationally oriented segments of the financial system and a continued uneasy coexistence between liberal and nonliberal regulatory modes. This scenario is more apparent in Germany, where the major banks are explicitly pursuing the goal of becoming global players in the investment banking area and have pulled back from servicing SMEs and lower-income households. These banks have also been the most important supporters of the introduction of liberal regulatory institutions on the Frankfurt stock exchange. At the same time, the public savings banks have been able to fight off attempts at privatization, have retained a corporatist form of regulation, and have introduced a broader set of financial services for SMEs and an expanded array of investment funds for their household customers.

The Japanese case is more complex, but this second scenario is also arguably the most likely outcome. The potential for creating global players is much smaller and thus support for full-blown liberal financial markets in Japan is weaker. The seriousness of the bad-debt situation also means that the need for heavy administrative guidance to support both troubled financial institutions and nonfinancial firms will persist into the medium term. Nevertheless, the potential for a more liberal, internationally oriented subsector of the financial system remains. Support for this subsector will be provided by the continuing core of low-debt, internationally competitive companies; Japanese financial institutions in alliances or partially owned by foreign financial institutions; and a private, capitalized pension system. The realization of this second scenario will amount to the achievement of coexistence of both bank-based and market-based finance within the same financial system.

Corporate Governance in Germany and Japan: Liberalization Pressures and Responses during the 1990s

Gregory Jackson

Corporate governance lies at the heart of debates over national varieties of capitalism. German and Japanese corporations were often admired for their strengths in building long-term commitments among shareholders, banks, suppliers, and employees. Their competitive success was related to institutional complementarities between capital and labor: the commitments of stable shareholders and banks to long-term capital investments helped foster a stable core of highly skilled employees with participation rights in company decisions (Aoki 1994a). Such beneficial constraints on short-term market rationality allowed managers to learn to cultivate long-term organizational capacities (Streeck 1997a). Corporations were successful in high-skill and high-quality markets through their dynamic (X-)efficiency in production and incremental innovation in products and process (Soskice 1999). These strengths mirrored perceived deficits of the United States and Britain during the 1980s, such as short-termism, opportunism, and breaches of employee trust.

Despite their success, Germany and Japan underwent far-reaching changes during the 1990s. Both countries faced pressure to liberalize their corporate governance institutions in line with prevailing Anglo-American practices to promote greater transparency and shareholder returns. Numerous factors drove these changes: the internationalization of capital

I thank the staff of the Ministry of International Trade and Industry (MITI) Research Institute for their generous assistance. I am also indebted to many others for comments, especially Masahiko Aoki, Ronald Dore, Nicola Ebert, Michael Faust, Joseph Foudy, Anke Hassel, Martin Höpner, Zenishi Shishido, David Stark, Wolfgang Streeck, Fujikazu Suzuki, Sigurt Vitols, Steven Vogel, Kozo Yamamura, and Rainer Zugehör. All errors are my own.

markets, pressures from institutional investors, regime competition between states to promote stock markets, and the renewed perception of
U.S. strength in information technology and venture capital entrepreneurship. After the mid-1990s, several major corporations surprisingly began to
proclaim shareholder value as their primary objective.

These developments are debated in terms of international convergence
toward a U.S. shareholder-oriented model. Convergence posits that the
growing international capital mobility exerts competitive pressures to
generate higher shareholder returns. Likewise, states are subject to regime
competition over shareholder rights and capital-market transparency. Even
when formal legal differences remain, corporate practices may undergo
functional convergence through self-regulatory instruments and strategic
choices, such as acquiring a listing on the New York Stock Exchange
(NYSE) (Coffee 1999).

Others argue that national differences will persist because corporate
governance exhibits features of path dependence (Guillén 2000; Soskice
1999). States may face strong political resistance to more active stock markets, because a corporate focus on share prices would threaten more egalitarian postwar conceptions of corporate responsibility. Corporate insiders
may also defend vested private benefits existing under the past system
(Bebchuk and Roe 1999). And since national systems may contain multiple complementary institutions, piecemeal change in a single institution
risks weakening the overall coherence and economic efficiency of corporate governance.

In addressing this debate, this chapter compares the liberalization pressures and responses in German and Japanese corporate governance
during the 1990s—to what extent and why did their past models change,
and does the emerging trajectory suggest convergence toward a single
model of corporate governance? This chapter offers a new interpretation
of the convergence debates by examining not just the rise of new investors,
but the independent roles of politics, labor representatives, and the changing social world and interests of top management in corporate strategy.
Two central claims are made:

- Germany and Japan have neither converged on a U.S. shareholder-
  oriented model nor maintained their past models. Despite a
  growing role of institutional investors, significant differences
  remain in company regulation, ownership, and the role of labor.
  The emerging pattern nonetheless represents a new path because
  core features of the past model have eroded and are unlikely to
  reemerge—particularly relational banking among large international firms.

- Germany and Japan are developing hybrid models to accommodate more marketized capital within regimes of industrial citizenship for employees. One scenario is an enlightened or weak version of the shareholder-value paradigm that stresses the positive-sum aspects of shareholder and employee interests. However, the stability of a hybrid model remains unclear and may be threatened by the emergence of a market for corporate control.

I first review the similarities and differences of corporate governance in Germany and Japan through the 1980s and examine the political dynamics of corporate reform during the 1990s. I next examine the changing roles of capital, labor, and management within the company. In the final section I address the future prospects of convergence or continued divergence.

Germany and Japan as Nonliberal Models

Germany and Japan are often seen as deviating from an economic model of shareholder control.[1] This chapter, instead, views corporate governance more sociologically as the patterns of control and decision making within corporations (Jackson 2000). Corporate governance involves coalitions among capital, labor, and management (Aoki 1986a) and how these coalitions are institutionally embedded by corporate law, accounting rules, financial regulation, pension finance, and industrial relations. Institutional configurations exert joint effects that may have strengths and weaknesses for different types of economic behavior (Aoki 2001). Institutions provide not only incentives and constraints for economic behavior; over time, they shape identities to reflect the social and political processes by which their interests are defined (socially constructed), aggregated, and represented.

Similarities

Germany and Japan share a number of functional similarities because their institutions limit the marketization of both capital and labor. In contrast to the liberal United States, postwar Germany and Japan each

---

1. Given the conventional focus of agency theory on how shareholders (principals) control management (agents), Germany and Japan appear exceptional in having concentrated share ownership and granting governance rights to employees.

Table 9.1 Comparison of Corporate Governance Patterns

	Germany and Japan	United States

Capital	Strategic/organizational interests
	Commitment, voice
	Intensive private information
	  sharing; implicit contracting
		Financial interests
		Liquidity, exit
		Extensive public disclosure;
		  formalized contracting

Labor	Industrial citizenship
	Legal or bargained rights to
	  information, consultation, and
	  codetermination
		Voluntarism
		Collective bargaining; low legal
		  intervention

Management	Contingent managerialism, internal
	  labor markets
	Modest salaries, stock options rare
		Capital market constraints, internal
		  and external labor markets
		High salaries tied to shareholder value

Mechanism of
  corporate
  control
	Internal coalitions	External takeovers

developed distinct versions of a nonliberal corporate governance model having three broad similarities: the financial commitment of capital, industrial citizenship of labor, and contingent managerialism (see table 9.1). Corporate governance is institutionalized through highly committed coalitions and organizational voice.

Financial Commitment of Capital

Corporate ownership is typically concentrated among banks and intercorporate networks rather than fragmented among individuals and institutional investors, as in the United States. Japanese *keiretsu* groups link corporations and banks in extensive patterns of horizontal cross-shareholding (Gerlach 1992); pyramidal conglomerate holding companies (*Konzern*) and dense bank-industry networks are important in Germany (Beyer 1998). Bank and intercorporate ownership typically involve high commitment relative to the more liquid trading of institutional investors (Jackson 2000). And whereas Anglo-Saxon institutional investors are oriented to financial gains from share-price appreciation and dividends, corporations and banks often pursue strategic organizational interests in promoting interfirm cooperation, reducing risks, and generating relationship-specific rents. Consequently, these features limit markets for corporate control as well as create incentives for owners to influence management through voice rather than exit.

Within this context, banks historically played the central governance role. Japanese main banks act as delegated monitors through direct equity stakes, credit, and dispatched directors (Sheard 1994). German universal banks are linked to business through credit, equity stakes, the exercise of proxy votes, and supervisory board representation (Edwards and Fischer 1994). In both cases, banks extend relational financing (see Aoki and Dinc 1997, 3; Elston and Albach 1995; Hoshi 1994), commingle debt and equity, and provide financial services. External corporate monitoring is often linked to bank loans, but it also complements a strong capacity for internal finance in the absence of shareholder pressure (Corbett and Jenkinson 1996).

Industrial Citizenship

In contrast to Anglo-Saxon countries, employees enjoy industrial citizenship within the corporation, participation rooted in asymmetric and reciprocal status rights and obligations that take account of differences in the interests and capacities of actors (Streeck 1997b, 12). Employee voice supports the commitment and integration of labor as a citizen within the corporation, as witnessed by employment that is more stable[2] and less sensitive to the business cycle than in the United States (Economic Planning Agency 1993). This mutual commitment to stable employment has proven indispensable for high-skilled and functionally flexible employment systems by protecting firm-specific investments in human capital from excessive short-term rationality.

German industrial citizenship is vested in the institution of codetermination (*Mitbestimmung*) that specifies legal rights to information, consultation, and codetermination for the works councils representing employees at the plant and company levels. Employees are also allocated between one-third and one-half of the seats on the supervisory board, placing them alongside shareholders in appointing and monitoring management, giving business advice, and ratifying important strategic decisions with the shareholder representatives. Compared to Germany, Japanese industrial citizenship is less formalized in law and more restricted to the core workforce among large corporations. Joint consultation is linked to collective bargaining, but often covers a very wide range of business decisions and subjects them to information, consultation, and sometimes codetermination. Consultation takes place in the context of lifetime-employment practices resting on strong legal claims to employment security. A wage system promotes the decommodification of labor within internal promotion systems. And employee opinion has considerable importance in the internal promotion of management.

---

2. Japanese employees have an average tenure of eleven years, compared to nearly ten years in Germany and seven years in the United States (OECD 1995a).

Contingent Managerialism and Coalitions for Organization Building

Facing voice from both capital and labor, management operates ex ante under a duality principle of balancing long-term returns to capital and labor (Aoki 1988). As long as distributional patterns are not undermined by very poor performance, management retains a high degree of autonomy. Management tends to be internally promoted, and compensation schemes lack strong shareholder-oriented incentives such as stock options in favor of more egalitarian pay scales. External intervention is contingent on low performance and can be mobilized in various ways: by banks, by the German supervisory board, or through the loss of cooperation with labor representatives.

The resulting governance coalitions offer a unique combination of distributional compromise and particular sorts of competitive advantage. Financial commitment provides reliable access to external capital at the lowest feasible cost (Ide 1998, 62–66), and small portions of value-added are paid to shareholders—declaring low profit rates, treating dividends as fixed payments rather than residuals to be maximized, and supporting high rates of internal reinvestment. This pattern generates stable returns for shareholders, although the market capitalization remains lower. Given the absence of a market for corporate control (De Jong 1996; Höpner and Jackson 2001), freedom from strong capital-market constraints opens a variety of company strategies that bestow possible competitive advantage:

- Firms can pursue a higher market share through forward-pricing of products below current marginal costs in anticipation of scale economies through gaining market share.
- Firms can service market segments offering lower returns but large sales and relatively low risk.
- Firms can spend more on continuous capital investments and research and development supporting incremental innovation (Soskice 1999).
- Firms can absorb higher labor costs and avoid layoffs during cyclical downturns, thus maintaining implicit contracts and protecting firm-specific human capital; industrial citizenship is accommodated as a beneficial constraint in support of high wages and high skills (Streeck 1997a).

Differences

Despite functional similarities, Germany and Japan's nonliberal variants had distinct structural features or institutional logic. The German model can be characterized in terms of enterprise constitutionalism—the voice of labor and capital is a matter of public interest and supported through politics. Unlike a purely private association, corporations have features of a social institution that assigns noncontractual status rights and obligations to its members independent of their will and independent of the exchange value of labor or capital. Governance involves externalization onto corporatist associations. But societal interests are also internalized by a densely regulated two-tier board system that legally separates management and shareholder control, and opens the supervisory board to employee representation. Law plays a strong role in institutionalizing and giving voice to public identities and class interests.

By contrast, Japanese corporations are often described as enterprise communities (Dore 2000). Unlike constitutionalized decision making, capital and labor exert voice on the basis of their close mutual dependence with the firm. Stakeholders face significant constraints on their ability to exit through mutual cross-shareholding or lifetime employment practices such as seniority-related wages and firm-specific skill formation. Although voice is preferred to exit, managerial power is very strong within the informally defined norms of performance, both in the contingent governance exercised by the main banks and in the consultation of enterprise unions. The structural differences between the constitutional and community models can thus be schematized with regard to the different role of legal coercion and the relative importance of horizontal class identities versus vertically segmented enterprise identities as an organizational basis for institutional compromise (Dore 1996).

The Politics of Corporate Governance Reform in the 1990s

Historically, national differences in corporate governance emerged as the legacy of political struggles over who should control the corporation. In the United States, for example, politics promoted the primacy of shareholders and the use of markets as the primary form of corporate control (Jackson 2001; Roe 1994). In Germany and Japan, nonliberal corporate governance was historically legitimated by the idea of the corporation as a community or an entity in itself comprising multiple constituents. However, the legacy of the resulting political compromises started to unwind during the 1990s, allowing a greater role for shareholders and capital markets.

Reform pressures stem both from external international pressure and from the changing ideas and interests of domestic actors. Liberalization is usually linked to the international capital markets: the growth of Anglo-Saxon institutional investors, public concern over outward foreign direct investment (FDI) by large corporations, the desire to attract inward FDI, and cross-border mergers and acquisitions. Given the regime competition to attract mobile capital, states may initiate market-oriented reforms in order "to make economic activities located within the national territory . . . more competitive in international or transnational terms" (Cerny 1997, 257). Unilateral U.S. pressure and the politics of building the EU common market have channeled such reform pressure and mobilized domestic actors. Germany and Japan have attempted to establish level playing fields for shareholders, particularly by moving their standards of information and disclosure toward the standards of the U.S. Securities and Exchange Commission (SEC).

The endogenous economic pressures on German and Japanese corporate governance are less well understood and often framed politically in terms of perceived strengths of the U.S. model. Specifically, it is argued that the information technology paradigm gives renewed competitive strength to the United States due to its liquid stock markets, venture capital, and strong external labor markets that rely on portable professional qualifications (see the essay by Kozo Yamamura in this volume). The privatization of state enterprises and impending reforms to public pensions by promoting private savings create new political support for the stock market. Dissatisfaction was prompted by corporate scandals: payments to Japanese corporate racketeers; the 1996 scandal over speculative copper trading losses at Sumitomo Corporation; and the failures of a main creditor, Deutsche Bank, to monitor during the 1993 speculation losses at Metallgesellschaft and the 1994 Jürgen Schneider real estate scandal. Finally, the Japanese banking crisis prompted political debate over transparency and relations between banks and industry.

The politics of liberalization thus reflects changing interests and coalitions among state actors, the investment community, and corporations. Yet political resistance remained given the interests of corporate management in preserving its own autonomy and public concern over the social and distributional consequences of shareholder value that precluded a direct political attack on the rights of labor. The resulting reforms enabled corporations to adopt many new capital market-oriented practices while retaining significant national differences in the powers of corporate boards and labor participation.

Corporate law reforms changed the ways corporations could use their equity, specifically by allowing managerial stock options and share buybacks. Accounting reforms also facilitated the adoption of international standards, which contrast with conservative and creditor-oriented rules by stressing market valuations and transparent profits. Voluntary self-regulation has also sought to promote best practices, but thus far creates only marginal normative pressures to implement new governance practices.

Corporate Law Reform

Japanese reform occurred through incremental amendments to the Commercial Code.[3] Major business associations, such as the industry association (Keidanren), the employer association (Nikkeiren), and the Japan Association of Corporate Executives (Keizai Dōyūkai), took moderate stances on reform that opposed major inroads against managerial autonomy (Keizai Dōyūkai 1996, 1998; Nikkeiren Kokusai Tokubetsu Iinkai 1998). For example, Keidanren opposed requiring independent outside directors and responded to reduced legal fees for shareholder derivative action suits by proposing an explicit business judgment rule, as in the United States, to preclude liability when adverse outcomes result from poor business judgment rather than from dishonesty or fraud. Thus, the early reform was limited to improving the independence of statutory auditors (see list at the end of this chapter)—addressing concern over illegal behavior, but unlikely to impact strategic control given the weak role of auditors.

Keidanren also actively promoted reforms to facilitate corporate reorganization, particularly by changing the use of corporate equity. The key measure lifted the ban on pure holding companies by revising the 1947 Antimonopoly Law.[4] Holding company structures facilitate centralized strategic management of multiple businesses, heighten flexibility in creating and terminating enterprises during mergers and acquisitions (M&A), and may differentiate employment conditions across business units (Aoki 2000; see also the essay by Steven Vogel in this volume). Holding companies are now spreading and being used to centralize strategic management within smaller corporate boards, creating more arm's-length relations between businesses, isolating risks, and decentralizing incentives and responsibility for performance. Although holding companies internalize the monitoring functions of subsidiary businesses, the question of ultimate control over the parent firm remains. Related reforms ease the adoption of holding company structures by facilitating reorganization through share swaps and spin-offs. Share buybacks and stock options were also legalized to enable firms to return free cash flow to shareholders.

3. This section draws on interviews conducted at Keidanren, Economic Law Group, March 1999, Tokyo, and the Department of Justice, General Secretariat, May 2000, Tokyo. I exclude discussion of the New Businesses Act of 1998 and the Act for Special Measures for Rehabilitation of Industry Power of 1999, which authorize the Ministry of Economy, Trade and Industry (METI) to apply a special set of rules regarding stock options, voting rights, and disposal of company assets to selected companies.

4. The U.S. occupation forces implemented this law because of concern about antitrust and as a public interest measure to prevent Japan's military-industrial collaboration (Jackson 2001).

In 2002, a series of major reforms continued this basic trend toward more varied use of corporate equity and attempts to improve the independence of supervisory functions. Previous restrictions on stock options were largely removed, and management liability toward the company was reduced. In terms of monitoring, statutory auditors were again made more independent. But initial proposals to introduce outside independent directors were dropped due to opposition by Keidanren. Corporations were instead given the option of implementing a U.S.-style system of board committees (compensation, nominations, and auditing) whose members would be a majority of outside nonexecutive directors. Such corporations would no longer be required to have statutory auditors. While too early to tell, indications are that few corporations currently plan to adopt this system. Thus, despite the high level of activity, these reforms represent rather incremental adjustments to increase active and independent supervision within the board.

German reform centered on the Law on Control and Transparency in Corporations of 1998 (Gesetz zur Kontrolle und Transparenz im Unternehmensbereich, hereafter KonTraG) (Donnelly et al. 2001).[5] During 1994, the governing coalition between the conservative Christlich Demokratische Union (CDU) and liberal Freie Demokratische Partei (FDP) considered improving the transparency and competitiveness of German firms in the global capital market. A perennial German debate about the power of banks also reemerged amid public outcry over scandals at Metallgesellschaft, Klöckner-Humboldt-Deutz, and Schneider real estate. An extensive debate followed over bank proxy votes, the size and practice of supervisory boards, and corporate disclosure.

The KonTraG aimed to improve auditor independence by requiring appointment by the supervisory board, as well as the disclosure of multiple supervisory-board memberships and ownership stakes exceeding 5 percent. Several provisions also increased shareholder influence: multiple voting rights and voting rights restrictions were eliminated, banks were barred from using proxy votes if their direct shareholding exceeded 5 percent, banks had to solicit more instructions from shareholders, and the supervisory board was given greater duties of financial oversight. Restrictions on share buybacks and stock options were removed.

Politically, the KonTraG represents a compromise. More far-reaching proposals by the Sozialdemokratische Partei Deutschlands (SPD) to curtail bank influence were rejected due to the opposition of German industry and banking associations (Ziegler 2000). German unions also successfully

5. The earliest measures were introduced in the context of the Single European Act to promote economic integration by liberalizing capital markets and ensuring equal protections for small investors across member states.

opposed reducing the size of the supervisory board; although a smaller board would retain parity codetermination, the balance among labor representatives between company employees and outside union representatives would be upset.

German reform is also influenced by debates over the European company statute. Since the 1970s, Europe has proposed a uniform legal form of incorporation as an important step in market integration. For example, administrative expenses would decline and help transnational companies avoid the psychologically difficult choices between two national corporate cultures. German supervisory board codetermination proved a central barrier; unions opposed measures that might weaken codetermination by allowing German firms to migrate to a new European corporate form. Likewise, numerous European countries opposed strong codetermination rules. The breakthrough of the Nice Summit in 2000 opened European incorporation only to multinational firms and required social partners to negotiate company-specific codetermination rules. If management and employee representatives failed to agree on the extent of employee board representation for the new company, the highest applicable level from national law would remain in force.

Accounting

Japanese accounting traditionally allows asset valuation at cost rather than market value. Germany also applies conservative prudence rules (*Vorsichtsprinzip*) and favors creditors through conservative asset valuation and allowing up to 50 percent of profits to be used as internal reserves. By contrast, both GAAP (U.S. generally accepted accounting practices) and IAS (International Accounting Standards) are significantly more shareholder-oriented by stressing market valuations and more precise definitions of profits. The U.S. SEC remains able to resist loosening its standards to facilitate uniform international rules. Whereas convergence theories posit that corporations will push for international accounting standards or voluntarily adopt them by obtaining a listing on a foreign stock exchange, others warn that market-valuation principles make balance sheets overly vulnerable to short-term market fluctuations.

Japanese companies have made no dramatic move to obtain listings on the NYSE—only seven of the seventeen Japanese firms on the NYSE listed between 1990 and 2001. Companies such as Honda were already listed in the 1970s but retain many Japanese corporate governance features. Accounting reforms were largely initiated by the Ministry of Finance as part of the financial Big Bang called for by Prime Minister Ryūtarō Hashimoto in 1996. The banking crisis helped mobilize political support for reform and opened a window to push changes in line with U.S.

pressure to adopt international standards. Despite high adjustment costs, parliamentary opposition would be politically costly. Keidanren (2001) now supports international harmonization through the recognition of SEC standards under domestic law.

Japan required the reporting of financial assets at market value in March 2001 and of cross-shareholdings in March 2002. Market valuation has revealed unfunded pension liabilities that require large payments into pension reserves—often done by donating ownership of cross-shareholdings to pension funds. New consolidated accounting promotes transparency by making it harder to hide losses in subsidiary firms. Whereas internationally oriented sectors may benefit from international standards, others become more vulnerable to balance-sheet volatility due to depressed stock prices. Accounting is thus a major force driving reductions in cross-shareholding. Banks especially must guard themselves in order to meet minimum capital adequacy and solvency requirements.

By contrast, German reforms were driven less by domestic crisis than by EU harmonization and lobbying by large international companies. Debate was sparked when Daimler-Benz and Deutsche Telekom became the first German companies seeking NYSE listing during the mid-1990s. Initially, corporations were forced to maintain two sets of calculations in fulfillment of both NYSE listing requirements and German tax law. The large discrepancies in the profit calculations of DM 2.5 billion at Daimler-Benz led to bad publicity and encouraged skepticism of German standards. Germany enabled corporations to adopt GAAP or IAS for domestic tax purposes until a uniform global standard emerges.[6] This flexible approach does not require a wholesale shift in accounting principles but allows firms to adopt rules according to their needs in accessing international capital markets or to continue a more creditor-oriented approach. By March 2002, eighteen German corporations were listed on the NYSE (2001a), and all the corporations listed on the Deutscher Aktien Index 30 (DAX 30) use international standards—seventeen use IAS and thirteen use either U.S. GAAP or both standards (Deutsches Rechnungslegungs Standards Committee 2001).

Voluntary Codes

Self-regulation has been important in promoting transparency and investor protection in Anglo-Saxon countries. During the 1990s, voluntary

6. These rules were introduced in the 1998 Kapitalaufnahmeerleichterungsgesetz (Investment Facilitation Act) for a period of six years. The International Accounting Standards Committee (IASC) and International Organization of Securities Commissions (IOSCO) are currently negotiating to bring the IAS and GAAP together.

codes proliferated internationally, being issued by the Organization for Economic Cooperation and Development (OECD), national stock exchanges, and various interest associations (Aguilera and Cuervo-Cazurra 2000). Voluntary codes promote institutional change through the diffusion of ideas, as well as creating normative pressures and sanctions (DiMaggio and Powell 1991). Self-regulation may thereby act as a functional substitute to law in promoting international convergence (Coffee 1999).

The Corporate Governance Forum of Japan (CGF), a private study group of academics and business leaders, issued a set of voluntary corporate governance principles (Corporate Governance Forum of Japan 1998) such as introducing independent outside directors and improved transparency and disclosure. The CGF hopes to win support from the Tokyo Stock Exchange to enforce its principles as listing requirements along SEC lines. Despite its ideology of shareholder control, the CGF remains cautious about Anglo-American practices such as hostile takeovers and corporate layoffs. Nor do its principles explicitly call for reductions of cross-shareholding, unlike many foreign investors such as the California Public Employees' Retirement System (CalPERS).

Self-regulation has been more widespread in Germany, where a voluntary takeover code in 1995 aimed to fill the legal gap regarding takeover bids given a deadlocked European Directive (Vitols et al. 1997). Because the Takeover Commission lacked sanctioning power, only 540 of 933 listed companies and 79 of the DAX 100 companies participate (Bundesministerium 2000, 62). The hostile takeover of Mannesmann in 1999 exposed the urgency of a binding regulation on bidding procedures and permissible defensive actions. The current SPD government opposed a subsequent European initiative in 2001 as being too restrictive of takeover defenses. Under pressure from unions and leading corporations, Germany adopted a national law in December 2001 allowing management to pursue some takeover defenses, as in the United States, if shareholders empower the board accordingly beforehand (Höpner and Jackson 2001). More generally, a government commission also developed a German Code of Corporate Governance in February 2002 (for details, see www.corporate-governance-code.de). The code follows several private codes of best practice[7] that were more far reaching in scope but largely without

---

7. Two codes were developed by the German Panel on Corporate Governance (available at www.dai.de) in January 2000 and the Berlin Initiative Group German Code of Corporate Governance (available at www.gccg.de) in June 2000. The former advocates a number of Anglo-American practices uncommon in Germany: stock-market-oriented compensation, rapid disclosure, the independence of supervisory board members from ongoing business relations, committee work among supervisory boards, and greater concern for conflicts of interests.

influence. The new code will act as soft law via a comply or explain rule in the forthcoming Transparency and Disclosure Law (Transparenz- und Publizitätsgesetz) of May 2002.

In sum, political reforms show substantial areas of convergence to Anglo-Saxon regulation, as well as other areas of continued divergence. Most measures enable rather than force change and focus on capital- market regulation rather than boardroom practices. Transparency and disclosure were increased, as was the range of allowable speculative man- agement practices (Krier 2001) oriented toward share prices (e.g., share buybacks, stock splits, foreign stock exchange listings, and reorganization through mergers and acquisitions).

Capital: Erosion of Financial Commitment?

Convergence arguments cite several types of capital market pressures as driving convergence. Corporations face greater competition for external finance and shareholder loyalty. Cross-border mergers and acquisitions create global corporations adopting international best practices. Share- holder activism by British and U.S. institutional investors is increasing, as are the threats of hostile takeovers. At the same time, ties between domes- tic banks and corporations are seen to be weakening.

How did monitoring by investors change during the 1990s? I argue that stable and committed capital are weakening. First, corporate owner- ship has begun to shift away from committed relationship-oriented shareholders to more financially oriented shareholders, particularly foreign institutional investors. Second, changes in corporate finance have weakened the creditor relations between large corporations and banks. Third, new institutional investors have created considerable pressures to respond to share prices and spurred the diffusion of generic forms of best practice such as transparency and investor relations. Institutional investors, however, tend not to intervene regarding specific corporate strategies and retain a preference for exit. This changing social organization of markets has increased turnover and volatility. Corporations respond by more active speculative management of share prices (Krier 2001) to guard against takeovers or facilitate active corporate reorganization.

Ownership and Stable Shareholding

Between 1990 and 2001, corporate ownership by stable investors declined in favor of institutional investors in Japan, whereas the German pattern remained stable on aggregate (table 9.2). The proportion of stable shares (owned by banks, insurance firms, corporations, and the state)

Table 9.2 Ownership of Listed Corporations, 1990s (%)

	Germany		Japan		United States	
	1990	2000	1990	2001	1990	1998
Banks	9.4	8.4	22.1	19.3	—	—
Nonfinancial firms	41.4	40.1	24.8	22.7	—	—
Government	6.0	6.5	0.7	0.4	0.0	0.0
Insurance firms	3.2	4.8	17.2	10.4	1.9	3.5
Pension funds	—	—	0.9	4.3	24.4	25.9
Investment firms and other[a]	3.3	4.7	7.8	3.8	15.8	22.3
Individuals	18.3	15.6	22.6	26.3	51.0	41.1
Foreign	18.6	19.9	3.9	13.2	6.9	7.2

Source: Tokyo Stock Exchange (1991–2001); Deutsche Bundesbank (2001); New York Stock Exchange (2001b). German data are estimated from heterogeneous sources using both market and book values. Japanese data based on number of unit shares in March of the year indicated.
[a] For Japan, includes investment trusts, securities companies, and other financial institutions. For the United States, data include bank personal trusts, mutual funds, and other nonhousehold investors.

decreased from 64.8 to 52.8 percent in Japan and from 60.0 to 59.8 percent in Germany. These groups tend to hold shares on a committed long-term basis and pursue strategic and organizational interests. Conversely, other groups (individuals, institutional investors, and foreigners) increased from 35.2 to 47.2 percent in Japan and from 40.0 to 40.2 percent in Germany. These groups trade shares more actively (creating greater market liquidity) and their orientation is more purely financial in terms of share price gains. Despite the mix of different shareholder groups, the structure falls short of the U.S. pattern in which finance-oriented investors dominate. What dynamics account for these patterns?

In Japan, a partial unraveling of ties between horizontal *keiretsu* groups is observable. Between 1987 and 2000, the proportion of shares in listed companies owned by stable shareholders declined from 46 to 33 percent and cross-shareholding from 18 to 10 percent (Kuroki 2001).[8] Intercorporate stakes were divested to the smallest extent, despite a growing number of strategic alliances forged outside traditional groupings. Since 1996, corporations began unilaterally selling stakes in the ailing banks, cutting their cross-shareholdings with banks by one-half. Due to the banking crisis, struggling firms faced difficulties obtaining loans and financed investment

---

8. The major horizontal *keiretsu* show different rates of change. Between 1987 and 1999, the Mitsubishi group was the most stable, whereas the Fuji group saw the greatest decline from 54.6 to 38.2 percent stable shareholders and from 39.9 to 23.4 percent in-group cross-shareholding (H. Inoue 2000).

by generating cash from equity sales.[9] By contrast, banks have divested to a lesser extent, although sometimes selling and repurchasing shares to cover losses on bad debt. Insurance companies divested to the greatest extent because postbubble declines in dividend yields and share prices have led to financial troubles in facing their growing liabilities in the aging Japanese society.

Further unwinding is driven by changed accounting rules that value equity at market rather than book values. This change will require unrealized losses to be reported, thus making balance sheets more volatile.[10] Stable shareholding is nonetheless unlikely to dissolve entirely. Business corporations are expected to slow their dissolution of cross-shareholdings because Japanese managers value them as protections against hostile takeovers. Only 23 percent of managers in one survey thought the stable shareholding ratio at their company should be decreased (Research Institute for the Advancement of Living Standards 1999).

In Germany, aggregate statistics show remarkable stability in ownership by banks, insurers, and corporations.[11] Ownership concentration remains high, as shown among the largest one hundred companies in 1998: only fifty-one are listed on the stock exchange (the rest are unlisted corporations or private limited companies) and just twenty-three had over 50 percent of their shares widely held. Behind this apparent stability has been a reorientation of banks and insurance companies to a more profit-oriented portfolio of companies, as well as some consolidation among intercorporate ownership that will probably accelerate after changes in tax law after 2002.

As stable shareholding weakens, institutional investors are becoming more important. In Japan, domestic institutional investors have grown slowly due to the postbubble slide in stock prices. But the proportion of foreign ownership increased very rapidly. Foreign investors are largely mutual funds and pension funds from the United States and Britain. Foreign shareholders influence price movements by very active trading— accounting for 13 percent of turnover in Japanese stocks during 1991 (a turnover rate of 289 percent) and nearly 28 percent in 1999 (a turnover rate of 198 percent) (Tokyo Stock Exchange 1991–2001). Foreign

9. Stronger corporations are loosening their bank ties by repaying loans and reducing interest-bearing debt.

10. To facilitate unwinding, the Financial Services Agency (FSA) proposed the creation of a state-backed stock-buying body to purchase shares owned by the banks in an effort to stabilize share prices (*Nikkei Weekly*, 2 July 2001).

11. The Bundesbank estimates the ownership of domestic shares held within Germany, but directly covers only approximately 60 percent of outstanding shares held in bank deposits. These statistics miss many large illiquid blocks. These estimates are supplemented with additional information on a firm-by-firm basis, making trends difficult to interpret due to inaccuracies in estimated market valuations.

investors focus on a narrow segment of export-oriented blue-chip companies with high market capitalization and liquidity (Jackson 2002a). In 1998, foreign owners held a majority of shares at 1 percent of Japanese nonfinancial listed corporations and controlled stakes of 33 percent or more at thirty firms (2.5 percent of the total). And between 1988 and 1998, the number of firms with foreign ownership of 10 percent or more increased dramatically from 9 to 25 percent.

In Germany, domestic institutional investors (such as investment and mutual funds) expanded dramatically following financial market liberalization and the promotion of equity culture through the privatization of Deutsche Telekom. Both through direct holdings and indirect holdings by institutional investors bound by fiduciary duties to maximize stock market gains, the percentage of German household assets invested in stocks grew from 5.5 percent in 1991 to 8.7 percent in 1998, and the percentage of the adult population owning shares increased from approximately 7 percent in 1988 to nearly 14 percent in 1999 (Deutsches Aktieninstitut 1999). Reforms to the public pension systems will continue to facilitate a strong flow of household savings into stock markets (Jackson and Vitols 2001). The composition of foreign ownership has changed from large direct investments to institutional holdings—the outstanding volume of the latter growing from DM 147 billion in 1995 to DM 514 billion in 1998. As in Japan, a focus on blue-chip companies is evident: data from twenty-four of the DAX 30 companies showed an average of 31 percent foreign ownership, compared to 18 percent at nineteen smaller DAX 100 companies (Hassel et al. 2000; Sherman and Kaen 1997).

Corporate Finance

Investor influence is shaped by the dependence of corporations on different sources of finance. Convergence theories posit a selection mechanism occurring though competition for access to internationally mobile external capital. Empirically, corporations do not appear to depend strongly on external equity capital. Nonetheless, bank lending has declined, particularly to large firms. Whereas Japanese firms are substituting bonds and internal finance for bank loans, German firms greatly increased internal finance but used bond markets to a lesser extent.

Japanese corporations had a net surplus of funds between 1994 and 1998 (Economic Planning Agency 1999). Corporations slowed investment while increasing finance from corporate bond markets and writing off or refinancing bank loans. Although small and medium-size enterprises (SMEs) remain dependent on bank loans, aggregate bank lending to large manufacturing firms has increased only moderately (Economic Planning Agency 1999, 181). The ratio of corporate debt to equity consequently declined from 69 percent in 1989 to 65.1 percent in 1997 (Bank of Japan 1999, 136), although remaining higher than in the United States or Germany.[12] Large firms increased their use of direct finance by issuing bonds, both to finance international expansion through local currency[13] and to tap low interest rates in Japan. Bonds issued by nonfinancial firms between 1992 and 1998 averaged 3.4 percent of gross domestic product in Japan, compared to 2.7 percent in the United States or just 0.04 percent in Germany (Bank of Japan 1999; my calculations).

Large German corporations also increased their financial autonomy. Corporate borrowing remained high during the early 1990s unification boom, followed by a sharp decline to under 9 percent of liabilities (Deutsche Bundesbank 2000, 39). Unlike smaller firms that continue to depend on Germany's regional savings banks, large corporations financed investments internally through retained earnings and pension reserves— pensions representing 15 percent of their balance sheet and bank credits only 7 percent (Sherman and Kaen 1997, 8). Securitized finance such as corporate bonds remains weak—in 1999 securitized corporate debt totaled 20 percent of GDP in Japan, 34 percent in the United States, 20 percent in Britain, and just 3 percent in Germany (Deutsche Bundesbank 2000, 5). Banks make greater use of securities to refinance debt through issuing bonds, accounting for 33 percent of GDP in Germany in 1999 compared to just 6 percent in Japan and 5 percent in the United States (Deutsche Bundesbank 2000, 35).

Share issues continue to make only a small contribution to corporate finance and cannot be seen as directly driving changes toward a share-holder-oriented model. During the 1980s, Japanese firms began to issue equity at market prices rather than par value as Ministry of Finance enforcement eroded. Equity finance proved strongly cyclical, being high during the bubble in 1987–90. But securities issues by nonfinancial companies between 1992 and 1998 averaged only 0.4 percent of GDP in Japan, compared to 0.8 percent in Germany and 1.4 percent in the United States (Bank of Japan 1999; my calculations). In Germany, the 1991–97 annual average of new shares issues was DM 18 billion, but surged to DM 84 billion in 1998 following the privatization of Deutsche Telekom and establishment of a new segment of the stock exchange (*Neuer Markt*). The bursting of the new-technology-stocks bubble sent share issues into a cyclical decline.

12. The Ministry of Finance survey on principal corporations confirms this trend. Between 1992 and 1998, the proportion of new funds from internal finance increased from 65 to 92 percent with a corresponding decline in loans from 33 percent toward a net repayment totaling 4.4 percent of gross new funds.

13. An average of 9.6 percent of Japanese equity financing was raised overseas between 1994 and 1998 (Tokyo Stock Exchange 1991–2001) compared to 15.9 percent of corporate and convertible bonds.

Table 9.3 Financial Systems, Selected Indicators

	United States	United Kingdom	Germany	Japan
Number of domestic listed companies				
1990	5,345	2,111	649	2,071
2000	6,495	2,371	1,034	1,993
Stock market capitalization (% GDP)				
1990	49	88	25	99
1999	181	201	68	104
Concentration of stock market capitalization on top 5% of firms				
1990	53	71	53	47
1998[a]	64	81	78	58
Concentration of stock market turnover on top 5% of firms				
1990	36	72	71	42
1999[a]	58	88	83	65
Currency and deposits (% total household sector assets)				
1990	23	31	48	59
1998	16	21	39	63
Banking sector assets, 1995 (proportion of total financial system assets)	24.6	ca. 25	74.3	63.6
Securitized liabilities (% total nonfinancial enterprise liabilities)				
1990	49	57	19	16
1998	67	73	37	28

Source: Bank of Japan (1999); Deutsches Aktieninstitut (1999). Figures rounded to the nearest percentage point. U.S. figures refer to the NYSE and NASDAQ combined. U.K. figures refer to Great Britain and Northern Ireland.
[a] U.S. figures refer to the New York Stock Exchange only in 1992. Japan refers to Tokyo Stock Exchange only.

Corporate finance changes in the context of larger financial systems (table 9.3). Japanese stock markets gained little financial weight because overall stock market capitalization declined relative to GDP, the number of listed firms increased only slightly, and households shifted savings to bank deposits despite zero interest rates. Beyond the postbubble downward correction in the market, slow growth rates and reduced levels of corporate investment contribute to stagnant stock markets. Since 2000, the two leading stock exchanges created new market segments such as Mothers (a loose abbreviation for market of the high-growth and emerging stocks) and NASDAQ Japan to promote investment in new technology companies. These markets listed thirty-three and fifty-seven companies, respectively, by mid-2001, but face share prices dropping below their initial public offering (IPO) levels.

Meanwhile, German stock markets benefited from the late 1990s boom in high-tech stocks. Starting from a lower level than Japan, market capitalization doubled relative to GDP. Households shifted savings away from banks and toward securities markets, increasing the proportion of individuals holding stock to a historical high. The number of listed companies grew, particularly through the *Neuer Markt* created in 1997 designed to facilitate high-tech IPOs through strict disclosure requirements. The *Neuer Markt* boasted 342 companies by mid-2001, but it also faces problems of small share-price capitalization, high volatility, and plummeting prices following the tech-stock boom and bust.

Who Monitors: Shareholders, Banks, or Markets for Corporate Control?

What impact have changes in ownership and finance had on the monitoring of corporate management? Contrary to the shareholder-oriented model, shareholder voice is weakening due to the decline of traditional bank monitoring. Institutional investors tend not to attend shareholder meetings or intervene actively given poor performance—their stakes remain too small and coordination costs too high. Rather, institutional investors often use voice to promote generic best practices such as accounting and board independence. As investors focus more on share prices and capital-market turnover increases, more corporations are becoming concerned about their vulnerability to hostile takeovers. Although markets for corporate control are not yet active on a large scale, barriers to takeovers are weakening and will be critical to future developments. In short, there is a gradual shift from direct monitoring by banks to indirect feedback via share prices. As the U.S. case shows, stock markets leave an unexpected scope for managerial action.

Banks

Relational contracting with banks traditionally involved multiplex relations mixing credit, large equity stakes, financial services and advice, representation of shareholders as a delegated monitor or through proxy votes, holding of seats on corporate boards, and being active in corporate rescues (Aoki and Patrick 1994).[14] Financial liberalization measures have eroded rents from relational contracting. A general account of financial

14. Aoki and Dinc describe "bank rents that contributed to the evolution of the Japanese main bank institution may be considered a mixture of policy-induced rents extracted from the household savers under financial restraint; monopolistic rents made possible by entry regulation, bond issue repression, and the institutionalization of financial keiretsu; as well as relation-specific rents yielded by corporate clients in exchange for the bank's information services and unique roles in contingent corporate governance" (1997, 21–22).

liberalization[15] is not attempted here (see essay by Sigurt Vitols in this volume); however, market-oriented reforms have reduced the advantages of private information underpinning relational contracting by increasing public disclosure and transparency. Liberalization also eased corporations' access to external capital markets and increased competition among financial intermediaries.

Japanese main bank relationships were dramatically weakened as a consequence of the bubble. Financial liberalization gave corporations greater access to bond markets and rising share prices led to cheap equity finance, consequently reducing the demand for bank credit by large corporations. Banks initially compensated by lending to smaller and riskier firms, which later resulted in bad loans estimated at ¥18 trillion, as well as unrealized losses on stocks purchased at the height of the bubble estimated at ¥4 trillion (Takao, Ikeda, and Fuchita 1998). As this banking crisis unfolded, banks reduced outstanding loans to meet capital adequacy ratios and created a credit crunch for smaller firms despite the Bank of Japan's zero interest rate policy. Banks also divested from shares or sold and repurchased holdings in order to improve balance sheets by booking unrealized gains.[16] As previously mentioned, market-based accounting further reinforces equity divestment.

Relational financing is being partially reconstituted with a focus on securities underwriting and risk management rather than on credit. Banking mergers[17] may help recapture scale and informational advantages, as well as eliminate excess competition. For example, new bank holding companies may increase ownership concentration by being allowed to hold 15 percent stakes rather than the previous 5 percent. Banking mergers bring together firms from competing *keiretsu* groups and may help organize the emerging M&A market by promoting consolidations across these same group lines. But banks are unlikely to regain their past monitoring capacity and thus fail to hinder a growing heterogeneity between large capital market-oriented firms and smaller credit-oriented firms.

German private banks have shifted away from industrial loans and deposits and toward highly profitable investment banking services (Deeg

15. German reform centered on three Financial Market Promotion Acts (Donnelly et al. 2001; Lütz 2000) and Japanese reform was implemented through the financial Big Bang (Ide 1998, 77; Pempel 1999).

16. Banks accounted for less than 5 percent of stock transactions between the mid-1970s and mid-1980s, increasing to 26.2 percent in 1998 (Tokyo Stock Exchange 1991–2001). For example, the Industrial Bank of Japan disposed of ¥268.8 billion in bad debt, nearly 77 percent of which was paid for through sales of stock.

17. These include the following major mergers: (1) Industrial Bank of Japan, Dai-ichi Kangyo Bank, and Fuji Bank; (2) Sumitomo Bank and Sakura Bank; (3) Sanwa Bank, Tokai Bank, and Asahi Bank; and (4) Bank of Tokyo-Mitsubishi and Mitsubishi Trust and Banking.

2001). Deutsche Bank and Dresdner Bank have acquired British and U.S. investment banks, shifted their equity holdings to subsidiary companies, and announced intentions to divest from large stakes. Banks are reducing the size of their largest stakes and diversifying their ties to large firms (Bundesverband deutscher Banken 1999; Böhm 1992, 49).[18] Whereas high taxes previously hindered sales of large stakes, tax reforms initiated by the SPD made capital gains tax-free in 2002. Banks have reduced stakes through innovative devices such as Deutsche Bank's 1997 issue of a long-term convertible bond linked to its holdings in Daimler-Benz.[19] Banks are also slowly reducing their supervisory board seats: private banks held 20 percent of seats in the largest one hundred companies during 1974, but only 8 percent in 1986 and 6 percent in 1993 (Sherman and Kaen 1997, 11–16).

Banks face growing dilemmas regarding their governance role as they shift from traditional *Hausbank* relations to investment banking services. This is well illustrated by the takeover of Hoesch by Krupp in 1991–92 and Thyssen in 1997. Krupp's house bank (WestLB) informally supported Krupp's takeover attempt through its 12 percent stake in Hoesch. Likewise, Deutsche Bank failed to defend Hoesch despite its role as Hoesch's house bank and its seat chairing Hoesch's supervisory board. Deutsche Bank was again active in advising Krupp-Hoesch in its unfriendly takeover bid for Thyssen, although its management held a seat in the target's supervisory board. The implied conflicts of interest drew sharp public criticism and protest from the metalworkers' union, the IG Metall.

Shareholders

As ownership dispersion increases among the largest international corporations, the voting power of shareholders at the annual general meeting (AGM) has remained weak. Japanese AGMs remain extremely short (roughly thirty minutes) and are all held on the same day to prevent *sokaiya* (corporate racketeer) interference. Domestic shareholder activism has made only a small start through the no votes cast by insurance companies regarding dividend policies or changes in management. Germany has a stronger culture of activism by shareholder associations and environmental groups. In neither country do foreign shareholders typically exercise

18. The ten largest banks reduced stakes over 10 percent from forty-six to thirty firms between 1986 and 1994. By 1996, only thirty-one bank stakes exceeding 5 percent existed among the one hundred largest firms (Sherman and Kaen 1997, 10). This does not reflect a strategy of maximizing returns but one of gaining advantages in competing for the banking business of these firms by holding over a 5 percent equity stake.

19. Full conversion would reduce the Deutsche Bank stake from 24.4 to 22.9 percent, raising over $500 million.

voting rights and thus contribute to the declining AGM participation. In Germany, for example, the percentage of share capital represented between 1980 and 1994 declined from 66.2 to 50.9 percent at BASF, 67.5 to 48.4 percent at Bayer, and 63.4 to 45.7 percent at Mannesmann (Bundesverband deutscher Banken 1999).[20]

Shareholder voice thus depends on the threat of exit. Institutional investors consult with management largely outside formal institutions. Such investors usually voice concern over general measures perceived to contribute to good governance, such as transparency or independence. But investors rarely intervene actively to remedy poor corporate performance, preferring exit over voice. Although a small segment of pension funds engages in relationship investing, its role should not be overestimated. Monitoring remains largely mediated via the market in the form of stock price signals.

Markets for Corporate Control

The potential market for corporate control remains a critical variable. The erosion of committed shareholders has slowly increased the number of potential target firms.[21] Conversely, corporations are engaging in external growth through horizontal mergers to cope with international competition, European integration, and deregulation. The worldwide volume of M&A transactions increased from $605 billion in the record year 1989 to an estimated $2,500 billion in 1999 (*Handelsblatt*, 3 December 1999, p. 30). Official German and Japanese statistics document a high number of M&A in the late 1990s (Höpner and Jackson 2001). The value of M&A transactions during 1998 totaled only 0.5 percent of GDP in Japan compared to 20.7 percent in the United States. German M&A totaled just 1.9 percent of GDP in 1996 before growing to 4.5 percent in 1997 and 11.6 percent in 1998, given the Daimler-Chrysler merger (*Handelsblatt*, 5 November 1999, p. 15). M&A are often financed through share swaps with higher share prices leveraging larger takeovers—a powerful motivation for management to maintain share prices. German and Japanese firms with concentrated ownership may use markets for corporate control asymmetrically to take over foreign companies without themselves being vulnerable

20. German banks thus remain the most formidable voting power, particularly when ownership is fragmented. One study of the twenty-four largest firms with fragmented ownership showed that banks accounted for an average of 84 percent of votes through proxies and direct stakes (Baums and Fraune 1995).

21. Japan has a very large pool of takeover candidates. According to ING Barings Brokerage, 47 percent of first section Tokyo Stock Exchange firms have a market value below book value (*Financial Times*, 24 January 2000). At two hundred companies, price-book ratios are less than 0.5, pointing to substantial hidden financial gains. Twenty-one companies are trading at values below their net cash flow.

to takeover bids and thus have survival advantages during international takeovers (Coffee 1999).

Japanese reforms eased corporate restructuring through share swaps, holding companies, corporate spin-offs, and business splits. Holding company structures help position businesses strategically for M&A. But barriers to hostile takeovers continue: cross-shareholding, the difficulty of integrating company-specific employment systems, the role of the Ministry of Economy, Trade and Industry and banks in mediating domestic mergers, restrictions on share swaps with foreign firms, and so on. No large-scale hostile takeover bids have been successful. For example, Yoshiaki Murakami (an ex-MITI official now of M&A International) launched a takeover bid for Shoei Corporation in January 2000. But Murakami did not overcome the opposition by stable shareholders such as Canon Corporation and the Fuji bank group and gained only a 6.5 percent stake. Nonetheless, the tender offer sparked debate, particularly about returning underperforming assets to shareholders.

Shoei may not remain an isolated incident. Cable & Wireless PLC (UK) won a contested takeover battle with NTT to gain a 98 percent stake in International Digital Communications Inc. in 1999 after Toyota sold its shares to the highest bidder rather than to the friendly domestic bidder. Boehringer Ingelheim pharmaceuticals also gained a controlling stake (35.9 percent) in SSP Co., a Japanese drug company (*Boerson Zeitung*, 17 February 2000, p. 12). Apparently motivated by strategic rather than financial interests, the stake surprised SSP management and disrupted patterns of stable shareholding by its customers. Notably, Japan still lags behind in cross-border M&A (see statistics in Ministry of International Trade and Industry 1998) despite the unprecedented participation of foreign companies at Mitsubishi Motors and Nissan.

In Germany, markets for corporate control were limited due to concentrated ownership, bank proxy votes and supervisory board seats, the two-tiered board structure, voting rights restrictions, accounting and disclosure rules, codetermination, and German corporate culture. However, the hostile takeover of Mannesmann by VodaphoneAirtouch in 2000 illustrates how the barriers have weakened (Höpner and Jackson 2001) to a greater extent than in Japan. Many DAX 30 companies have fragmented ownership with a large proportion of international investors. Voting rights caps used by many such firms were abolished through the KonTraG. Mannesmann's size, excellent share performance, and use of less transparent accounting standards failed to protect it from takeover through a cashless share swap from its smaller but highly capitalized U.K. competitor. The case shows that neither banks nor employee representatives were willing or able to mount effective resistance, leading the hostile bid to ultimately be fought with arguments about shareholder value by both management teams.

Labor: Shareholder Value and the Shrinking Core of Industrial Citizenship

How have changes in the role of capital markets impacted long-term employment and industrial citizenship in Germany and Japan? New shareholder groups and regulatory reforms favor the diffusion of a shareholder-value (SV) paradigm of corporate management. As a criterion of business rationality, SV runs contrary to the participation rights and sharing of organizational rents that characterize nonliberal models. The exclusive focus on shareholders contradicts the egalitarian or solidaristic normative notions of the firm embodied in codetermination or enterprise community. Growing managerial orientation to capital markets and shareholder interests typically provokes a number of conflicts (see also Vitols 2000):

- Focus on core competencies creates conflicts with employees over the definition of core business units and the strategies of growth by diversification used to stabilize employment. Divestment from non-core units raises issues of finding good buyers who honor existing employment agreements.
- Ending the cross-subsidization of business units and establishing equity-oriented performance targets create conflicts over performance criteria, profitability hurdles, time horizons, and disciplining poor performance. Greater independence of business units may weaken solidarity among employees who are more directly exposed to market risks and rewards.
- Performance-oriented pay raises issues of balancing individual and group incentives, defining performance criteria, and the risks of contingent pay. Managerial stock options provoke controversy over income inequality and short-termism.
- Increased disclosure and market-oriented accounting may conflict with buffering risks through internal reserves and favor a higher distribution of profits to shareholders. However, disclosure may also increase transparency for employee representatives.

Three areas are impacted by these changes: the strength of labor participation in top management decisions, the security of long-term employment, and contingent pay schemes. Labor continues to play a central corporate governance role by aiming to preserve employment for core employees; however, labor's position is weakening at the margin. Existing institutions no longer display the same capacity for effective participation within new company structures. The mechanisms of negotiated employment adjustment may also be reaching their limits. Meanwhile, contingent pay may weaken employee solidarity by creating differential rewards across business units and a greater consciousness of share prices.

The Organizational Effectiveness of Industrial Citizenship

Corporate restructuring is changing the organizational relation between the business units and employee representation. Effective participation presupposes access to management at the level where strategic decisions are made. Strategic information is needed to engender employees toward a long-term perspective and an active role concerning managerial issues such as investment and human resource planning. Japanese enterprise unions thus face new questions about their boundaries (Sako 1999) and tensions arise between the various levels of German codetermination, such as plant and enterprise. International corporate structures present another dimension because parent firms and foreign subsidiaries are not subject to the same legal and contractual institutions. Overseas workers may not be represented by domestic unions or works councils bargaining with parent firms. Taken together, labor faces growing difficulties in aggregating employee interests and representing them at the level where key managerial decisions are made.

Japanese union density shrank to approximately 22.4 percent across the economy and 30.4 percent in manufacturing by 1998. Joint-consultation agreements remain a core feature maintained by 78 percent of unions and all unions with over 5,000 members (Nikkeiren 1999). Thus, industrial relations at large firms have remained highly cooperative and the number of strikes very low. A major challenge remains the deregulation of holding companies. Previously, Japanese firms often cross-subsidized operations and maintained homogeneous labor contracts across divisions. Holding companies increase centralized financial control while decentralizing operational management. Such reorganization is often intended to differentiate wages in line with the marginal productivity of the divisions.

It is unclear to what extent enterprise unions will bargain centrally with holding companies, who are composed almost exclusively of nonunion managerial employees. Some companies such as Mitsubishi Chemical and NTT retain one union but negotiate separate contracts for group companies. It is an open question to what degree unions will defend uniform wages and working conditions as their own member interests become more heterogeneous. For example, the strong NTT union (nearly a 100 percent organization rate) has maintained similar basic wages and quarterly consultation between the president of the holding company and top union members. Alternatively, separate enterprise unions may establish federations. For example, Nissan developed union federations among related companies and achieved a fair degree of coordination (Sako 1999). The union position was strengthened by a last-minute amendment to the spin-off legislation (pushed by unions through minority parties such as the Democratic Party of Japan) protecting existing labor agreements.

In Germany, codetermination rights are vested in legal rules that constitutionalize participation within formally defined organizational units. Trends toward centralized strategic decision making and decentralized operations often create mismatches with legal rights for works councils vested at the plant and enterprise levels—managers may not be competent bargaining partners when parameters are determined from above and information problems make employees unsure what role their plant has within the overall corporate strategy. Unlike the plant and enterprise level, works councils at the conglomerate level (*Konzernbetriebsrat*)[22] remain voluntary and only their information and consultation rights are legally protected. Labor has attempted to defend the substance of codetermination through contractual agreements that adjust codetermination to new organizational structures (Leminksy 1996, 44) and informal coordination and information across organizational boundaries. This contractualization of industrial citizenship is unlikely to prevent its partial erosion.

International corporations also pose problems for constitutionalized decision making. The European Works Council Directive provides some formal rights for representing European workforces, although their strength depends on being an extended arm of national labor representatives. Board-level codetermination is also threatened by the migration of corporation headquarters to other countries or internationalized corporate boardrooms. For example, Daimler and Chrysler merged under German law, thereby retaining codetermination and the two-tiered board. Because U.S. employees are not entitled to elect supervisory board representatives, the IG Metall offered one of its seats to the United Auto Workers (UAW). DaimlerChrysler also established a novel integration committee to consult with shareholders outside the supervisory board (Gordon 2000),[23] provoking the establishment of a parallel labor committee with the labor bench of the supervisory board plus additional North American labor representatives.[24] Another example is the merger of Hoechst and French Rhone-Poulenc to form the life sciences company Aventis in 1999. Management opposed board codetermination because it is not required under French law. After protracted negotiations, a weakened form of contractually based codetermination was settled on, giving labor four board seats (to the ten shareholder-representative seats). It remains unclear to what extent the European Company Statute will help guard against such de facto erosion through new company-specific codetermination regimes in the future.

22. Little is known systematically about the conglomerate level participation.

23. This committee has no formal decision-making power, but functions somewhat in the manner of a U.S. board, meeting six times per year and providing shareholder advice to the cochairmen.

24. This is not a global employee council with negotiating or decision-making power, as found at Volkswagen, for example.

Corporate reorganization thus often leads to a growing heterogeneity of employee interests and modes of representation within the firm, as well as to weakened access to top-level management decisions over production and investment. A consequence of this is a growing internal competition between different subsidiary companies or production sites over strategic resources (e.g., decisions over whether to upgrade through internal reinvestment). For example, diversified corporations often make substantial divestments from noncore business units in response to capital-market pressures (Zugehör 2000). Labor may strongly oppose company breakups in which employees are commonly transferred between businesses (e.g., NTT moving personnel to its mobile communications company; interview with the secretary general of the All NTT Workers Union of Japan, March 1999, Tokyo). But labor may also support spin-offs when the resources of old businesses are drained to finance new ones (e.g., Mannesmann used its steel division to finance growth of mobile communications; interview with a supervisory board member of Mannesmann, March 2000, Köln) or when they can negotiate positive employment outcomes (e.g., the VEBA works council was active in negotiating with potential buyers to avoid the breakup of business units or sale to competitors aiming at the elimination of excess capacity; interviews with a works council member of VEBA, July 2000, Marl; and an investor relations department member of VEBA, July 2000, Düsseldorf). Other examples include concessions made by works councils to guarantee increased production at their plants (Nagel et al. 1996). Such trends can be interpreted in terms of a functional change in institutions from favoring employee interests as producers to supporting firm competitiveness through active comanagement.

Employment Security

Japanese corporations have maintained strong commitments to lifetime employment (Dore 2000, 104–7; Ministry of Labor 1999, 80–81). Despite the prolonged recession, few companies announced major layoffs and employment adjustment remained much slower than in the United States (Economic Planning Agency 1999, 144, 238). Corporations focused on controlling the rate of accessions and using casual employment rather than increasing separations (Ministry of Labor 1999, 49).[25] However, benevolent employment adjustment faces limits (Yoshitomi 1996, 286–87;

---

25. One study shows the following methods of employment adjustment at Japanese firms: limits on overtime (29.6 percent), hiring freezes (27.4 percent), intrafirm transfers (23.1 percent), transfers to other enterprises (20.2 percent), voluntary retirements (3.7 percent), and, only very rarely, dismissals (1.9 percent) (Japan Institute of Labour 1995).

see also the essay by Kathleen Thelen and Ikuo Kume in this volume). Wage reduction was achieved by reducing overtime working hours and making employment transfers (*shukkō*) to related companies offering lower wages and sometimes subsidizing pay differentials. Such transfers extend across networks of firms rather than within single large companies (Dirks 1997; Sato 1996). But consolidated accounting makes in-group transfers less attractive, and strategies of internal diversification to maintain employment are being abandoned (illustrated for the case of Hitachi in the essay by Kathleen Thelen and Ikuo Kume in this volume). Many large companies are left with very skewed age distributions and incur the high costs associated with Japan's seniority-wage system.

German corporations are also shedding labor through negotiated employment adjustment. In the largest one hundred companies, domestic employment declined 5.8 percent between 1986 and 1996 despite their net employment increase of 10.3 percent worldwide (Hassel et al. 2000, 17).[26] Firms could previously shift the costs of employment adjustment onto the welfare state through early retirement, a practice used to manage the decline in the coal and steel industries. Early retirement schemes paid the differential between state retirement benefits and past salary; for example, VEBA shed 29,000 employees through early retirement with 90 percent salary. This system has reached its limits due to the burdens on the social insurance system and the resulting high nonwage labor costs.

Works councils increasingly negotiate site pacts to keep high value-added production in Germany and protect jobs (Rehder 2001). First, in order to assure investment in core plants, works councils may grant cost-cutting concessions: lower social standards, the elimination of premium wages above collective bargaining rates, and cuts in bonuses for overtime and shift work (Nagel et al. 1996, 99; see the essay by Thelen and Kume in this volume for the implications of cost-cutting pacts for collective bargaining). For example, labor representatives in Audi's supervisory board consented to a new motor plant in Hungary in exchange for reinvesting a portion of the labor cost and investment savings in two large German plants. Second, employment alliances may involve concessions on wages or working hours in exchange for employment guarantees over a period of two to four years.[27] Work may be redistributed through reduced or flexible working time or made cheaper by reducing company premiums above the industrywide rates established by collective bargaining.

26. The data relate to firms that were among the one hundred largest in both time periods, excluding privatized state companies. The largest one hundred companies accounted for 15.8 percent of domestic employment in 1996.

27. Pioneering examples can be found at Mercedes Benz, Bayer, Continental, and Adam Opel.

Contingent Pay and Participation through Share Ownership?

New capital market-oriented practices often involve contingent pay and employee stock ownership programs (ESOPs) to create incentives and promote greater shareholder consciousness within corporate culture.[28] In Japan, lifetime employment practices among large firms were supported by seniority-related wage components, and wage costs have risen because of slowed economic growth and aging corporate workforces. The slow introduction of contingent or merit pay is aimed at controlling costs without damaging incentives for employee loyalty. Wage growth at listed companies slowed in the 1990s and led to a growing dispersion among companies (Economic Planning Agency 1999, 129–30). ESOPs have also become widespread but are limited in scope—covering 96 percent of listed companies and an average of 49.7 percent of their employees in 1998, although representing only approximately 1 percent of the total stock market value (Tokyo Stock Exchange 2000).

In Germany, wage rates are generally set by sectoral collective bargaining arrangements that leave small scope for company-specific variation by setting bonuses. Moreover, works councils have codetermination rights regarding the remuneration methods used in contingent pay. Unions have resisted share ownership because it erodes class consciousness or transfers income risks onto employees. One study documents that 70 percent of the largest one hundred corporations have adopted performance-related pay and 57 percent have ESOPs (Kurdelbusch 2001). These plans were introduced or enlarged in the context of internationalization and the diffusion of an SV management paradigm.

Japanese and German unions are discussing whether ESOPs are a potential means of influence within shareholder-oriented corporations. Following the Mannesmann takeover, worker representatives at other widely held companies such as Siemens attempted to organize the voting rights of employee-owned shares into blocks. Likewise, Mitsubishi Heavy Industries organized its ESOP plan through a delegated employee (in consultation with the enterprise union) to become the company's eleventh largest shareholder with a 1 percent stake (interview with an executive committee member of Mitsubishi Heavy Industries Workers Union, June 2000, Tokyo). But given their small size, ESOPs have only a limited potential as a new source of participation.

In sum, labor has not blocked corporate restructuring but has played a subtle role in shaping the implementation of new SV strategies (see also Höpner 2001; Höpner and Jackson 2001). Such comanagement has, on

---

28. For venture capital companies, ESOPs create a deferred payment to firm-specific investments, but involve risk sharing rather than bureaucratic employment protections.

the one hand, assured a basic continuity in cooperative industrial relations and a core of long-term employment; when the legitimacy of employee participation is not fundamentally in question, labor has accepted economic constraints and sought to make adjustment socially acceptable (sometimes altering management's course) (Kotthoff 1998). On the other hand, this continuity should not overshadow both the shrinking core of employees enjoying such industrial citizenship and the institutional erosion of participative institutions toward more voluntaristic arrangements.

Management: Governance Paradigms within Shifting Coalitions

Managers now intensified investor pressure alongside a continued importance of employee voice in corporate governance. Understanding how these conflicting demands (or declining institutional coherence) play out requires a deeper look into the changing identities and interests of management itself: corporate boards, managerial pay, and the diffusion of SV practices. I discuss changes to smaller boards and the growing dominance of managers with financial backgrounds, rising managerial salaries and the spread of stock options, and the gradual diffusion of an SV paradigm as a new managerial ideology. These changes should not be seen only as a response to external shareholder pressure but as an interrelated set of changes in the social world of managers—the contestation and spread of a new conception of control (Fligstein 1990).

Board of Directors

Japanese boards are typically very large bodies, sometimes totaling forty internally promoted directors who remain closely involved with operational management. The president often retains strong control but may be monitored by outside dispatched directors from the main bank, particularly in a crisis. Since 1997, many leading companies drastically reduced board sizes in order to speed decision making and make meetings less cumbersome. Board restructuring is often related to the introduction of holding companies: strategic management is performed by a smaller board that internalizes monitoring over its subsidiaries. Despite insistence from foreign investors and the Corporate Governance Forum, only a few companies such as Sony have independent outside directors. Managers doubt whether outside directors have enough company knowledge to make effective contributions, and underdeveloped external labor markets present daunting problems for recruiting qualified external directors. Labor unions have advocated outside directors in exceptional cases, such as Ajinomoto, in which a director was found guilty of making payments to *sokaiya*. It remains to be seen whether smaller board sizes lead to changes in the system of internal managerial promotion because a smaller board may decrease the incentives inherent in a quasi-bureaucratic system of advance.

By contrast, German boards have a much stronger monitoring role due to the two-tier structure dividing supervisory and management functions. Debate has focused less on outside directors because supervisory board members represent major shareholders and industrywide unions. The KonTraG made only incremental changes, such as limiting the number of mandates held by particular individuals, improving the information and preparation of the board, and requiring more meetings. More significant are two longer-term trends: the number of bank representatives is declining in favor of former management board members (Bundesverband deutscher Banken 1999; Höpner 2002) and board subcommittees are increasingly used but widely perceived to circumvent parity codetermination. Both factors increase the power of managerial insiders relative to external control.

German management boards (*Vorstand*) are generally smaller compared with Japan, although also differing from the United States in using collegial decision making and lacking strong CEOs. Managers are mostly insiders and industrial management is dominated by technical and scientific backgrounds. However, management careers have been changing—the average tenure declined from thirteen years in the 1980s to just six years in the 1990s, and the number of directors with outside work experience increased from 17 to 35 percent (Höpner 2002). More finance officers often become speakers of the board, an unprecedented move at many science- and engineering-oriented companies such as Hoechst and DaimlerChrysler.

Managerial Pay

German and Japanese management receive modest compensation compared with other countries. In 1991, the total CEO pay was 7.8 times higher in Japan than an average manufacturing employee, 10.2 in Germany, and 25.8 in the United States. By 1999, the gap rose to 11 times higher in Japan, 13 in Germany, and 34 in the United States (Towers Perrin 2000). An important factor behind these differences involves the degree of performance-related pay and stock options, representing over 140 percent of the basic salary in the United States compared to 60 percent in Germany and just 13 percent in Japan during 1999. Although stock options are often viewed as promoting shareholder interests, the evidence of performance effects is mixed at best. Stock options are also criticized as contributing to the excessive growth of managerial pay in the United States, as well as rewarding short-term thinking and behavior contrary to the interests of other stakeholders. Although stock options have been liberalized, it remains open whether the spread of stock options yields differences from Anglo-American practices.

Following the legal reform in June 1997, Toyota was one of the first Japanese companies to introduce managerial stock options (Dore 2000). According to a survey by Nikko Securities, approximately 10 percent of listed companies have managerial stock option schemes (*Nikkei Weekly*, 17 April 2000, p. 23). Many companies view stock options as inappropriate to their corporate culture, too volatile, or a poor measure of performance. The regulations remained restrictive—the National Tax Authority applied a high-rate income tax and companies could not issue the stock options of a parent company to officers and employees of their subsidiaries. Stock options also required explicit approval from the shareholder meeting, as well as specific mention of the individuals and amounts to be received, in strong contrast to the powers of U.S. corporate boards to determine remuneration. Business leaders and the U.S. Chamber of Commerce criticized these various restrictions as inflexible and hindering the recruitment of outside staff. Further liberalization in 2002 removed most of these restrictions.

German management salaries traditionally had small variable components linked to dividend payments. Daimler-Benz and Deutsche Bank were leaders in introducing stock options valued at DM 40 million during 1996. Prior to liberalization, only six companies issued stock options through a very cumbersome procedure using convertible bonds. Large firms lobbied intensely to ease legal restrictions as part of the 1998 KonTraG to link managerial incentives to share price performance, make German managerial positions more attractive relative to better-paid Anglo-American positions, and promote venture capital start-ups (interview with research and legal officers of Deutsches Aktieninstitut, April 1999, Frankfurt am Main). Stock options spread quickly thereafter, particularly among *Neuer Markt* companies.

Stock options are a symbolic point of conflict over the appropriate role of SV and have even been portrayed as the end of postwar social consensus. At Daimler-Benz in 1995, the introduction of managerial stock options led to dramatic employee protest that succeeded in gaining ESOPs for all employees. This event appeared to set the important precedent of using stock options in a democratic way, as opposed to creating divergent incentives between management and labor. The KonTraG addressed some concerns by requiring explicit performance targets and two-year vesting periods before exercising options. Compensation plans are also left to the supervisory board and thereby open to the scrutiny of employee representatives. German companies are thus perceived to set stricter performance criteria and retain more modest remuneration than U.S. companies. For example, BASF requires investment on the part of managers and limits the level of the profits realized (*Handelsblatt*, 8 October 1999).

The Diffusion of Shareholder-Value Practices

As a cognitive and normative model, the SV paradigm serves as a template for interpreting organizational problems, as well as guiding experiments in search of new best practices under conditions of rapid environmental change and high uncertainty. Diffusion and imitation are aided by professional standard setting, consultants, personal networks, and the media (DiMaggio and Powell 1991). The dominance of agency theory among academic economists helps legitimate the view of shareholders as having ultimate control rights and being residual risk bearers in the firm.[29]

Challenged by this new model, some managers defend the merits of what has diffusely been termed a stakeholder approach. The commitment to employees remains strong among Japanese managers (Research Institute for the Advancement of Living Standards 1999), even if less consensus exists on other issues such as the appropriate role of corporate boards. Kenzaburo Mogi, CEO of Kikkoman, argues for "preserving employment, thus providing incentive to work hard for the long-run survival and growth of the firm." These sentiments are echoed in leading Japanese financial publications: "there is no future for a firm that places its first priority on increasing share value to please stockholders" because doing so "would neglect Japan's most valuable resource—its employees" (quoted in Kōsaki 2000, 72).

In Germany, a survey also showed that only 7 percent of top managers viewed creating SV as the goal of the firm, compared to 72 percent who put the interests of shareholders, employees, and the public good on equal footing (*Handelsblatt*, 17 March 2000). Managers such as Hubertus von Grünberg (ex-board chairman of Continental) also defend public responsibility toward stakeholders: "Management must have its employees and customers in mind in addition to the shareholders, otherwise it is not doing justice to its responsibility" (quoted in Nölting 2000, 42). Likewise, Nikolaus Schweickart (board chairman of Altana) made bold statements against the efficiency of SV principles: "We see in the shareholder value theory an opposition to cultural and social engagement. . . . We know the markets are easy to excite for cleaning portfolios and divesting, since these effects can be easily calculated. Investments, restructuring, and long-term

---

29. Despite powerful critiques of this theory (Parkinson and Kelly 2001), the stakeholder model of the firm remains less well theorized.

research and development are harder to calculate and are not popular among powerful new investors. . . . For this reason, I recommend calm and long-term thinking as well as more resolve against capital-market actors who wish to force their rules of the game onto the company" (quoted in Nölting 2000, 116).

Other prominent corporations have nonetheless advocated SV as the future paradigm of management—for example, DaimlerChrysler, Hoechst, and VEBA in Germany and Sony and Orix in Japan. SV refers to a diverse spectrum of corporate strategies to improve the value of shares and establish the creation of value for shareholders as an overarching performance criterion (Rappaport 1986). SV practices include upgrading investor relations and corporate disclosure. Beyond its symbolic gesture, SV also involves deeper operational measures, such as decentralized profitability targets related to return on equity. For example, Sony now evaluates six division companies with Stern Stewart's economic value-added (EVA) concept. And in Germany, VEBA introduced a value-oriented controlling concept in 1994 developed with Boston Consulting—it monitors forty business units according to the level of capital invested, return on investment, and SV creation (return beyond imputed capital costs at market rates according to similar risk investments).

Only a small segment of internationalized Japanese companies have adopted these practices. Meanwhile, SV has diffused more rapidly among German companies and is highly correlated with capital-market pressures (e.g., ownership by foreign or institutional investors and vulnerability to takeovers) and international product-market competition (e.g., sheltered and export-oriented sectors) (Höpner 2001).[30] SV is nonetheless not solely a response to external pressures. As previously argued, capital-market constraints may be rather soft—corporations are largely internally financed, markets for corporate control are limited, and institutional investors focus on generic issues rather than proactive intervention. Even within the shareholder model in the United States, strong remnants of managerial capitalism remain—markets for corporate control have been limited by corporate lobbies of state legislatures, independent outside directors have little impact on performance, management salaries show little correlation with performance, and managers retain considerable scope to employ speculative management techniques to impact the liquidity and value of their share prices.

A fuller account should recognize that promoting SV does not necessarily limit managerial power and may often further managerial objectives or interests. First, managers benefit from high share prices not only as a

---

30. Bank influence (ownership and board seats) or strength of codetermination had no effect on the adoption of SV.

guard against hostile takeovers, but as a means of fueling expansion by taking over other companies through share swaps. Using stock as a currency of mergers and acquisitions helps corporations manage competition and gain strategic inroads into new market segments. Second, the rhetoric of SV may legitimate measures necessary for product-market competition vis-à-vis middle management and employees. SV is often part of larger attempts to change organizational cultures or turn around performance. Third, managerial stock options are associated with large growth in management salaries, as illustrated dramatically at DaimlerChrysler.

New management paradigms at German companies such as Daimler-Chrysler and Hoechst were associated with the rise of new management teams having greater international experience and expertise in finance. Although capital-market pressures may create demand for financial skills, finance experts also use SV to further their own careers and power within the organization relative to other management groups. Here, SV serves as a set of principles (a cognitive model or ideology) giving meaning to new behaviors by identifying them as solutions. By using the language of SV, managers can mobilize support of new external coalitions among institutional investors and gain internal legitimacy relative to rivals. Generational change and new managerial education and careers, particularly exposure to U.S. business schools and corporate practices, are important in promoting new management paradigms.

It remains an open question to what degree SV will serve as a model and diffuse outside of the largest international corporations. Where traditional managers have stayed entrenched, corporations are more cautious and selective in adopting new management practices. Mitsubishi Chemical Corporation represents this pattern of conservative renewal through adopting a smaller board and holding company structure, but continuing to reject stock options and external directors (interviews with the director of Mitsubishi Chemical Corporation, March 1999 and June 2000, Tokyo). Such selective experimentation with SV practices is very instructive due to the multiplicity of motives and their result as firm-specific governance arrangements. This type of hybridization process involves negotiated combinations wherein SV may be adapted or weakened to fit with other existing institutions, particularly industrial citizenship.

Conclusion: Hybridization and Heterogeneity within National Models

Much public debate attributes change in nonliberal models of corporate governance to the internationalization of capital markets—corporations are subjected to the pressures of competitive selection driving convergence toward an Anglo-Saxon shareholder model. This chapter adds substance to this general notion by examining internationalization in terms of changing coalitions between state actors, new shareholder groups, labor, and management. A more differentiated picture emerges of how market pressures are refracted through distinct sets of national institutions, as well as the active role of labor, management, and state actors in negotiating elements of a new shareholder model.

The comparison contrasts slower liberalization in Japan in the context of its severe macroeconomic situation and the more rapid pattern in Germany pushed by the political and market integration of Europe. The empirical parallels are nonetheless notable. First, regulatory reform increased transparency and disclosure, as well as changing the use of corporate equity to allow new methods of speculative management and corporate reorganization; however, national diversity remains in corporate boards and labor participation. Second, new institutional investors created greater pressure for financial returns through relatively active trading, in contrast to the strategic and committed shareholders of the past. At the same time, the monitoring role of banks eroded as relationship banking faced declining returns culminating in the Japanese banking crisis and strategic reorientation of German commercial banks. The impact of more indirect investor monitoring via the market still depended on whether large-scale markets for corporate control emerge. Third, labor continued to play a significant corporate governance role. Employment adjustment and corporate restructuring remained largely negotiated rather than unilateral. Labor also shaped how corporations implemented SV measures at the margin. Last, management actively initiated SV practices, reflecting important changes in their careers, remuneration, and conception of control.

These trends hold three key implications for the future: (1) Germany and Japan have neither retained their past models in a path-dependent manner nor converged to the shareholder model found in Anglo-Saxon countries, (2) these changes can be interpreted as a process of hybridization, particularly between marketized capital and industrial citizenship, and (3) whether the future builds on past competitive strengths depends on the degree that corporations learn to adopt an enlightened approach to SV by stressing the positive-sum interests with labor. This model nonetheless presents new challenges to public policy as well as new risks and social costs.

National Models between Path Dependence and Convergence

The patterns of change observed in German and Japanese corporate governance fit uncomfortably with current theories of institutional change. On the one hand, theories of institutional path-dependence generally posit that (1) national institutions display complementarities (positive feedback or increasing returns) that make systemic change difficult and piecemeal changes unlikely to fit efficiently within existing institutional contexts and/or (2) the vested political interests of corporate insiders such as banks, blockholders, and corporate management will prevent shifts toward a market-oriented system. Given such barriers, systemic change is unlikely without an exogenous shock. This chapter demonstrates both endogenous institutional erosion, such as declining returns to relationship banking, and that internationalization may create political realignments. Key elements of Germany and Japan's national models have changed and represent a distinct institutional path. Both the rules of the game and strategies of major actors have shifted in ways unlikely to reverse back to the previous model.

On the other hand, liberalization and internationalization are not leading to strong convergence to a single model of best practices (see Bratton and McCahery 1999; Guillén 2000). Convergence theories claim that international capital markets exert competitive selection pressures on corporations and these force convergence to the U.S. model of corporate governance because of its greater ability to produce high returns to shareholders. Empirically, little evidence points to strong mechanisms of competitive selection. Corporations have not increased their dependence on external equity finance under the current condition of low economic growth and slowed capital investment, nor have markets for corporate control emerged on a large scale.

Differences relative to the United States continue along each dimension compared. Political reforms facilitate greater capital-market orientation but face significant political limits preserving distinct rules for corporate boards and employee representation. Institutional ownership is concentrated in a small segment of large international companies, whereas ownership generally remains more concentrated. Labor plays a much stronger role in corporate reorganization than in liberal countries. Management pay remains more modest and boardroom practices distinct. Decisive is, however, that these are not differences of degree. Rather, the interaction among these elements is argued to follow an overall logic quite distinct from current U.S. practice or theories of shareholder primacy.

Hybridization and Heterogeneity

These transformations are interpreted here as a process of institutional and organizational hybridization, "the ways in which forms become separated from existing practices and recombine with new forms in new practices" (Pieterse 1994, 165). The new hybrid forms of corporate governance involve mixing shareholder or market-oriented practices developed within Anglo-American economies with nonliberal practices, particularly the institutions fostering industrial citizenship. The concept rejects both an economic determinism of a single best model and arguments of societal determinism suggesting that practices can never be transferred. Given the strong internal complementarity among the elements of past nonliberal models in sustaining particular profiles of competitive advantage, hybridization has puzzling implications.

Historically, German and Japanese corporate governance developed through an uneasy tension between liberal and nonliberal organizational principles (Jackson 2001). For example, the historical experience of importing U.S. institutions after World War II did not result in convergence but rather in the modification of foreign practice to develop new hybrid forms with varying degrees of success (Zeitlin 2000, 41–50). Likewise, management did not see postwar industrial citizenship as a beneficial governance tool but rather as a threat to private property and managerial discretion. The results were not coherent by design; rather, complementarities resulted through an unintended fit between different practices. Corporations had to discover how to reconcile competing principles and thereby learn to realize latent institutional complementarities. Institutional efficiency was an emergent phenomenon involving organizational learning and change over a relatively long period.

For participants and observers alike, the degree of tension or complementarity among institutions is thus often difficult to predict. New hybrids may be unstable if their components lack complementarities—resulting in further institutional change, inefficient outcomes, or abandonment of an initial change. Alternatively, hybrids may prove stable if existing practices can be reconfigured to fit within a firm-specific competitive environment, existing firm coalitions, or a national institutional context. Conflicting logics may even help balance one another and preserve beneficial requisite variety in the long run. Both dynamics are relevant to the ongoing changes.

One issue concerns the erosion of relationship banking. Liberalization inserts different sorts of rules—those that level the playing field through information, disclosure, and arm's-length relationships. Transparency erodes rents available to insiders through private information while requiring greater neutrality in mediating market-oriented transactions. German banks faced role conflicts in acting as traditional house banks and simultaneously as investment banks while markets for corporate control emerged. Likewise, Japanese banks faced declining policy-induced rents that sustained main-bank relations and faced enormous challenges to put such relations on a new footing. Thus, a viable hybrid between relationship banking and market-oriented control has been hard to achieve. The result seems to be a bifurcation between sectors within national models—itself a type of hybridization. Large international firms and banks are increasingly moving toward market-oriented control, whereas small firms and the regional and cooperative banks seek to uphold more traditional relations (Deeg 2001).

Another issue concerns whether SV practices among large corporations will ultimately undo existing patterns of industrial citizenship or be accommodated in a new hybrid. Although no definite conclusions can be drawn, this chapter has illustrated numerous attempts at accommodation along the lines of weak or enlightened SV. Here labor has given conditional support to SV measures, but has used its influence to codetermine their substance to either improve managerial accountability or lessen class conflict. Labor generally favors greater transparency to enhance employee participation and thus improve managerial accountability. Labor has also pushed accountability in managerial remuneration in efforts to prevent excessive inequality that damages employee morale and foreclose short-term misincentives. Moreover, in accepting the legitimacy of managerial stock options, labor gained a springboard to implementing ESOPs. Of course, the success of such efforts has been mixed. But the examples suggest that strong labor may potentially play a positive role by lessening the class-conflict aspects of SV and stressing its positive-sum potential.

This positive-sum potential for capital and labor within a shareholder model depends on the degree that labor constraints force managers to resist the temptations of pleasing shareholders in the short term without considering long-term strategic consequences (e.g., rapid downsizing of personnel, mergers, or spin-offs). Performance targets may be reached by improving productivity rather than short-term cost-cutting or balance-sheet manipulation. Or, faced with corporate restructuring (e.g., a focus on core competence), labor may promote good buyers during spin-offs (e.g., those who intend to act as good employers rather than the highest bidder). Such measures may be compatible with the long-term interest of capital, even when short-term returns are sacrificed. Just as labor acts as a beneficial constraint for product-market competition by promoting a high-road strategy, labor also helps block the temptations of excessive short-term rationality in responding to capital markets.

The stability of enlightened SV appears greater in Germany than Japan. In Germany, SV entered a constitutional governance regime and was accommodated by contractualizing existing arrangements. When the legal checks and balances remain strong, negotiated outcomes have a more stable footing. By contrast, Japanese industrial citizenship depended more on patient shareholders than on channeling control into a constitutionalized regime of checks and balances within the corporate board. Without legal guarantees, Japanese practice may be less resilient in the face of strong shareholder pressures. Conversely, labor may be more resistant to managerial initiatives. Thus when labor is weak, SV probably intensifies adversarial relations; when labor has been a strong partner, employees may positively influence SV strategies. Even such a successful recombination of institutions promotes a functional change toward employees engaging in active comanagement to promote their company-related producer interests, as opposed to more solidaristic class interests.

A further consequence of hybridization is the growing heterogeneity of organizational practices within national systems. Corporations choose their corporate governance practices within the boundaries of prevailing institutional constraints and past organizational coalitions. Although national models were never entirely homogeneous, the capacity to generate relatively isomorphic practices across companies and sectors within a particular country is declining. Inherent institutional tensions facilitate deviant patterns of behavior (Whitley 1992, 248) and greater firm-specific experimentation in combining elements of different models. Even as nations retain distinct profiles of corporate practices, the range of internal variation is growing, particularly between large internationalized corporations and more protected domestically oriented or private corporations. Heterogeneity itself entails a de facto element of convergence (Streeck 2001).

Which Future Model: A Coexistence of Markets and Citizenship?

Nobody can predict with certainty which corporate governance model will prove most well adapted within the rapidly evolving international economy. New information technologies (IT) and internationalization raise fundamental questions about the appropriate scale and boundaries of corporate organization as well as the legitimate criteria of rationality to guide decisions. Facing high uncertainty about the appropriate model, corporations engage in decentralized processes of experimentation. Corporations may seek to imitate perceived best practices (DiMaggio and Powell 1991). But any future paradigm remains a moving target, and firms may not necessarily become competitive by replicating the strategies of successful first-movers. Corporations must also differentiate themselves from their competitors by distinct profiles of competence and strategy.[31] Given

---

31. The sociology of markets suggests that markets are not characterized by the convergence of firms around the same schedules of output and price but by a process of finding niches differentiated vis-à-vis other producers (White 2002).

diverse organizational and institutional endowments, market pressures can initiate searches for new opportunities and learning that lead to further specialization rather than convergence (Hollingsworth and Streeck 1994, 284).

What prospects exist for a hybrid model to sustain a distinct profile of competitive advantage? In the past, nonliberal models derived their competitive advantage from the complementary relation between committed capital and industrial citizenship. Complementarities created increasing returns, reinforcing a stable path of organizational learning and innovation. As a more conflictual interface with marketized capital emerges, institutional tensions may undermine some past strengths but fail to provide for new ones. In sectors exposed to the capital market, German and Japanese firms may find it more difficult to pursue strategies of low risk and return or accommodate high labor or research and development (R&D) costs.

The potential strengths of enlightened SV rest on a positive-sum view of power stressing the common interests of shareholders and employees in managerial accountability. To the extent that industrial citizenship promotes accountability and can lessen the class conflicts surrounding corporate restructuring, Germany and Japan can preserve some past strengths. As radical innovation in IT slows, the skill and information structures supported by industrial citizenship may see renewed importance in the continuous coordination and incremental innovation necessary to integrate IT technologies into new sorts of hybrid products (see the essay by Kozo Yamamura in this volume; see also Aoki 2000). Thus, it is premature to assume that a stronger role of the capital market necessitates market-based labor relations with high external mobility and low participation rights. In fact, movement to such a model would probably destroy hard-won organizational competencies crucial to competitiveness. A more constructive approach involves labor helping to constrain management within the context of international capital markets by reining in temptations to please capital markets by short-term measures.

Yet the risks and social costs of a shareholder-oriented model should not be overlooked. Creating the institutions for market-based finance is likely to expand the supply of capital trading in the secondary market for existing corporate shares more rapidly than the current growth of real economic activity. Such financialization (Dore 2000) subjects corporations to pressures for higher profits, but penalizes them with greater volatility when expectations are not met, as witnessed by the IT stock bubble in the late 1990s. Conversely, market actors have little responsibility to contribute to active monitoring. A long way remains to close the gap between the demands of the market and the indirect monitoring it provides—one consequence being a reassertion of managerial capitalism under the guise of shareholder control. The long-term beneficiaries will probably be those corporate managers whose fortunes come to be tied to the stock market, but who remain largely emancipated from careful stakeholder scrutiny.

Meanwhile, industrial citizenship is becoming less of a politically or socially guaranteed right and more a contractual arrangement used by firms to increase productivity. The shrinking core enjoying membership in the corporation as comanagers and coowners contrasts with the growing social closure at its boundaries (see Streeck 2001). A smaller core no longer has the same weight within national economies to sustain positive macroeconomic externalities as during much of the postwar era—notwithstanding the high demands corporations now make on the institutional infrastructure of society to sustain their competitiveness. This raises serious questions of corporate accountability to the public interest. A consequence will be a rising inequality in wealth and incomes.

Politically, the future prospects depend on the will and capacity to internationally establish a level playing field for labor. Whereas shareholder protection has become a major part of the international political agenda, less has been done to address basic rights of industrial citizenship. However, the experience of EU directives on works councils and European companies shows that Germany had little success in exporting features of its corporate model to Europe. Meanwhile, Japan is embedded in a less integrated regional setting and subject to greater bilateral pressure from the United States (see the essay by Peter Katzenstein in this volume), thus making Japan an unlikely strongman in promoting an alternative to the Anglo-Saxon model within international corporate governance standards.

Major Amendments to Japanese Corporate Law, 1990s (Commercial Code of Japan)

1993, Derivative Actions, Strengthening Auditors' Function: Effectively lowers fees for shareholder derivative law suits. Introduced requirement for a Board of Auditors and at least one outside statutory auditor who has not been a director, manager, or employee of the company and its subsidiaries for five years. Also decreases the minimum stockholding for inspection of company accounts.

June 1994, Share Buybacks: Removes prohibition on the purchase of the company's own shares. If transferred to employees, the purchase is limited to 10 percent of issued shares and within profit available for dividends, as well as being subject to approval of the shareholder meeting. Corporations can also use profits to purchase and cancel issued shares.

June 1997, Stock-Option System (Initiated by Diet): Allows Treasury (or Warrant) stock options to be granted to employees and directors pending a general resolution (extraordinary resolution) of the shareholder meeting. The total number must not exceed 10 percent of issued shares. The proposal must specify the name of the director or employee, the number of shares, transfer price, exercise period, and conditions of exercise. The Securities and Exchange Law was amended to require disclosure of stock option plans.

October 1997, Deregulation of Share Buybacks: Allows changes in company articles to empower board of directors to carry out stock repurchases.

December 1997, Liberalization of Holding Companies: Fair Trade Commission revises antimonopoly law to allow the establishment of pure holding companies.

March 1998, Deregulation of Share Buybacks: Allows funds for stock repurchase to be expanded beyond profit to include capital reserves.

October 1999, Stock-Swap System: Facilitates cashless mergers by allowing a parent firm (A) to buy subsidiary (B) through an exchange of shares (company B's shareholders get shares in company A). Requires two-thirds majority of the respective shareholder meetings. Minority shareholders have right to sell shares back to company at a "fair price." Law aimed to facilitate formation of holding companies.

January 2001, Spin-Off Legislation: Allows corporations to transfer business to a separate company without capital ties or to a third company. Requires two-thirds majority of shareholders.

March 2001, Market-Based Valuation in Accounting: Requires assets to be reported at current market values. The law applies to stable shareholdings beginning in 2002.

June 2001, Deregulation of Share Buybacks: Allows corporations to engage in buybacks for unspecified purposes and hold shares for an unlimited duration.

April 2002, Deregulation of Share Issues and Stock Options, Electronic Disclosure: Relaxes conditions for issuing new shares and increases the variety of stock, such as shares with limited voting rights. Abolishes certain restrictions on stock options. Extends use of electronic disclosure.

May 2002, Strengthening Statutory Auditors and Reduction of Directors' Liabilities: Requires one-half of auditors to be outsiders who have never been a director or employee of the corporation. Reduces the liabilities of directors and relaxes procedure for such waivers.

Passed May 2002, Introduction of Committee System and Relaxation of Quorum Requirement of Shareholders' Meeting: Allows corporations to adopt committees for nominations, auditing, and compensation of which more than one-half the members may be outside directors (nonexecutive directors)—along lines of U.S. practice. Such companies are not required to have a statutory auditor. Reduces quorum for shareholders' meeting to one-third of total number of voting shares.

The Re-Organization of Organized Capitalism: How the German and Japanese Models Are Shaping Their Own Transformations

Steven K. Vogel

The German and Japanese models of capitalism are fundamentally transforming, yet they are neither collapsing nor converging to the liberal market model. Rather, they are "re-organizing," charting distinctive paths of adaptation. But which analytical perspective is most useful in describing and explaining the trajectory of institutional change? In this chapter, I contend that the best way to understand the transformation of German and Japanese capitalism is to focus on the preexisting institutions of the models themselves because these institutions powerfully condition patterns of change. I develop a simple model of institutional change and apply it to changes in two core components of the German and Japanese models: labor relations and financial systems.

The German and Japanese Models

For present purposes, I define the German and Japanese models as constellations of institutions (including political institutions, intermediate associations, financial systems, labor relations systems, and interfirm networks) linked together into distinct national systems of economic

I thank Robert Fannion for field research collaboration and feedback; Kenneth Haig, Keith Nitta, and Masaya Ura for research assistance; participants in the Germany-Japan Project and the Harvard Government Department Workshop on Comparative and International Political Economy for comments; and the Abe Fellowship Program, the U.S.-Japan Program at Harvard University, and the Center for Japanese Studies at the University of California, Berkeley for financial support.

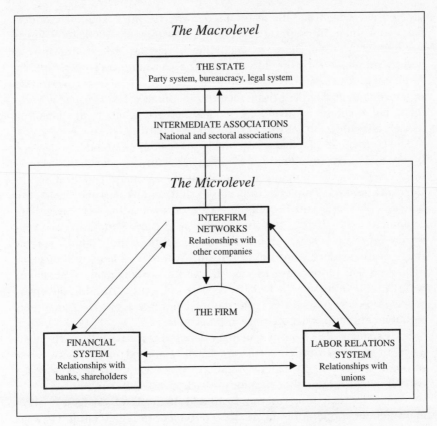

Figure 10.1 Simple Model of an Organized Market Economy

governance (see figure 10.1). Organized market economies (OMEs) such as Germany and Japan differ from liberal market economies (LMEs) in that they foster more long-term cooperative relationships between firms and labor, between firms and banks, and between different firms. And the state and intermediary associations play a critical role in establishing and maintaining the framework for this private-sector coordination. Although there is considerable variation across sectors and across firms within individual countries, OMEs remain sufficiently different from LMEs to make this a useful distinction. These governance structures affect everything from corporate strategy to public policy and economic performance (e.g., Albert 1993; Hollingsworth, Schmitter, and Streeck 1994; Kitschelt et al. 1999; Porter 1996).

The German and Japanese variants of the OME model also differ from one another. German firms, banks, and unions are more inclined to coor-

dinate their activities at the sectoral level, whereas their Japanese counterparts coordinate through intersectoral groups (Soskice 1999, 106). Japan
has denser interfirm networks, including horizontal industrial groups as
well as supply and distribution chains. The German government merely
facilitates private-sector coordination, whereas the Japanese government
organizes and guides the private sector more directly. The German government has codified its economic model into law, whereas the Japanese
model relies more on informal norms and standard practices.

The German and Japanese labor relations systems combine broad agreements on wage moderation in exchange for employment security
with firm-level pacts that promote labor-management cooperation. In
Germany, sectoral employer associations and unions negotiate collective
bargains on wages and benefits. In Japan, a few leading firms negotiate
settlements with their enterprise-based unions during the annual spring
wage offensive (*shuntō*), and other firms then follow within a fairly narrow
range of the leaders. These labor relations systems can benefit both sides:
employers win moderation in wage demands, workers gain employment
security, and both benefit from fewer labor disputes. In addition, firms
avoid competing in wages or undermining labor-management cooperation
through contentious negotiations at the firm level.

Both systems also feature systematic labor representation in the management process. German firms are legally required to represent labor
through a system of codetermination, whereas Japanese companies
typically incorporate labor despite the lack of a legal requirement to do
so. Labor participation at the firm and plant level facilitates labor-
management cooperation on the shop floor, a critical element in German
and Japanese firms' ability to continuously raise productivity. Long-term
cooperative relations between labor and management also give firms the
incentive to invest in human resources. German firms typically do this
through a distinctive dual (firm and school) vocational training system,
whereas Japanese firms train their workers directly. In the political realm,
German employer associations and unions are both represented in most
important decision-making bodies, whereas Japanese business enjoys
better access than labor to central ministries and the ruling party.

Germany and Japan both have credit-based financial systems in which
banks have dominated the long-term financing of industry. The Japanese
government has actively directed the allocation of credit through government financial institutions and private banks, whereas the German government has left the banks with greater freedom. In both countries, however,
firms have developed long-term relationships with their primary banks,
known as *Hausbanken* in Germany and main banks in Japan. The banks
monitor firm performance and aid firms in distress. The firms, in turn, remain loyal clients—they conduct a large and stable share of their borrow-

ing and transaction business with their lead bank. German banks exercise influence over industrial firms through ownership stakes, proxy votes, and direct representation on company boards, whereas Japanese banks are restricted to 5 percent ownership and rely more on industrial group ties and informal channels of influence.

The Forces for Change

Before we look at how Germany and Japan are responding to their respective predicaments, let us briefly review the common forces driving change in the two systems. First, the increase in trade and capital flows between nations is breaking down the relative insulation of the German and Japanese markets.[1] Manufacturers and financial institutions are less dependent on exclusive relationships with domestic business partners, because they can pursue other opportunities in international markets. Domestic markets are increasingly infiltrated by foreign companies that do not behave according to local norms, and domestic companies are exposed to new patterns of behavior as they move abroad. The growing mobility of capital and corporate activity not only undermines the ability of national authorities to control corporate behavior, but encourages the governments to reform regulations so as to prevent capital or corporate flight. Capital mobility also directly affects labor relations because it means firms can exit from long-term relations with labor partners by shifting to foreign suppliers or moving production abroad, whereas labor lacks a comparable exit option. Meanwhile, financial disintermediation disrupts bank-industry relations because firms rely less on their banks as they shift from borrowing to equity finance.

Second, the U.S. government, other national governments, and international organizations such as the World Trade Organization (WTO) and the European Union (EU) are promoting further market liberalization and regulatory harmonization. Third, both countries have experienced a long-term appreciation of their currencies, especially in the late 1980s and early 1990s, increasing pressure on corporations to cut costs to compete in international markets. Fourth, technological change and related marketplace developments are forcing German and Japanese ministries, associations, and companies to adapt. New products and production techniques have emerged that do not play to traditional German or Japanese strengths, and the growing importance of the service sector challenges countries such as Germany and Japan that have their primary strength in manufacturing (see the essay by Kozo Yamamura in this volume). Com-

1. For evidence of internationalization, see Milner and Keohane (1996).

pounded with internationalization, technological change increases the costs of dualistic economic systems, in which a highly competitive export sector, primarily in manufacturing, is combined with an uncompetitive sheltered sector, primarily in services.

Finally, Germany and Japan have experienced a decline in economic performance, with slower growth, declining export competitiveness, and high (in Germany) and rising (in Japan) unemployment. This has generated enormous political pressure for economic reform. In particular, slow economic growth and government budget constraints have encouraged political leaders to promote deregulation, privatization, and other reforms that promise to improve economic performance without increasing spending (Vogel 1996, 39–41).

Germany and Japan also face pressures unique to their particular circumstances. Germany has confronted the daunting challenge of reunification with the former East Germany, which not only strains the country's financial resources but also entails the incorporation of a region with a completely different institutional legacy. Germany must cope with integration into the EU, which mandates market liberalization and regulatory harmonization and imposes stiff requirements for fiscal policy. Japan faces greater political change, with the end of Liberal Democratic Party (LDP) hegemony, the introduction of a new electoral system, and the ongoing realignment of political parties. And Japan suffers a far more serious economic crisis, with a prolonged recession and a full-fledged financial crisis.

Understanding Institutional Change

The various schools of new institutionalism have been more successful in explaining why institutions persist than how they change. The new institutional economics (NIE) stresses the equilibrium nature of governance systems, the new institutionalism in sociology identifies normative and cognitive constraints on change, and the historical institutionalism in political science highlights path dependency. Nevertheless, some work offers insights into the process of institutional change as well (e.g., Boyer and Hollingsworth 1997; Knight 1992; North 1990). Here I outline one perspective on institutional change and apply it to Germany and Japan. Toward the end of the chapter, I suggest how it might be refined by incorporating further insights from political science and sociology (see Hall and Taylor 1996, especially 938–42, on calculus versus cultural approaches).

Incentives and Constraints

Building on the new institutional economics and the varieties of capitalism literature, let us view the German and Japanese (hereafter G-J) models of capitalism as systems of incentives and constraints (Aoki 1988; North 1990; Soskice 1999; Williamson 1985). That is, actors within these systems (firms, banks, and unions) use institutions such as the *Hausbank* (main bank) system, collective bargaining, and interfirm networks to reduce transaction costs. They then incorporate these institutions into their cost-benefit calculus as they adapt to new circumstances. Corporations will only abandon their stable partners, such as unions, banks, or other corporations, when the efficiency gains from doing so outweigh the cost of forgoing future benefits from cooperation with these partners. And in most cases, the marginal increase in efficiency will not justify the large fixed cost of exit from these relationships. This perspective not only helps to explain why the G-J models are slow to change, but it also helps to explain when and how they do change.

This model assumes for now that firms make rational cost-benefit calculations about corporate adjustments or their positions on government reform policies, but it incorporates insights from work in institutional economics to provide a broader and more realistic picture of this calculus. We could describe this in terms of broadening circles of rationality. In the first circle, a manager simply calculates the estimated costs of financing with the firm's main bank versus the costs with a competing financial institution. If the competitor is less costly, he abandons the main bank. In the second circle, however, he weighs the potential cost savings from switching against damage to the long-term cooperative relationship with the main bank, including preferential services and the insurance the bank provides in the form of a commitment to assist the firm in a crisis. And in the third circle, he further broadens the calculus to include possible costs beyond the main-bank relationship, such as damage to the firm's reputation or strains in relationships with workers, other business partners, intermediary associations, or the government. As the circle of rationality expands, the chances that a firm will exit from relationships diminishes. Because G-J firms rely so heavily on long-term relations with workers, banks, and other firms to maximize their performance, they are almost certain to broaden their calculus beyond the first circle and quite likely beyond the second.

In this view, institutional change occurs when an exogenous shock pushes actors to reassess the balance between the costs and benefits of the status quo.[2] Institutional change is a function of the level of the shock and

---

2. North (1990) describes this in terms of a shift in relative prices or preferences.

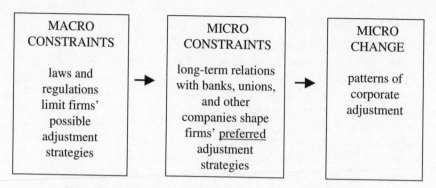

Figure 10.2 Microlevel: Factors Shaping Patterns of Corporate Adjustment

the incentives and constraints built into the existing system. This means that even when the shock is big enough to impose change, preexisting institutions still shape the substance of change. For our purposes, the forces for change make up the exogenous shock and the G-J models themselves constitute the incentives and constraints that shape the response to this shock.

In practice, the task of analyzing institutional change is made all the more difficult because it operates simultaneously at many different levels of a given political-economic system. That is, German and Japanese firms are renegotiating agreements with their workers, banks, and business partners; industry associations and union federations are reorganizing and redefining their missions; and the governments are revising regulatory procedures and passing reform legislation—all at the same time. To make the situation even more complex, adjustments at one level have ramifications for further adjustments at other levels. In order to make sense of this analytically, I simplify the picture somewhat and focus on adjustments at two levels: the firm and the government.

The Microlevel: Corporate Adjustment

At the firm (micro)level, the forces for change translate primarily into increased pressure to cut costs. But as G-J firms strive to cut costs, they are constrained from laying off workers, abandoning their main banks, and cutting off stable suppliers by the logic of the G-J models themselves (see figure 10.2 and table 10.1). Their options for adjustment are limited by legal and regulatory constraints, such as laws governing the dismissal of workers. Moreover, their preferred strategies for adjustment within these legal constraints are shaped by their preexisting relations with workers, banks, and other firms. That is, they are situated within a network of long-term

Table 10.1 How German and Japanese Models Shape Their Own Transformations

	Characteristics	Outcomes
Microlevel (corporate adjustment)	Firms are constrained by long-term relationships with workers, banks, other firms	Firms strive to adapt within the existing institutional structure
	Firms are constrained by their own internal governance structures	Firms try to leverage the advantages of existing institutions
Macrolevel (policy reform)	Industry demands for liberal reform are modified by internal governance structures and long-term relationships with workers, banks, other firms	Governments promote liberal reforms cautiously, consulting and often compensating groups opposed to reform
	Industry associations and political parties aggregate demands in a manner that further modifies pressure for liberal reform	Governments design reforms to preserve valued institutions
Micro-macro interaction	Corporate adjustments alter firm preferences regarding further policy reform	
	Policy reforms facilitate or constrain further corporate adjustments	

relationships with these partners from which they benefit, so when they face new challenges they are likely to go to considerable lengths to adjust without abandoning these partners. They are likely to renegotiate with these partners (to exercise voice) rather than to break with them (exit), and they are likely to leverage the benefits of these long-term relationships and perhaps even reinforce these ties in order to ride out their problems (Hirschman 1970). In short, G-J firms respond to new challenges neither by clinging to the status quo nor by converging to Anglo-American practices but rather by charting their own distinctive patterns of adjustment.

The Macrolevel: Policy Reform

At the national (macro)level, the G-J governments are also constrained from moving toward the liberal market model (figure 10.3). Just as firms' preferred business strategies reflect the incentives and constraints of the G-J models, so do their preferences on policy reform. I build here on the basic insight of the historical institutionalist school that suggests that institutions shape actors' preferences (Steinmo, Thelen, and Longstreth 1992; see also Hall 1999; Pierson 2000). In this case, I contend that there is a micro logic to macro preferences—industry policy preferences reflect the institutions of German and Japanese capitalism, such as labor relations and financial systems. Many firms derive comparative institutional

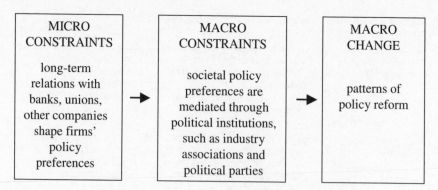

Figure 10.3 Macrolevel: Factors Shaping Patterns of Policy Reform

advantage from these institutions, so they have to weigh the expected efficiency gains from policy reforms against the possible costs of undermining these institutions (Soskice 1999).

Jeffrey Frieden and Ronald Rogowski (1996) offer a useful model for deducing societal preferences regarding liberal economic reform, focusing especially on sectoral cleavages. According to standard economic analysis, economic liberalization should reduce prices and expand choices for consumers, lower costs for producers, and boost economic growth. It not only improves efficiency in the short run, but also can bring more dynamic long-term benefits by stimulating business activity and innovation. Protection has both a distributive cost, in that it punishes consumers in favor of producers, and a social welfare cost, in that it distorts the allocation of resources within the economy. The higher the level of protection and regulation, the greater the potential benefits from reform. Frieden and Rogowski suggest that internationalization should intensify domestic groups' preference for liberalization. They focus primarily on the liberalization of international trade and financial transactions, but they note that the argument applies to domestic structural barriers as well. As international trade and capital flows expand, the gap between domestic prices of protected goods and world market prices widens, meaning that the welfare costs of protection (and hence the potential benefits of liberalization) increase. Moreover, they hypothesize that internationalization should increase conflict among sectors, specifically among those relatively competitive on world markets, which favor liberalization, and those relatively uncompetitive, which demand protection. They expect internationalization to strengthen the hand of those groups favoring liberalization at the expense of those opposing it.

In contrast, I argue that in Germany and Japan even the competitive sectors do not fully support liberal reform. The institutional context of

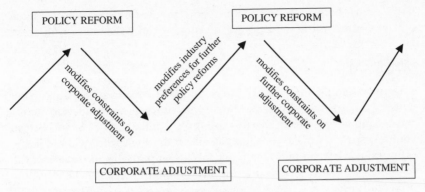

Figure 10.4 Micro-Macro Interaction

German and Japanese capitalism modifies industry preferences—fewer firms advocate reform than we would otherwise expect, and those firms that do advocate it are more ambivalent than we would otherwise expect. Moreover, these preferences are aggregated in the political (macrolevel) arena in a manner that further moderates demands for liberal reform. The major industry associations and political parties represent both the advocates and opponents of reform, so they are not likely to push for the all-out victory of one side but, rather, to arrange delicate compromises between the two. And if anything, they tend to favor the potential losers from liberal reform. As a result, when contemplating liberalization, German and Japanese government leaders are likely to move cautiously; to package delicate compromises, including considerable compensation for those who might be disadvantaged by the reforms; and to design reform to preserve the core institutions of the G-J models as much as possible (Vogel 2001).

Micro-Macro Interaction

Thus the G-J models themselves generate relatively predictable patterns of corporate adjustment and government reform. But the actual trajectory of change over the longer term is complicated by the fact that the two levels interact. As governments enact policy reforms, these reforms create new opportunities and constraints for further corporate adjustment. And as firms adjust to new challenges, these adjustments may modify the firms' policy preferences and thereby affect future policy reforms (figure 10.4).

Patterns of Corporate Adjustment

Let us now turn to examples from developments in labor relations and finance to illustrate how our model might play out: how preexisting institutions shape corporate adjustment, how preexisting institutions shape policy reform, and how corporate adjustment and policy reform interact.

Labor Relations

German and Japanese firms have responded to increased pressure to cut costs in remarkably predictable ways given the enormous diversity across sectors and companies in the two countries. Unlike their U.S. and British counterparts, they make considerable efforts to reduce costs without laying off workers. German and Japanese firms accomplish this in somewhat different ways, however, reflecting the institutional differences between the two countries.

As previously noted, when a German or Japanese firm considers laying off workers, it does not simply weigh the benefit of reducing operating expenses versus the cost of shrinking the workforce. It also must consider how this decision might impair its ability to mobilize the remaining workers to enhance productivity, to recruit new workers in the future, and to project a positive image in the business community. It is also likely to encounter more substantial legal and regulatory barriers to laying off workers than its U.S. counterpart. Moreover, the G-J models themselves provide troubled corporations with other options: they can rely on their close cooperative relationship with workers to raise productivity or call on their lead bank to help obtain more credit or reduce financing costs.

In both countries, corporations have focused first on raising productivity and lowering nonlabor costs. They have leveraged their relationships with workers to enhance productivity, they have simplified the production process, and they have pressured suppliers to reduce costs. When they have sought to reduce labor costs, they have done so through a predictable series of steps, with layoffs as the last step in the chain. In Germany, for example, companies worked with the unions to shorten work hours and to design early retirement plans. With this strategy exhausted, they moved on to more creative solutions that build on one of the strengths of the German system, the ability of management and labor to negotiate solutions that benefit both sides. For example, many employers agreed to preserve job security or to forgo plans to move production abroad in exchange for greater flexibility in working hours. Some firms have devised elaborate schemes in which they pay workers constant wages over a year, but the workers' actual hours vary considerably so as to better match production cycles.

Meanwhile, the peak employer and labor organizations have agreed to allow greater flexibility in collective bargains. Specifically they have established clauses allowing companies that meet certain hardship criteria to diverge from the bargains. Employers and unions are working on a longer-term compromise solution that would preserve collective bargaining but permit more leeway at the plant level. This approach naturally builds on the strengths of the German system: peak organizations able to negotiate broad agreements combined with good working relations between management and labor at the plant level. The system is coming under increasing stress, however, because a growing number of employers are not abiding by the agreements or are defecting from their associations altogether. But even firms covered by the bargains often use these agreements as a reference point in determining wages and benefits (see the essay by Kathleen Thelen and Ikuo Kume in this volume).

Large Japanese corporations are also striving to cut labor costs without laying off workers. They accomplish this primarily by reducing new hires and offering early retirement, not by opting for the German solution of cutting working hours. Japanese firms also tend to reduce management salaries and bonuses before cutting blue-collar wages and to reduce workforces more rapidly overseas than at home. Japanese firms enjoy some built-in flexibility because they can shed temporary and/or part-time workers without threatening lifetime employment for the core workforce and they can shift the burden of adjustment to suppliers outside the system of long-term employment guarantees. Beyond this, large Japanese firms have developed a distinctively Japanese method of reducing labor costs by putting their corporate networks to a new use. In the past, they have used these networks as channels for reemploying workers after retirement. Now they are extending this practice as a means of coping with excess labor. In fact, some companies have diversified with precisely this goal in mind—to create subsidiaries and affiliates that can serve as employment networks.[3]

Finance

As German and Japanese firms seek to reduce costs and bolster profits, they naturally look to lowering financing costs. In Germany, large firms have markedly decreased their reliance on loans as a source of funding since the 1980s, shifting more to equity markets and self-financing (Deeg 1993). And as they shift to equity financing, they become more dependent on outside investors, often including foreign investors. Meanwhile, many small and medium-size enterprises still depend on loans and rely on a close working relationship with their *Hausbanken* as much as ever.

But even large corporations have not simply severed their long-term relationships with their banks. German banks are universal banks (i.e., they

3. Hirokuni Tabata (1996) offers a fascinating case study of how Japanese auto unions have worked with management to reduce costs and increase productivity.

can provide the full range of financial services, including banking and brokerage), so they can adapt to their clients' changing needs by transforming from providers of loans to underwriters of debt (Roe 1993). Although underwriting implies less oversight and control than lending, it does leave the banks with a continuing role in meeting these corporations' financial needs. Moreover, the banks have many other channels of influence over industrial corporations, including substantial shareholding positions, representation on supervisory boards, and proxy voting rights. Many banks have been decreasing their ownership stakes in client firms, but they appear to be decreasing their largest stakes while increasing other shares, leaving the overall level of ownership relatively steady (Deeg 1993). They are not only reluctant to sell off shares of companies with which they have long-term business relationships, but they are also deterred from doing so by the possibility that they might drive share prices down if they sell too much at one time. Likewise, banks have not substantially reduced their positions on corporate supervisory boards or given up their proxy voting rights (see the essay by Gregory Jackson in this volume).

Rather than abandon one another (exit), German corporations and banks have been more likely to manipulate the changing business environment by renegotiating the terms of their relationships (voice). The banks have retained substantial equity shares in long-term business partners, but have pressed these firms to increase profitability. The corporations still give the bulk of their banking business to their long-term banking partners, but demand lower costs and better service in exchange. Meanwhile, banks are trying to reduce the financial burden of bailing out client corporations in trouble, but they have not abandoned this role. Bankers argue that they serve their own enlightened self-interest in doing so in many cases—they may lose more by allowing a firm to fail than by bailing it out because its failure could spread to affect other corporate clients. Banks have become more stingy in funneling cash into rescue operations, but they remain critical intermediaries in most mergers, acquisitions, and other forms of corporate restructuring.

Likewise, German corporations' well-publicized newfound attention to shareholder value has gone further in rhetoric than in reality. A few prominent firms have set targets for profitability, created departments for investor relations, adopted international standards of accounting, and otherwise sought to make themselves more attractive to international investors (Marsh 1996). Even so, most German companies have a substantial proportion of their shares in stable hands and relatively little in foreign hands. This means they can continue business as usual without being punished too brutally by fickle international investors. And of course German firms are constrained from making some of the moves that would most please their shareholders—such as shedding excess workers—by the constraints of the labor-relations system.

Japanese companies have also moved away from reliance on bank loans, but they too are renegotiating their relationships with their main banks rather than abandoning them. As in Germany, smaller corporations remain heavily reliant on banks. In fact, the banks are trying to strengthen their ties with medium-size firms in order to compensate for business lost from the larger corporations. Japanese banks are not universal banks, and therefore disintermediation has posed a greater threat to their business than in Germany. Not surprisingly, they lobbied to enter the securities business, gaining the right to underwrite debt through separate subsidiaries in 1992. They have since leveraged their main-bank relationships to seize a substantial share of the corporate bond market.

Japanese corporations still give much of their banking business to their traditional main banks, and the banks retain ownership shares in these corporations. Japanese bankers describe an elaborate ritual in which the banks and their main-bank clients renegotiate the terms of the relationship. The guiding principles are twofold: prior consultation and reciprocity. If a bank wants to sell shares of a corporation, it consults the corporation first. As a result, it can expect to lose a proportionate share of the corporation's banking business. Likewise, a corporation that shifts some of its banking business to other financial institutions can expect that the bank will divest some shares. In either case, the bank does not divest all of its shares and the corporation does not completely drop the main bank, so the long-term relationship continues. When banks vie for underwriting business, a similar logic applies. The banks expect their favored clients to give them the largest share of this business, but the client companies do so on the condition that the banks offer terms, expertise, and a menu of financial instruments nearly comparable to the top securities firms. And the companies continue to pressure the banks to enhance their services.

Banks continue to play a role in corporate restructuring, yet they are much less capable of providing funds given the current financial crisis. When banks do intervene to help firms in crisis, they do so in accord with the principles of reciprocity previously described. That is, they gauge their commitment to a firm in terms of the level of cross-ownership and the firm's loyalty as a banking customer. As the financial crisis has deepened, many firms are actually reinforcing their ties with their main banks. As their bond ratings have deteriorated, they have been forced to shift back from equity financing to borrowing. And although the banks' ability to bail out the firms may have diminished, the firms' reliance on the banks' generosity has only increased.

Patterns of Policy Reform

German and Japanese firms' choices are limited not only by informal constraints, such as commitments to long-term relationships, but also by the formal laws and regulations that underlie the G-J models. So any substantial transformation of the models requires policy reform. As Peter Gourevitch (1996) has noted, the microinstitutions of capitalism rest on macro (political) foundations, and thus major reforms to these institutions must survive the political process. Yet just as the microinstitutions of the models themselves affect firms' preferred strategies for adjustment, these institutions also shape firm preferences about policy reform.

Labor Market Reform

Given the cost pressures they face, we expect German and Japanese employers to favor labor deregulation, which should give them access to a wider pool of workers at a lower cost. Commentators in both countries now blame rigid labor markets for high labor costs, decreasing competitiveness, and high unemployment. Politically, therefore, we expect the battle over labor deregulation to pit firms, employer federations, and the conservative parties against workers, union federations, and the parties of the left. Yet in both countries firms have been ambivalent about labor market reforms, fearing that these reforms might undermine the advantages of the German and Japanese labor relations systems.[4] Moreover, firm preferences have been aggregated through employer federations and political parties that represent opponents as well as advocates of reform.

In Germany, economists, journalists, and other opinion leaders have called for the abolition of the collective bargaining system altogether. But most firms feel that they benefit from the present system and prefer to preserve it while introducing modest reforms to allow more flexibility. German companies are wary of abandoning the collective bargaining system because they fear that shifting wage and benefit negotiations to the plant level will undermine the cooperative atmosphere on the shop floor. In addition, labor market reforms could force companies to compete for workers on the basis of wages, dilute their incentive to invest in human resources, and otherwise erode their productivity advantage (see Soskice 1999; Thelen 1999b). Meanwhile, the employer associations and the trade unions strongly support the system; after all, they have a huge institutional stake in preserving it. The conserva-

---

4. The logic of the present argument also applies to welfare reform. That is, we expect most firms to favor reforms to reduce mandatory spending on employee benefits and otherwise lower the overall tax burden. But German and Japanese firms are more ambivalent than we might normally expect because many feel that welfare provisions help to sustain productivity pacts on the shop floor (see Manow 1999).

tive government under Chancellor Helmut Kohl did not attempt to reform the collective bargaining system, but did take several smaller steps (Thelen 1999b).In1996,thegovernmentreducedlegallymandatedsick-payallowances from 100 to 80 percent of salary. This created a major uproar, with unions arguing that companies would be violating their labor contracts if they implemented the change. Interestingly enough, Kohl himself encouraged companies with such provisions in their contracts to maintain this commitment, whereas Freie Demokratische Partei (FDP) leaders were alone in pressing companies to take advantage of the new law (*Financial Times*, 30 September 1996, p. 2). As it turns out, the vast majority of German companies have simply continued to pay the 100 percent rate. Then, in the autumn 1997, the government enacted two additional measures: one easing requirements for terminating workers and the other allowing more flexibility in short-term (one- to two-month) contracts. The Sozialdemokratische Partei Deutschlands (SPD)-Green government has since reversed all three of these measures.

In Japan, employers have not proposed any wholesale change in the employment system but instead only piecemeal reforms coupled with more active adjustment polices and new protections for workers. The government has moved forward with modest deregulation measures in the context of a governmentwide deregulation movement that began in the 1980s and has accelerated since 1993. In 1997, the government removed some special protections for female workers, such as those governing overtime and nighttime work. Then in September 1998, it revised portions of the Labor Standards Law to give employers more flexibility with employment contracts and overtime pay, but it coupled this with increased regulation of termination notices, working conditions, and overtime hours. And in July 1999, it revised the Worker Dispatching Law and the Employment Security Law to give employers greater freedom in dispatching workers, to allow private companies to provide employment placement services, and to increase legal protection for job seekers. Nevertheless, the Japanese legal system still gives employers considerable flexibility in managing human resources within the firm by transferring employees to subsidiaries or increasing work time, for example, while sharply constraining their ability to hire and fire workers. In particular, the Japanese courts have developed a case law doctrine that deters employees from dismissing workers (Yamakawa 1999).

Financial Reform

Here again, we expect firms to advocate financial and corporate governance reforms designed to make equity markets operate more efficiently because this will reduce financing costs and stimulate financial innovation.

But German and Japanese firms derive distinct advantages from their existing financial systems. Many German and Japanese managers value their freedom to hide profits and losses or to manipulate reporting to smooth out earnings over time, so they are reluctant to embrace financial reforms that would bring stricter requirements for information disclosure. Others worry that further financial liberalization might undermine the advantages of close working relations with their banks. They count on these banks for preferential access to credit at special rates, a wide range of free services such as providing information and brokering business alliances, and for assistance in the event of a financial crisis. Despite the firms' reservations, however, Germany and Japan have both moved forward with substantial financial reforms in the face of powerful forces for change.

Germany lagged behind other advanced industrial countries in financial liberalization, especially with respect to securities markets. The big banks supported measures to promote new financial instruments and to centralize equity trading activity in Frankfurt, whereas the smaller financial institutions and the *Länder* opposed these. Meanwhile, the Bundesbank opposed the introduction of money-market instruments for fear these might affect monetary policy. And when the Bundesbank finally did permit these instruments, it did so in a manner such that the banks could dominate the new products (Vitols 1997). Nevertheless, the German government pushed through substantial reforms in the 1990s in response to political pressure from the large banks; increasing competition from other financial centers, especially London; and EU directives on financial services. In 1994, the government passed an omnibus financial reform bill that reorganized the stock exchange; created a new regulatory agency, the Supervisory Office for Securities; set criminal penalties for insider trading; and established the legal foundation for the introduction of money-market funds (Story 1996; Vogel 1996).

In Japan, some of the biggest banks favored more rapid liberalization in the 1980s and early 1990s, but they moderated their demands for reform because they recognized that rapid reform could threaten other financial institutions with whom they have strong long-term working relationships. They also realized that articulating demands too strenuously could undermine their relationship with the Ministry of Finance. The ministry moved very deliberately, packaging elaborate political compromises among the various groups within the financial sector (city banks, securities houses, insurance companies, regional banks, credit associations, and cooperatives) (Vogel 1996, 93–117). With the financial crisis and the widespread loss of faith in the ministry, however, the political pressure for further reform increased substantially.

In response, Prime Minister Ryūtarō Hashimoto proposed a Big Bang reform in which the government would liberalize foreign exchange restrictions; open up the mutual fund, pension, and trust markets; deregulate brokerage commissions; allow banks, securities houses, and insurance companies to enter one another's lines of business through holding companies; and delegate some of the Ministry of Finance's supervisory duties to a new finance agency. Even so, the Big Bang does not represent a complete break with past patterns of financial regulation because the government is phasing in these measures gradually and paying special attention to their impact on domestic financial institutions. Moreover, the government has gained leverage over the financial sector as a result of the banking crisis. It is playing a major role in allocating funds to banks in crisis, monitoring troubled banks' behavior, and orchestrating the reorganization of the financial sector.

Germany and Japan both have large public-sector components of their financial systems, representing approximately one-half of total savings, that strongly resist reform. In Germany, the public-sector regional banks and cooperatives are highly popular and politically powerful at both the regional and the national levels. Despite pleas for reform from the private banks, conservative politicians have resisted reforms that would threaten this sector. Meanwhile, government officials and public bank executives are working together to increase economies of scale through business tie-ups and mergers within the network of public banks. Likewise, the Japanese bureaucracy has allied with powerful LDP politicians to fight back calls for reforming the postal savings system. Prime Minister Jun'ichirō Koizumi finally began to push through his long-anticipated reform program in 2002.

The German and Japanese governments have both made progress on corporate governance reform as well, but have compromised on the terms of those reforms that have gone through and have yet to address many other regulations that impede a more decisive move toward shareholder capitalism. In Germany, politicians debated major reform legislation for over a year before reaching a compromise in November 1997. The bill abolishes enhanced and maximum voting rights (special voting rights not accorded to all shareholders); restricts banks from exercising proxy voting rights in firms in which they have a greater than 5 percent ownership share; requires banks to report transfers of their own personnel to firms in which they have a greater than 5 percent stake; allows firms to buy back up to 10 percent of their own shares; reduces restrictions on shareholders' ability to receive compensation for management misconduct; and increases the duties of supervisory boards, especially with respect to coordination with auditors. In announcing these measures, Economics Minister Günther Rexrodt was careful to stress that the legislation would not undermine the positive role of banks in providing capital to growing industrial firms and supporting firms in times of crisis (*Business Law Europe*, 12

November 1997, p. 8). The government considered but ultimately rejected proposals to impose legal restrictions on bank share ownership. In addition, Labor Minister Norbert Blüm blocked proposals to reduce the size of supervisory boards due to powerful resistance from unions that feared this might undercut their influence.

In Japan, the authorities have gradually phased in a shift toward market value–based accounting. But many firms have resisted these reforms because they fear this will make it more difficult to manipulate return on equity figures, to smooth out earnings over time, to ignore contingent or unfunded liabilities, or to camouflage the cross-subsidization of business operations (Shinn 1999). The Ministry of Finance and the Financial Services Agency have also been reluctant to move too far for fear they might lose the ability to supervise and restructure the financial sector in a discretionary and discreet fashion. Meanwhile, both the Federation of Economic Organizations (Keidanren) and the LDP have proposed measures to allow corporations to restructure their cross-shareholdings without causing the stock market to collapse or allowing outside shareholders to buy up the shares. Yet these measures violate the very purpose of market-oriented corporate governance reform—to facilitate stock market adjustments and corporate contests for control (10–11).

Micro-Macro Interaction

Let us now turn to concrete examples of how these two levels of adjustment interact, beginning with some stylized facts from postwar Japanese history and then moving on to speculation about how current changes might evolve in the future. As noted in figure 10.4, policy reforms alter the incentives for and constraints on corporate adjustment; and corporate adjustments in turn shift industry preferences regarding further policy reforms. For example, when the Japanese government relaxed capital controls in the 1960s, this prompted Japanese firms to dramatically increase their cross-shareholdings, creating what is considered to be a primary feature of the Japanese model. In doing so, Japanese firms helped to preserve features of the Japanese system—such as industrial policy, administrative guidance, and interfirm collaboration—that function best in a market protected from foreign capital. And they were only able to accomplish this in the context of close government-industry collaboration, relatively weak antitrust regulation, and well-organized interfirm networks.

Then in the 1970s, when the Japanese government moved forward with trade liberalization, some industries replaced tariffs and quotas with private-sector substitutes, including preferential procurement practices, exclusive dealerships, and cartels. Kodak argued this point in its WTO case against Fuji Film, contending that the Ministry of International Trade and Industry (MITI) had worked with Fuji to establish exclusive dealer networks that effectively shut out foreign suppliers (Dewey Ballantine 1995; Johnson 1982; Tilton 1996).

Then in 1985, the G-5 governments launched a substantial appreciation of the yen with the Plaza Accord. Many Japanese firms responded by shifting manufacturing activity to southeast Asia so as to reduce production costs. But rather than abandoning their favored suppliers, large manufacturers moved abroad in tandem with their suppliers, extending national supply networks into the Asian region (Hatch and Yamamura 1996). In each of these cases, the Japanese model transformed, yet did not converge with, a liberal market model. In fact, the government and industry interacted to produce an adjustment of the model (institutional change) conditioned by the incentives and constraints of the model itself.

I contend that this has been happening once again since the 1990s. Germany and Japan have made little progress in labor-market reforms (macrolevel), meaning that the governments have not substantially expanded opportunities for private-sector adjustment (microlevel). So the two levels of change are not interacting in a way that is likely to dramatically accelerate the rate of change. In fact, we could even argue that feedback mechanisms are reducing the prospects for radical change in Germany. That is, as firms gain more flexibility in applying collective agreements and those firms most dissatisfied with the system simply defect, the firms left within the employer associations are even less likely to press for major reform. In finance, however, the two governments have enacted reforms in accounting, pension systems, and other areas that are spurring more substantial changes at the firm level. As German and Japanese corporations adjust to more international regulatory standards and deeper ties with foreign institutions, they are likely to become more favorably disposed toward future financial reforms.

Looking to the future, Japan's decision to lift the ban on holding companies could profoundly affect the long-term evolution of the Japanese model. Most countries already have holding companies, but this new option could solve Japan-specific problems in distinctive ways. For example, the holding company option will help companies to extend their practice of using interfirm links and diversification in managing labor costs without layoffs. They will be able to develop multiple tiers of wages and benefits for permanent employees and to reallocate workers across firms within the holding company structure. Likewise, holding companies may be able to develop a functional substitute for venture capital by funneling investments into virtually autonomous subsidiaries with new forms of organization and structures of compensation designed to foster innovation. Japanese firms may be able to develop a new approach to mergers and acquisitions in which two firms integrate gradually within a holding company rather than fusing more abruptly. This could alleviate the problem of distinctive corporate cultures and ingrown resistance to mergers, which is especially acute in Japan. Commentators joke about merged banks that have twin branches across the street from one another because neither partner will shut down its branch or about executives who identify with one partner firm and not the other decades after a merger. Of course, companies that slow down the process of integration will also forestall the efficiency benefits from merging, but this may be a price they are willing to pay.

By looking at the interaction effects in this way, we begin to see both the strengths and the limits of the model presented here. By focusing on institutions, we can go quite far in explaining the distinctive German and Japanese patterns of corporate adjustment and policy reform over the short to medium term. We can also show how adjustments at one time reshape the possibilities and constraints for change at a later time. But we cannot predict the long-term evolution of these institutions because micro and macro adjustments interact and cumulate over time. I argue that this does not imply a failure of the model but simply reminds us of the inherent limits of social-scientific models in explaining complex interactions over time.

Refining the Model

Before summarizing the patterns of institutional change, let us look briefly at two ways we might enhance the model presented thus far.

A More Political Perspective

The model outlined so far is inherently political because it suggests that corporate adjustments are subject to legal and regulatory constraints and that changes in these constraints must survive the political process. It emphasizes how institutions shape societal preferences, but also suggests that intermediate associations and political parties play an important role in aggregating these preferences. Nonetheless, we could easily imagine a perspective that would bring politics much more to the forefront, and Herbert Kitschelt (in his essay in this volume) suggests just how this might be done.

For present purposes, we might simply add that the German and Japanese political systems both have built-in propensities toward immobilism. In Germany, the weakness of coalition government makes it hard for a ruling coalition to impose change, and the federal structure of government makes it difficult for the central government agencies to impose change on the *Länder* (Webber 1992). In Japan, the bureaucracy-led process of packaging political bargains can be painfully slow and prone to elaborate compromises. Likewise, the LDP route in policy formulation leans toward solutions that reflect a delicate balance among multiple constituent groups (Stockwin et al. 1988).[5] The Japanese government faces less formidable obstacles than its German counterpart in passing reform legislation, but is more prone to building in compromises and concessions before legislation reaches the Diet. And bureaucrats are often less than zealous in implementing liberal reforms.

Moreover, the two systems both rest on a power structure in which multiple groups are given privileged status. This means that to the extent that change takes place through the political process, the primary beneficiaries of the status quo are well represented and thus have a substantial say in the terms of change. In Germany, labor has a privileged status at every level of the political structure (national, *Länder*, sectoral, and firm), and thus it can try to shape decisions that do not destroy those institutions it values. In Japan, the sheltered sectors of the economy, such as agriculture and small business, have privileged relations with the LDP and/or the bureaucracy, so they too have a substantial say in determining the mode of adaptation. Thus although both governments must package reforms that are sensitive to the demands of the protected sectors of the economy, the German government must be especially sensitive to labor, whereas the Japanese government caters more to farmers and small businesses.

Even so, I argue that the microinstitutions that shape industry preferences are even more important in shaping the distinctive patterns of reform in the two countries than the macroinstitutions that mediate these preferences (see figure 10.3). Opinion leaders such as the president of the Federation of German Industries (Bundesverband der Deutschen Industrie, BDI), Hans-Olaf Henkel, and Liberal Party leader, Ichirō Ozawa, have proposed constitutional changes to break the reform logjam in their respective countries. But even with constitutional changes, it is hard to imagine how a democratic government in either country could push through reforms that societal actors do not want.

A More Sociological Perspective

We could also argue that the model developed here is too rationalistic—it views the German and Japanese models as systems of incentives and constraints rather than systems of norms. From a more sociological perspective, we might suggest that actors facing new circumstances do not rationally calculate costs and benefits as much as they fall back on preexist-

5. On the bureaucracy-led process, see F. Schwartz (1993); Vogel (1994).

ing norms and routines (Powell and Dimaggio 1991). The two perspectives, the economic and the sociological, overlap with one another up to a point. That is, systems of incentives and constraints reflect underlying norms, and formal incentives and constraints (such as laws or regulations) can reshape norms over time. For example, we could explain a G-J firm's reluctance to lay off workers either way; that is, the firm may be calculating the cost savings against the potential damage to its cooperative relationship with the remaining workers or its ability to recruit workers in the future, or it may simply be adhering to prevailing social norms of acceptable firm behavior.

Although the two perspectives are consistent with one another up to a point, there are real differences. I prefer the economic perspective for my present purposes because it is more useful in moving beyond an explanation of why institutions are slow to change toward an explanation of the substantive patterns of change. Nonetheless, I readily concede that a rationalist logic misses the ways normative factors affect the trajectory of change. Specifically, a deeper appreciation of these factors might alter our expectations about patterns of change in three ways.

First, a sociological perspective leads us to expect an even slower process of institutional change. The economic perspective implies that firm managers are reluctant to cut off a stable supplier because this will entail a substantial cost in terms of the loss of the long-term cooperative relationship. But once they determine that the efficiency benefits outweigh these long-term costs, then presumably they act decisively. The sociological perspective suggests, however, that firm managers may not respond even to very clear shifts in economic payoffs due to normative commitments. They might hesitate because they view certain actions as inappropriate or because they fear societal disapproval. One Japanese manager recalls an internal debate in which several board members proposed that the firm cut off a stable supplier in favor of a lower-cost foreign supplier—the board member with closest personal relationships with the domestic supplier's managers successfully fought off the proposal because he felt he could not betray these partners (interview, February 1997, Tokyo).

Second, a sociological approach might help us to understand the consistency in corporate adjustment strategies within each country across diverse sectors. That is, the economic approach leads us to expect substantial variation across sectors because the economic rationale for stable employment, for example, varies considerably by sector, depending on the level of training required and the nature of the work. Yet German and Japanese firms trying to cut labor costs have followed remarkably similar patterns of adjustment across diverse sectors. This suggests that firms are not simply rationally choosing the best strategy, but instead are imitating one another and minimizing dissent by not diverging too far from standard practice.

Third, a sociological approach suggests a perspective on the mechanisms of change that focuses more on the diffusion of norms than on a shift in incentives. Specifically, it predicts more rapid change when foreign firms or domestic opinion leaders disseminate new ideas widely enough to alter the prevailing discourse about corporate adjustment or policy reform, thereby shifting actors' judgments about what constitutes an appropriate response. It provides insight about the tipping points, at which isolated incidents of defection might cumulate into broader institutional change, suggesting that the key lies not in rational calculus but in legitimacy. This helps to explain why certain changes may be slow to take hold but then may diffuse very rapidly. Thus, many German companies suddenly embraced shareholder value in the early 1990s, and many Japanese companies abruptly shifted toward merit-based wage systems in the late 1990s.

The Comparative Context

At this point, I propose three tentative conclusions about patterns of institutional change in Germany and Japan that can be further tested against evidence in future research: Germany and Japan have not converged to the Anglo-American model, they have each responded differently, and they have both moved further in finance than in labor relations.

Germany and Japan versus the Liberal Market Economics

Despite popular cries of the end of German and Japanese capitalism, these two economies have preserved many of their distinctive features. Compared to the United States and Britain, they continue to maintain greater cooperation amarg labor and management, closer ties between banks and industry, denser networks of relationships among firms, and closer coordination between government and industry. But have Germany and Japan moved closer to the liberal market model? If we view the liberal market model in static terms, then Germany and Japan have indeed moved in the direction of more competitive market systems. If we compare them to the moving targets of the United States and Britain, however, they may not have narrowed the gap at all.[6] If anything, U.S. and U.K. firms have been moving further toward the LME ideal: reducing costs, maximiz-

6. Using a statistical index, James Gwartney and Robert Lawson (1997) find that economic freedom did not rise at all in Germany from 1990 to 1995, actually fell in Japan, and rose substantially in the United States and Britain. Then from 1995 to 2000, economic freedom fell in both Germany and Japan, remained stable in the United States, and rose in the United Kingdom (O'Driscoll, Holmes, and Kirkpatrick 1999).

ing short-term profits, relying more on equity markets for finance, and increasingly participating in markets for corporate control. Whereas Germany and Japan have been cautiously moving ahead with liberal policy reforms, the United States and Britain have been surging forward more boldly. In labor markets, for example, the United States and Britain have aggressively deregulated, but Germany and Japan have not (Golden, Wallerstein, and Lange 1999; Soskice 1999). As Desmond King and Stewart Wood (1999) demonstrate, the micrologic of industry policy preferences in the LMEs is strikingly different from that of the OMEs. Because firms in the LMEs compete more on the basis of cost than quality, they strongly advocate market liberalization and other policies designed to lower costs.

Germany versus Japan

Shifting to the comparison between Germany and Japan, we find substantial differences as well as similarities. Germany has moved further toward the liberal market model than Japan, especially in finance. Although a full explanation for this divergence is beyond the scope of this essay, I suggest that four factors are salient. First, in Germany the EU gives greater urgency to corporate adaptation as firms fight off new competitors in their home markets and move into foreign markets. The EU serves as a political force driving liberalization and regulatory harmonization that is sometimes able to supersede the normal logic of German domestic politics. Second, German politics is more infiltrated by international interests and views than Japanese politics. Foreign firms have a stronger presence in Germany than Japan and play a greater role in advocating reform. Third, the German bureaucracy has not shaped the substance of reform nearly as much as has its Japanese counterpart. Japanese officials have been especially zealous in designing reforms so as not to undermine their own regulatory discretion, a critical source of leverage over industry. And finally, Japanese firms are linked to banks, other firms, and government agencies in even denser networks of interrelationships than their German counterparts, making them more reluctant to undermine these ties or to support reforms that might jeopardize them.

Furthermore, the logic of the argument presented here suggests that we should find considerable differences between Germany and Japan, reflecting differences in the structure of the two economies. As noted at the outset, both systems are organized, but in different ways. The German labor market is organized through a massive array of national, regional, and plant-level associations, whereas the Japanese labor market relies more on private-sector networks. So German firms have used their corporatist institutions to renegotiate bargains with labor, whereas Japanese firms have leveraged their dense corporate networks to reallocate workers without laying them off. Likewise, the German labor relations system is more codified into law. This means that German firms have less freedom in a legal sense to adjust their practices than their Japan counterparts, but it also means that the German government has a greater ability to impose changes in these practices through legislation.

Differences in economic governance at the sectoral level also influence patterns of reform. For example, Japan's separation of commercial and investment banking made the process of financial reform more contentious and protracted than it was in Germany. Because Japanese commercial banks could not enter the securities business prior to 1992, they had very different views from German universal banks on financial reform. They wanted to slow down the liberalization of securities markets until they could fully participate in these markets. Meanwhile, securities firms fought to prevent banks from invading their turf.

Labor versus Finance

Not surprisingly, Germany and Japan have moved furthest in those areas in which market pressures are the greatest and in which the reform debate has not become highly politicized. They have enacted substantial financial and corporate governance reforms, although they are more tightly constrained with labor and welfare reform. In addition, Germany and Japan have made substantial reforms in more technical areas that have not become as politicized, such as accounting. The German government was able to move forward with a major corporate governance reform bill with relatively little political resistance. Likewise, the Japanese government almost pushed through its new holding company bill without the labor unions or opposition parties even taking notice. At the eleventh hour, however, Japanese Trade Union Confederation (Rengō) officials suddenly realized the ramifications of this bill and mobilized to win a delay. As financial and corporate governance reforms continue, this will create more leeway in corporate adjustments, contributing to greater feedback effects between policy reform and corporate adjustment (micro-macro interaction) and greater institutional change overall.

If reform is in fact moving more quickly in finance and corporate governance than in labor, this then raises the question of how tightly the different parts of the German and Japanese systems are linked. For example, we could argue that the German or Japanese labor-relations systems are linked to their financial systems (Aoki 1994a). Firms are only able to make long-term commitments to their workers because the financial system shields them from shareholder demands for short-term profits, but patient capital in turn relies on stable labor relations. If this is true, then we should find that shocks to one side reverberate to the other. Will more

competitive financial markets and tougher information disclosure requirements force German and Japanese firms to shift from stakeholder to shareholder governance? And if so, does this mean that these firms will have
to abandon or loosen their long-term commitments to their workers?
Changes in finance in the late 1990s have put additional pressure on companies to reduce costs and raise returns, but they have not forced German
and Japanese firms to abandon the core features of their respective
labor-relations systems. That is, financial developments have created new
challenges in German and Japanese labor relations, but have not been so
powerful as to dictate the nature of the response to these challenges.

Whither Germany and Japan?

Thus far I have described and explained patterns of corporate adjustment
and policy reform in Germany and Japan. But what *should* Germany and
Japan be doing? If we take institutional legacies seriously, as this chapter
suggests we should, this could lead us to either of two radically different
conclusions. First, we could argue that Germany and Japan are doing just
what they should be doing—searching for the right mix of continuity and
change. They are making incremental adjustments to refine their models,
building on their strengths when possible, and avoiding radical moves
toward the liberal market model that would be doomed to fail in the
absence of complementary institutions. Jonah Levy (1999) tells a delightful
tale about how French leaders tried to shift the institutions of *dirigisme* from
the national to the local and the EU level and to replace state sponsorship
of industry through selective credit allocation with the cultivation of
German-style industrial banks. But for the most part, he argues, they failed
because they could not find the necessary complementary institutions at
either of these levels. Likewise, we could argue that British attempts to
develop an industrial policy in the 1960s and 1970s were destined to fail
because Britain lacked the close working relationship between government
and industry necessary for such a policy to work (Vogel 1996). We might
conjecture, then, that German and Japanese attempts to create a U.S.-style
venture capital market cannot succeed because Germany and Japan lack
the unique institutional infrastructure of Silicon Valley. German reformers
might be better served to adapt handicraft production to the needs of
the twenty-first century, and Japanese reformers might be better off trying
to use partnerships between government and special research-oriented
subsidiaries of large companies to promote innovative research.

Alternatively, however, we might argue that Germany and Japan may be
proceeding along the wrong path—failing to adjust to a fundamental shift
in the dominant production paradigm from flexible manufacturing to a

new paradigm centered on global finance and information technology. They may have mastered the challenges of the late twentieth century so well that they have failed to prepare for the new challenges of the twenty-first century. In this view, Germany and Japan share the fate of seventeenth-century Spain, nineteenth-century Britain, and perhaps the mid-twentieth-century United States—they were so successful that they naturally built on existing strengths rather than shifting resources toward a new paradigm that would eventually supersede the one they had mastered (see Landes 1999).

So which is it: right mix or wrong path? We cannot know at this point; the answer depends on technological and societal shifts yet to come (see the essay by Kozo Yamamura in this volume). We know how Germany and Japan are adjusting to new challenges, but we cannot evaluate the long-term results of these patterns based on a few good or bad quarters of growth or a jump or blip in the stock market. German and Japanese business and political leaders clearly recognize the weaknesses of their respective economic models, and they will continue to strive to adapt them to a changing world. But they will do so by reorganizing rather than dismantling the institutions that have brought them so much success.

Competitive Party Democracy and Political-Economic Reform in Germany and Japan: Do Party Systems Make a Difference?

Herbert Kitschelt

What role did the arena of electoral and legislative party competition play in accelerating or slowing down the reform of the German and Japanese nationally embedded capitalisms in the 1990s? I detail four general conditions that encourage politicians to consider policy reforms, even if such reforms tend to be unpopular because they impose painful losses of benefits on large constituencies. First, all parties defending the status quo have become unpopular themselves and/or have been discredited by weak economic performance when they held executive office. Second, there are no new (blackmail) parties waiting in the wings to benefit hugely by promising a painless economic policy when governing parties implement unpopular and painful economic reforms. Third, at least one party with sufficient electoral support to advance reform eludes control by rent-seeking special interests. And fourth, the issue structure of competitive political alignments allows parties to focus on economic reforms without fearing deep internal divisions among their activists and voters.

The upshot of my analysis of German and Japanese party competition in the 1990s is that both party systems operated more as fetters than as catalysts of reform. This general tendency applies to Japan with greater force than to Germany. Of course, the party systems, by themselves, do not fully determine the outcomes of political-economic reform efforts. A variety of other economic and political actors outside the arenas of party competition affect the ultimate policies so that there is no simple one-to-one relationship between electoral-competition-induced reform propensities and actual reform outcomes. Nevertheless, party systems reinforce path dependence and incrementalism in the prevalent problem-solving techniques of national polities.

My chapter complements the general gist of the analyses by Steven Vogel, Sigurt Vitols, Gregory Jackson, and Kathleen Thelen and Ikuo Kume in this volume, namely that German and Japanese political-economic reform proceeded incrementally, if at all, and without touching the basic institutional organizing principles of the nationally embedded market economies. This chapter first identifies one of the challenges to these organizing principles and sketches political-economic reform efforts with an eye to the role of competition among elected politicians and parties. I then develop a framework of partisan incentives to administer bitter economic reform and apply it to the two cases.

Challenges of Structural Economic Reform in Germany and Japan

Cooperative market economies such as Germany and Japan build on long-term, incompletely specified contractual relations among market actors. Therefore, innovation takes place through continuous incremental mutual adjustment and compromise among a given set of players.[1] The long-term nature of economic relations reduces transaction costs and opportunism by the contractual partners, but makes dramatic departures from the status quo difficult to engineer.[2] Joseph Schumpeter's animal spirits of capitalist entrepreneurial innovation rarely make an appearance in such systems, but they perform well as long as the major technological and marketing challenges involve stepwise, incremental improvements in decomposable components of economic production and distribution. Such systems, however, cannot cope well with radical innovations that proceed in leaps and bounds based on quasi-randomized trial-and-error exploration of wholly new technological processes and products. Economic actors cannot easily decompose and sequence innovation strategy within an incremental framework of learning.[3] Unfortunately, many late-twentieth-century frontiers of technological and market innovation, such as computer software development, information technology, biotechnology, electronic media culture industries, and, more broadly, all those symbol-producing economic sectors thriving in increasingly affluent postindustrial economies (multimedia, entertainment, travel and related

1. For a concise characterization of embedded market economies, see Soskice (1999, 101–34) and Streeck (1997c, 33–54).

2. For this argument in neoinstitutional economics, see Williamson (1985).

3. For a general application of this contingency theory of national comparative institutional advantage in innovation processes, see Kitschelt (1991).

services, and fashion and design) involve processes of learning and diffusion inimical to the incremental operating practices of nationally embedded market economies. Whereas embedded market economies reward resource pooling among firms, close relations between manufacturers and banks, and long-term careers within companies, market innovation puts a premium on venture capitalism, a relatively free rein of individualist competition with innovative entrepreneurs defying conventional corporate wisdom, relying on short-term and fleeting interfirm contractual relations, and attracting a labor force ready to engage in flexible cooperative networks that can quickly dissolve.

Pushed to their extreme, such circumstances of innovation yield short-term labor contracts rather than sustained organizational careers, episodic organizational affiliations and cooperation on projects to which individuals lend their skills and names for defined periods. Based on their personal general human capital, labor-market participants move across employment relations and collaborative ventures on different corporate campuses. Corresponding systems of education, training, and research also build on flexibility, horizontal mobility, and competition among decentralized units, in stark contrast to the current bureaucratic hierarchical systems of higher education in Germany and Japan, which tend to stifle creative spirits because they dull competitive incentives. Setting aside more subtle differences between Germany's and Japan's innovation regimes (see especially Boyer 1998b), what unites both countries is the incongruity of their existing cooperative market institutions with the incentive structures that would promote the new-frontier technologies and (post)industrial sectors, particularly in the areas of communications and information technology and their cultural applications, broadly conceived and thus encompassing a significant proportion of the service sector.[4]

Of course, not all economic performance issues originate in problems of technological innovation. Particularly in Germany, for example, the existing labor market regime has stifled the expansion of employment in the personal-services sector, a major source of job growth in liberal market economies. This regime results in wage compression, making low-skill labor in personal services relatively expensive and unaffordable to most. Given that Germany, unlike Scandinavia, has not resorted to an expansion of public-sector employment to meet the demand for jobs, higher unemployment rates are the result (see Iversen and Wren 1998; Scharpf 1997).

---

4. Walter Eltis, an Oxford economist writing in the November 1998 issue of the *International Bank Credit Analyst*, estimated that in 1996 the United States spent approximately 4.1 percent of GDP on information technology, whereas Japan spent 2.4 percent and Germany only 2.1 percent in the same area (*The Economist*, 14 November 1998, p. 114).

I have detailed the challenges to nationally embedded market economies to identify a baseline for the trajectory of reform against which we can assess the appeal and potential impact of party politics in Germany and Japan. If there were no institutional and strategic impediments, office-seeking politicians in both countries would support policies designed to enhance the access of risk-taking market actors to scarce resources (capital and highly trained labor) and differentiate economic payoffs to reward such activities.

As can be demonstrated with Danish and Dutch labor market policies in the 1990s, greater flexibility of labor markets does not imply a wholesale adoption of U.S.- or British-style market liberalism, sacrificing a baseline of socioeconomic equality. Means-tested tuition systems, for example, in a higher education reform could make compatible imperatives of flexibility and competition among students, faculties, and research units with values of social equality. The same applies to reforms of pension systems or health care, each of which would permit politicians to build in safeguards to protect the weakest in a more competitive, innovation- and performance-oriented institutional governance structure. As a practical application of the Rawlsian difference principle, neosocial democratic visions, as advanced but not fully fleshed out by Britain's New Labour Party, attempt to claim the virtues of competition and efficiency for a leftist program while also attending to problems of inequality, social disenfranchisement, and poverty traps.[5] By contrast, the absence of a powerful new vision that would transcend both unencumbered market liberalism and the status quo of nationally embedded market economies tends to be the story of Germany and Japan in the 1990s and calls for an explanation.

Political-Economic Reform and Partisan Politics in Germany and Japan in the 1990s

To give a rough approximation of the strategies to create embedded capitalism, the German political economy primarily protects labor, but exposes business to domestic and international competition, whereas Japan has chosen to protect business selectively from competition while shielding labor only indirectly, for example, by allowing protected corporations to buy labor peace with favorable employment contracts. Therefore, in Germany policy battles about institutional economic reform primarily revolve around questions of labor-market rigidities, industrial relations,

5. I am drawing here on the mushrooming Third Way literature inspired by various British social scientists politically close to the New Labour Party; see, for example, Giddens (1994).

and social policy schemes, whereas in Japan they concern trade protection; domestic regulation of business competition; relations among government, business, and the financial sector; and the collusion between politicians and private firms.

Germany

The critical arenas for political reform in Germany concern the facilitation of entry into and exit from the labor market, the system of industrial relations, and social policy–social wage levels. In the area of labor-market flexibility, German governments have slightly lowered the wage-replacement level of unemployment benefits since the 1980s, but extended the duration of eligibility for unemployment insurance benefits, particularly for beneficiaries approaching retirement age (for an overview of German social policy, see Manow and Seils 1999). At the same time, few policy changes have made fixed-term employment contracts or part-time work more attractive options for employers who are reticent to incur the potential costs and stickiness of entering open-ended full-time contracts with new employees (see Regini 1999). Overall, government policies have encouraged neither demand-side business propensity to hire nor supply-side flexibility of the unemployed to consider a range of job opportunities broader and less favorable than that held during the previous period of employment. Both the Social Democrats (Social Democratic Party, SPD) and Christian Democrats (Christian Democratic Union, CDU; and Christian Social Union, CSU) have supported incremental modifications of the status quo, primarily by pushing older redundant workers into early retirement. Only the small liberals (Free Democratic Party, FDP) have called for structural reform.

The German system of higher education and research-oriented education suffers from rigidities and performance problems widely recognized by analysts and policymakers. Again, the parties have been unable to advance a reform agenda that would bring substantial reforms. As in previous decades, the institutional configuration of federalism exacerbates the inertia of education policy evident in the conduct of the major parties (see Katzenstein 1987, chap. 7).

With regard to industrial relations, the German system of sectoral wage agreements (*überbetrieblicher Flächentarifvertrag*) has stayed in place, but has been hollowed out by the defection of employers from their association and the willingness of firm-level works councils to accept productivity-boosting work hours or company-specific wage schemes. By hollowing out the operational bite of sectoral wage agreements, economic change takes place despite institutional rigidities, a development that may have made the extension of the social partnership framework to eastern Germany more acceptable to business (see Turner 1998). Although unit labor costs in Germany rose considerably relative to the international field of competitors until the mid-1990s (see Carlin and Soskice 1997, 59), in manufacturing these costs declined by approximately 10 percent from the 1996 peak until spring 1998 (see *The Economist*, 5 December 1998, p. 70), defining the moment at which German labor unions began a major campaign to obtain a significant real wage increase.[6]

In terms of social policy, Germany is one of very few countries where favorable demographic changes (small age cohorts, reduced by casualties and low birth rates during the world wars, are entering retirement), a relatively good economic performance, and linear, proportional benefit reductions from the late 1970s through the early 1990s made possible a small reduction in public social expenditure as a percentage of GDP (see Alber 1998; see also Clayton and Pontusson 1998; Pierson 1996; Pierson and Smith 1993; Stephens, Huber, and Ray 1999). Changing the formulas to calculate benefits (e.g., pegging pensions to net rather than gross wages) was the dominant mode of problem solving, not the wholesale reform of the benefits structure (see Klammer and Rolf 1998).

In the 1990s, the demographic prospect of steeply falling contributor/ beneficiary ratios in the pension system, together with heavy corporate lobbying, prompted the CDU-FDP government in 1997 to pass a nonincremental pension reform that implied a potential fall of benefits from 70 to 64 percent of final income. The defeat of the government parties in 1998 in part constitutes a punishment for this reform, widely criticized by the then-opposition SPD. The incoming SPD-Green government undid the reform, but hesitated from 1998 into 2000 over the choice of an alternative policy that remained unavoidable, given the skyrocketing costs of social security and of health care, if no changes were made in the system. Then, in a period of extraordinary CDU-CSU weakness in the aftermath of a cumulation of party finance scandals in the CDU that severely compromised its once-revered leader and chancellor Helmut Kohl, the SPD pushed ahead with a rather substantial reform in 2000–2001.

Although the burden of German social insurance that employers must pay for each employee may lower employment and investment in export-oriented and import-competing manufacturing activities only at the margin, the real problem is that German social policy discourages the creation of new domestic service-sector jobs that can thrive only if wage rates are lower or subsidized by local or state-level funds (see Scharpf 1997). None

6. Even in 1998, however, German unit labor costs in manufacturing were 45 percent higher than in the United States. In a similar vein, French, Japanese, and British unit labor costs exceed those of the United States, whereas Dutch, Australian, and even Swedish unit labor costs were much closer to U.S. levels (see *The Economist*, 19 December 1998, p. 148).

of the major political parties has dared to address that issue, from either a market-liberal or a neosocial democratic vantage point.

In health care, the Structural Reform Law (Gesundheitsstrukturgesetz) of 1992 assembled a grand coalition of the major parties, business, labor, and insurers against doctors and the pharmaceutical industry to undercut the capacity of health-care providers to inflate expenses to their own advantage (see Schmidt 1998a, 141). But also in this policy area, after a bold beginning, further reforms failed due to disagreement among the major parties. In 1996, the SPD majority in the Federal Council, the upper house of the German parliament that represents state governments, blocked legislation to create competition among public and private health insurers. In the same year, a law passed by the CDU-FDP government coalition failed due to a strike wave that forced employers to guarantee full wage replacement based on a collective bargaining agreement.

Overall, the German system of social protection is geared to an outdated demographic profile and model of labor markets in which a single full-time wage earner with continuous employment throughout his adult life cares for a "normal" family with a stay-at-home spouse and children (see Schmidt 1998b, 546). Compared to the challenges faced by the inflexible German labor regime, German business regulation appears to involve fewer anticompetitive practices that can be addressed by public policy. Certainly, the belated privatization and deregulation of public utilities (rail, telecommunications, and electricity), often opposed jointly by business and labor, have delayed economywide efficiency gains. In a similar vein, the European deregulation of banking and insurance has yet to produce efficiency gains and lower costs for consumers. And the abolished capital gains tax on the sale of company equity kept large commercial banks with large equity holdings in the business of propping up ailing companies. But many of the challenges of innovation faced by German business are not in the realm of public policy but of private corporate governance, such as the creation of venture capital markets, the authority and responsibility of senior company management, and the facilitation of new business formation.

Japan

Compared to Germany, Japan has always had a lean or residual welfare state, placing the burden of protecting citizens from the major risks of life onto corporate welfare provisions or informal assistance in the family system (Pempel 1997). Nevertheless, until the 1990s, Japan delivered political-economic outcomes that looked like those of Scandinavian social democracy—low unemployment and relative income equality. It relied on segmented labor markets with large firms providing lifetime wage contracts and private social security and small firms extending less generous labor contracts and benefits packages, complemented by residual public benefits and the family system (Shalev 1990). Only in the 1970s, when the ruling Liberal Democrats briefly faced stiffer electoral competition, did the Japanese government improve pension and health-care provisions. It scaled down these commitments in the 1980s when party competition subsided and the government asserted the need for fiscal restraint (see Pempel 1998; Shinkawa 1990, chap. 8; Tanabe 1997).

After the real estate and stock market bubble burst in 1990, and in an environment of overcapacity and shrinking consumer demand, fiscal retrenchment in the residual welfare state could hardly make more than a marginal difference for the country's medium-term economic performance. In the long run, the reorganization of public pension entitlements in line with increasing demographic dependency ratios, however, looks inevitable (Pempel 1998, 151). The flexibility of labor markets is also not a priority concern for Japan's politicians.[7] Economic growth, labor-market segmentation, and the protection of failing sectors, such as agriculture and retail, pacified and divided an initially militant post–World War II labor movement in partisan and sectoral terms.[8]

The main focus of the institutional reform of the Japanese embedded cooperative economy concerns the (de)regulation of business. With considerable simplification, the prolonged economic crisis of the 1990s, to a large measure, was due to decades of government-induced excess savings and overinvestment in industrial capacity and real estate, combined with an accommodating public regulation of the finance sector and a clientelist party system that protected inefficient sectors such as agriculture, construction, and commercial retail. Of course, macroeconomic developments in an open economy, such as the inexorable currency appreciation induced by Japan's favorable trade balance, reinforced these developments.

The extraordinarily high Japanese saving rate is in part a function of a tax system that treats unearned income (interest earnings, dividends, and capital gains) preferentially. Even after the end of government-subsidized industrial loan programs, this tax treatment of unearned income helped to lower the cost of domestic capital in relatively closed capital markets

7. Whereas German businesspeople find German labor markets quite inflexible by comparative standards, Japanese business respondents believe labor markets have intermediate flexibility. On a 100-point scale, the lowest flexibility appears in Greece (score 30.28), the highest flexibility in the United States (score 72.66), with Germany at 41.49 and Japan at 55.43 (see Di Tella and MacCulloch 1998, table A).

8. Also the unification of the labor unions under the moderate umbrella organization, Rengō, has not changed that (see Pempel 1998, 163).

(see Mikuni 1998).[9] Cheap capital encouraged investments in marginally productive industrial and real estate venues. This became problematic only when Japan's central bank raised real interest rates in the late 1980s.

A second causal chain leads from the *keiretsu* networks, configured around house banks that extend credits to member firms on generous conditions, to overinvestment in low-yield industrial and real estate projects. The appreciation of the yen ultimately revealed the buildup of excess capacity in the late 1980s.[10] An opening of Japanese capital markets further weakened the financial system, because strong firms obtained cheap international financing and the *keiretsu* banks got stuck with less viable network companies or had to accept extremely low margins (see *The Economist*, 13 March 1999, p. 87; see also the essays by Sigurt Vitols and Gregory Jackson in this volume). The lax regulatory oversight of financial institutions (including life insurance companies and savings and loans institutions) by the Ministry of Finance (MOF) exacerbated the bad-loan problem further. The emergence of an independent organ of financial oversight, the Financial Supervisory Agency, arrived too late and initially had too little bite to prevent the weakening of Japan's financial institutions. In a similar vein, Japan installed a Securities and Exchange Surveillance Commission (SESC) to counteract insider trading in equities markets in 1992, but MOF granted it only limited resources and powers (see Keehn 1998).

Weak regulation permitted other financial institutions to hide their true risk exposure and fund overinvestment. The postal savings and insurance system funneled its enormous financial resources into industry and then into infrastructure investments with very low returns, such as toll roads and bridges (see Noguchi 1995; see also *The Economist*, 12 December 1998, p. 71). Moreover, a large share of postal savings funds has been loaned by the Japan Development Bank, which invested in low-yield assets and supported many loss-making companies, such as Nissan. The privatization of the postal savings system (suggested by economists) and the removal of its obligation to lend to public institutions have been controversial (Carlile 1998, 102) and may ultimately reveal more bankruptcies in the Japanese economy.

Japanese politicians only belatedly tightened bank and financial-sector regulation, combined with an enormous package of public subsidies to help banks address their bad-loan problem, but evidently it was not gener-

9. In this regard, Mikuni comments, "both the savings themselves and the productive capacity they financed were protected from the risk of failure by every tool the government could command" (1998, 159).

10. The pattern of cross-shareholding between *keiretsu* banks and industrial concerns further weakened the efficiency control that banks could otherwise exercise over debt-financed investment decisions.

ous enough to address the deep-seated problems in the late 1990s. Banks obtained low-interest loans with few strings attached to unload bad debt, but generated little incentive for lasting and efficient restructuring (*The Economist*, 28 November 1998, p. 79). Only a gradual strengthening of the banking regulator, the Financial Supervisory Agency, relative to the banking lobby may force banks to deal squarely with their high debt burden.

A similar story of muffled reform can be told about the various efforts to rationalize the Japanese bureaucracy itself (Carlile 1998). Bureaucratic efficiency and accountability have been the hobbyhorse of many a rising politician of the Liberal Democratic Party (LDP) since the 1970s, but this has accomplished little. The salience of pork-barrel politics and the intimate ties among bureaucratic offices, private corporations, and individual politicians, particularly but not exclusively those of the ruling party, stand in the way (see the revealing recollections of one of the ultimate insiders of Japanese politics, Tanaka 1996). Privatizing public companies (the railroads and telecommunications) will not address this issue. Only a change of governance structures, dissociating business interests from those of public regulatory agencies, could (see the general evaluation in Carlile and Tilton 1998). The various waves of fiscal deficit spending that the Japanese government initiated after the worsening of the economic crisis in many ways only reinforced the structural entrenchment of overlapping business-agency networks. Much public money goes into public-infrastructure investments, enabling politicians to serve their local corporate networks and to grease the wheels linking parties, bureaucracy, and corporate Japan. Japanese citizens therefore experienced a progressive "politicization of economic policies" in which the well-being of political networks, encompassing private businesses and elected politicians, trumped efforts for reform and promoted a "sectionalization" of politics and policy (Pempel 1998, 182, 185).

Overall, neither German nor Japanese politicians tackled their structural and institutional challenges for reform in the 1990s, but relied on fiscal and monetary policies. In Germany, this incrementalism amounted to marginal welfare state retrenchment plus fiscal austerity, whereas in Japan it implied an expansionary fiscal policy through large infrastructure public works projects intended to soften the blow of gradual regulatory tightening and more exposure to market competition in the financial and industrial sectors.

A Model of Party-Competition-Induced Economic Policy Change

Following Anthony Downs (1957), in two-party systems with strategic voters supporting the party closest to their policy ideal points and office-seeking politicians, but no entry of blackmail parties, politicians will adopt appeals closely conforming to those of the median voter. Hence, they support economic reforms only if the median voter renounces the status quo and embraces reform.[11] In multiparty systems, individual vote- and office-seeking parties may not necessarily appeal to median-voter preferences, but minimum winning majority coalition governments are likely to include the party winning the median voter, if we assume a unidimensional space of salient policy issues, ideological connectedness, and/or minimal ideological distance among the parties as likely criteria of coalition formation (see Laver and Schofield 1990). The decisiveness of the party capturing the median voter for making or breaking winning coalitions empowers it to become the dictator of coalition policy strategy and thus moves that policy toward its own ideal point near the median voter.

Contrary to simple spatial models of party competition, in which policy reversals depend on the preference change of the median voter, in real political life democratically elected leaders often enact reforms against the voter majority's preference. This was the case for the neoliberal reforms of the Ronald Reagan and Margaret Thatcher administrations and many of the stabilization and liberalization programs in Latin America and the postcommunist east.

In Germany and Japan in the late 1990s, popular majorities affirmed the need for change beyond the business-as-usual approach to economic and social policy, but they opposed painful adjustments that would expose them to greater market risks, particularly employment and wage uncertainties, and would require more initiative and flexibility on their part.[12] Given the small size of its welfare state, a majority in Japan, in fact, asked for an extension of social programs. In the 1990 World Values Survey, with data collected shortly after the economic bubble burst in Japan, only 34 percent of Japanese respondents felt the economy should provide greater incentives for individual effort (Germany, 52 percent; average of forty-two countries, 56 percent), but 55 percent thought the state should take more responsibility to ensure that everyone is provided for (Germany, 22 percent; average of 42 countries, 33 percent) (reported in Inglehart, Basanez, and Moreno 1998). But in neither Japan nor Germany did opinion polls evidence a strong desire to retrench, if not dismantle, the welfare state, to expose business to more international competition, or to remove the protection of businesses from the risks of bankruptcy.

Even if politicians believe that policies initially supported by minorities will eventually be endorsed by majorities, they may face a problem of

11. These are just some of the most important (but certainly not all) of the assumptions necessary to derive the median voter theorem in a strictly logical fashion.

12. Survey evidence demonstrates continuing high levels of support for specific programs of the welfare state. See Pettersen (1995) and Roller (1995).

time-inconsistency. If public support for a new policy were to occur after the next election, office-seeking politicians would refrain from it because it would make electoral defeat likely. Examining patterns of party competition more closely, there are at least four contingencies that affect the willingness of politicians to embrace market reform: (1) the lack of a credible alternative to an incumbent government (coalition) that engages in unpopular reform, (2) the facing by parties of only mild electoral trade-offs in the pursuit of political-economic reform, (3) the weakness of rent-seeking groups affiliated with the party organization, and (4) the salience and polarization of economic-distributive conflict for party competition.

No Credible Alternative to an Incumbent Government That Engages in Unpopular Reform

Opposition parties may have been in government and delivered bad economic performance before. Or they may have never been in government at all and thus present a risky choice because they lack a track record.[13] In all these instances, only a very severe and sustained crisis might induce a critical mass of citizens to vote opposition parties into office. Incumbent government parties thus have a relatively free hand to impose unpopular policies up to a certain threshold of pain when voters defect to old and new alternatives previously considered unacceptable.

Government incumbents may get away with unpopular policies also when their competitors embrace radical alternatives far removed from median-voter preferences. This happens when a government party is taken over by radical ideological stalwarts, such as the British Labour Party after 1979 or the conservatives after 1998. Even if the incumbent government party or parties deliver unpopular policies and results, electoral majorities may back them for want of a centrist alternative.[14] Left or social democratic governments may in fact pursue economic liberalization policies situated to the right of the median voter as long as no credible challenger can displace them on the left (see the second contingency). Policies of privatization, reduction of social expenditure, and deregulation, pushed by social democratic incumbents, may preempt a centrist-conservative con-

---

13. For a fascinating analysis of how incumbency creates a logic of credibility that undermines permanent opposition forces, see Magaloni (1997).

14. Opposition parties lacked credibility and sufficiently diverged from the preferred policy position of the median voter to allow governing parties to pursue unpopular reforms in the case of the U.S. Republicans and British conservatives in the 1980s. In the same decade, the Dutch and Belgian Liberal-Christian Democratic coalitions thrived on the weak credibility and competence ratings of their adversaries in the opposition.

tender from winning elections and indirectly help to isolate more radical market-liberal conservatives by taking the wind out of their sails.[15]

By embracing liberalizing reform programs, left social democratic parties benefit from the Nixon-in-China effect—a conservative hawkish president made concessions to China that did not raise popular anxieties about the government caving in to communist demands. In a similar vein, only a party with a strong record of defending the welfare state can retrench social policies without losing the confidence of voter majorities firmly committed to a dense network of social security.

Parties That Face Only Mild Electoral Trade-Offs in the Pursuit of Political-Economic Reform

In multiparty competition, a party may need to pursue different strategies to maximize the size of its legislative group (vote seeking) or the likelihood of its participation in government (office seeking). Winning the median voter definitely maximizes office-seeking ambition, but may require giving up a large share of more radical voters to competitors and thus reduce the moderate party's electoral support. For example, moderate social democrats may lose votes to radical socialist blackmail parties waiting in the wings to mop up a large share of the former social democratic electorate (see Kitschelt 1994, 125–28, especially chap. 4). For social democrats, the less sharp the trade-off between vote seeking versus office seeking, the more willing they may be to embrace more market liberalization than endorsed by their stalwarts or even more than the median voter. Conversely, more market-liberal parties may assert their reform program if no centrist alternative is likely to emerge that could take office and the failure to cater to market-liberal beliefs results in the appearance of a credible competitor on the right.

Weakness of Rent-Seeking Groups Affiliated with the Party Organization

A party's propensity to embrace market-liberal or neosocial democratic reform presupposes strategic leadership flexibility to adopt new appeals, particularly if they initially are unpopular with the party's core supporters.

---

15. In different variations, this logic of preemptive leftist strategic policy strikes itself out, for example, in Spain under the socialists after 1982, in France in the late 1980s, in Britain under Tony Blair's leadership of the Labour Party, and in the Australian and New Zealand labor parties. In newly democratizing countries, the examples in which leftist parties have tried this strategy are legion, including Argentina, Chile, Hungary, and Poland. Whether social democratic parties can choose this strategy depends on a variety of other conditions that reinforce their courage to experiment with novel reform strategies.

Leadership in a highly institutionalized mass-party organization with tight accountability to a broad and diversified rank-and-file ties a party to the policies of its median party activist (McGann 1999), whereas framework parties with small and malleable, fluid cores of activists enhance the strategic mobility of leaders.

A large party apparatus often has a further disadvantage for reform-minded politicians because it frequently has the character of organized rent-seeking groups with a vested interest in the continuation of antireform economic policies. In conservative parties, this resistance to reform may come from regulated and subsidized sectors of the economy (agriculture, small business, and domestically protected industries) and in social democratic parties primarily from public- or quasi-public-sector employees, particularly those in social services, and from state-owned and domestically regulated industries with strong labor unions (railroads, telecoms, etc.)

The effectiveness of such groups in fighting political-economic policy reform increases if they are tied to party leaders and elected politicians by clientelist networks of exchange. In democratic politics, a clientelist linkage between electoral constituencies involves two types of exchanges (see Kitschelt et al. 1999, 46–61, especially 47–49): resource-poor but vote-rich constituents provide votes and labor in exchange for targeted selective favors that accrue only to party supporters (public jobs, public housing, gifts in kind, entertainment, etc.) and vote-poor but resource-rich constituents furnish campaign funds in exchange for favorable targeted decisions that award them a rent in market settings (favorable regulatory decisions, government procurement contracts, export or import licenses, etc.). Clientelist linkages are economically inefficient and often increase social inequality, but they may satisfy politicians' survival strategies when they are sufficiently powerful. Clientelist groups fight against neosocial democratic reform agendas in leftist parties and against market-liberal reform programs in conservative parties.

Salience and Polarization of Economic-Distributive Conflict for Party Competition

In many democracies, major political parties support rather similar middle-of-the-road economic policies in support of a mixed economy, but divide more sharply on sociocultural issues, such as church-state relations, multiculturalism, gender, ecology, disarmament, foreign aid, and participatory democratic institutional reform. The decisiveness of sociocultural divides in discriminating among partisan supporters gives leading politicians in all parties little incentive to abandon centrist economic stances in favor of market-liberalizing reform.

At first sight, this is a counterintuitive proposition. Should it not be easier to make a party's loyalists accept unpopular socioeconomic reform when their partisan ties are primarily defined by noneconomic sociocultural programmatic appeals? Moreover, should parties that repeatedly lose in the competitive electoral struggle waged on the dominant-issue divide not have a powerful incentive to undercut an entrenched governing party by trying to invent a new issue dimension of partisan competition to break up the majority garnered by the dominant party (Riker 1982, chap. 8)? When sociocultural alignments are dominant, however, electorates of both governing and opposition parties will internally split, if economic-distributive issues gain salience. Consequently, all established parties may fight against a new competitive dimension for fear of facing the internal disorganization of its electorate and legislative party cohesion. New challengers therefore usually champion new issue dimensions. Furthermore, the prominence of noneconomic-issue divides typically coincides with the endorsement of a mixed economy by all established competitors. If that remains the median-voter position, each of them can credibly present itself as a protector of the popular policy status quo and electorally punish defectors from the hegemonic position. A defecting party may therefore lose as many or more voters due to its appeal to economics as it wins from its new strategy of recasting the salience of issue alignments. Conversely, middle-of-the-road economic stand-patters may win more defectors from parties newly advocating economic policy innovation than they lose from the ranks of their conventional electorate.

When sociocultural alignments polarize parties that are quite close to one another in their economic policy positions, unpopular liberal market reform has the character of a prisoner's dilemma—either party can embrace unpopular reforms only with the support of the other party. Although in the long run all parties might be better served if they pursued incentives-compatible market-oriented reform of some kind with beneficial effects for long-term growth, none of the major players individually has the incentive to provide that collective good because such an altruistic player would be punished by electoral defeat. This dilemma applies particularly forcefully when the number of iterations in the game tends to be low and the actors' discount rates, shaped by the rhythm of electoral terms, may be too high to make them favorably disposed toward the gains of cooperation.

Moving from noncooperative to cooperative game theory, of course, we might empirically expect a bargaining solution that entails political-economic reform. In a system with dominant sociocultural divides, such reform would be forthcoming only if the major centrist parties—those that could credibly threaten one another to exploit their competitor's move toward unpopular reform—enter a pact or a grand coalition that jointly commits them to unpopular reform and institutes mechanisms to police their mutual compliance with this pact. Of course, a serious economic crisis might turn the economic reform prisoner's dilemma into a coordination game in which neither of the parties can afford to be seen as supporter of the economic status quo.

Party Competition in Germany and Japan

At first sight, the German and the Japanese party systems are profoundly different on a wide range of attributes that shape their respective competitive dynamic. Yet on closer inspection, both polities display mechanisms that undercut the propensity of the major parties to initiate political-economic reform. These mechanisms are structurally different and involve rational actor strategies specific to each system. At the same time, they are functionally equivalent in that they foster economic policy stability and, at most, incremental adjustment in the realm of political-economic reform.

Credible Defense of the Status Quo

Unlike countries with electorally powerful parties with long track records advocating market-liberal reforms, neither Germany nor Japan has a strong and credible natural party of political-economic reform that insists on reinforcing market incentives. The absence of a firmly anchored liberal party with a strong reputation for reform slows the competitive stimulus that other major established parties might have to recast their programs and policies when faced with the performance problems of conventional economic policies. But in the postwar period, and against the backdrop of semiplanned war economies until 1945, neither Germany nor Japan offered favorable conditions for the rise of a strong market-liberal party.[16]

Overall, in Germany the status quo orientation of the party system may be even greater than in Japan. Germany has two major parties that can credibly claim to have built the status quo. Japan, by contrast, in the 1990s no longer had a credible opposition party that could present itself as defender of the status quo if the dominant LDP embraced political-economic reform. As a consequence, judging by this first factor only, the electoral punishment the LDP might face for pursuing unpopular reforms may be less harsh and swift than the corresponding fate of partisan-led political-reform initiatives in Germany.

16. Pempel (1990) has cogently argued that postauthoritarian and posttotalitarian democracies after 1945 crafted ruling parties around broad coalitions of agriculture, business, and segments of labor. The LDP and CDU are major manifestations of such political strategies to assert a new dominant party.

The German party that comes closest to the market-liberal pole is the small FDP. But it generally attracts less than one-tenth of the electorate and it highlights its distinctiveness from the other parties often as much (or more) in terms of its socioculturally and politically libertarian credentials, such as in the defense of the rule of law, civil liberties, or the rights of immigrants, as in terms of a strictly economic program of market liberalization. Moreover, many of its economic proposals have the air of advancing the financial fortunes of a thin stratum of affluent independent professionals (such as lawyers and doctors) rather than promoting a broad-based effort to improve the efficiency of the German economy.

Against this backdrop, it would be up to one or both of the two major parties, the SPD and the CDU, to seize the initiative and push forward encompassing programs of political-economic institutional reform. Both of these parties, however, contributed to the construction of the German welfare state in decisive and cumulative ways in different historical periods and therefore each can present itself as a credible defender of the average citizen's welfare, were its main competitor to withdraw from the current institutional arrangements and propose alternatives that expose citizens to more market risks.

In a similar vein, both the CDU and the SPD have been political pillars of the German system of labor relations. Both parties have advocated and implemented legislation that would induce employers and employees to engage in cooperative conduct within the framework of the firm. At the margin, of course, the SPD pushed harder to extend the rights of employees in decision making on the factory floor through works councils and at the heights of corporate management through codetermination in the boardroom. Given both parties' track records of promoting class compromise and the institutions of the cooperative market economy, it would be costly for either of them to make a decisive move toward a market-liberal or even a neosocial democratic program of political-economic reform.

At the level of partisan voters, the similarity of the SPD and CDU strategic positions is reflected in their electorates' moderate economic-policy stances (for evidence, see Kitschelt 1994, 168–69; Kitschelt and McGann 1995, 222–23; Stöss 1997, 182–83). If there is a conflict between parties in German politics, the gap tends to be greater on sociocultural issues (discussed later). Neither of the major parties could withdraw from supporting current political-economic institutions without risking major electoral defeats.

As always, exceptions prove the rule. In 1999 and 2000, the CDU suffered a spectacular implosion of support when it was revealed that former chancellor Helmut Kohl had accepted financial contributions to his party from business and was unwilling to disclose the sources of these funds. As a consequence, the CDU temporarily lost credibility as Germany's second main party. Its financial scandal diverted attention from interparty policy conflict and for close to two years gave the SPD an almost invincible-looking electoral lead over its main competitor in the opinion polls. Under these circumstances, Chancellor Gerhard Schröder and his supporters in the SPD dared to pushed through a rather significant reform of the German social security system. Against fierce resistance from the traditionalist wing of his own party and from the labor unions, the reform package reduced the pay-as-you-go benefits component accruing to future social security recipients. Furthermore, it obliged recipients to pay into contributions-defined individual retirement accounts in order to make up for the loss of coverage under the conventional German public pension system. To compensate labor unions for their concessions, however, Schröder abstained from major reforms of labor-market regulation that would have made it easier to hire and fire workers in Germany. Moreover, the SPD extended corporate codetermination laws that give employees and unions a voice in company management against the vocal objections of the business community. The government thus seized an unprecedented and transitory configuration of party competition in order to push the envelope of market-liberal reforms at least on one prominent issue, but gave up on others.

Japanese party competition opens up somewhat different opportunities for reform. The system became one party dominated by the LDP in the 1950s. Since the 1960s, the main opposition party, the Japan Socialist Party (JSP), has atrophied and given way to a scattering of often internally divided centrist and leftist parties too much at odds with one another to launch a coordinated challenge on the LDP's grip on the government.

In Japan's political economy, the LDP managed to forge a class compromise through subsidies and favorable regulation benefiting lagging sectors and the collective benefits of economic growth fueled by a mixture of free-market competition and an activist state. The LDP's political compact initially centered on business and agriculture in the 1950s and 1960s, but left out labor. Yet, economic growth gradually enabled the party to attract growing working-class support as well (Pempel 1998, 164). Japan's economic positive-sum game in a regulated capitalist market economy that delivered high growth until 1991, with a brief intermission in the aftermath of the first oil crisis, allowed the LDP to become a cross-class coalition of diverse socioeconomic interests.

The decline of the LDP's erstwhile main competitor, the JSP, was the result of a number of developments. Not only did the JSP perform very badly when briefly in government in the 1940s, but it also proved unable to wean itself from a radical Marxian socialism in the 1950s and 1960s, a time when the German SPD embraced the mixed economy in its Bad Godesberg program. Further, the competition and electoral trade-off with the politically significant Japan Communist Party (JCP) always restricted the electoral incentives for the JSP to move to a centrist economic position (Kohno 1997). The incentives for moderation further declined when reformist Social Democrats in the JSP cut themselves loose from the party and formed their own moderate alternative that cemented a further fragmentation of the left.

The single nontransferable vote system (SNTV) in Japan became an impediment to the party's strategic mobility only in the context of this competitive configuration. Given the presence of other leftist party candidates in the small multimember electoral districts, the JSP was increasingly restricted to nominating one candidate for a single seat with some prospect of success in each district, thus locking itself into a permanent minority position. The candidates for these safe seats tended to be socialist stalwarts, most of the time supported by the orthodox public-sector union association Sōhyō, and their competitive prospects, confined to a socialist niche constituency, gave them little reason to reach out to a centrist electorate.

The inability of the JSP to build itself up into a serious alternative to the LDP rests on two other factors as well. In the legislature, JSP members often engaged in a pragmatic bargaining style with the hegemonic LDP in order to protect the left's own electoral constituencies, particularly in the public sector. By the end of the 1980s, the JSP was just as much a party built on support from the state-protected economic sectors as the LDP and thus unfit for policy innovation, particularly public-sector reform (Yayama 1998, 91–92). Furthermore, with the end of the cold war, the major noneconomic divides on which the Japanese party system had rested since 1945 and that supported the JSP-LDP antagonism vanished, namely, the conflict over the constitution and the defense alliance with the United States (Pempel 1998, 156). This opened the door to a short-lived coalition government of the LDP and JSP against reform in 1994 that gave the JSP the final *coup de grâce* and removed its *raison d'être*.

In an extension of Barbara Geddes's (1994) analysis of public-sector reform in Latin America, reforms that hurt entrenched political-economic interests are more likely to move ahead when there is bipolar competition among two major parties such that both eventually see the advantages of reform. The presence of a strong market-liberal party thus may induce social democrats to embrace market-incentive-enhancing reforms on their own, although of a neosocial democratic variety with a baseline social-equality criterion. In Japan and Germany, the competitive configuration for reform initiatives has been much less favorable than in bipolar systems in which parties have incentives to innovate. In Japan, important segments of the LDP are beholden to entrenched protected business interests and the party did not face the competitive stimulus of a credible alternative until the mid-1990s.

In Germany, both major parties are in one way or another wedded to the status quo of the political-economic institutions and fear that one party's defection in favor of unpopular reform strategies will be exploited by the other's vigorous defense of that status quo. This logic was very much confirmed by the experience of the 1998 federal election. Recall that the CDU-CSU-FDP cabinet's willingness to push through unpopular reforms of sickness wage compensation and pension benefits in 1995–97, against the resistance of the party's own labor wing, resulted in the SPD's fierce and credible opposition against the new policy. The SPD benefited from the conflict in its landslide victory of September 1998, but then, as the governing party, faced the same problem that the opposition party might credibly oppose the new government's own version of benefits-reducing pension reform. Until the CDU became entangled in financial scandals in 1999–2000, it could employ its opposition role by presenting the party as the true protector of the elderly against social democratic treason. Once the CDU came under the cloud of scandal, these appeals lost their credibility and put the SPD in a position to pass an unpopular social security reform without immediate harm to its electoral standing.

Electoral Trade-Offs Faced by Political-Economic Reform Parties

What strengthens the arguments of strategic stand-patters in the main German and Japanese parties is the presence of considerable electoral trade-offs faced by any of the major parties choosing a strategy of political-economic reform. It is very difficult to quantify these trade-offs with sufficient precision to identify whether the German or Japanese parties face the greater downside of economic policy reform. But it appears to me that, on balance, in the second half of the 1990s these risks were greater in Germany than in Japan.

In Germany, the only party that could embrace political-economic reform without any electoral cost was the market-liberal FDP. By contrast, the two major parties faced major electoral downsides. As demonstrated so vividly by the 1998 national parliamentary election, even modest moves of the CDU/CSU toward a market-liberalizing institutional framework contributed to the party's severe electoral losses and to the strong gains of the SPD. The SPD, in turn, faced a considerable voter trade-off in competition with the Greens. If the Greens pursued moderation as their rational vote- and office-maximizing strategy, then the SPD's office-maximizing strategy was moderation to capture the median voter. This strategy, however, might lead to net voter losses because more leftist supporters defect from the SPD to the Greens than the SPD wins back on the center-right from CDU/CSU or FDP. This pattern of trade-offs presupposes that the Greens do not pursue a radical strategy of intransigent antagonism toward the SPD. When the radical Green wing asserts itself, the party loses votes to the SPD, no matter where the SPD positions itself relative to its more tradition-alist leftist supporters.[17] In this situation, it is often difficult for SPD leaders and party-internal currents to persuade their fellow partisans to sacrifice votes for the advantage of more bargaining power over govern-ment formation. Fortunately for the party's reformist tendencies support-ing Gerhard Schröder, the contradictory strategy of the Greens, wavering between radical intransigence and reformist moderation, in the events leading up to the 1998 election liberated the SPD from the predicament of a sharp trade-off between vote- and office-seeking objectives and helped the Schröder wing to assert its moderate appeal.

In Japan's party competition, the LDP faced only limited electoral trade-offs at least from the late 1970s, when it reasserted itself after a temporary weakness due to the fallout of the oil crises, until well after the stock market and real estate bubble burst in 1990. But given the broad electoral support the LDP enjoyed in that time, it had no reason to consider painful reform programs, whether in a neosocial democratic or a market-liberalizing direction. Since the late 1980s, electoral trade-offs of the LDP's political-economic appeal have become more severe, but the nature of these trade-offs is unclear. According to expert panels rating the Japanese party alternatives in 1996, the then briefly second-largest party in parliament, the New Frontier Party (NFP), supported center-right policy positions on the most salient issues (social policy, citizens' rights, environmental policy, and regulatory policy, in that order) almost identical with those of the LDP or very fractionally more market liberal (on regulation). The other relevant opposition parties, by contrast, above all the new Democratic Party (DP), which has added legislators and public support since 1996, and the JCP and the fading Japan Social Democratic Party, by contrast, generally endorsed positions far to the left of the LDP and NFP on most economic issues (see Kato and Laver 1998).[18] The exception is the DP's position on regulation, which is close to that of the NFP, but according to experts DP politicians attribute little salience to that issue.[19]

Between the widely dispersed opposition parties NFP, on the one side, and DP and JCP, on the other, the LDP may thus still control the median

17. This strategic constellation occurred in the 1990 and 1998 federal elections.

18. The former JSP, now renamed the Social Democratic Party, receives so little support that it is hardly worth mentioning any more.

19. Curiously, in Kato and Laver's (1998) survey, the opposition parties attribute little salience to all issues! They obtain their relatively highest, but absolutely still modest, salience scores on issues not in the center of political-economic policy debates, such as defense and national identity. I do not trust these scores. It is possible that some experts have confused salience with positional scores.

voter with a cross-class, moderate, status-quo-oriented position that calls neither for vigorous market liberalization nor the belated construction of a European-type welfare state. The data suggest that any move toward the right (market liberalism) or the left (economic redistribution) endangers the LDP's control of the median voter.

The resurgence of the LDP in the years following 1996 in public opinion (Mair and Sakano 1998, 189) and in subnational elections suggests that the control of the median voter, mandating a policy of cautious, incremental political-economic adjustment, is the electorate's favorite approach and certainly the approach that maximizes the LDP's bargaining power over policymaking. The LDP's supremacy with this incremental approach was further confirmed in the 1996–2000 legislative period by the entry of the New Komeitō and Ichirō Ozawa's Liberal Party into the LDP cabinet in 1999, giving the LDP-led government a majority in both houses of parliament.

Flashier alternatives on the right and the left quickly run out of steam, especially when they cannot negotiate broad-based coalitions among opposition parties that can raise the confidence of voters in the opposition's capacity to govern Japan. A split opposition has always been the gift of grace for hegemonic parties (Castles 1978; McGann 1999), a rule that appears to be confirmed by Japan. This competitive configuration, however, also implies that the likely electoral trade-offs of strategic policy innovation dissuade LDP politicians from rocking the boat and opting for profound political-economic reform. Moreover, the political hegemony of the LDP lured back ambitious office-seeking dissident LDP politicians, such as Ozawa, when they eventually determined that their personal political prospects would be brighter inside the LDP framework.

Party Organization and Rent-Seeking Constituencies

Even if vote- and office-seeking parties have collective incentives offered by the opportunities of external party competition to embrace unpopular economic policies, the same may not apply to internal majorities of individual politicians, whether they are elected officials or not. The internal politics of interest aggregation inside parties is not always congruous with the external incentives for strategic maneuvering shaped by the party system and its institutions. Mass party organization in Germany and clientelist voter-party linkages in Japan both undercut the incentives for a large proportion of office-seeking politicians inside the relevant parties to support painful political-economic reform.

In Germany, the organization of the major parties, the CDU and the SPD, at least in the western part of Germany involves a mass membership and the participation of economic interest groups, particularly of labor unions, business, and professional associations. Although the inclusiveness of mass-membership organizations, together with functional interest representation, has increased the stability of the parties' strategic appeals, it has made politicians accountable to a host of status-quo-oriented interests entrenched inside the parties.

In addition to different currents inside each party that represent socio-economic and ideological constituencies, German federalism leads to internal territorial center-periphery divides between party segments over questions of program and strategy that make it difficult to work out and stick to a consistent national social and economic policy party strategy. Both CDU and SPD chancellors had trouble holding their parties together around a distinctive, consistent economic and social policy strategy. These divisions reached a dramatic climax in the SPD after its return to national executive power in autumn 1998. The contrast with Tony Blair's Labour Party is instructive. Whereas the latter put in charge of the New Labour Party a strong moderate National Executive Council in the 1990s and renewed its small membership base by the influx of new moderate militants that tended to displace the older hard-core Labour militants, the German SPD had a mass organization with many groups subscribing to an entrenched social democratic traditionalism. These tendencies have been represented all the way to the top of the party leadership. By ousting Oskar Lafontaine from the cabinet, Chancellor Schröder scored points against his traditionalist rivals, but the aversion of broad currents in the party against a neosocial democratic strategy made this cabinet reshuffle only the opening shot in what was to become a fierce ongoing intraparty controversy rather than the final capstone of the neosocial democrats' victory.

In Japan, the critical impediment to the strategic mobility of the LDP lies less in party program and ideology than in the clientelist voter-politician linkages that are reinforced by old and new electoral institutions of Japanese politics. Such bonds more powerfully condition the party's strategic actions than the thin veneer of programmatic lip service to economic efficiency might suggest. Given that politicians compete as individuals not only against politicians of other parties, but also against their own party, they seek to build local electoral district ties that induce voters through material incentives to support a particular candidate in elections. This has several consequences. On the one hand, over the years the costs of electoral campaigns have spun out of control and have increased the sectorization of Japanese politics (Pempel 1998, 184). On the other, the local entrenchment of individual candidates makes elected politicians less dependent on the national party apparatus than on their local base. This enables members of parliament to leave their party when they believe an association with the party label will reduce their prospects of reelection (Cox and Rosenbluth 1995). Thus, after 1992, for a brief period, a mad scramble, in part orchestrated by a dissatisfied contender for the LDP leadership, Ichirō Ozawa, ensued in which both politicians benefiting from clientelism as well as their antagonists in the progressive reform coalition left the LDP in order to protect their turf and obstruct plans for an unfavorable reform of the electoral law.

The new electoral law first tested in the 1996 Japanese election really does not improve substantially on the clientelist logic of the old system. Thus, functionalist arguments that Japan chose a new electoral system in order to enable Japanese governing parties to deliver economic policies that improve Japan's international competitiveness and efficiency by undercutting the parties' clientelist linkages are empirically incorrect on two counts (for this functionalist view, see Rosenbluth 1996; Shugart 1998). First, there is little evidence that Japan's trade exposure has increased or that a declining performance of export-oriented industries, induced by the transaction costs of a clientelist economy, would have made domestic political arrangements less viable. Second, Japan's electoral law of 1994 does not really improve electoral efficiency because it continues to orient politicians toward cultivating their localized clientelist networks. This applies not just to the first-past-the-post tier of legislative seats allocated under the new electoral law, but even to those elected in the proportional representation (PR) tier of multimember districts, in which seats are allocated according to the percentage of the vote each party receives. In this electoral tier, parties need not rank-list candidates and can field the same candidates in both single-member and PR districts. Those candidates on a party's list who won the highest ratio of votes relative to the winner in their single-member district races will then obtain PR legislative seats. At least indirectly, this rule pits candidates of the same party against one another across several electoral districts. Electoral rules continue to make politicians seek their electoral fortunes as individual entrepreneurs, in competition with candidates of their own party. Candidates therefore will continue to offer selective incentives to electoral constituencies in their own districts (see McKean and Scheiner 1996).

Both in Germany and in Japan, the micrologic of intraparty organization and competition for electoral office, shaped by the state structure and the electoral laws, boosts the leverage of constituencies that fight against more market incentives in the economy, whether of a liberal laissez-faire or a neosocial democratic institutional type. Intraparty organization and electoral incentives, of course, are not the only forces that shape parties' strategic dispositions, but they are an important element we must take into account.

The Alignment of Party Competition: How Costly Is It for Politicians to Configure Party Competition around Political-Economic Reform?

The theoretical arguments and empirical observations advanced so far assume that policies affecting political-economic production and distribution have great salience for interparty competition. But what if all major parties subscribe to centrist economic policies that take profound socio-economic conflict out of the picture? As my theoretical argument suggests, in that case politicians have even further disincentives to rock the boat by embracing unpopular economic reform programs to increase market incentives. Both German and Japanese politics approximate situations in which the space of party competition over economic issues is rather narrow and other issues have contributed more to polarize competition. In the 1990s, this narrowing of the political-economic competitive space was probably greater in Japan than in Germany.

Similar to many other advanced postindustrial democracies, German party competition configured salient political alignments more around sociocultural than socioeconomic issues in the 1980s and 1990s, although the two overlapped to some extent. Those parties and voters who tended to subscribe to libertarian sociocultural ideas affirming the autonomy of groups and individuals from collective cultural and institutional restrictions and emphasizing participatory modes in which collective decision making is necessary also tended to endorse the more redistributive political-economic institutions of the welfare state and the corresponding economic policy. Conversely, supporters of authoritarian conformity and hierarchical decision making leaned toward market mechanisms of economic allocation (Kitschelt 1994, chaps. 1, 4). Data on German party positions and the attitudes of the parties' electorates suggest that the policy distance between the CDU and SPD was usually greater on sociocultural issues than on political-economic issues (for mid-1980s and 1990 data, see Kitschelt 1994; Kitschelt and McGann 1995; for 1994 survey data, see especially Stöss 1997).

Nevertheless, neither in Germany nor elsewhere in Europe has the political-economic dimension of competition completely evaporated. Among other things, the electoral success of social democratic parties appears to depend on their ability to revoke their traditional leftist program without embracing an unqualified market-liberal agenda (see Kitschelt 1999). This is a strategy easier to adopt and electorally more effective for social democrats, whose conservative adversaries primarily compete on economic issues and invoked market-liberal positions in the 1980s and 1990s. When economic issues divide the electorate, the conservatives' moves toward market liberalism will not internally divide their supporters to the extent that is likely in polities where conservatives emphasize their sociocultural distinctiveness but try to assemble a very broad centrist socioeconomic coalition of voters. In Germany, in contrast to Britain, Australia, and New Zealand, conservative parties never vacated positions in the political-economic policy center and derive the coherence of their electorate to a large extent from their sociocultural appeal. Here, as well as in other countries with centrist conservative parties, it has been difficult for social democrats to win additional voters merely through centrist political-economic appeal. Why vote for an unproved opposition party that promises the same economic policies as the incumbent?

Only a combination of additional circumstances enables social democrats to dislodge incumbent conservative governments with a centrist economic policy thrust. One such circumstance is that voters perceive the incumbents to be ineffective in economic policymaking (indicated by rising unemployment). In response, such governments begin to experiment with unpopular social reform policies. This creates an opening for social democrats to make their claim that new economic policy initiatives will enable them to lead the country back to a golden age of full employment and an expanding welfare state appear credible. In a party system where the non–social democratic competitor by and large defends the welfare state, social democratic policy cannot entirely abandon its distinctiveness from that of the conservatives or leapfrog the latter using a neosocial democratic program with greater emphasis on market incentives than that of mixed economy conservatism. The danger is that the conservatives then can present themselves as the voters' advocates against unpopular reforms.

Social democrats in Germany, and also in other countries with strong centrist Christian democratic or secular parties but weak market-liberal parties, therefore must attempt to walk a fine line, avoiding traditional welfare-state rhetoric while still distinguishing their economic policy appeal from that of centrist conservatives. The difficulty of this balancing act was demonstrated by the strategic volatility of the new German red-green coalition government in fall and winter 1998–99. The traditionalist wing, led by Oskar Lafontaine as finance minister and party leader, insisted on the need to distinguish red-green economic policy from the preceding conservative government through redistributive measures, something the neosocial democratic wing under Gerhard Schröder wished to tone down in favor of neosocial democratic, market-incentive-enhancing reform strategies.

For the incoming SPD, another way to cope with the legacy of CDU economic policy centrism was to engage in sociocultural policy change in which the two major parties had programmatic identities that were more sharply polarized. The red-green push for a revision of German citizenship and immigration laws in order to permit the children of immigrants to become dual citizens until they became adults was one such initiative. In a previous era, under Chancellor Willy Brandt, the SPD engaged in a similar shift of attention from socioeconomic reform to sociocultural and political innovation. Although Brandt's government expanded the welfare state, it distinguished itself most from the preceding government through its new *Ostpolitik* vis-à-vis the Soviet block. In the late 1990s, probably even more so than in the 1970s, the strong noneconomic element in the alignment of German party politics reduced politicians' inclinations to pursue unpopular economic and social policy reforms.

Whereas Germany's party competition incorporates a considerable economic left-right divide, although intertwined with sociocultural policy conflict, in Japan the most fundamental feature of the party system of the 1990s appears to have been the all but complete disappearance of policy-based alignments. Economic growth, the entrenchment of a clientelist system that also benefited some constituencies of the main opposition party (the JSP), and the protection of business and employees through regulatory institutions, particularly in the financial sector, undercut the economic policy divide over questions of redistribution in the 1960s and 1970s. When the foreign policy and constitutional conflicts that inspired postwar Japanese party divides evaporated with the end of the cold war, the party system essentially had been stripped of any recognizable programmatic alignments (Kato and Laver 1998).

Although an expert poll by Junko Kato and Michael Laver reveals considerable programmatic differences among political parties, two major qualifications apply. First, experts rated only the programmatic appeal of the Japanese parties relative to one another. As a consequence, they may have overstated marginal differences that would shrink into insignificance, if Japanese parties were compared to the programmatic issue divides found among parties in other polities. Second, the two major electoral parties in 1996, the LDP and the NFP, had policy positions virtually indistinguishable in all the salient policy fields. In the October 1996 Lower House parliamentary election, they received over 60 percent of the list vote and almost 80 percent of the combined single-member district (SMD) and PR seats. By contrast, the three parties with more leftist social and economic policy positions failed to win even one-third of the list vote and ended up with only one-fifth of the combined PR-SMD seats. And the largest of these three, the new DP, with 17.5 percent of the vote and 10.4 percent of the seats, tended to support positions on economic liberalization very similar to those of the NFP and LDP.

In Japan, the virtual evaporation of meaningful programmatic alignments in the arena of party politics facilitated industry-centered adjustment, coordinated by a bureaucracy that aimed at the dispersal of costs and benefits across a wide variety of groups (Hiwatari 1998). These techniques, in turn, have promoted further convergence among parties, but undercut the implementation of far-reaching political-economic reform. Every party may be talking about the need to change regulatory arrangements, for example, in the financial sector. But in light of the withering of past political alignments, voters and parties appear to lack an ideological system of coordinates that would enable them to highlight meaningful and credible policy differences among the contenders in the arena of party competition.

Against this backdrop, it is comprehensible why the LDP always held onto at least one-third of the vote and in fact staged a comeback after the October 1996 election.[20] In a political environment in which programmatic partisan alignments evaporated, particularly those configured around questions of economic distribution, what counts for politicians' and parties' success is not positional but valence competition. Valence competition rewards parties whose lead politicians command credibility and the popular perception of competence in pursuing the good policies every politician claims to want. This perception of competence and credibility is always much easier to achieve for a governing party than for an untested, recently emerged opposition force. Consequently, if an economic crisis eventually prompts politicians to make painful reforms, it is more likely that such initatives will come from challenging factions within the old ruling party rather than from a new party building credibility while confined to the opposition benches of the Diet.

At least four mechanisms hobble the credibility and electoral prospects of Japanese opposition parties. First, they have difficulty manufacturing a new issue dimension where none exists to build on, particularly no strong economic-distributive dimension. The idea that a sectoral divide between competitive and noncompetitive industries, city and countryside, could supply a new partisan alignment is an interesting hypothesis but there is little evidence to back it up.[21] Second, when the opposition to the LDP does subscribe to issue positions on the economic left-right divide, such positions tend to divide the opposition parties among themselves, thus boosting the bargaining power of a centrist LDP and certainly not giving the hegemonic party a reason to engage in profound political-economic reform. Third, electoral laws and clientelist networks enable individual politicians to defect from parties with ease when they reckon the party label does not give them value-added for their personal campaigns. This autonomy of electoral candidates is likely to hurt emerging opposition parties more than the hegemonic party, except in episodes of acute crises

---

20. This comeback, of course, was not a smooth uninterrupted affair, as became clear in the 1998 Upper House legislative elections.
21. Pempel (1998, 166) suggests some indirect empirical indicators.

of governance. Fourth, the continuous reconfiguration of opposition forces makes it hard for the opposition parties to gain credibility in the eyes of critical electoral constituencies. Voters are unlikely to attribute the competence of governance to parties that appear unable to protect their own internal cohesion.

Conclusion

I began this chapter with the question of what, if anything, party competition can contribute to political-economic institutional reform in nationally embedded capitalist Germany and Japan. My tentative answer in light of the theoretical model developed here and the empirical evidence cited is that in the 1990s partisan politics was more effective at slowing down than at promoting reform in both countries. Beyond this retrospective, what are the prospects of partisan politics and political-economic reform in the two countries?

Although it is difficult to calculate and to compare a summary balance sheet of the propensities each country's parties develop toward political-economic reform, I am inclined to argue that Japan faces greater obstacles to reform than Germany. What drives my judgment is particularly the weight I attribute to the persistent entrenchment of clientelist relations between politics and business and the evaporation of previous programmatic dimensions of competition in Japan. In Germany, mass party organization constitutes an obstacle to policy reform, but it has clearly less independent weight in forcing politicians to abstain from reforms than the clientelism of rent-seeking groups. Also in Germany, party competition is not entirely or even always primarily configured around economic issues and the two main parties display more convergence than divergence on this dimension, but the continued presence of a left-right political-economic partisan discourse puts reform on the agenda in a different, more contentious fashion than in Japan. In both countries, however, the absence of an electorally powerful market-liberal party reduces the stimulus that would make the dominant parties rethink current arrangements of cooperative market capitalism. At the same time, the LDP in principle would face fewer threats from existing or new parties were it to embrace radical reform.

All of this, however, does not imply the prediction that, from the vantage point of the year 2010 or so, Japan will have displayed less political-economic reform than Germany. After all, the mechanisms of party competition are only one set of forces that impinge on policy reform. Economic crises and the public atmosphere and perception of crisis might compel politicians to act regardless of partisan considerations (Vogel 1998, 19).

In this regard, Japan's weak economic performance and spectacular business failures in the late 1990s certainly generated a sense of urgency about reform programs unequaled by the apprehension about the performance of political-economic institutions among Germany's politicians. Responses to the crisis have come primarily from small and large corporations and are hastened by the failure of banks and lending agencies. Even under conditions of crisis in which the self-organizing and adaptive potential of market participants themselves is crucial, however, the nature of political leadership in Japan or in Germany and the configurations of political and economic power remain critical. They suggest that changes in existing institutions will be path dependent. A radical break with cooperative market capitalism in favor of a liberal economic order is highly unlikely.

Moreover, the democratic decision-making process does not entirely revolve around party competition in national politics. The way judiciaries, parliaments, and bureaucracies affect policymaking and policy implementation may be independent of whatever partisan alignments prevail in a country. The subnational territorial division of political jurisdictions in a federalist system, for example, may enable opponents of reform to fight more tenaciously against national political initiatives than in a centralist polity. Conversely, local and regional reform efforts may compensate for immobilism at the national or the supranational level, for example, within the framework of the European Union. These are all questions on which my essay cannot throw light. Nevertheless, students of political economy should appreciate the configuration of party competition in democratic polities as one force that may facilitate, restrict, or direct policymakers' efforts to cope with institutions that no longer appear to serve the interests that led to their emergence.

References

Abernathy, William J. 1978. *The Productivity Dilemma: Roadblock to Innovation in the Automobile Industry.* Baltimore: Johns Hopkins University Press.

Abo, Tetsuo. 1994. *The Hybrid Factory: The Japanese Production System in the United States.* Oxford: Oxford University Press.

Abramson, Albert. 1987. *The History of Television, 1880–1941.* Jefferson, N.C.: McFarland & Co.

Acs, Zoltan, and David Audretsch, eds. 1993. *Small Firms and Entrepreneurship: An East-West Perspective.* Cambridge, UK: Cambridge University Press.

Adams, T. F. M. 1964. *A Financial History of Modern Japan.* Tokyo: RESEARCH (Japan) Ltd.

Aglietta, Michel. 1982. *Regulation and Crisis of Capitalism.* New York: Monthly Review Press.

Aglietta, Michel, André Orléan, and Gilles Oudiz. 1980. "Contraintes de change et régulations macroéconomiques nationales." *Recherches Economiques de Louvain* 46(3): 175–206.

Aguilera, Ruth V., and Alvaro Cuervo-Cazurra. 2000. Codes of Good Governance Worldwide. Paper presented at the Society for the Advancement of Socio-Economics, 15 July, London.

Alber, Jens. 1998. "Der deutsche Sozialstaat im Licht international vergleichender Daten." *Leviathan* 26: 199–227.

Albert, Michel. 1993. *Capitalism vs. Capitalism: How America's Obsession with Individual Achievement and Short-Term Profit Has Led It to the Brink of Collapse.* New York: Four Walls Eight Windows.

Alexander, Suzanne. 1991. "Japanese Firms Embark on a Program of Lavish Giving to American Charities." *Wall Street Journal,* 23 May, p. B1.

Amable, Bruno. 1989. "Economies d'échelle dynamiques, effet d'apprentissage et progrès technique endogène: Une comparaison internationale." *La Revue de l'IRES* 1: 31–54.

Amable, Bruno, Rémi Barré, and Robert Boyer. 1997. *Les systèmes d'innovation à l'ère de la globalisation.* Paris: Economica/OST.

Amable, Bruno, and Robert Boyer. 1992. "The R&D-Productivity Relationship in the Context of New Growth Theories: Some Recent Applied Research." In *Proceedings of the Workshop on Quantitative Evaluation of the Impact of R&D Programmes*, edited by Henri Capron, 45–74. Brussels: Commission of the European Communities.

Amable, Bruno, Robert Boyer, and Frederic Lordon. 1996. "The Ad Hoc in Economics: The Pot Calling the Kettle Black." In *Is Economics Becoming a Hard Science?* edited by Antoine d'Autume and Jean Cartelier, 252–73. Cheltenham: Edward Elgar.

Amable, Bruno, and Michel Juillard. 1995. "Innovation and Endogenous Growth: Study of a Long-Term Relationship in the U.S.A." Ronéotypé CEPREMAP, Paris.

Aoki, Masahiko. 1986a. *The Co-Operative Game Theory of the Firm*. Oxford: Clarendon Press.

——. 1986b. "Horizontal versus Vertical Information Structure of the Firm." *American Economic Review* 76: 971–83.

——. 1988. *Information, Incentives, and Bargaining in the Japanese Economy*. Cambridge, UK: Cambridge University Press.

——. 1994a. "The Japanese Firm as a System of Attributes: A Survey and Research Agenda." In *The Japanese Firm: The Sources of Competitive Strength*, edited by Masahiko Aoki and Ronald Dore, 11–40. Oxford: Oxford University Press.

——. 1994b. "Toward an Economic Model of the Japanese Firm." In *Business Enterprise in Japan*, edited by Ken'ichi Imai and Ryutaro Komiya, 39–72. Cambridge, Mass.: MIT Press.

——. 1995. *Keizai shisutemu no shinka to tagensei: Hikaku seido bunseki josetsu*. Tokyo: Tōyō Keizai Shinpōsha.

——. 2000. *Information, Corporate Governance and Institutional Diversity: Competitiveness in Japan, the U.S.A. and the Transitional Economies*. Oxford: Oxford University Press.

——. 2001. *Toward a Comparative Institutional Analysis*. Cambridge, Mass.: MIT Press.

Aoki, Masahiko, and Serdar Dinc. 1997. "Relational Financing as an Institution and Its Viability under Competition." CEPR Publication no. 488. Center for Economic Policy Research, Stanford University.

Aoki, Masahiko, and Masahiro Okuno. 1996. *Keizai shisutemu no hikaku seido bunseki*. Tokyo: University of Tokyo Press.

Aoki, Masahiko, and Hugh Patrick, eds. 1994. *The Japanese Main Bank System: Its Relevance for Developing and Transforming Economies*. Oxford: Oxford University Press.

Applebaum, Eileen, and Rosemary Batt. 1994. *The New American Workplace: Transforming Work Systems in the United States*. Ithaca: ILR Press.

Asahi shinbun. 1999. 1 March, p. 1.

Asmus, Ronald D. 1991. "Fragen unter Freunden." *Die Zeit*, 15 February.

——. 1992. *Germany after the Gulf War*. Santa Monica: RAND.

——. 1995. *Germany's Contribution to Peacekeeping: Issues and Outlook*. Santa Monica: RAND.

Atkinson, Anthony, Lee Rainwater, and Timothy Smeeding. 1995. *Income Distribution in OECD Countries*. Paris: OECD.

Avery, Robert, and Gregory Elliehausen. 1986. "Financial Characteristics of High-Income Households." *Federal Reserve Bulletin* 72(3): 163–77.

Ball, Desmond. 1993–94. "Arms and Influence: Military Acquisitions in the Asia-Pacific Region." *International Security* 18(3): 78–112.

Bank of Japan. 1999. *Comparative Economic and Financial Statistics: Japan and Other Major Countries*. Tokyo: International Department, Bank of Japan.

Baring, Arnulf, and Masamori Sase, eds. 1977. *Zwei zaghafte Riesen—Deutschland und Japan seit 1945*. Stuttgart: Belser.

Barou, Yves, and Bernard Keizer. 1984. *Les grandes economies.* Paris: Editions du Seuil.

Barro, Robert J., and Xavier Sala-I-Martin. 1995. *Economic Growth.* New York: McGraw-Hill.

Baslé, Maurice, Jacques Mazier, and Jean François Vidal. 1999. *When Economic Crises Endure.* Armonk, N.Y.: M. E. Sharpe.

Baums, Theodor, and Christian Fraune. 1995. "Institutionelle Anleger und Publikums-gesellschaft: Eine empirische Untersuchung." *Die Aktiengesellschaft* 3: 97–112.

Bebchuk, Lucian A., and Mark J. Roe. 1999. A Theory of Path Dependence in Corporate Governance and Ownership. Working paper no. 131. Center for Law and Economic Studies, Columbia Law School, New York.

Beeson, Mark, and Kanishka Jayasuriya. 1997. The Politics of Regionalism: APEC and the EU in Comparative Perspective. Working paper no. 59, November. Development Research Series, Research Center on Development and International Relations (DIR), Department of Development and Planning, Aalberg University, Aalberg, Denmark.

Bendix, Reinhard. 1956. *Work and Authority in Industry: Ideologies of Management in the Course of Industrialization.* New York: John Wiley & Sons.

Benz, Winfried. 1998. Science Policy in Germany and the Role of the Wissenschaftsrat in Advising the Federal and Länder (State) Governments. Paper presented at the Tenth Anniversary International Conference of the National Institute of Science and Technology Policy, 8–9 October, Tokyo.

Berger, Suzanne. 1996. "Introduction." In *National Diversity and Global Capitalism,* edited by Suzanne Berger and Ronald Dore, 1–25. Ithaca: Cornell University Press.

Berger, Suzanne, and Ronald Dore, eds. 1996. *National Diversity and Global Capitalism.* Ithaca: Cornell University Press.

Berger, Thomas U. 1996. "Norms, Identity and National Security in Germany and Japan." In *The Culture of National Security: Norms and Identity in World Politics,* edited by Peter J. Katzenstein, 317–56. New York: Columbia University Press.

Berggren, Christian, and Masami Nomura. 1997. *The Resilience of Corporate Japan: New Strategies and Personnel Practices.* London: Paul Chapman.

Bergner, Jeffrey T. 1991. *The New Superpowers: Germany, Japan, the U.S. and the New World Order.* New York: St. Martin's Press.

Berry, Steven, James Levinsohn, and Ariel Pakes. 1999. "Voluntary Export Restraints on Automobiles: Evaluating a Trade Policy." *American Economic Review* 89(3): 400–430.

Beyer, Jürgen. 1998. *Managerherrschaft in Deutschland? "Corporate Governance" unter Verflechtungsbedingungen.* Opladen: Westdeutsche Verlag.

Böhm, Jürgen. 1992. *Der Einfluß der Banken auf Großunternehmen.* Hamburg: Steuer und Wirtschaftsverlag.

Born, Karl Erich. 1967. *Die deutsche Bankenkrise 1931: Finanzen und Politik.* München: Piper.

Borrus, Michael, and John Zysman. 1992. "Industrial Competitiveness and American National Security." In *The Highest Stakes: The Economic Foundations of the Next Security System,* edited by Wayne Sandholtz, Michael Borrus, John Zysman, Ken Conca, Jay Stowsky, Steven Vogel, and Steve Weber, 7–52. New York: Oxford University Press.

Bouissou, Jean-Marie. 1994. "Japan and the Quest for Legitimacy." In *Power and Purpose after the Cold War,* edited by Zaki Laïdi, 55–81. Oxford: Berg.

Boyer, Robert. 1988. "Formalizing Growth Regimes within a *Régulation* Approach: A Method for Assessing the Economic Consequences of Technological Change." In *Technical Change and Economic Theory: The Global Process of Development,* edited by Giovanni Dosi, Christopher Freeman, Gerard Silverberg, and Luc Soete, 608–30. London: Frances Pinter.

——. 1990. *The Regulation School: A Critical Introduction.* New York: Columbia University Press.

——. 1996. "The Convergence Hypothesis Revisited: Globalization but Still the Century of Nations?" In *National Diversity and Global Capitalism,* edited by Suzanne Berger and Ronald Dore, 29–59. Ithaca: Cornell University Press.

——. 1998a. "Hybridization and Models of Production: Geography, History, and Theory." In *Between Imitation and Innovation: The Transfer and Hybridization of Productive Models in the International Automobile Industry,* edited by Robert Boyer, Elsie Charron, Ulrich Jürgens, and Steven Tolliday, 23–56. Oxford: Oxford University Press.

——. 1998b. Will the Japanese and the German Innovation Systems Cope with the Challenges of the 21st Century? Paper presented at the Economic Research Center of the School of Economics, Nagoya University, November, Nagoya.

——. 1999a. *Le gouvernement économique de la zone euro.* Paris: La Documentation Française.

——. 1999b. "The Variety and Dynamics of Capitalism." In *Institutions and the Evolution of Capitalism,* edited by John Groenewegen and Jack Vromen, 122–40. Cheltenham: Edward Elgar.

——. 2000a. "La formation professionnelle tout au long de la vie: Analyse macro-économique et comparaisons internationales." *Conseil d'Analyse Economique* 22: 89–122.

——. 2000b. "The Unanticipated Fallout of the European Monetary Union: An Essay on the Political and Institutional Deficits of the Euro." In *After the Euro: Shaping Institutions for Governance in the Wake of European Monetary Union,* edited by Colin Crouch, 24–88. Oxford: Oxford University Press.

——. 2000c. What Constraints on European Growth: Innovation, Institutions and Economic Policy. Paper presented at the conference What Do We Know about Institutions and Innovation in Europe? organized by the Saint Gobain Centre for Economic Studies, 9–11 November, Paris.

Boyer, Robert, and Eve Caroli. 1993. Production Regimes, Education and Training Systems: From Complementarity to Mismatch? Unpublished paper.

Boyer, Robert, Elsie Charron, Ulrich Jürgens, and Steven Tolliday. 1998. *Between Imitation and Innovation: The Transfer and Hybridization of Productive Models in the International Automobile Industry.* Oxford: Oxford University Press.

Boyer, Robert, and Michel Didier. 1998. "Innovation et croissance." *Conseil d'Analyse Economique* 10: 11–132.

Boyer, Robert, and Jean-Pierre Durand. 1997. *After Fordism.* London: Macmillan.

Boyer, Robert, and Michel Freyssenet. 1995. "Emergence de nouveaux modeles industriels: Problématique et démarche d'analyse." *Actes du GERPISA* (Université d'Évry—Val d'Essonne) 15: 9–73.

Boyer, Robert, and J. Rogers Hollingsworth. 1997. "From National Embeddedness to Spatial and Institutional Embeddedness." In *Contemporary Capitalism: The Embeddedness of Institutions,* edited by Robert Boyer and J. Rogers Hollingsworth, 433–84. Cambridge, UK: Cambridge University Press.

Boyer, Robert, and Michel Juillard. 1991. "The New Endogeneous Growth Theory versus a Productivity Regime Approach: One Century of American Economic History Revisited." Couverture Orange CEPREMAP no. 9210, December, Paris.

——. 2000. "The Wage Labour Nexus Challenged: More the Consequence than the Cause of the Crisis." In *Japanese Capitalism in Crisis,* edited by Robert Boyer and Toshio Yamada, 119–37. London: Routledge.

Boyer, Robert, and Pascal Petit. 1991. "Technical Change, Cumulative Causation and Growth: Accounting for the Contemporary Productivity Puzzle with Some Post Keynesian Theories." In *Technology and Productivity: The Challenge for Economic*

Policy, edited by Directorate for Science, Technology and Industry, 47–67. Paris: OECD.

Boyer, Robert, and Yves Saillard. 2001. *Regulation Theory: The State of Art*. London: Routledge.

Boyer, Robert, and Toshio Yamada. 2000. *Japanese Capitalism in Crisis: A Regulationist Interpretation*. London: Routledge.

Bratton, William W., and Joseph A. McCahery. 1999. "Comparative Corporate Governance and the Theory of the Firm: The Case against Global Cross Reference." *Columbia Journal of Transnational Law* 38: 213–97.

Brendt, Ernst R., and Catherine J. Morrison. 1995. "High-Tech Capital Formation and Economic Performance in U.S. Manufacturing Industries: An Exploratory Analysis." *Journal of Econometrics* 65(1): 9–43.

Bresnahan, Timothy F., and Peter Reiss. 1991. "Entry and Competition in Concentrated Markets." *Journal of Political Economy* 99(5): 977–1009.

Broadberry, Steven N., and Karin Wagner. 1996. "Human Capital and Productivity in Manufacturing during the 20th Century: Britain, Germany and the United States." In *Quantitative Aspects of Post-war European Economic Growth*, edited by Nicholas F. R. Crafts and Bart van Ark, 244–70. Cambridge, UK: Cambridge University Press.

Bruce, W. Don. 1998. Helping Improve S&T Policy in the United States: Some Future Issues to Be Considered in Analysis. Paper presented at the Tenth Anniversary International Conference of the National Institute of Science and Technology Policy, 8–9 October, Tokyo.

Bundesministerium der Finanzen. 2000. "Entwurf eines Gesetzes zur Regelung von 'Unternehmensübernahmen.'" Available at http://www.bundesfinanzministerium.de; INTERNET.

Bundesverband deutscher Banken. 1999. Available at http://www.bdb.de; INTERNET.

Bundesvereinigung der Deutschen Arbeitgeberverbände (BDA). 1996. Reform von Tarifpolitik und Tarifrecht. 3 July. Unpublished document.

Burawoy, Michael. 1985. *The Politics of Production: Factory Regimes under Capitalism and Socialism*. London: Verso.

Burniaux, JeanMare, Thai-Thanh Dang, Douglas Fore, Michael Foerster, Marco Mira d'Ercole, and Howard Oxly. 1998. Income Distribution and Poverty in Selected OECD Countries. Economic Department OECD Working paper no. 189, 10 March, OECD, Paris.

Büschgen, Hans E. 1983. "Zeitgeschichtliche Problemfelder des Bankenwesens der Bundesrepublik Deutschland." In *Deutsche Bankengeschichte*, edited by Institut für Bankhistorische Forschung e.V. Frankfurt am Main: Fritz Knapp Verlag.

Calder, Kent E. 1982. "Opening Japan." *Foreign Policy* 47(summer): 82–97.

——. 1993. *Strategic Capitalism: Private Business and Public Purpose in Japanese Industrial Finance*. Princeton: Princeton University Press.

Campbell, John Y., and Yasushi Hamao. 1994. "Changing Patterns of Corporate Financing and the Main Bank System in Japan." In *The Japanese Main Bank System: Its Relevance for Developing and Transforming Economies*, edited by Masahiko Aoki and Hugh Patrick, 325–49. Oxford: Oxford University Press.

"The Car Industry: Downhill Racers." 2001. *Economist*, 31 March, p. 60.

Carlile, Lonny E. 1998. "The Politics of Administrative Reform." In *Is Japan Really Changing Its Ways?* edited by Lonny E. Carlile and Mark C. Tilton, 76–110. Washington, D.C.: Brookings Institution.

Carlile, Lonny E., and Mark C. Tilton. 1998. "Regulatory Reform and the Developmental State." In *Is Japan Really Changing Its Ways?* edited by Lonny E. Carlile and Mark C. Tilton, 1–15. Washington, D.C.: Brookings Institution.

Carlin, Wendy, and David Soskice. 1997. "Shocks to the System: The German Political Economy under Stress." *National Institute Economic Review* 159: 57–76.

Caroli, Eve. 1994. "Croissance et formation: Le rôle de la politique éducative." *Economie et Prévision* 116(5): 49–61.

Casper, Steven, Mark Lehrer, and David Soskice. 1999. "Can High-Technology Industries Prosper in Germany?" *Industry and Innovation* 6(1): 5–24.

Castles, Francis G. 1978. *The Social Democratic Image of Society*. London: Routledge and Kegan Paul.

Cerny, Philip G. 1997. "Paradoxes of the Competition State: The Dynamics of Political Globalization." *Government and Opposition* 32: 251–74.

Chandler, Alfred D. 1977. *The Visible Hand: The Managerial Revolution in American Business*. Cambridge, Mass.: Belknap Press.

Chikuma, Tadao. 1999. "Hataraku katachi to hyōka no shikata o kaeru." *Jitsugyō no Nihon* 102(April): 12–20.

Choate, Pat. 1990. *Agents of Influence: How Japan's Lobbyists in the United States Manipulate America's Political and Economic System*. New York: Knopf.

Christensen, Thomas J. 1999. "China, the U.S.-Japan Alliance, and the Security Dilemma in East Asia." *International Security* 23: 49–80.

Clark, Kim B., and Takahiro Fujimoto. 1991. *Product Development Performance: Strategy, Organization, and Management in the World Auto Industry*. Boston: Harvard Business School Press.

Clayton, Richard, and Jonas Pontusson. 1998. "Welfare State Retrenchment Revisited: Entitlement Cuts, Public Sector Restructuring, and Inegalitarian Trends in Advanced Capitalist Societies." *World Politics* 51(1): 67–98.

Coffee, John C. 1999. "The Future as History: The Prospects for Global Convergence in Corporate Governance and Its Implications." *Northwestern University Law Review* 93: 641–708.

Cook, Don. 1989. *Forging the Alliance: NATO, 1945–1950*. New York: Arbor House.

Corbett, Jennifer, and Tim Jenkinson. 1996. "The Financing of Industry, 1970–1989: An International Comparison." *Journal of the Japanese and International Economies* 10: 71–96.

Cordesman, Anthony H. 1988. *NATO's Central Region Forces: Capabilities/Challenges/Concepts*. London: Jane's Publishing.

Corporate Governance Forum of Japan. 1998. *Corporate Governance Principles: A Japanese View (Final Report)*. Tokyo: Corporate Governance Forum of Japan.

Cox, Gary W., and Frances Rosenbluth. 1995. "Anatomy of a Split: The Liberal Democrats of Japan." *Electoral Studies* 14(1): 355–76.

Cronin, James E. 1998. What the Cold War Made Possible: Constraints and Opportunities within the Postwar Settlement. Paper presented at the Eleventh International Conference of Europeanists, 26–28 February, Baltimore.

Crouch, Colin, and Wolfgang Streeck. 1997. *Political Economy of Modern Capitalism: Mapping Convergence and Diversity*. Thousand Oaks: Sage.

David, Paul A. 1988. "Path-Dependence: Putting the Past in the Future of Economics." IMSSS Technical Report no. 533, Stanford University.

Deeg, Richard. 1992. Banks and the State in Germany: The Critical Role of Subnational Institutions in Economic Governance. Ph.D. diss., Massachusetts Institute of Technology.

——. 1993. "The State, Banks, and Economic Governance in Germany." *German Politics* 2(August): 149–76.

——. 2001. Institutional Change and the Uses and Limits of Path Dependency: The Case of German Finance. Discussion paper 01/6, Max-Planck-Institut für Gesellschaftsforschung, Köln.

De Jong, Henk W. 1996. "European Capitalism between Freedom and Social Justice." In *International Regulatory Competition and Coordination: Perspectives on Economic Regulation in Europe and the United States,* edited by Joseph McCahery, William W. Bratton, Sol Picciotto, and Colin Scott, 185–206. Oxford: Clarendon Press.

Dertouzos, Michael L., Robert M. Solow, and Richard K. Lester. 1989. *Made in America: Regaining the Productive Edge.* Cambridge, Mass.: MIT Press.

Deutsch, Karl W., Sidney A. Burrell, Robert A. Kann, Maurice Lee, Jr., Martin Lichterman, Raymond E. Lindgren, Francis L. Lowenheim, and Richard W. Van Wagenen. 1957. *Political Community and the North Atlantic Area.* Princeton: Princeton University Press.

Deutsche Bundesbank. 1992. "Longer Term Trends in the Financing Patterns of West German Enterprises." *Monthly Report* 44(10): 25–39.

———. 1995. "The Trend in and Significance of Assets Held in the Form of Investment Certificates." *Monthly Report* 47(10): 49–71.

———. 2000. "Die Beziehung zwischen Bankkrediten und Anleihemarkt in Deutschland." *Monatsbericht* 52(1): 33–48.

———. 2001. "Ergebnisse der gesamtwirtschaftlichen Finanzierungsrechnung für Deutschland 1991 bis 1999." *Statistische Sonderveröffentlichung* 4.

Deutsches Aktieninstitut. 1999. *DAI-Factbook 1999.* Frankfurt am Main: Deutsches Aktieninstitut.

Deutsches Rechnungslegungs Standards Committee. 2001. Available at http://www.drsc.de/; INTERNET.

Dewatripont, Mathias, and Jean Tirole. 1994. *The Prudential Regulation of Banks.* Cambridge, Mass.: MIT Press.

Dewey Ballantine. 1995. Privatizing Protection: Japanese Market Barriers in Consumer Photographic Film and Consumer Photographic Paper. Unpublished paper.

DiMaggio, Paul J., and Walter W. Powell. 1991. "The Iron Cage Revisited: Institutional Isomorphism and Collective Rationality in Organization Fields." In *The New Institutionalism in Organizational Analysis,* edited by Walter W. Powell and Paul J. DiMaggio, 63–82. Chicago: University of Chicago Press.

Dirks, Daniel. 1997. "The Japanese Employment System in Transition: Five Perspectives." Working paper 97/3, German Institute for Japanese Studies, Economic Section, Tokyo.

Di Tella, Rafael, and Robert MacCulloch. 1998. The Consequences of Labour Market Flexibility: Panel Evidence Based on Survey Data. Unpublished paper.

Dohse, Knuth, Ulrich Jürgens, and Thomas Malsch. 1985. "From 'Fordism' to 'Toyotism'? The Social Organization of the Labor Process in the Japanese Automobile Industry." *Politics and Society* 14(2): 115–46.

Dollfus, Olivier. 1994. "Networks and Territories: Integration Processes in Europe and East Asia." In *Regional Strategies in East Asia: A Comparative Perspective,* edited by François Gipouloux, 141–48. Tokyo: Maison Franco-Japonaise.

Donnelly, Shawn, Andrew Gamble, Gregory Jackson, and John Parkinson. 2001. *The Public Interest and the Company in Britain and Germany.* London: Anglo-German Society for the Study of Industrial Society.

Dore, Ronald. 1973. *British Factory, Japanese Factory: The Origins of National Diversity in Industrial Relations.* Berkeley: University of California Press.

———. 1986. *Flexible Rigidities: Industrial Policy and Structural Adjustment in the Japanese Economy, 1970–1980.* Stanford: Stanford University Press.

———. 1996. "Unions between Class and Enterprise." *Industrielle Beziehungen* 3.

———. 2000. *Stock Market Capitalism, Welfare Capitalism: Japan and Germany versus the Anglo-Saxons.* Oxford: Oxford University Press.

Dosi, Giovanni. 1983. "Technological Paradigm and Technological Trajectories." In *Long Waves in the World Economy*, edited by Christopher Freeman, 78–101. London: Butterworths.

Dower, John. 1988. Psychological Aspects of Contemporary U.S.-Japan Relations. Unpublished paper.

Downs, Anthony. 1957. *An Economic Theory of Democracy*. New York: Harper and Row.

Duignan, Peter, and L. H. Gann. 1994. *The USA and the New Europe 1945–1993*. Oxford: Basil Blackwell.

Durand, Jean-Pierre, Paul Stewart, and Juan José Castillo, eds. 1999. *Teamwork in the Automobile Industry: Radical Change or Passing Fashion?* Houndmills: Macmillan.

Ebbinghaus, Bernhard, and Philip Manow. 2001. *Comparing Welfare Capitalism: Social Policy and Political Economy in Europe, Japan and the USA*. London: Routledge.

Economic Planning Agency. 1993. *Economic Survey of Japan*. Tokyo: Economic Planning Agency.

——. 1999. *Economic Survey of Japan*. Tokyo: Economic Planning Agency.

Economic Report to the President. 1999. Washington, D.C.: Government Printing Office.

Edwards, Jeremy, and Klaus Fischer. 1994. *Banks, Finance and Investment in Germany*. Cambridge, UK: Cambridge University Press.

Eicher, Theo S., and Stephen J. Turnovsky. 1999. "Nonscale Model of Economic Growth." *Economic Journal* 109: 394–415.

Eisenstadt, S. N. 1996. *Japanese Civilization: A Comparative View*. Chicago: University of Chicago Press.

Elbaum, Bernard, and William Lazonick, eds. 1986. *The Decline of the British Economy*. Oxford: Clarendon Press.

Elger, Tony, and Chris Smith, eds. 1994. *Global Japanization? The Transnational Transformation of the Labour Process*. London: Routledge.

Elston, Julie A., and Horst Albach. 1995. "Bank Affiliations and Firm Capital Investment in Germany." *Ifo-Studien* 41: 3–16.

Elvander, Nils. 1997. *The Swedish Bargaining System in the Melting Pot*. Solna: Arbetslivsinstitutet.

Ermarth, Michael. 1993. "Introduction." In *America and the Shaping of German Society, 1945–1955*, edited by Michael Ermarth, 1–22. Providence: Berg.

"The Erosion of Employers' Associations and Industry-Level Bargaining in Eastern Germany." 1997. August. Available at EIROnline, www.euro.eurofound.ie; INTERNET.

European Central Bank. 1999. *Monthly Report*. February.

European Commission. 1997. *Second European Report on S&T Indicators*. Luxembourg: EUR 17369, Science Research Development.

"Europe's New Capitalism." 2000. *Economist*, 12 February, p. 72.

Farnsworth, Clyde H. 1989. "Japan's Loud Voice in Washington." *New York Times*, 10 December, pp. F1, F6.

Fearon, James D. 1994. "Domestic Political Audiences and the Escalation of International Disputes." *American Political Science Review* 88(3): 577–87.

——. 1995. "Rationalist Explanations for War." *International Organization* 49(3): 379–414.

——. 1997. "Signaling Foreign Policy Interests: Tying Hands versus Sinking Costs." *Journal of Conflict Resolution* 41(1): 68–90.

Fedder, Edwin H. 1973. *NATO: The Dynamics of Alliance in the Postwar World*. New York: Dodd, Mead.

Fichter, Michael. 1981. "U.S. Policy on Trade Unions in Occupied Germany, 1945–48." In *The Role of the United States in the Reconstruction of Italy and West Germany*,

1943–1949, edited by Ekkehart Krippendorff, 105–19. Berlin: John F. Kennedy Institut für Nordamerikastudien, Freie Universität Berlin.

———. 1997. The German System of Labor Relations: Still a Model or a Passing Phenomenon? Unpublished paper.

Fine, Charles H., Richard St. Clair, John C. Lafrance, and Don Hillebrand. 1996. *The U.S. Automobile Manufacturing Industry.* Washington, D.C.: U.S. Department of Commerce, Office of Technology Policy.

Flecker, Jörg, and Thorsten Schulten. 1999. "The End of Institutional Stability." *Economic and Industrial Democracy* 20: 81–115.

Fligstein, Neil. 1990. *The Transformation of Corporate Control.* Cambridge, Mass.: Harvard University Press.

———. 2001. "Social Skill and the Theory of Fields." *Sociological Theory* 19: 105–25.

Florida, Richard, Davis Jenkins, and Donald F. Smith. 1998. "The Japanese Transplants in North America: Production Organization, Location, and Research and Development." In *Between Imitation and Innovation: The Transfer and Hybridization of Productive Models in the International Automobile Industry,* edited by Robert Boyer, Elsie Charron, Ulrich Jürgens, and Steven Tolliday, 189–215. Oxford: Oxford University Press.

Floud, Roderic, and Donald N. McCloskey, eds. 1994. *The Economic History of Britain since 1700.* 2 vols. Cambridge, UK: Cambridge University Press.

Forsyth, Douglas, and Ton Notermans, eds. 1997. *Macroeconomic Policy and Financial Regulation in Europe from the 1930s to the 1990s.* Providence: Berghahn Books.

Frankel, Jeffrey A., and Miles Kahler. 1993. "Introduction." In *Regionalism and Rivalry: Japan and the United States in Pacific Asia,* edited by Jeffrey A. Frankel and Miles Kahler, 1–18. Chicago: University of Chicago Press.

Freeman, Christopher. 1987. *Technology Policy and Economic Performance: Lessons from Japan.* London: Pinter Publishers.

Freyssenet, Michel, Andrew Mair, Koichi Shimizu, and Giuseppe Volpato, eds. 1998. *One Best Way? Trajectories and Industrial Models of the World's Automobile Producers.* Oxford: Oxford University Press.

Friedberg, Aaron. 1993–94. "Ripe for Rivalry: Prospects for Peace in a Multipolar Asia." *International Security* 18(3): 5–33.

Frieden, Jeffrey, and Ronald Rogowski. 1996. "The Impact of the International Economy on National Policies: An Analytical Overview." In *Internationalization and Domestic Politics,* edited by Robert O. Keohane and Helen V. Milner, 25–47. Cambridge, UK: Cambridge University Press.

Fujimoto, Takahiro. 1997. "Strategies for Assembly Automation in the Automobile Industry." In *Transforming Automobile Assembly: Experience in Automation and Work Organisation,* edited by Koichi Shimokawa, Ulrich Jürgens, and Takahiro Fujimoto, 211–37. Berlin: Springer-Verlag.

———. 1999. *The Evolution of a Manufacturing System at Toyota.* Oxford: Oxford University Press.

Fukai, Shigeko N. 1992. The Role of "Gaiatsu" in Japan's Land Policymaking. Paper presented at the Annual Meeting of the American Political Science Association, 3–6 September, Chicago.

Galbraith, James K. 1998. *Created Unequal: The Crisis in American Pay.* New York: Free Press.

Gall, Lothar, Gerald D. Feldman, Harold James, Carl-Ludwig Holtfrerich, and Hans E. Büschgen. 1995. *Die Deutsche Bank, 1870–1995.* Munich: C. H. Beck.

Gao, Bai. 1997. *Economic Ideology and Japanese Industrial Policy: Developmentalism from 1931 to 1965.* Cambridge, UK: Cambridge University Press.

Gardener, Edward, and Philip Molyneux. 1993. *Changes in Western European Banking*. London: Routledge.

Garten, Jeffrey E. 1992. *A Cold Peace: America, Japan, Germany, and the Struggle for Supremacy*. New York: Times Books.

Geddes, Barbara. 1994. *Politicians' Dilemma*. Berkeley: University of California Press.

Georghiou, Luke. 1998. Science Policy Advice in the UK and the Work of PREST. Paper presented at the Tenth Anniversary International Conference of the National Institute of Science and Technology Policy, 8–9 October, Tokyo.

Gerlach, Michael L. 1992. *Alliance Capitalism: The Social Organization of Japanese Business*. Berkeley: University of California Press.

Gesamtmetall. 1999. *Geschäftsbericht 1997–99*. Köln: Gesamtmetall.

Giddens, Anthony. 1994. *Beyond Left and Right: The Future of Radical Politics*. Stanford: Stanford University Press.

Gipouloux, François. 1994. "Introduction: Globalization and Regionalization in East Asia: Stakes and Strategies." In *Regional Strategies in East Asia: A Comparative Perspective*, edited by François Gipouloux, 13–43. Tokyo: Maison Franco-Japonaise.

Gloannec, Anne-Marie. 1994. "The Purpose of German Power." In *Power and Purpose after the Cold War*, edited by Zaki Laïdi, 35–53. Oxford: Berg.

Golden, Miriam, Michael Wallerstein, and Peter Lange. 1999. "Postwar Trade-Union Organization and Industrial Relations in Twelve Countries." In *Continuity and Change in Contemporary Capitalism*, edited by Herbert Kitschelt, Peter Lange, Gary Marks, and John D. Stephens, 194–230. Cambridge, UK: Cambridge University Press.

Goldman, Steven L., Roger N. Nagel, and Kenneth Preiss. 1995. *Agile Competitors and Virtual Organizations: Strategies for Enriching the Customer*. New York: Van Nostrand Reinhold.

Goodin, Robert E., Bruce Headey, Ruud Muffles, and Henk-Jan Dirven. 1999. *The Real Worlds of Welfare Capitalism*. Cambridge, UK: Cambridge University Press.

Gordon, Jeffrey N. 2000. Pathways to Corporate Convergence? Two Steps on the Road to Shareholder Capitalism in Germany: Deutsche Telekom and DaimlerChrysler. Working paper no. 161, Center for Law and Economics, Columbia Law School, New York.

Gospel, Howard. 1994. Whatever Happened to Apprenticeship Training? A British, American, Australian Comparison. Discussion paper no. 190, Centre for Economic Performance, London School of Economics.

Goto, Akira, and Hiroyuki Odagiri, eds. 1997. *Innovation in Japan*. Oxford: Clarendon Press.

Gourevitch, Peter. 1996. "The Macropolitics of Microinstitutional Differences in the Analysis of Comparative Capitalism." In *National Diversity and Global Capitalism*, edited by Suzanne Berger and Ronald Dore, 239–59. Ithaca: Cornell University Press.

Gowa, Joanne. 1994. *Allies, Adversaries, and International Trade*. Princeton: Princeton University Press.

Granovetter, Mark. 1985. "Economic Action and Social Structure: The Problem of Embeddedness." *American Journal of Sociology* 91: 481–510.

Green, Carl J. 1995. "APEC and Trans-Pacific Dispute Management." *Law and Policy in International Business* 26(3): 719–34.

Grieco, Joseph M. 1997. "Systemic Sources of Variation in Regional Institutionalization in Western Europe, East Asia, and the Americas." In *The Political Economy of Regionalism*, edited by Edward D. Mansfield and Helen V. Milner, 164–87. New York: Columbia University Press.

——. 1999. "Realism and Regionalism: American Power and German and Japanese Institutional Strategies during and after the Cold War." In *Unipolar Politics: Realism and State Strategies after the Cold War*, edited by Ethan Kapstein and Michael Mastanduno, 319–53. New York: Columbia University Press.

Gries, Thomas, Berthold Wigger, and Claudia Hentschel. 1994. "Endogenous Growth and R&D Models: A Critical Appraisal of Recent Developments." *Jahrbücher für National Ökonomie und Statistik* 231(1): 64–84.

Guillén, Mauro F. 2000. "Corporate Governance and Globalization: Is There Convergence across Countries?" *Advances in International Comparative Management* 13: 175–204.

——. 2001. "Is Globalization Civilizing, Destructive or Feeble? A Critique of Five Key Debates in the Social-Science Literature." *Annual Review of Sociology* 27: 235–60.

Gurowitz, Amy I. 1998. Mobilizing International Norms: Domestic Actors, Immigrants, and the State. Ph.D. diss., Cornell University, Ithaca.

Gwartney, James, and Robert Lawson. 1997. *Economic Freedom of the World 1997 Annual Report*. Vancouver: Fraser Institute.

Hall, Peter. 1999. "The Political Economy of Europe in an Era of Interdependence." In *Continuity and Change in Contemporary Capitalism*, edited by Herbert Kitschelt, Peter Lange, Gary Marks, and John D. Stephens, 135–63. Cambridge, UK: Cambridge University Press.

Hall, Peter A., and David Soskice. 2001. "An Introduction to Varieties of Capitalism." In *Varieties of Capitalism: The Institutional Foundations of Comparative Advantage*, edited by Peter A. Hall and David Soskice, 1–70. Oxford: Oxford University Press.

Hall, Peter, and Rosemary Taylor. 1996. "Political Science and the Three New Institutionalisms." *Political Studies* 44: 936–57.

Hamada, Koichi, and Akiyoshi Horiuchi. 1987. "The Political Economy of the Financial Market." In *The Political Economy of Japan*, Vol. 1, *The Domestic Transformation*, edited by Kozo Yamamura and Yasukichi Yasuba, 223–60. Stanford: Stanford University Press.

Hanada, Masanori, and Yasuro Hirano. 2000. "'Industrial Welfare' and 'Company-ist' *Régulation*: An Eroding Complementarity." In *Japanese Capitalism in Crisis*, edited by Boyer Robert and Toshio Yamada, 87–103. London: Routledge.

Hancké, Bob. 1999. "Varieties of Capitalism Revisited: Globalisation and Comparative Institutional Advantage." *Lettre de la Régulation* 30: 1–3.

Hassel, Anke, Martin Höpner, Antje Kurdelbusch, Britta Rehder, and Rainer Zugehör. 2000. Dimensionen der Internationalisierung: Ergebnisse der Unternehmensdatenbank "Internationalisierung der 100 größten Unternehmen in Deutschland." Working paper 1/00, Max-Planck-Institut für Gesellschaftsforschung, Köln.

Hassel, Anke, and Thorsten Schulten. 1998. "Globalization and the Future of Central Collective Bargaining: The Example of the German Metal Industry." *Economy and Society* 27(4): 486–522.

Hatch, Walter, and Kozo Yamamura. 1996. *Asia in Japan's Embrace: Building a Regional Production Alliance*. Cambridge, UK: Cambridge University Press.

Hein, Laura E. 1993. "Growth versus Success: Japan's Economic Policy in Historical Perspective." In *Postwar Japan as History*, edited by Andrew Gordon, 99–122. Berkeley: University of California Press.

Herz, John H., ed. 1983. *From Dictatorship to Democracy*. Westport: Greenwood Press.

Higgott, Richard. 1995. "Economic Cooperation in the Asia Pacific: A Theoretical Comparison with the European Union." *Journal of European Public Policy* 2(3): 261–83.

Hirasawa, Ryo. 1998. Workshop Contribution of Supporting Institutions to the National Science and Technology Policies, and the Future Perspectives of Policy Studies: Introductory Remarks. Paper presented at the Tenth Anniversary International Conference of the National Institute of Science and Technology Policy, 8–9 October, Tokyo.

Hirschman, Albert. 1970. *Exit, Voice and Loyalty: Responses to Decline in Firms, Organizations, and States.* Cambridge, Mass.: Harvard University Press.

Hiwatari, Nobuhiro. 1998. "Adjustment to Stagflation and Neoliberal Reformism in Japan, the United Kingdom, and the United States." *Comparative Political Studies* 31(5): 602–32.

Hollingsworth, J. Rogers, and Robert Boyer. 1997. *Contemporary Capitalism: The Embeddedness of Institutions.* Cambridge, UK: Cambridge University Press.

Hollingsworth, J. Rogers, Philippe Schmitter, and Wolfgang Streeck, eds. 1994. *Governing Capitalist Economies.* New York: Oxford University Press.

Hollingsworth, J. Rogers, and Wolfgang Streeck. 1994. "Countries and Sectors: Concluding Remarks on Performance, Convergence, and Competitiveness." In *Governing Capitalist Economies: Performance and Control of Economic Sectors,* edited by J. Rogers Hollingsworth, Philippe C. Schmitter, and Wolfgang Streeck, 270–300. Oxford: Oxford University Press.

Holtfrerich, Carl-Ludwig. 1995. "The Deutsche Bank 1945–1957: War, Military Rule and Reconstruction." In *The Deutsche Bank: 1870–1995,* edited by Lothar Gall, Gerald D. Feldman, Harold James, Carl-Ludwig Holtfrerich, and Hans E. Büschgen, 357–521. London: Weidenfeld and Nicolson.

Höpner, Martin. 2001. Corporate Governance in Transition: 10 Empirical Findings on Shareholder Value and Industrial Relations in Germany. Discussion paper 01/5. Max-Planck-Institut für Gesellschaftsforschung, Köln.

——. 2002. Wer beherrscht die Unternehmen? Shareholder Value, Managerherrschaft und Mitbestimmung in großen deutschen Unternehmen. Ph.D. diss., Fern Universität Hagen.

Höpner, Martin, and Gregory Jackson. 2001. The Political Economy of Takeovers in Germany: The Case of Mannesman. Discussion paper 1/4, Max-Planck-Institut für Gesellschaftsforschung, Köln.

Hoshi, Takeo. 1994. "The Economic Role of Corporate Grouping and the Main Bank System." In *The Japanese Firm: Sources of Competitive Strength,* edited by Masahiko Aoki and Ronald P. Dore, 285–309. Oxford: Oxford University Press.

Hosokawa, Morihiro. 1998. "Are U.S. Troops in Japan Needed?" *Foreign Affairs* (July–August): 1–5.

Howe, Russell Warren, and Sarah Hays Trott. 1977. *The Power Peddlers: How Lobbyists Mold America's Foreign Policy.* Garden City, N.Y.: Doubleday.

Ide, Masasuke. 1998. *Japanese Corporate Finance and International Competition: Japanese Capitalism versus American Capitalism.* London: Macmillan.

Ifo Institut für Wirtschaftsforschung and Sakura Institute of Research. 1997. *A Comparative Analysis of Japanese and German Economic Success.* Tokyo: Springer.

"IG BCE and Employers Adopt Joint Declaration on Partnership and Branch-Level Bargaining." 1999. *EIROnline,* February. Available at www.eiro.eurofound.ie; INTERNET.

Imai, Ken'ichi, and Ryutaro Komiya. 1994. "Characteristics of Japanese Firms." In *Business Enterprise in Japan,* edited by Ken'ichi Imai and Ryutaro Komiya, 19–38. Cambridge, Mass.: MIT Press.

Imai, Masaaki. 1986. *Kaizen: The Key to Japan's Competitive Success.* New York: Random House.

Inglehart, Ronald, Miguel Basanez, and Alejandro Moreno. 1998. *Human Values and Beliefs: A Cross-Cultural Sourcebook.* Ann Arbor: University of Michigan Press.

Inoue, Hideaki. 2000. "Companies Continue to Unwind Cross-Shareholdings—The Fiscal 1999 Cross-Shareholding Survey." *NLI Research* (October): 11–20.

Inoue, Yasuo. 2000. "Beyond the East Asia Economic Crisis." In *Japanese Capitalism in Crisis,* edited by Robert Boyer and Toshio Yamada. London: Routledge.

International Monetary Fund (IMF). 1996. *International Financial Statistics Yearbook, 1996.* Washington, D.C.: International Monetary Fund.

Ireland, Timothy P. 1981. *Creating the Entangling Alliance: The Origins of the North Atlantic Treaty Organization.* Westport: Greenwood Press.

Ito, Takatoshi. 1992. *The Japanese Economy.* Cambridge, Mass.: MIT Press.

Iversen, Torben, and Anne Wren. 1998. "Equality, Employment, and Budgetary Restraint: The Trilemma of the Service Economy." *World Politics* 50(4): 507–46.

Jackson, Gregory. 2000. "Comparative Corporate Governance: Sociological Perspectives." In *The Political Economy of the Company,* edited by Andrew Gamble, Gavin Kelly, and John Parkinson, 265–87. Oxford: Hart Publishers.

——. 2001. "The Origins of Nonliberal Corporate Governance in Germany and Japan." In *The Origins of Nonliberal Capitalism: Germany and Japan in Comparison,* edited by Wolfgang Streeck and Kozo Yamamura, 121–70. Ithaca: Cornell University Press.

——. 2002a. Organizing the Firm: Corporate Governance in Germany and Japan, 1870–2000. Ph.D. diss., Columbia University, New York.

——. 2002b. Varieties of Capitalism: A Review. Discussion paper, Max-Planck-Institut für Gesellschaftsforschung, Köln.

Jackson, Gregory, and Sigurt Vitols. 1998. Pension Regimes and Financial Systems: Between Social Security, Market Liquidity and Corporate Governance. Paper prepared for the conference on Varieties of Welfare Capitalism in Europe, North America and Japan, Max-Planck-Institut für Gesellschaftsforschung, 11–13 June, Köln.

——. 2001. "Between Financial Commitment, Market Liquidity and Corporate Governance: Occupational Pensions in Britain, Germany, Japan and the USA." In *Comparing Welfare Capitalism: Social Policy and Political Economy in Europe, Japan, and the USA,* edited by Bernhard Ebbinghaus and Philip Manow, 171–89. London: Routledge.

Jacobi, Otto, Berndt Keller, and Walther Müller-Jentsch. 1998. "Germany: Facing New Challenges." In *Changing Industrial Relations in Europe,* 2nd ed., edited by Anthony Ferner and Richard Hyman, 190–238. Oxford: Basil Blackwell.

Jacobs, Michael. 1991. *Short-Term America: The Causes and Cures of Our Business Myopia.* Boston: Harvard Business School Press.

Japan Economic Research Center. 1998. *Heisoku yarubu IT sangyō.* Tokyo: Nihon Keizai Shinbun.

Japan Institute of Labour. 1995. "Rengo Releases Survey on Employment Check." *Japan Labor Bulletin* 34(7).

Japanisch-Deutsches Zentrum Berlin. 1992. *Symposium: Die deutsch-japanischen Beziehungen in den 30er und 40er Jahren.* Berlin: Japanisch-Deutsches Zentrum Berlin.

Jervis, Robert. 1978. "Cooperation under the Security Dilemma." *World Politics* 30(2): 167–214.

Johnson, Chalmers. 1982. *MITI and the Japanese Miracle: The Growth of Industrial Policy, 1925–1975.* Stanford: Stanford University Press.

Jonas, Manfred. 1984. *The United States and Germany: A Diplomatic History.* Ithaca: Cornell University Press.

Jones, Christopher D. 1984. "National Armies and National Sovereignty." In *The Warsaw Pact: Alliance in Transition?* edited by David Holloway and Jane M. O. Sharp, 91–102. Ithaca: Cornell University Press.

Jürgens, Ulrich. 1997. "Rolling Back Cycle Times: The Renaissance of the Classic Assembly Line in Final Assembly." In *Transforming Automobile Assembly: Experience in Automation and Work Organisation*, edited by Koichi Shimokawa, Ulrich Jürgens, and Takahiro Fujimoto, 255–73. Berlin: Springer-Verlag.

——. 1998. "Implanting Change: The Role of 'Indigenous Transplants' in Transforming the German Productive Model." In *Between Imitation and Innovation: The Transfer and Hybridization of Productive Models in the International Automobile Industry*, edited by Robert Boyer, Elsie Charron, Ulrich Jürgens, and Steven Tolliday, 319–41. Oxford: Oxford University Press.

Jürgens, Ulrich, and Inge Lippert. 1997. "Schnittstellen des deutschen Produktionsregimes: Innovationshemmnisse im Produktentstehungsprozeß." In *Ökonomische Leistungsfähigkeit und institutionelle Innovation: Das deutsche Produktions- und Politikregime im globalen Wettbewerb* (WZB Jahrbuch 1997), edited by Frieder Naschold, David Soskice, Bob Hancké, and Ulrich Jürgens, 65–94. Berlin: edition sigma.

Kagan, Robert. 1991. "Adversarial Legalism and American Government." *Journal of Policy Analysis and Management* 10: 369–406.

Kahler, Miles. 1997. Does Legalization Have Regional Limits? The Asia-Pacific Case. Paper presented at the Annual Meeting of the American Political Science Association, 28 August, Washington, D.C.

Kaiser, Karl. 1970. "Das internationale System der Gegenwart als Faktor der Beeinträchtigung demokratischer Aussenpolitik." *Politische Vierteljahresschrift* (Sonderheft 1/1969): 340–58.

——. 1971. "Transnational Relations as a Threat to the Democratic Process." *International Organization* 25(3): 706–20.

——. 1991. "Germany's Unification." *Foreign Affairs* 70(1): 179–205.

Kaldor, Nicholas. 1966. *Causes of the Slow Rate of Growth in the United Kingdom.* Cambridge, Mass.: Cambridge University Press.

Kapstein, Ethan. 1996. "Workers and the World Economy." *Foreign Affairs* 75(3): 16–37.

"Kartellamt: WTO soll Fusionen kontrollen." 1999. *Handelsblatt,* 5 January, p. 3.

Kato, Junko, and Michael Laver. 1998. "Party Policy and Cabinet Portfolios in Japan, 1996." *Party Politics* 4(2): 253–60.

Kato, Kozo. 1998. Open Regionalism and Japan's Systemic Vulnerability. Unpublished paper.

Kato, Tetsuro, and Rob Steven, eds. 1993. *Is Japanese Management Post-Fordism?* Tokyo: Mado Sha.

Katz, Harry, and Owen Darbishire. 1999. *Converging Divergences.* Ithaca: Cornell University Press.

Katz, Richard. 1998. *Japan, the System That Soured: The Rise and Fall of the Japanese Economic Miracle.* Armonk, N.Y.: M. E. Sharpe.

Katzenstein, Peter J., ed. 1978. *Between Power and Plenty: Foreign Economic Policies of Advanced Industrial States.* Madison: University of Wisconsin Press.

——. 1985. *Small States in World Markets: Industrial Policy in Europe.* Ithaca: Cornell University Press.

——. 1987. *Policy and Politics in West Germany: The Growth of a Semisovereign State.* Philadelphia: Temple University Press.

———. 1993a. "Regions in Competition: Comparative Advantages of America, Europe, and Asia." In *America and Europe in an Era of Change*, edited by Helga Haftendorn and Christian Tuschoff, 105–26. Boulder: Westview Press.

———. 1993b. "A World of Regions: America, Europe and Asia." In *Beginnings of the Soviet-German and the U.S.-Japanese Wars and 50 Years After*, edited by Sophia University Institute of American and Canadian Studies, 63–84. Tokyo: Sophia University Institute for the Culture of German-Speaking Areas.

———. 1996. *Cultural Norms and National Security: Police and Military in Postwar Japan.* Ithaca: Cornell University Press.

———. 1997a. "Introduction: Asian Regionalism in Comparative Perspective." In *Network Power: Japan and Asia*, edited by Peter J. Katzenstein and Takashi Shiraishi, 1–46. Ithaca: Cornell University Press.

———. ed. 1997b. *Tamed Power: Germany in Europe.* Ithaca: Cornell University Press.

———. 1997c. "United Germany in an Integrating Europe." In *Tamed Power: Germany in Europe*, edited by Peter Katzenstein, 1–48. Ithaca: Cornell University Press.

Katzenstein, Peter J., and Takashi Shiraishi. 1997a. "Conclusion: Regions in World Politics, Japan and Asia—Germany in Europe." In *Network Power: Japan and Asia*, edited by Peter J. Katzenstein and Takashi Shiraishi, 341–81. Ithaca: Cornell University Press.

———. eds. 1997b. *Network Power: Japan and Asia.* Ithaca: Cornell University Press.

Katzenstein, Peter J., and Yutaka Tsujinaka. 1995. "'Bullying,' 'Buying,' and 'Binding': US-Japanese Transnational Relations and Domestic Structures." In *Bringing Transnational Relations Back In: Non-State Actors, Domestic Structures and International Institutions*, edited by Thomas Risse-Kappen, 79–111. New York: Cambridge University Press.

Keck, Otto. 1993. "The National System for Technical Innovation in Germany." In *National Innovation Systems: A Comparative Analysis*, edited by Richard Nelson, 115–57. New York: Oxford University Press.

Keehn, E. B. 1998. "The Myth of Regulatory Independence in Japan." In *Unlocking the Bureaucrats' Kingdom*, edited by Frank Gibney, 204–19. Washington, D.C.: Brookings Institution.

Keidanren. 2001. "A Proposal for Better Corporate Accounting." 27 March. Available at www.keidanren.or.jp/english/policy/2001/013.html; INTERNET.

Keizai Dōyūkai. 1996. *Kigyo hakusho 12-kai: Nihon kigyo no keiei-kozo kaikaku.* Tokyo: Keizai Dōyūkai.

———. 1998. *Kigyo hakusho 13-kai: Shihon-koritsu-jushi keiei.* Tokyo: Keizai Dōyūkai.

Keizai Senryaku Kaigi. 1998. "Nihon keizai saisei e no senryaku." 23 December. Available at www.kantei.go.jp/jp/senryaku/981224interim.html; INTERNET.

Kelleher, Catherine M. 1990. "Fundamentals of German Security: The Creation of the Bundeswehr—Continuity and Change." In *The Bundeswehr and Western Security*, edited by Stephen F. Szabo, 13–30. New York: St. Martin's Press.

Kenney, Martin, and Richard Florida. 1988. "Beyond Mass Production: Production and the Labor Process in Japan." *Politics and Society* 16(1): 121–58.

———. 1993. *Beyond Mass Production: The Japanese System and Its Transfer to the U.S.* New York: Oxford University Press.

Keohane, Robert O., and Joseph S. Nye. 1977. *Power and Interdependence: World Politics in Transition.* Boston: Little Brown.

Kern, Horst, and Michael Schumann. 1989. "New Concepts of Production in West German Plants." In *Industry and Politics in West Germany: Toward the Third Republic*, edited by Peter J. Katzenstein, 87–110. Ithaca: Cornell University Press.

King, Desmond, and Stewart Wood. 1999. "The Political Economy of Neoliberalism: Britain and the United States in the 1980s." In *Continuity and Change in Contemporary*

Capitalism, edited by Herbert Kitschelt, Peter Lange, Gary Marks, and John D. Stephens, eds., 371–97. Cambridge, UK: Cambridge University Press.

Kitschelt, Herbert. 1991. "Industrial Governance Structures, Innovation Strategies, and the Case of Japan." *International Organization* 45(4): 453–93.

———. 1994. *The Transformation of European Social Democracy*. Cambridge, UK: Cambridge University Press.

———. 1999. "European Social Democracy between Political Economy and Electoral Competition." In *Continuity and Change in Contemporary Capitalism*, edited by Herbert Kitschelt, Peter Lange, Gary Marks, and John D. Stephens, 317–45. Cambridge, UK: Cambridge University Press.

Kitschelt, Herbert, Peter Lange, Gary Marks, and John D. Stephens, eds. 1999. *Continuity and Change in Contemporary Capitalism*. Cambridge, UK: Cambridge University Press.

Kitschelt, Herbert, Zdenka Mansfeldova, Radek Markowski, and Gabor Toka. 1999. *Post-Communist Party Systems*. Cambridge, UK: Cambridge University Press.

Kitschelt, Herbert, and Anthony J. McGann. 1995. *The Radical Right in Western Europe*. Ann Arbor: University of Michigan Press.

Kjellberg, Anders. 1998. "Sweden: Restoring the Model?" In *Changing Industrial Relations in Europe*, edited by Anthony Ferner and Richard Hyman, 74–117. Oxford: Basil Blackwell.

Klammer, Ute, and Gabriele Rolf. 1998. "Auf dem Weg zu einer gerechteren Alterssicherung? Rentenreformpolitik in Deutschland und Italien im Vergleich." *Zeitschrift für Sozialreform* 44(11–12): 308–38.

Knapp, Manfred. 1975. "Zum Stand der Forschung über die deutsch-amerikanischen Nachkriegsbeziehungen." In *Die deutsch-amerikanischen Beziehungen nach 1945*, edited by Manfred Knapp, 7–85. Frankfurt am Main: Campus.

Knight, Jack. 1992. *Institutions and Social Conflict*. Cambridge, UK: Cambridge University Press.

Knoke, David, Franz U. Pappi, Jeffrey Broadbent, and Yutaka Tsujinaka. 1996. *Comparing Policy Networks: Labor Politics in the U.S., Germany, and Japan*. New York: Cambridge University Press.

Kodama, Fumio. 1995. *Emerging Patterns of Innovation: Source of Japan's Technological Edge*. Boston: Harvard Business School Press.

Kohaut, Susanne, and Lutz Bellmann. 1997. "Betriebliche Determinanten der Tarifbindung: Eine empirische Analyse auf der Basis des IAB-Betriebspanels 1995." *Industrielle Beziehungen* 4(4): 317–34.

Kohaut, Susanne, and Claus Schnabel. 1998. "Flächentarifvertrag im Westen sehr viel weiter verbreitet als im Osten: Ergebnisse aus dem IAB-Betriebspanel." *IAB Kurzbericht* 19 (23 December). Available at *EIROnline*, www.eiro.eurofound.ie/1999/02/features/DE9902196F.html; INTERNET.

Kohno, Masaru. 1997. "Electoral Origins of Japanese Socialists' Stagnation." *Comparative Political Studies* 30(1): 55–77.

Koike, Kazuo. 1987. "Human Resources Development and Labor-Management Relations." In *The Political Economy of Japan*. Vol. 1, *The Domestic Transformation*, edited by Kozo Yamamura and Yasukichi Yasuba, 289–330. Stanford: Stanford University Press.

———. 1993. *Shigoto no keizaigaku*. Tokyo: Tōyō Keizai Shinpōsha.

Koike, Kazuo, and Takenori Inoki. 1990. *Skill Formation in Japan and South East Asia*. Tokyo: University of Tokyo Press.

"Kontrolle von internationalen Fusionen gefordert." *Frankfurter Allgemeine*, 3 January, p. 33.

Kōsaki, Rin'ichi. 2000. "Kabuka chōjūshi no keiei shifuto de 'shain o mamoru koto wa furukusai': Kore de yoinoka?" *Ekonomisuto*, 14 March, pp. 72–73.

Kotthoff, Hermann. 1998. "Mitbestimmung in Zeiten interessenpolitischer Rückschritte: Be-triebsräte zwischen Beteiligungsofferten und 'gnadenlosem Kostensenkungsdiktat.' " *Industrielle Beziehungen* 5: 76–100.

Koyama, Osamu. 1994. "La politique scientifique et technologique et la politique de l'enseignement supérieur au Japon." *IRIG: La Revue de l'Institut de Recherches Industrielles et de Gestion* 13(3): 27–69.

Kozmetsky, George, and Piyu Yue. 1997. *Global Economic Competition*. Boston: Kluwer Academic Publishers.

Kramer, Alan. 1991. *The West German Economy*. New York: Berg.

Krasner, Stephen D. 1999. *Sovereignty: Organized Hypocrisy*. Princeton: Princeton University Press.

Krier, Dan. 2001. Practices Used to Manage Share Prices of Large American Firms in the Late 20th Century. Paper presented at the Annual Meeting of the Society for the Advancement of Socio-Economics, 28 June–1 July, Amsterdam.

Kristof, Nicholas D. 1998. "Japan Sees Itself as a Scapegoat of Washington in the Asia Crisis." *New York Times*, 21 September, pp. A1, A6.

Kudo, Akira. 1998. *Japanese-German Business Relations: Cooperation and Rivalry in the Inter-War Period*. London: Routledge.

Kuhlmann, Martin, and Michael Schumann. 1997. "Patterns of Work Organisation in the German Automobile Industry." In *Transforming Automobile Assembly: Experience in Automation and Work Organisation*, edited by Koichi Shimokawa, Ulrich Jürgens, and Takahiro Fujimoto, 289–304. Berlin: Springer-Verlag.

Kuhn, Thomas S. 1970. *The Structure of Scientific Revolutions*, 2nd ed. Chicago: University of Chicago Press.

Kumazawa, Makoto. 1996. *Portraits of the Japanese Workplace: Labor Movements, Workers, and Managers*. Boulder: Westview Press.

Kume, Ikuo. 1998. *Disparaged Success: Labor Politics in Postwar Japan*. Ithaca: Cornell University Press.

Kumon, Shumpei, and Henry Rosovsky, eds. 1992. *The Political Economy of Japan*. Vol. 3, *Cultural and Social Dynamics*. Stanford: Stanford University Press.

Kurdelbusch, Antje. 2001. The Rise of Variable Pay in Germany: Evidence and Explanations. Paper presented at the Annual Meeting of the Society for the Advancement of Socio-Economics, 28 June–1 July, Amsterdam.

Kuroki, Fumiaki. 2001. "The Present Status of Unwinding Cross-Shareholding: The Fiscal 2000 Survey of Cross-Shareholding." *NLI Research* 157: 24–36.

Kurth, James R. 1989. "The Pacific Basin versus the Atlantic Alliance: Two Paradigms of International Relations." *Annals of the American Academy of Political Science* 505 (September): 34–45.

Kurzer, Paulette. 1993. *Business and Banking*. Ithaca: Cornell University Press.

Kusano, Atsushi. 1992. *Amerika gikai to Nichibei kankei*. Tokyo: Chūōkōronsha.

Kuznets, Simon. 1965. *Modern Economic Growth*. New Haven: Yale University Press.

LaFeber, Walter. 1997. *The Clash: A History of U.S.-Japan Relations*. New York: W. W. Norton.

Lake, David. 1988. *Power, Protection, and Free Trade: International Sources of U.S. Commercial Strategy, 1887–1939*. Ithaca: Cornell University Press.

Lanciano, Caroline, Hiroatsu Nohara, and Eric Verdier. 1998. The Societal Analysis of Engineers: Socialisation, Hierarchy and Knowledge Creation: Comparison between France and Japan. Paper presented at the Tenth International Conference of the Society for Advanced of Socio-Economics, 13–16 July, Vienna.

Landes, David. 1999. *The Wealth and Poverty of Nations: Why Some Are So Rich and Some So Poor*. New York: W. W. Norton.

Laver, Michael, and Norman Schofield. 1990. *Multiparty Government*. Oxford: Oxford University Press.

Lee, Chung Hee. 1988. *Foreign Lobbying in American Politics*. Seoul: Seoul National University.

Lehmkuhl, Ursula. 1999. *Pax Anglo-Americana: Machtstrukturelle Grundlagen anglo-amerikanischer Fernostpolitik in den 1950er Jahren*. Munich: Oldenbourg.

Leibenstein, Harvey. 1976. *Beyond Economic Man*. Cambridge, Mass.: Harvard University Press.

Leminksy, Gerhard. 1996. *Mitbestimmen—Wie wir in Zukunft arbeiten und leben durch Mitgestaltung und Management des Wandels*. Düsseldorf: Hans Böckler Stiftung.

Lenoir, Timothy. 1998. "Revolution from Above: The Role of the State in Creating the German Research System, 1810–1910." *American Economic Review* 88(2): 22–27.

Levy, Jonah. 1999. *Tocqueville's Revenge: State, Society, and Economy in Contemporary France*. Cambridge, Mass.: Harvard University Press.

Lewis, Melissa. 1997. "Certified Training Breeds Better Workers: The National Institute of Metalworking Skills' Certification Program Is Making a Name for Itself in Both Industry and Education." *American Machinist* 141(12): 68–72.

Liberman, Peter. 1998. Do Germany and Japan Rely Too Much on the United States for Their Own Good? Unpublished paper.

Liker, Jeffrey K., W. Mark Fruin, and Paul S. Adler. 1999. *Remade in America: Transplanting and Transforming Japanese Management Systems*. New York: Oxford University Press.

Lincoln, Edward J. 1993. *Japan's New Global Role*. Washington, D.C.: Brookings Institution.

Linnenkamp, Hilmar. 1992. "The Security Policy of the New Germany." In *The New Germany and the New Europe*, edited by Paul B. Stares, 93–125. Washington, D.C.: Brookings Institution.

Lundvall, Bengt. 1988. "Innovation as an Interactive Process: From User-Producer Interaction to National Systems of Innovation." In *Technical Change and Economic Theory: The Global Process of Development*, edited by Giovanni Dosi, Christopher Freeman, Gerard Silverberg, and Luc Soete, 361–83. London: Frances Pinter.

——, ed. 1992. *National Systems of Innovation: Towards a Theory of Innovation and Interactive Learning*. London: Pinter Publishers.

Lütz, Susanne. 1996. The Revival of the Nation-State? Stock Exchange Regulation in an Era of Internationalized Financial Markets. Discussion paper 96/9, Max-Planck-Institut für Gesellschaftsforschung, Köln.

——. 2000. From Managed to Market Capitalism? German Finance in Transition. Discussion paper 00/2, Max-Planck-Institut für Gesellschaftsforschung, Köln.

Mackintosh, Malcolm. 1984. "The Warsaw Treaty Organization: A History." In *The Warsaw Pact: Alliance in Transition?* edited by David Holloway and Jane M. O. Sharp, 41–58. Ithaca: Cornell University Press.

Maddison, Angus. 1964. *Economic Growth in the West*. New York: Twentieth Century Fund.

Magaloni, Beatriz. 1997. The Dynamics of Dominant Party Decline: The Mexican Transition to Multipartism. Ph.D. diss., Duke University, Durham, N.C.

Mahnkopf, Birgit. 1991. "Vorwärts in die Vergangenheit? Pessimistische Spekulationen über die Zukunft der Gewerkschaften in der neuen Bundesrepublik." In *Wirtschaftspolitische Konsequenzen der deutschen Vereinigung*, edited by Andreas Westphal. Frankfurt am Main: Campus.

Maier, Charles S. 1978. "The Politics of Productivity: Foundations of American International Economic Policy after World War II." In *Between Power and Plenty: Foreign Economic Policies of Advanced Industrial States*, edited by Peter J. Katzenstein, 23–50. Madison: University of Wisconsin Press.

Mair, Peter, and Tomokazu Sakano. 1998. "Japanese Political Realignment in Perspective: Change or Restoration?" *Party Politics* 4(2): 177–202.

Manow, Philip. 1999. Comparative Institutional Advantages of Welfare State Regimes and New Coalitions in Welfare State Reforms. Unpublished paper.

——. 2001a. Globalization, Corporate Finance, and Coordinated Capitalism: Pension Finance in Germany and Japan. Working paper 01/5, Max-Planck-Institut für Gesellschaftsforschung, Köln.

——. 2001b. "Welfare State Building and Coordinated Capitalism in Japan and Germany." In *The Origins of Nonliberal Capitalism: Germany and Japan in Comparison*, edited by Wolfgang Streeck and Kozo Yamamura, 94–120. Ithaca: Cornell University Press.

Manow, Philip, and Eric Seils. 1999. Adjusting Badly: The German Welfare State, Structural Change, and the Open Economy. Unpublished paper.

Markovits, Andrei S. 1986. *The Politics of West German Trade Unions*. Cambridge, UK: Cambridge University Press.

Marsh, David. 1996. "Reinventing German Capitalism." *German Politics* 5(December): 402–3.

Marston, Richard C. 1991. "Price Behavior in Japanese and U.S. Manufacturing." In *Trade with Japan: Has the Door Opened Wider?* edited by Paul Krugman, 121–41. Chicago: University of Chicago Press.

Martin, Bernd, ed. 1987. *Japan's Weg in die Moderne: Ein Sonderweg nach deutschem Vorbild?* Frankfurt am Main: Campus.

——. 1995. *Japan and Germany in the Modern World*. Providence: Berghahn.

Maull, Hans. 1990–91. "Germany and Japan: The New Civilian Powers." *Foreign Affairs* 69(1): 91–106.

Maurice, Marc, Francois Sellier, and Jean-Jacques Silvestre. 1986. *The Social Foundations of Industrial Power: A Comparison of France and Germany*. Cambridge, Mass.: MIT Press.

McGann, Anthony J. 1999. The Modal Voter Result: Preference Distributions, Intra-Party Competition and Political Dominance. Ph.D. diss., Duke University, Durham, N.C.

McKean, Margaret, and Ethan Scheiner. 1996. Can Japanese Voters Ever Throw the Rascals Out? Electoral Reform Enhances Permanent Employment for Politicians. Unpublished paper.

Mearsheimer, John. 1990. "Back to the Future: Instability in Europe after the Cold War." *International Security* 15(1): 5–56.

Merton, Robert K. 1963. *Social Theory and Social Structure*. Glencoe: Free Press.

Mikuni, Akio. 1998. Why Japan Can't Reform Its Economy. Working paper 44/1998, Japan Policy Research Institute, Cardiff, Calif.

Milgrom, Paul R., and John M. Roberts. 1994. "Complementarities and Systems: Understanding Japanese Economic Organisation." *Estudios Economicos* 9: 3–42.

Milner, Helen V. 1997. *Interests, Institutions, and Information: Domestic Politics and International Relations*. Princeton: Princeton University Press.

Milner, Helen V., and Robert O. Keohane. 1996. "Internationalization and Domestic Politics: An Introduction." In *Internationalization and Domestic Politics*, edited by Robert O. Keohane and Helen V. Milner, 3–24. Cambridge, UK: Cambridge University Press.

Ministry of Economy, Trade and Industry [METI]. 2001. "A Proposal for Commercial Code Reform for Business Management in the 21st Century." Background material for JETRO conference on Japan's Changing Foreign Direct Investment and Corporate Environment, 25 April, New York.

Ministry of International Trade and Industry. 1998. *White Paper on International Trade, 1998*. Tokyo: Ministry of International Trade and Industry.

Ministry of Labor. 1995. *Chingin rōdō jikan seidotō sōgō chōsa*. Tokyo: Ministry of Labor.

——. 1999. *White Paper on Labor 1999*. Tokyo: Japan Institute of Labor.

Mitbestimmung. 1996. 42(1): 34–35.

Miyamoto, Mitsuharu. 1998. *Nihon no koyō o dō mamoru ka*. Tokyo: PHP.

Monden, Yasuhiro. 1983. *Toyota Production System: Practical Approach to Production Management*. Atlanta: Industrial Engineering and Management Press.

Montgomery, John. 1957. *Forced to Be Free: The Artificial Revolution in Germany and Japan*. Chicago: University of Chicago Press.

Moravcsik, Andrew. 1998. *The Choice for Europe: Social Purpose and State Power from Messina to Maastrict*. Ithaca: Cornell University Press.

Morishima, Motohiro. 1995. "Embedding HRM in a Social Context." *British Journal of Industrial Relations* 33(December): 617–40.

Morse, Ronald A. 1989. "Japanese Lobbynomics: Shaping America's Political Agenda." *Venture Japan* 1(4): 29–35.

Moulton, Harold G. 1944. *The Control of Germany and Japan*. Washington, D.C.: Brookings Institution.

Mowery, David C., and Nathan Rosenberg. 1998. *Paths of Innovation: Technological Change in 20th-Century America*. Cambridge, UK: Cambridge University Press.

Murakami, Yasusuke. 1982. "The Age of New Middle Mass Politics: The Case of Japan." *Journal of Japanese Studies* 8: 29–72.

——. 1983. "Henkansuru sangyō bunmei to nijūisseiki e no tenbō." *Ekonomisuto*, 5 April.

——. 1986. "Technology in Transition: Two Perspectives on Industrial Policy." In *Japan's High Technology Industries*, edited by Hugh Patrick, 211–41. Seattle: University of Washington Press.

——. 1996. *An Anticlassical Political-Economic Analysis: A Vision for the Next Century*. Stanford: Stanford University Press.

Nagel, Bernhard, Birgit Tiess, Stefan Rüb, and Andreas Beschorner. 1996. *Information und Mitbestimmung im internationalen Konzern*. Baden-Baden: Nomos.

Nakamura, Takafusa. 1998. *A History of Showa Japan, 1926–1989*. Tokyo: University of Tokyo Press.

National Institute for Science, Technology and Economic Policy (NISTEP). 1990. *Choice of University Applicants among Fields of Study*. Report no. 12. Tokyo: NISTEP.

——. 1997. *State of Japan's Technology Exports*. Report no. 53. Tokyo: NISTEP.

——. 1998. *A Collection Celebrating the 10th Anniversary of NISTEP*. Tokyo: NISTEP.

NATO Review. 1996. no. 1: D14.

Nelson, Richard. 1988. "Institutions Supporting Technical Change in the United States." In *Technical Change and Economic Theory*, edited by Giovanni Dosi, Christopher Freeman, Richard Nelson, Gerald Silverberg, and Luc Soete, 312–29. London: Pinter Publishers.

——, ed. 1993. *National Innovation Systems: A Comparative Analysis*. Oxford: Oxford University Press.

Nelson, Richard, and Nathan Rosenberg. 1993. "Technical Innovation and National System." In *National Innovation Systems: A Comparative Analysis*, edited by Richard Nelson, 3–21. Oxford: Oxford University Press.

New York Stock Exchange (NYSE). 2001a. Available at www.nyse.com/listed/listed.html; INTERNET.

——. 2001b. *Share Ownership 2000*. New York: NYSE.

Nikkeiren. 1998. "Rōdōryoku ryūdoka ni taiōsuru jinji rōmukanri no arikata." *Kōyō Tokubetsu Iinkai hōkokusho*, 25 November.

———. 1999. *The Current Labor Economy in Japan.* Tokyo: Japan Federation of Employer Associations.

Nikkeiren Kokusai Tokubetsu Iinkai. 1998. *Nihon-kigyo no kōporōto gabanansu kaikaku no hoko: Shihon-shijo kara mo rōdō shijo kara mo sentaku sareru kigyo o mezashite.* Tokyo: Nikkeiren.

Nishioka, Koichi, and Fumihiro Nagaoka. 1998. *Fukkatsu Nihon keizai.* Tokyo: Nikkei Shinbunsha.

Noguchi, Yukio. 1995. "The Role of the Fiscal Investment and Loan Program in Postwar Japanese Economic Growth." In *The Japanese Civil Service and Economic Development: Catalysts of Development,* edited by Hyung-Ki Kim, Michio Muramatsu, T. J. Pempel, and Kozo Yamamura, 261–87. Oxford: Clarendon Press.

Nölting, Andreas. 2000. *Die Supermacht Börse—Wie Fondsmanager unsere Welt verändern.* Reinbeck bei Hamburg: Rohwolt.

Nomura, Masami, and Ulrich Jürgens. 1995. *Binnenstrukturen des japanischen Produktivitätserfolgs: Arbeitsbeziehungen und Leistungsregulierung in zwei japanischen Automobilunternehmen.* Berlin: edition sigma.

Nonaka, Ikujiro. 1990. "Redundant, Overlapping Organization: A Japanese Approach to Managing the Innovation Process." *California Management Review* 32(3): 27–38.

———. 1994. "Product Development and Innovation." In *Business Enterprise in Japan,* edited by Ken'ichi Imai and Ryutaro Komiya, 209–24. Cambridge, Mass.: MIT Press.

North, Douglass C. 1990. *Institutions, Institutional Change and Economic Performance.* Cambridge, UK: Cambridge University Press.

Odagiri, Hiroyuki. 1992. *Growth through Competition, Competition through Growth: Strategic Management and the Economy in Japan.* Oxford: Clarendon Press.

Odagiri, Hiroyuki, and Akira Goto. 1993. "The Japanese System of Innovation: Past, Present, and Future." In *National Innovation Systems: A Comparative Analysis,* edited by Richard Nelson, 76–114. Oxford: Oxford University Press.

O'Driscoll, Gerald, Kim Holmes, and Melanie Kirkpatrick. 1999. *2000 Index of Economic Freedom.* New York: Heritage Foundation/Wall Street Journal.

Ohmae, Kenichi. 1995. *The End of the Nation State: The Rise of Regional Economies.* New York: Free Press.

Ohno, Taiichi. 1988. *Workplace Management.* Cambridge, Mass: Productivity Press.

Okada, Yoshitaka. 1998. Cooperative Learning and Japan's Techno-Governance Structure: Exploratory Case Studies. Paper presented at the Tenth International Conference of the Society for Advanced of Socio-Economics, 13-16 July, Vienna.

Okazaki, Tetsuji, and Masahiro Okuno-Fujiwara, eds. 1999. *The Japanese Economic System and Its Historical Origins.* Oxford: Oxford University Press.

Okubo, Yoshiko. 1996. *La Science Japonaise en Question.* Paris: Economica.

Okumura, Kōchi. 1998. "Tahatsusuru chōdaigata kokusai M&A: Beikoku shihon obiyakasu Ōshuzei no kōgekiteki bōgyo." *Ekonomisuto*, 29 December 1998–5 January 1999, pp. 40–45.

———. 2001. "Ōbei de futtōshita M&A būmu ga Nihon ni honkaku jōriku." *Ekonomisuto,* 26 June, pp. 39–41.

Oliver, Nick, Daniel T. Jones, and Peter Roberts. 1994. *Worldwide Manufacturing Competitiveness Study: The Second Lean Enterprise Benchmarking Report.* London: Andersen Consulting.

O'Loughlin, John, and Luc Anselin. 1996. "Geo-Economic Competition and Trade Bloc Formation: United States, German, and Japanese Exports, 1968–92." *Economic Geography* 72(2): 131–60.

Organization for Economic Cooperation and Development (OECD). 1989. *Foreign Trade by Commodities.* Paris: OECD.

——. 1991. *Technology and Productivity: The Challenge for Economic Policy.* Paris: OECD.

——. 1995a. *Employment Outlook.* Paris: OECD.

——. 1995b. *Foreign Trade by Commodities.* Paris: OECD.

——. 1996. *OECD Employment Outlook.* Paris: OECD.

——. 1997a. An Empirical Comparison of National Innovation Systems: Various Approaches and Early Findings. DSTI/STP/TIP(97)13, 8–9 December, Paris. Mimeographed.

——. 1997b. *Information Technology Outlook.* Paris: OECD.

——. 1997c. National Innovation Systems: Background Report. DSTI/STP/TIP(97)2, Paris. Mimeographed.

——. 1997d. *Policy Evaluation in Innovation and Technology: Towards Best Practices.* Paris: OECD.

——. 1997e. *The Soft-ware Sector: A Statistical Profile for Selected OECD Countries.* Paris: OECD.

——. 1998. Technology, Productivity and Job Creation—Best Policy Practices. DSTI/IND/STP/ICCP(98)/PART2, March, Paris. Mimeographed.

——. 1999a. *Economic Outlook.* Paris: OECD.

——. 1999b. *The Knowledge Based Economy: A Set of Facts and Figures.* Paris: OECD.

——. 1999c. "Training of Adult Workers in OECD Countries: Measurement and Analysis." In *Employment Outlook*, 134–75. Paris: OECD.

Orwell, George. 1949. *Nineteen Eighty-Four: A Novel.* London: Secker and Warburg.

Pape, Wolfgang. 1994. "Elements of Integration in Europe and Asia." In *Regional Strategies in East Asia: A Comparative Perspective*, edited by François Gipouloux, 221–26. Tokyo: Maison Franco-Japonaise.

Parker, Michael, and Jane Slaughter. 1988. *Choosing Sides: Unions and the Team Concept.* Boston: South End Press.

Parkinson, John, and Gavin Kelly. 2001. "The Conceptual Foundations of the Firm." In *The Political Economy of the Company*, edited by John Parkinson, Andrew Gamble, and Gavin Kelly, 113–40. Oxford: Hart Publishing.

Paul, T. V. 1996. Great Powers without Nuclear Weapons? Explaining the Non-Nuclear Policies of Germany and Japan. Paper presented at the Annual Meeting of the American Political Science Association, 29 August–1 September, San Francisco.

Pauly, Louis W., and Simon Reich. 1997. "National Structures and Multinational Corporate Behavior: Enduring Differences in the Age of Globalization." *International Organization* 51(1): 1–30.

Pempel, Aaron. 1991. From the Bottom Up: Understanding Business-Government Relations from a Corporate Perspective. Undergraduate honors thesis, Cornell University.

Pempel, T. J. 1982. *Policy and Politics in Japan: Creative Conservatism.* Philadelphia: Temple University Press.

——. 1990. "Exclusionary Democracies: The Postauthoritarian Experience." In *Comparative Theory and Political Experience: Mario Einaudi and the Liberal Tradition*, edited by Peter J. Katzenstein, Theodore Lowi, and Sidney Tarrow, 97–118. Ithaca: Cornell University Press.

——. 1997. Labor Exclusion and Privatized Welfare: Two Keys to Asian Capitalist Development. Paper presented at the Conference on Comparative Capitalism, 23–25 May, Durham, N.C.

——. 1998. *Regime Shift: Comparative Dynamics of the Japanese Political Economy.* Ithaca: Cornell University Press.

———. 1999. "Structural Gaiatsu: International Finance and Political Change in Japan." *Comparative Political Studies* 32(8): 907–32.

Pempel, T. J., and Keiichi Tsunekawa. 1979. "Corporatism without Labor?" In *Trends toward Corporatist Intermediation*, edited by Philippe C. Schmitter and Gerhard Lehmbruch, 231–70. Beverly Hills: Sage.

Pettersen, Per Arnt. 1995. "The Welfare State: The Security Dimension." In *The Scope of Government*, edited by Ole Borre, 198–233. Oxford: Oxford University Press.

Pierson, Paul. 1996. "The New Politics of the Welfare State." *World Politics* 48(2): 143–79.

———. 2000. "Increasing Returns, Path Dependence, and the Study of Politics." *American Political Science Review* 94(2): 251–67.

Pierson, Paul, and Miriam Smith. 1993. "Bourgeois Revolutions? The Policy Consequences of Resurgent Conservatism." *Comparative Political Studies* 25(4): 487–520.

Pieterse, Jan Nederveen. 1994. "Globalization as Hybridization." *International Sociology* 9: 161–84.

Pil, Frits K., and Saul Rubinstein. 1998. "Saturn: A Different Kind of Company?" *In Between Imitation and Innovation: The Transfer and Hybridization of Productive Models in the International Automobile Industry*, edited by Robert Boyer, Elsie Charron, Ulrich Jürgens, and Steven Tolliday, 361–73. Oxford: Oxford University Press.

Piore, Michael J., and Charles F. Sabel. 1984. *The Second Industrial Divide: Possibilities for Prosperity.* New York: Basic Books.

Pohl, Manfred. 1973. *Wiederaufbau: Kunst und Technik der Finanzierung 1947–1953. Die ersten Jahre der Kreditanstalt für Wiederaufbau.* Frankfurt: Fritz Knapp.

Polanyi, Karl. 1944. *The Great Transformation.* Boston: Beacon Press.

Porter, Michael. 1990. *The Competitive Advantage of Nations.* New York: Free Press.

———. 1992. *Capital Choices.* Washington, D.C.: Council on Competitiveness.

Powell, Walter, and Paul Dimaggio, eds. 1991. *The New Institutionalism in Organizational Analysis.* Chicago: University of Chicago Press.

Pyle, Kenneth B. 1984. "Advantages of Followership: German Economics and Japanese Bureaucrats, 1890–1925." *Journal of Japanese Studies* 1(1): 127–64.

Rappaport, Alfred. 1986. *Creating Shareholder Value: The New Standard for Business Performance.* New York: Free Press.

Reed, John A., Jr. 1987. *Germany and NATO.* Washington, D.C.: National Defense University Press.

Regini, Marino. 1999. Between De-Regulation and Social Pacts: The Responses of European Economies to Globalization. Unpublished paper.

Rehder, Britta. 2001. The Impact of Plant-Level Pacts for Employment and Competitiveness on the Institutional Change of the German System of Industrial Relations. Paper presented at the Annual Meeting of the Society for the Advancement of Socio-Economics, 28 June–1 July, Amsterdam.

Research Institute for the Advancement of Living Standards. 1999. How Top Managers See the Japanese Corporation: An Interim Report of the Survey on Corporate Governance to the Top Management (February 1999). Paper presented at the conference on The Political Economy of Corporate Governance in Europe and Japan, Robert Schuman Centre, European University Institute, 10–11 June, Florence.

Reuters. 1994. Reuters Asia Pacific Business Report. 16 March. Available at Lexis online database.

Riker, William. 1982. *Liberalism against Populism.* Prospect Heights: Waveland Press.

Risse, Thomas, Maria Green Cowles, and James A. Caporaso, eds. 2001. *Transforming Europe: Europeanization and Domestic Change.* Ithaca: Cornell University Press.

Risse-Kappen, Thomas, ed. 1995. *Bringing Transnational Relations Back In: Non-State Actors, Domestic Structures and International Institutions.* New York: Cambridge University Press.

Roach, Stephen. 1997. "Angst in the Global Village." *Challenge* 40(5): 95–108.

Rodney, Alan M. 1998. A ((Very) Brief) History of Advice and Advisors. Paper presented at the Tenth Anniversary International Conference of the National Institute of Science and Technology Policy, 8–9 October, Tokyo.

Roe, Mark. 1993. "Some Differences in Corporate Structure in Germany, Japan, and the United States." *Yale Law Journal* 102: 1958–65.

——. 1994. *Strong Managers, Weak Owners: The Political Roots of American Corporate Finance.* Princeton: Princeton University Press.

Roller, Edeltraut. 1995. "Political Agendas and Beliefs about the Scope of Government." In *The Scope of Government,* edited by Ole Borre, 55–86. Oxford: Oxford University Press.

Romer, Paul M. 1986. "Increasing Returns and Long-Run Growth." *Journal of Political Economy* 94(5): 1002–37.

——. 1987. "Growth Based on Increasing Returns Due to Specialization." *American Economic Review* 77(2): 56–62.

——. 1990. "Endogenous Technological Change, Part II." *Journal of Political Economy* 98(5): S71–S102.

Rosecrance, Richard. 1986. *The Rise of the Trading State: Commerce and Conquest in the Modern World.* New York: Basic Books.

Rosen, Rüdiger von. 1997. *Chancengemeinschaft: Deutschland braucht die Aktie.* Munich: Wirtschaftsverlag Langen Müller/Herbig.

Rosenberg, Nathan. 1976. *Perspective on Technology.* New York: Cambridge University Press.

Rosenbluth, Frances McCall. 1989. *Financial Politics in Contemporary Japan.* Ithaca: Cornell University Press.

——. 1996. "Internationalization and Electoral Politics in Japan." In *Internationalization and Domestic Politics,* edited by Robert O. Keohane and Helen V. Milner, 137–54. Cambridge, UK: Cambridge University Press.

Ross, George, and Andrew Martin, eds. 1999. *The Brave New World of European Labor: European Trade Unions at the Millennium.* New York: Berghahn.

Roth, Siegfried. 1997. "Labor's Perspective on Lean Production." In *After Lean Production: Evolving Employment Practices in the World Auto Industry,* edited by Thomas A. Kochan, Russell D. Lansbury, and John Paul Macduffie, 117–36. Ithaca: Cornell University Press.

Rybczynski, T. M. 1988. "Financial Systems and Industrial Restructuring." *National Westminster Bank Quarterly Review* (November): 3–13.

Sakakibara, Eisuke. 2000. Asian Regional Cooperation in the Digital Age. Paper presented at the Sixth Annual Asia-Pacific Conference on Central Banking Policy, 27 July, Tokyo.

Sako, Mari. 1999. What Is the Boundary of the Firm for Enterprise Unions in Japan? Paper presented at the conference on The Political Economy of Corporate Governance in Europe and Japan, Robert Schuman Centre, European University Institute, 10–11 June, Florence.

Sala-I-Martin, Xavier. 1997. "I Just Ran Two Million Regressions." *American Economic Review: Papers and Proceedings* 87(2): 178–83.

Sato, Hiroki. 1996. "Keeping Employees Employed: Shukko and Tenseki Job Transfers: Formation of a Labor Market within Corporate Groups." *Ministry of Labour Bulletin* 35(12). Available at www.jil.go.jp/bulletin/1996/vol35-12/06.htm; INTERNET.

Sato, Yukio. 1998. The Changing Framework for the S&T Policy in Japan. Paper presented at the Tenth Anniversary International Conference of the National Institute of Science and Technology Policy, 8–9 October, Tokyo.

Schaller, Michael. 1997. *Altered States: The United States and Japan since the Occupation.* New York: Oxford University Press.

Scharpf, Fritz. 1997. Employment and the Welfare State: A Continental Dilemma. Working paper no. 97/7, Max-Planck-Institut für Gesellschaftsforschung, Köln.

Schlesinger, Arthur. 1989. "Our Problem Is Not Japan or Germany." *Wall Street Journal,* 22 December, p. A6.

Schmidt, Gustav, and Charles F. Doran, eds. 1996. *Amerikas Option für Deutschland und Japan. Die Position und Rolle Deutschlands und Japans in regionalen und internationalen Strukturen. Die 1950er und die 1990er Jahre im Vergleich.* Bochum: Universitätsverlag Dr. N. Brockmeyer.

Schmidt, Manfred G. 1998a. *Sozialpolitik in Deutschland: Historische Entwicklung und Internationaler Vergleich,* 2nd ed. Opladen: Leske & Budrich.

———. 1998b. "Thesen zur Sozialpolitik in Deutschland." *Zeitschrift für Sozialreform* 44(8): 525–69.

Schmitter, Phillippe C., and Wolfgang Streeck. 1985. "Community, Market, State—and Associations? The Prospective Contribution of Interest Governance to Social Order." *European Sociological Review* 1(2): 119–38.

Schnabel, Claus, and Joachim Wagner. 1996. "Ausmass und Bestimmungsgruende der Mitgliedschaft in Arbeitgeberverbaenden: Eine empirische Untersuchung mit Firmendaten." *Industrielle Beziehungen* 3(4): 293–306.

Schneider, William, Jr. 1989. *The Future Role of Germany and Japan: Challenges and Opportunities for the United States.* Project on the Role and Responsibilities of Japan and the Federal Republic of Germany in the International System. Berlin: Aspen Institute.

Schoppa, Leonard J. 1993. "Two-Level Games and Bargaining Outcomes: Why Gaiatsu Succeeds in Japan in Some Cases but Not Others." *International Organization* 47(3): 353–86.

———. 1997. *Bargaining with Japan: What American Pressure Can and Cannot Do.* New York: Columbia University Press.

———. 1999. "The Social Context in Coercive International Bargaining." *International Organization* 53(2): 307–42.

Schroeder, Wolfgang. 1996. "Industrielle Beziehungen in Ostdeutschland: Zwischen Transformation und Standortdebatte." *Aus Politik und Zeitgeschichte* 40: 25–34.

Schulten, Thorsten. 1998. "New Collective Agreement in the East German Steel Industry." January. Available at *EIROnline,* http://www.eiro.eurofund.ie/1998/01/feature/DE9801243F.html; INTERNET. Accessed 26 August 2002.

Schulten, Thorsten, and Stefan Zagelmeyer. 1998. "1998 Annual Review for Germany." December. Available at *EIROnline,* http://www.eiro.eurofund.ie/1998/12/feature/DE9812287F.html; INTERNET. Accessed 26 August 2002.

Schwartz, Frank. 1993. "Of Fairy Cloaks and Familiar Talks: The Politics of Consultation." *In Political Dynamics in Contemporary Japan,* edited by Gary D. Allinson and Yasunori Sone, 217–41. Ithaca: Cornell University Press.

Schwartz, Thomas A. 1993. "Reeducation and Democracy: The Policies of the United States High Commission in Germany." In *America and the Shaping of German Society, 1945–1955,* edited by Michael Ermarth, 35–46. Providence: Berg.

Seitz, Richard. 1992. *NATO's New Troops: Overcoming Obstacles to Multinational Ground Forces.* Carlisle Barracks, Penn.: Strategic Studies Institute.

Seligman, Joel. 1995. *The Transformation of Wall Street: A History of the Securities and Exchange Commission and Modern Corporate Finance.* Boston: Northeastern University Press.

Sey, Anne. 1998. "Zur empirischen Aufarbeitung von Gruppenarbeit in Japan." In *Innovative Arbeitspolitik? Zur qualifizierten Produktionsarbeit in Japan*, edited by Norbert Altmann, 291–303. Frankfurt am Main: Campus.

Shalev, Michael. 1990. "Class Conflict, Corporatism, and Comparison: A Japanese Enigma." In *Japanese Models of Conflict Resolution*, edited by S. N. Eisenstadt and Eyal Ben-Ari, 60–95. London: Kegan Paul.

Sheard, Paul. 1994. "Interlocking Shareholdings and Corporate Governance." In *The Japanese Firm: Sources of Competitive Strength*, edited by Masahiko Aoki and Ronald Dore, 310–49. Oxford: Oxford University Press.

Sherman, Heidemarie C., and Fred R. Kaen. 1997. "Die deutschen Banken und ihr Einfluß auf Unternehmensentscheidungen." *Ifo Schnelldienst* 23: 3–20.

Shiers, George, ed. 1977. *Technical Development of Television*. New York: Arno Press.

Shimada, Haruo, and Kiyoshi Ota, eds. 1997. *Rōdōshijo kaikaku*. Tokyo: Tōyō Keizai Shinpōsha.

Shimizu, Koichi. 1998. "New Toyotaism?" In *One Best Way? Trajectories and Industrial Models of the World's Automobile Producers*, edited by Michel Freyssenet, Andrew Mair, Koichi Shimizu, and Giuseppe Volpato, 63–90. Oxford: Oxford University Press.

Shingo, Shigeo. 1981. *Study of Toyota Production System from Industrial Engineering Viewpoint*. Tokyo: Japan Management Association.

Shinkawa, Toshimitsu. 1990. The Political Economy of Social Welfare in Japan. Ph.D. diss., University of Toronto.

Shinn, James. 1999. Corporate Governance Reform and Trade Friction. Paper for the Study Group on U.S.-Japan Economic Relations, Council on Foreign Relations, March, Washington, D.C.

Shugart, Matthew Soberg. 1998. Efficiency and Reform: A Theory of Electoral System Chance in the Context of Economic Liberalization. Paper presented at the Annual Meeting of the American Political Science Association, 3–6 September, Boston.

Silvia, Stephen. 1996. Globalization and the German Economy. Paper presented at the Annual Meeting of the American Political Science Association, 29 August–1 September, San Francisco.

——. 1999. "Every Which Way but Loose: German Industrial Relations since 1980." In *The Brave New World of European Labor*, edited by Andrew Martin and George Ross, 75–124. New York: Berghahn.

Sloan, Stanley R. 1990. "Perspectives on the German Contribution to Western Defense." In *The Bundeswehr and Western Security*, edited by Stephen F. Szabo, 52–70. New York: St. Martin's Press.

Smith, O. Eric. 1994. *The German Economy*. London: Routledge.

Smith, Tony. 1998. "The International Origins of Democracy: The American Occupation of Japan and Germany." In *Democracy, Revolution, and History*, edited by Theda Skocpol, George Ross, Tony Smith, and Judith Eisenberg Vichniac, 191–209. Ithaca: Cornell University Press.

Soete, Luc. 1999. The Challenges and the Potential of the Knowledge Based Economy in a Globalised World. Unpublished paper.

Soeya, Yoshihide. 1998. "Japan: Normative Constraints versus Structural Imperatives." In *Asian Security Practice: Material and Ideational Influences*, edited by Muthiah Alagappa, 198–233. Stanford: Stanford University Press.

Sohn, Yul. 1998. "The Rise and Development of the Japanese Licensing System. " In *Is Japan Really Changing Its Ways? Regulatory Reform and the Japanese Economy*, edited by Lonny E. Carlile and Mark C. Tilton, 16–32. Washington, D.C.: Brookings Institution.

Solow, Robert M. 1956. "A Contribution to the Theory of Economic Growth." *Quarterly Journal of Economics* 70: 65–94.

——. 1994. "Perspectives on Growth Theory." *Journal of Economic Perspectives* 8(1): 45–54.

Sorge, Arndt, and Wolfgang Streeck. 1988. "Industrial Relations and Technical Change: The Case for an Extended Perspective." In *New Technology and Industrial Relations*, edited by Richard Hyman and Wolfgang Streeck, 19–47. Oxford: Basil Blackwell.

Sorge, Arndt, and Malcom Warner. 1986. *Comparative Factory Organization: An Anglo-German Comparison of Manufacturing, Management and Manpower.* Aldershot: Gower.

Soskice, David. 1996. German Technology Policy, Innovation, and National Institutional Frameworks. Discussion paper, FS I 96-319, Wissenschaftszentrum Berlin, Berlin.

——. 1999. "Divergent Production Regimes: Coordinated and Uncoordinated Market Economies in the 1980s and 1990s." In *Continuity and Change in Contemporary Capitalism*, edited by Herbert Kitschelt, Peter Lange, Gary Marks, and John D. Stephens, 101–34. Cambridge, UK: Cambridge University Press.

Stares, Paul B. 1990. *Allied Rights and Legal Constraints on German Military Power.* Washington, D.C.: Brookings Institution.

Statistics Bureau, General Affairs Agency. 1990–2000. *Sekai no tōkei.* Tokyo: Ministry of Finance Printing Bureau.

Steinmo, Sven, Kathleen Thelen, and Frank Longstreth, eds. 1992. *Structuring Politics: Historical Institutionalism in Comparative Analysis.* Cambridge, UK: Cambridge University Press.

Stephens, John D., Evelyne Huber, and Leonard Ray. 1999. "The Welfare State in Hard Times." In *Continuity and Change in Contemporary Capitalism*, edited by Herbert Kitschelt, Peter Lange, Gary Marks, and John D. Stephens, 164–93. Cambridge, UK: Cambridge University Press.

Stockwin, J. A. A., Alan Rix, Aurelia George, James Horne, Daiichi Itō, and Martin Collick. 1988. *Dynamic and Immobilist Politics in Japan.* London: Macmillan.

Story, Jonathan. 1996. "*Finanzplatz Deutschland*: National or European Response to Internationalization?" *German Politics* 5(December): 371–94.

Stöss, Richard. 1997. *Stabilität im Umbruch.* Opladen: Westdeutscher Verlag.

Streeck, Wolfgang. 1987. "The Uncertainties of Management in the Management of Uncertainty." *Work, Employment, and Society* 1(3): 281–308.

——. 1989. "Successful Adjustment to Turbulent Markets: The Automobile Industry." In *Industry and Politics in West Germany: Toward the Third Republic*, edited by Peter J. Katzenstein, 113–56. Ithaca: Cornell University Press.

——. 1992. *Social Institutions and Economic Performance: Studies of Industrial Relations in Advanced Capitalist Economies.* London: Sage.

——. 1996. "Lean Production in the German Automobile Industry: A Test Case for Convergence Theory." In *National Diversity and Global Capitalism*, edited by Suzanne Berger and Ronald Dore, 138–70. Ithaca: Cornell University Press.

——. 1997a. "Beneficial Constraints: On the Economic Limits of Rational Voluntarism." In *Contemporary Capitalism: The Embeddedness of Institutions*, edited by J. Rogers Hollingsworth and Robert Boyer, 197–219. Cambridge, UK: Cambridge University Press.

——. 1997b. Citizenship under Regime Competition: The Case of the European Work Councils, Jean Monnet chair papers, Robert Schuman Centre, European University Institute, San Domenico di Fiesole, Italy.

——. 1997c. "German Capitalism: Does it Exist? Can it Survive?" In *Political Economy of Modern Capitalism: Mapping Convergence and Diversity*, edited by Colin Crouch and Wolfgang Streeck, 33–54. London: Sage.

———. 1997d. Das Zukunftsmodell—Der Flächentarifvertrag. Vortrag bei der tarifpolitischen Tagung der IG Metall, 20–22 November, Darmstadt.

———. 1998. "The German Social Market Economy: External Competitiveness and Internal Cohesion." In *Ten Paradigms of Market Economy and Land Systems,* edited by Lee-Jay Cho and Yoon-Hyung Kim, 59–98. Kyonggi-do: Korean Research Institute for Human Settlements.

———. 1999. Competitive Solidarity: Rethinking the "European Social Model." Working paper 99/8, Max-Planck-Institut für Gesellschaftsforschung, Köln.

———. 2001. "The Transformation of Corporate Organization in Europe: An Overview." Working paper 01/08, Max-Planck-Institut für Gesellschaftsforschung, Köln.

Streeck, Wolfgang, and Kozo Yamamura, eds. 2001. *The Origins of Nonliberal Capitalism: Germany and Japan in Comparison.* Ithaca: Cornell University Press.

Stubbs, Richard. 1998. "Asia-Pacific Regionalism versus Globalization: Competing Forms of Capitalism." In *Regionalism and Global Economic Integration: Europe, Asia and the Americas,* edited by William D. Coleman and Geoffrey Underhill, 68–80. London: Routledge.

Sturgeon, Timothy J. 1997. Turnkey Production Networks: A New American Model of Industrial Organization? Working paper 92A, Berkeley Roundtable on the International Economy, University of California, Berkeley.

Tabata, Hirokuni. 1996. Gurobaraizēshon to jidōsha sangyō—jidōsha sōren no sangyō seisaku. Discussion paper J-52, June, Institute of Social Science, University of Tokyo.

Tachibanaki, Toshiaki. 1989. "Japan's New Policy Agenda: Coping with Unequal Asset Distribution." *Journal of Japanese Studies* 15(2): 345–70.

———. 1992. "Higher Land Prices as a Cause of Increasing Inequality: Changes in Wealth Distribution and Socio-Economic Effects." In *Land Policy in Japan: A Policy Failure?* edited by John O. Haley and Kozo Yamamura, 175–93. Seattle: Society for Japanese Studies.

———. 1996. *Wage Determination and Distribution in Japan.* Oxford: Oxford University Press.

———. 1998. *Nihon no keizai kakusa.* Tokyo: Iwanami Shoten.

Takanashi, Akira. 1994. *Kawaru Nihongata koyō.* Tokyo: Nihon Keizai Shinbunsha.

Takao, Yoshikazu, Yunosuke Ikeda, and Yasuyuki Fuchita. 1998. "Revitalizing Japan's Financial Markets." *Nomura Research Institute Quarterly* (winter) 2–23.

Takeuchi, Yasuo. 1998. *Nihon no owari.* Tokyo: Nihon Keizai Shinbunsha.

Tanabe, Kuniaki. 1997. "Social Policy in Japan: Building a Welfare State in a Conservative One Dominant Party System." In *State and Administration in Japan and Germany,* edited by Michio Muramatsu and Frieder Naschold, 107–31. New York: Walter de Gruyter.

Tanaka, Mikio. 1996. "Juristische, historische und kulturelle Aspekte administrativer Reformen in Japan: Von der Herrschaft der Bürokratie zur Herrschaft des Rechts." *Zeitschrift für japanisches Recht* 1(2): 110–27.

Thelen, Kathleen. 1999a. "Historical Institutionalism in Comparative Politics." *Annual Review of Political Science* 2: 369–404.

———. 1999b. "Why German Employers Cannot Bring Themselves to Dismantle the German Model." In *Unions, Employers, and Central Banks,* edited by Torben Iversen, Jonas Pontusson, and David Soskice, 138-69. New York: Cambridge University Press.

Thelen, Kathleen, and Ikuo Kume. 1999. "The Rise of Nonmarket Training Regimes: Germany and Japan Compared." *Journal of Japanese Studies* 25(1): 33–64.

———. 2001. "The Rise of Nonliberal Training Regimes: Germany and Japan Compared." In *The Origins of Nonliberal Capitalism: Germany and Japan in Comparison,* edited by Wolfgang Streeck and Kozo Yamamura, 200–227. Ithaca: Cornell University Press.

Thomas, Ian Q. R. 1997. *The Promise of Alliance: NATO and the Political Imagination.* Boulder: Rowman & Littlefield.

Thomas, L. G., III, and Geoffrey Waring. 1999. "Competing Capitalisms: Capital Investment in American, German and Japanese Firms." *Strategic Management Journal* 20(8): 729–48.

Thurow, Lester. 1992. *Head to Head: The Coming Economic Battle among Japan, Europe, and America.* New York: Murrow.

Tilton, Mark. 1996. *Restrained Trade: Cartels in Japan's Basic Materials Industries.* Ithaca: Cornell University Press.

Tokyo Stock Exchange. 1991–2001. *Tokyo Stock Exchange Fact Book.* Tokyo: Tokyo Stock Exchange.

Touraine, Alan. 1969. *La Societe Post-Industrielle.* Paris: Gontheir.

Towers Perrin. 2000. *1999 Worldwide Total Remuneration.* New York: Towers Perrin.

Turner, Lowell, ed. 1997. *Negotiating the New Germany: Can Social Partnership Survive?* Ithaca: ILR Press.

———. 1998. *Fighting for Partnership: Labor and Politics in Unified Germany.* Ithaca: Cornell University Press.

Tüselmann, Heinz-Josef. 1998. "Standort Deutschland: German Direct Foreign Investment—Exodus of German Industry and Export of Jobs." *Journal of World Business* 33(3): 295–313.

Ueda, Kazuo. 1994. "Institutional and Regulatory Frameworks for the Main Bank System." In *The Japanese Main Bank System: Its Relevance for Developing and Transforming Economies,* edited by Masahiko Aoki and Hugh Patrick, 89–108. Oxford: Oxford University Press.

Uemura, Hiroyasu. 2000. "Growth, Distribution and Structural Change in the Postwar Japanese Economy." In *Japanese Capitalism in Crisis,* edited by Robert Boyer and Toshio Yamada, 138–61. London: Routledge.

Uni, Hiroyuki. 2000. "Disproportionate Productivity Growth and Accumulation Regimes." In *Japanese Capitalism in Crisis,* edited by Robert Boyer and Toshio Yamada, 54–70. London: Routledge.

U.S. Department of Commerce. 1999. *Survey of Current Business* 79 (February). Washington, D.C.: U.S. Department of Commerce.

Varsori, Antonio. 1991. "The First Stage of Negotiations: December 1947 to June 1948." In *The Atlantic Pact Forty Years Later: A Historical Appraisal,* edited by Ennio Di Nolfo, 19–40. Berlin: Walter de Gruyter.

Vitols, Sigurt. 1996. Modernizing Capital: Financial Regulation and Long-Term Finance in the Postwar U.S. and Germany. Ph.D. diss. University of Wisconsin, Madison.

———. 1997. Beneficial Constraints and Industrial Finance in the Postwar German and Japanese Financial Systems. Unpublished paper.

———. 2000. The Reconstruction of German Corporate Governance: Reassessing the Role of Capital Market Pressures. Paper presented at the Annual Meeting of the Research Network on Corporate Governance, 23–24 June, Berlin.

———. 2001. "The Origins of Bank-Based and Market-Based Financial Systems: Germany, Japan, and the United States." In *The Origins of Nonliberal Capitalism: Germany and Japan in Comparison,* edited by Wolfgang Streeck and Kozo Yamamura, 171–99. Ithaca: Cornell University Press.

Vitols, Sigurt, Steven Casper, David Soskice, and Stephen Woolcock. 1997. *Corporate Governance in Large British and German Companies: Comparative Institutional Advantage or Competing for Best Practice?* London: Anglo-German Foundation for the Study of Industrial Society.

Vogel, Steven. 1994. "The Bureaucratic Approach to the Financial Revolution: Japan's Ministry of Finance and Financial System Reform." *Governance* 7(3): 219–43.

———. 1996. *Freer Markets, More Rules: Regulatory Reform in Advanced Industrial Countries.* Ithaca: Cornell University Press.

———. 1998. Can Japan Disengage? Winners and Losers in Japan's Political Economy, and the Ties That Bind Them. Working paper no. 111, Berkeley Roundtable on the International Economy, University of California, Berkeley.

———. 2001. "The Crisis of German and Japanese Capitalism: Stalled on the Road to the Liberal Market Model?" *Comparative Political Studies* 34(December): 1103–33.

Waltz, Kenneth. 1979. *Theory of International Politics.* New York: McGraw-Hill.

Wan, Ming. 1995. "Spending Strategies in World Politics: How Japan Has Used Its Economic Power in the Past Decade." *International Studies Quarterly* 39(1): 85–108.

Ward, Robert. 1975. "The Legacy of Occupation." In *The United States and Japan,* edited by Herbert Passin, 19–40. 2rd rev. ed. Washington, D.C.: Columbia Books.

Webber, Douglas. 1992. "Kohl's *Wendepolitik* after a Decade." *German Politics* 1: 149–80.

Weder, Rolf, and Herbert G. Grubel. 1993. "The New Growth Theory and Coasean Economics: Institutions to Capture Externalities." *Weltwirtschaftliches Archiv* 129(3): 488–511.

Weiss, Linda. 1998. *The Myth of the Powerless State.* Ithaca: Cornell University Press.

Wever, Kirsten S. 1995. "Human Resource Management and Organisational Strategies in German and US-Owned Companies." *International Journal of Human Resource Management* 6(3): 606–26.

White, Harrison C. 2002. *Markets from Networks: Socioeconomic Models of Production.* Princeton: Princeton University Press.

Whitford, Jon, and Thomas-Durell Young. 1997. "Command Authorities and Multi-nationality in NATO: The Response of the Central Region's Armies." In *Command in NATO after the Cold War: Alliance, National, and Multinational Considerations,* edited by Thomas-Durell Young, 53–73. Carlisle Barracks, Penn.: Strategic Studies Institute.

Whitley, Richard. 1992. *Business Systems in East Asia: Firms, Markets and Societies.* London: Sage.

———. 1999. *Divergent Capitalisms: The Social Structuring and Change of Business Systems.* Oxford: Oxford University Press.

Williamson, Oliver. 1985. *The Economic Institutions of Capitalism.* New York: Free Press.

Womack, James P., and Daniel T. Jones. 1996. *Lean Thinking: Banish Waste and Create Wealth in Your Corporation.* New York: Simon & Schuster.

Womack, James P., Daniel T. Jones, and Daniel Roos. 1990. *The Machine That Changed the World.* New York: Rawson.

Woo-Cumings, Meredith, ed. 1999. *The Developmental State.* Ithaca: Cornell University Press.

Woodall, Brian. 1992. The Calculus of Collusion: External Pressure and Collusive Action in Japanese Public Works. Paper presented at the Annual Meeting of the American Political Science Association, 3–6 September, Chicago.

World Bank. 1983. *World Tables.* 3rd ed. Washington, D.C.: World Bank.

———. 1992. *World Tables.* Washington, D.C.: World Bank.

———. 1995. Stars Data Set, CD-ROM. Washington, D.C.: World Bank.

———. 1999a. *Global Development Finance.* Washington, D.C.: World Bank.

———. 1999b. *World Development Indicators.* Washington, D.C.: World Bank.

"The World in 1999." 1999. *Economist,* 5 January, pp. 17–25.

Yamada, Toshio. 2000. "Japanese Capitalism and the Companyist Compromise." In *Japanese Capitalism in Crisis,* edited by Robert Boyer and Toshio Yamada, 19–31. London: Routledge.

Yamakawa, Ryuichi. 1999. Labor Law Reform in Japan: A Response to Recent Socio-Economic Changes. Paper presented at the Fourth Sho Sato Conference on Japanese and U.S. Law, 4–5 November, University of California, Berkeley.

Yamamura, Kozo. 1982. "Success That Soured: Administrative Guidance and Cartels in Japan." In *Policy and Trade Issues of the Japanese Economy,* edited by Kozo Yamamura, 77–112. Seattle: University of Washington Press.

——. 1985. "The Cost of Rapid Growth and Capitalist Democracy in Japan." In *The Politics of Inflation and Economic Stagnation,* edited by Leon N. Lindberg and Charles S. Maier, 467–508. Washington, D.C.: Brookings Institution.

——. 1997. "The Japanese Political Economy after the 'Bubble': Plus Ca Change?" *Journal of Japanese Studies* 23(2): 291–331.

Yashiro, Naohiro. 1997. *Nihonteki kōyōkankō no owari.* Tokyo: Nihon Keizai Shinbunsha.

Yayama, Taro. 1998. "Who Has Obstructed Reform?" In *Unlocking the Bureaucrat's Kingdom: Deregulation and the Japanese Economy,* edited by Frank Gibney, 91–115. Washington, D.C.: Brookings Institution.

Yoshikawa, Hiroyuki. 1996. *Made in Japan: Revitalizing Japanese Manufacturing for Economic Growth.* Cambridge, Mass.: MIT Press.

Yoshitomi, Masaru. 1996. "Labour Market Implications of Changing Corporate Governance in Japan." In *Macroeconomic Policies and Structural Reform,* edited by the Organization for Economic Cooperation and Development. Paris: OECD.

Young, Thomas-Durell. 1997a. "Centralizing German Operational Command and Control Structures." In *Command in NATO after the Cold War: Alliance, National, and Multinational Considerations,* edited by Thomas-Durell Young, 135–56. Carlisle Barracks, Penn.: Strategic Studies Institute.

——. 1997b. "Introduction." In *Command in NATO after the Cold War: Alliance, National, and Multinational Considerations,* edited by Thomas-Durell Young, 1–8. Carlisle Barracks, Penn.: Strategic Studies Institute.

Zagelmeyer, Stefan. 1998. "New Conflict Resolution Procedures Discussed for Labour Disputes." April. Available at *EIROnline,* www.eiro.eurofound.ie; INTERNET.

——. 1999. "Private Sector Collective Bargaining Coverage Analyzed." February. Available at *EIROnline,* www.eiro.eurofound.ie; INTERNET.

Zeitlin, Jonathan. 2000. "Introduction: Americanization and Its Limits: Reworking US Technology and Management in Post-War Europe and Japan." In *Americanization and Its Limits: Reworking US Technology and Management in Postwar Europe and Japan,* edited by Jonathan Zeitlin and Gary Herrigel, 1–52. Oxford: Oxford University Press.

Ziegler, J. Nicholas. 2000. "Corporate Governance and the Politics of Property Rights in Germany." *Politics and Society* 28(2): 195–221.

Zugehör, Rainer. 2000. Die neue Macht des Kapitalmarktes—Einfluss des Kapitalmarktes auf das Investitionsverhalten deutscher Großunternehmen: Eine empirische Analyse. Unpublished paper.

Zysman, John. 1983. *Governments, Markets and Growth: Financial Systems and the Politics of Industrial Change.* Ithaca: Cornell University Press.

Index

Cornell Studies in Political Economy

A series edited by

Peter J. Katzenstein

International Governance: Protecting the Environment in a Stateless Society
by Oran R. Young

Polar Politics: Creating International Environmental Regimes
edited by Oran R. Young and Gail Osherenko

Governing Ideas: Strategies for Innovation in France and Germany
by J. Nicholas Ziegler

Internationalizing China: Domestic Interests and Global Linkages
by David Zweig

Governments, Markets, and Growth: Financial Systems and the Politics of Industrial Change
by John Zysman

American Industry in International Competition: Government Policies and Corporate Strategies
edited by John Zysman and Laura Tyson